**Political Philosophy
and the
Issues of Politics**

PPPPPPPPPPPPPPPPPPPPPPPPPPPPPPPPPP
PPPPPPPPPPPPPPPPPPPPPPPPPPPPPPPPPP
PPPPPPPPPPPPPPPPPPPPPPPPPPPPPPPPPP
PPPPPPPPPPPPPPPPPPPPPPPPPPPPPPPPPP
PPPPPPPPPPPPPPPPPPPPPPPPPPPPPPPPPP
PPPPPPPPPPPPPPPPPPPPPPPPPPPPPPPPPP
PPPPPPPPPPPPPPPPPPPPPPPPPPPPPPPPPP
PPPPPPPPPPPPPPPPPPPPPPPPPPPPPPPPPP
PPPPPPPPPPPPPPPPPPPPPPPPPPPPPPPPPP
PPPPPPPPPPPPPPPPPPPPPPPPPPPPPPPPPP
PPPPPPPPPPPPPPPPPPPPPPPPPPPPPPPPPP
PPPPPPPPPPPPPPPPPPPPPPPPPPPPPPPPPP
PPPPPPPPPPPPPPPPPPPPPPPPPPPPPPPPPP
PPPPPPPPPPPPPPPPPPPP PPPPPPPPPPPPPPP
PPPPPPPPPPPPPPPPPPPP PPPPPPPPPPPPPP
PPPPPPPPPPPPPPPPPPPP PP PPPPPPPPPPPP
PPPPPPP PP PPPPPPPP PP PPPPPPP PPPPP
PPPPPPP PP PPPPPP PP PP PPP PPP PPPPP
PPP PPP PP PPPPPP PP PP PPP PPP PP PP
PPP PPP PP PP PPP PP PP PPP PPP PP PP
PPP P P PP PP PPP PP PP PPP P P PP P
PPP P P PP PP P P PP PP PPP P P PP P
P P P P P PP P P PP PP P P P P P P
P P P P P P P P PP P P P P P
P P P P P P P P P P
P P P P P P P
P P P P
P P
P

Joseph Cropsey   **Political Philosophy
                                  and the
                                  Issues of Politics**

113590

The University of
Chicago Press
Chicago and London

Joseph Cropsey is professor of political science at
the University of Chicago.

The University of Chicago Press, Chicago 60637
The University of Chicago Press, Ltd., London

Printed in the United States of America
81 80 79 78 77   9 8 7 6 5 4 3 2 1

Library of Congress Cataloging in Publication Data

Cropsey, Joseph.
  Political philosophy and the issues of politics.

  1. Political science—Addresses, essays, lectures.
I. Title.
JA71.C75   320.5   76-22960
ISBN 0-226-12123-2

Contents

Preface

This book consists of papers that were written during a period of almost twenty five years. None of them was designed to be part of a book such as this; the book itself was envisioned after most of its parts already existed. Yet the parts have proved submissive to a simple arrangement that distributes them under the main headings of critical reflections on some social sciences, characterization of leading or conspicuous political positions, comment with a moral intention on certain issues of public policy, and interpretation of philosophic texts. This plan is heavily influenced by the fact that political philosophy as I first encountered it consisted in large measure of critique of modernity through and alongside interpretation of texts. The critique of modernity was partly critique of social science, partly critique of modern politics, and partly critique of the texts of political philosophy written in and since the fifteenth century. The other large component of political philosophy as I was introduced to it by my late teacher and lamented friend, Leo Strauss, was the relevant literature of classical antiquity. In brief, the plan of this book resembles a sketch of political philosophy and its concerns as those have appeared to me during most of a working life.

The critique of modernity presupposes the significance of modernity, hence the significance of the distinction between modernity and the ages that preceded it. Since that presupposition is as indispensable to historicism as to the refutation of historicism, the terms on which it is being adopted need to be made clear. A lengthening experience with the texts persuades me that, however consequential the gap between antiquity and modernity may be, it is not so radical as to have made philosophy itself impossible. By philosophy, or at any rate political philosophy, I mean the benign, sober, incisive, and wise investigation of the problems of human life for which no age has found—and perhaps no age can find—unproblematic solutions. If I discover in Aristotle the terrestrialization of man's existence that is supposed to be a mark of the modern understanding, I conjecture with more satisfaction that there is an enduring human scene which reveals itself to intelligence than that ancients anticipated or surpassed every modern insight. The critique of modernity that runs in these papers is to that extent in the interest of philosophy rather than of antiquity. Of the critique of social science, much the same can be said.

A number of the essays consist of attempts to understand political issues and developments, as well as the important political alternatives, that have opened up in modern times. In every such case, I began by reminding myself that if a theme (for example liberal commercial society, or "modernization") belongs seriously to modernity, then it should be thought about with a view to the meaning of modernity. Thus the notion behind the papers on practical matters corresponds to the perception of political philosophy itself as dominated by a distinction between antiquity and modernity. In contemplating that distinction, one soon rediscovers that neither antiquity nor modernity is homogeneous. Modernity is so far from homogeneous that some of its most striking features can be best explained as extrusions from the pressure of one element of our epoch against another, or by reference to what I have called modernity's self-dissatisfaction. If, as I maintain, modernity has, in its thoughts and deeds in the practical realm, shown a disposition to cure itself by intensifying what may have been the original disorder, that fact would only verify the urgency of beginning with as clear a view as possible of the meaning, and thus the complexity, of modernity. Perhaps this sounds like an argument to the effect that in the essence itself of modernity there is prefigured a term to modernity's existence. My argument does have that implication, but it should transpire as no surprise, for what comes into being has "always" been expected to pass away.

The tendency of these papers as a whole is to view the relation between antiquity and modernity as a disjunction modified by continuity, and the internal constitution of each epoch as a heterogeneity in a state of tension. The complexity of the modern age is displayed in the wide literature of the last five centuries, that of the ancient time is indicated by the Platonic corpus, that critical conspectus of human types, schools, and arts which would lose in dignity if it exempted so looming a presence as that of Socrates. To the Platonic corpus, as the serious trial of Socrates by the wisest of his beneficiaries, must be added the scrutiny of Plato by Aristotle in order to gain a sense of the tensions that gave to classical thought its constitution and its energy. There is of course no way to arrive at any such sense except through the interpretation of texts, for which it would therefore be inappropriate to offer an apology.

Standing in the place of an Introduction is a recent paper in which a number of the notions that run through the remaining essays converge on a concrete political theme, the polity of the United States. The gathering of speculations—on the meaning of a regime, on the stresses and forces within modernity, on the autonomy of politics and the direction of history—and their projection toward a concrete moral concern within that paper give it a synthetic character that, added to its vantage of retrospect over the other essays, encourages me to let it serve as a gateway to the rest.

Introduction: The United States as Regime and the Sources of the American Way of Life

Paper presented at the 1975 annual meeting of the American Political Science Association, San Francisco.

As a nation, we are rather given to asking what we are, what we stand for, what our goals are. It is surprising that this should be so, for we have a national existence of two centuries during which our true being might well have become clearly manifest to us; and we have a written Constitution that was deliberately framed, extensively debated, and has been voluminously interpreted, and which is the official definition of our political essence. Our difficulties in this regard are probably not greater than those of other nations, but our experience is so long and our fundamental law so amply interpreted in civil war, jurisprudence, and scholarship that we are led to wonder not only about the meaning of our essence but about its elusiveness.

As we reflect on the peculiarities of our national self-scrutiny, we must own that our introspection is not on the whole complacent. On the contrary, much of it is darkened by self-dissatisfaction. We appear to be in the uneasiest of moods: at once unsatisfied by and dissatisfied with our self-knowledge. What is the meaning of our being vexed with uncertainty over what we are and with misgivings that we are what we are?

We find a clue in the recurrence of the expression "what we are." What we are as equivalent to what we stand for, what our goals are, is not necessarily the same as what we are in the sense of what kind of human beings we are in fact, and what is our way of life or mode of existence as we observe it and can experience it. To learn what we stand for as a nation and what end or ends our united existence is meant to promote, one must consult the documents of our political life. Some of those are authoritative in having the force of law; others are authoritative simply by reason of their gravity, nobility, or provenience.

Both together—the Constitution, laws, judicial opinions; and the Declaration of Independence and great public utterances of eminent men—articulate the conception that constitutes the American regime. But the regime is what we stand for, the expression of what our goals are— freedom, equality, and rights. Why is our political essence obscure to us if it is embodied in words that can be studied and comprehended? Experience shows that the words are subject to construction, and that the unchanging text of the First Amendment, for example, means different things to different judges. Apparently something, call it for the moment thought, mixes itself with the documents that embody the regime—in fact, then, mixes itself with the regime—and in so doing clarifies but also perplexes our understanding of the regime, and hence of ourselves—what we stand for and what our goals are.

This could be said no doubt of many regimes, probably of regimes as such. More characteristic of our own is its self-limitation in the name of freedom. It is obvious that regulation of religion, of art, of thought and the expression of it, of science, and of many aspects of private life is intentionally ruled out by the regime. But religion, art, thought, science, private life are a large part of what we are, for they and their like hover over and penetrate our way of life and help fix us in a mode of existence. But what governs and fixes our way of life is certainly entitled to be called our regime.

It follows from this that our regime has apparently two dimensions, the one consisting of the meaning embedded in the public utterances, coercive or solemn, the other consisting of the meaning embedded in our private— though not thereby necessarily individual—psychic existences. But the meaning embedded in the great public utterances is infiltrated with thought, i.e., with ongoing, changing thought; and our private psychic existence is, if the word "thought" be allowed an extended significance, largely made up of thought. These reflections expose a peculiarity of the regime. If the regime is the political fraction of what forms us and our way of life, then we must face the fact that we have an imperfect regime. It is imperfect in the sense that, as having been deliberated and as laid down, it neither can maintain itself in the direction that it selected nor can it, therefore, keep us without disruption on the course that it has set for us. It is powerfully, decisively, complemented or completed by thought. It is imperfect also in the sense that it by no means extends comprehensively over the whole of our way of life. But if the regime be conceived as not merely the political fraction of what presides over our way of life, but is taken necessarily to mean the ensemble of all decisive influences, then we must face the fact that we have an imperfect regime in another sense: while the coercive fragment of the political fraction can be thought of as under our deliberate control through suffrages and process of known law, every other element of the regime is subject to ongoing thought, which, in its political effect, if not in its origin, has so much in common with chance that we may for the moment count the two as equivalent. In recognizing that the regime includes an "ungovernable," we recognize that what governs us, the very regime, is imperfect. It is imperfect by virtue of the action within it, and upon us, and eventually upon itself, of what we vaguely call thought.

We have been pursuing the question, What is the meaning of our discomfort over the elusiveness of what we are? and we have arrived at the speculation that our discomfort is in fact over the effect produced by the imperfection of our regime, an imperfection identical with the invasion of the regime by thought. On reflection, it appears that we have also arrived at a point from which we can see the answer to the accompanying question, which was, What is the meaning of our dissatisfaction with what we are? Men become dissatisfied with themselves when, and only if, what they are does not possess them exhaustively and to the exclusion of a power to scrutinize what they are. It is tautologous but it is not useless to say that when men are dissatisfied with what they are, then what they are includes the power of self-dissatisfaction. In the case of a nation, that power is thought, still in a wide and indistinct sense. The reflexive thought that goes before and becomes indistinguishable from self-dissatisfaction does not originate in the regime as Constitution and laws, though evidently the coercive regime must enable such thought to find a place. Where the self-critical thought does originate is either outside the regime in its narrower meaning or in the ungoverned and ungovernable area of the regime in its broadest meaning. Stated somewhat differently, the regime is what teaches us to be what we are, and intrusive thought, alien to the regime but unrepressed by the regime, teaches us to be dissatisfied with what we are and, incidentally, with the regime that teaches us to be what we are. Alternatively, the regime, as what truly and comprehensively teaches us to be what we are, includes both what we are dissatisfied with and what provokes us to see that we must be dissatisfied with it—with our way of life and its support in the regime. The inescapable conclusion, by either understanding of regime, is that the regime is problematic with a view to its own persistence and to the manner in which it determines the way of life of the nation; that there is an extra-political which is decisive for the meaning of regime, and which may provisionally be called "thought"; and, as a corollary, that it is inappropriate to speak of the American regime and to imply in so doing that our way of life flows positively from authoritative politics—Constitution, laws, judicial opinions, and the speeches of public men.

If the discussion thus far has shed any light at all, it is on the question concerning the meaning of our uncertainty about ourselves, not on the question concerning the meaning of our dissatisfaction with ourselves. Perhaps we are condemned by the nature of regimes as such to be in doubt of some kind about what we are. But it is a certainty that we and our foreign observers perceive something about us that can be blamed and sometimes praised. What is it that is available to be seen, and that can be the basis for the judgments and self-judgments, especially the adverse self-judgments?

Visible in the nation are human beings and their parchment. Immediately our old problem recurs: are the human beings—their doings and relations—not merely the parchment made flesh? Why distinguish the American people from the Declaration of Independence, the Constitution, and Lincoln's Second Inaugural, for example? For one thing, because we might fail to embody our ideals, from which we must therefore be distinguished. But this is adequate only so far as it goes, for we and the world have reached a point at which the criticism directed against us, and not only from without, is not a reflection on our fidelity to our documents but rather supposes a sufficient harmony between men and their documentary or official norms. Whereas to begin with a difficulty arose over the elusiveness of the regime, and then over the mutual articulation of the official documentary regime and the people, the argument is now at a stage where those difficulties are overridden by abstracting equally from the elusiveness of the regime and from any possible disjunction between people and regime. This means simply that observers content themselves with a characterization of the American way of life and the American regime that is adequate for the purpose of passing a broad judgment on both—abstracting, to repeat, from the possible failure of the two to coincide. My purpose in what follows is not to quarrel with the easygoing ways of those who abstract so broadly in order to cut so sharply, but rather to extract what can be learned if one starts with the criticisms of us that are, indeed, especially informative as self-criticism or self-dissatisfaction.

Abstracting from the possible agreement of the human beings to their parchment regime might make the reasoning easier, but it does not do away with the fact that what one sees in looking at people is not the same as what one sees when studying the documents. Looking at people, one sees family and property. Looking at the documents, one sees life, liberty, and the pursuit of happiness. Where do these observations lead? "Family" means the human unit which has as its principle the generation and preservation of the young through the closest affiliation to each other of a small number of adults, whose needs too are satisfied by it at the same time. The intimacy of the family has made it the locus of that privacy that has been portrayed as drawing men's loyalties away from the larger societies, political or transpolitical. The family is the setting for the private calculations that promote the preservation of life. It is, therewith, the setting in which property performs its ultimate function, the support of human life. The family means privacy, calculation, preservation. And what do life, liberty, and the pursuit of happiness mean if not the freedom of private calculation of the means to preservation and, to be sure, other gratifications as well? As it appears, what one sees when looking at the people is consistent with what one sees when one looks at the parchment regime. And what one sees while looking at both is proto-modernity, the classic modernity of Hobbes and Locke.

How can it be maintained that the family, to say nothing of property, belongs peculiarly to classic modernity? ⊦ does so in that, by contrast with pagan antiquity and Christian pre-modιʼnity, only classic modernity is without a strong element of reservation against property and the family. In pagan antiquity, this found expression in the communism of Plato's *Republic*. In Catholic Christianity, it found expression in the celibacy and poverty of the few who lived the most Christ-like lives. Protestant Christianity begins, in this regard, to participate in a view that bears a similarity to that of classic modernity. It goes without saying that modernity has generated radical reservations against property and the family, but these had to arise in the course of the development of modernity, a development that must be considered by itself if the American "regime" is to be understood. Before reflecting on the meaning of the development of modernity for American existence, the meaning of that development for modernity itself can be noted in a word; modernity has scrutinized itself with some dissatisfaction virtually from its inception, and, through thinking about itself, has more or less continually modified itself. A mere sign of this is the changing stance of modernity toward property and family. But the discussion of these matters must wait until we have satisfied ourselves that we have in fact looked at America.

When one looks at America, one sees more than property and family, and more than the workings of a belief in the natural rights to life, liberty, and the pursuit of happiness. For one thing, one sees the presence of scriptural religion. And then one sees, in all their imponderable influence, natural science, socialism, existentialism, psychoanalysis, and their numerous derivatives in literature, art, journalism and elsewhere. One sees, in brief, some things known and other things wholly unknowable by the founders of the American regime. One sees a medley of thoughts old and modern that help to comprise our effectual regime, if that means what presides over our way of life. But the case is more complex than that. To consider Christianity itself for a moment, no one who is aware of the tendencies stirring in schools of divinity can doubt that actual Christianity is not free of every trace of influence coming from natural science, social-ism, existentialism, and psychoanalysis. Furthermore, it is not in their pure forms but rather as they have sunk down into common under-standing that science, socialism, existentialism, and psychoanalysis have come to bear not only on Christianity but, through Christianity or directly in their own names, on life itself. Thus we are surrounded by an array of thoughts, some old and some recent, the old permeated by the new—and doubtless vice versa—and the new already in a state of decay. This ensemble is part of our "regime." Is there a discernible order about it? Do the parts of the "regime" consist intelligibly with one another?

As often happens, it is not the facts that elude us but their meaning. The formula "life, liberty, and the pursuit of happiness" grew out of the great act of self-emancipation on the part of European mankind that was the opening of the modern age. Machiavelli called on men to take their earthly existences seriously, and thus to win release for themselves from the worst of their cares. He breathed high-heartedness on men by politi-cizing minds that had hitherto been fixed on eternity. He naturalized man in the world, restoring him to nature, so to speak, while presupposing innovations in the meaning of nature that it would be impossible to take up here, but that entered into Hobbes' formulations of natural rights and the state of nature. Inseparable from those formulations is Hobbes' reser-vation to men of the right to preserve life, and their natural freedom to seek the means thereto, as well as the large measure of private discretion that belongs to men as they deliberate on the ends of their actions and seek their satisfactions, if not their contentment, in life.

While the transition from Machiavelli to Hobbes might appear to be a simple evolution or even a kind of repetition, it in fact includes a develop-ment that should not be overlooked. Machiavelli can be understood as teaching a lesson intended to harden and inspirit men. Hobbes, teaching life, liberty, and the pursuit of happiness, prepared what came to be known as the bourgeoisification of life, and the expansion of the private sphere of existence in all ways that did not produce private encroachment on sovereignty. From its inception, modernity has exhibited two moral meanings or tendencies, one inspiriting, reminding man of his earth-bound solitude and presenting the world as an opportunity for greatness of some description, the other pointing toward survival, security, and free-dom to cultivate the private and privately-felt predilections. At its worst, the latter shows itself as acquisitive self-indulgence. The tension between the two dispositions present at the outset of modernity persists throughout the modern age. It concerns us immediately because it manifests itself decisively in our history and indeed it is crucial in the definition of our "regime." It is the thesis of this paper that the parchment regime is dominated by the strand of modernity that invokes preservation and privacy—life, liberty, the pursuit of happiness—but that the United States, any more than any Europeanized nation, could not be insulated against the shocks generated within modernity as the western mind scrutinized its heritage, scrutinized therewith itself, and could not find contentment. In brief, the currents of thought that have run through Europe have been at the same time the writhing of self-dissatisfied modernity and the source of every major non-scriptural ingredient of the American regime outside what I have called the parchment regime. The United States is an arena in which modernity is working itself out. The founding documents are the premise of a gigantic argument, subsequent propositions in which are the decayed or decaying moments of modern thought, superimposed on relics of antiquity. Knowing this helps us to consider more concretely those elements of our "regime" that surround the official or documentary regime; for we are aware that the two elements of the comprehensive regime do not simply coexist side by side but live in a condition of energetic tension.

Classic modernity, the modernity of Hobbes and Locke, provided for the preservation of life, for liberty, and for the pursuit of happiness through a doctrine that reached its practical consummation in man's passage out of the state of mere nature and into the condition of political society. Classic modernity provided for life, liberty, and the pursuit of happiness by means of politics, or it provided for them so far as the means available to essentially liberal politics will reach, perhaps only so far as any parchment regime can reach. But this provision gave rise to misgivings almost immediately. Spinoza saw the need to speak of life and liberty in terms that pointed to the happiness of a private man as such, of a philosopher on whose part an act of introspection would accomplish what citizenship could at best claim to prepare. Rousseau rejected the conception of life that attached it simply to preservation, and denied that the liberty and happiness that are afforded by Hobbesian politics are worthy of the names, for they ignore the amplitude of development of a man's powers of self-sufficiency, of action, feeling, and discipline—in brief, life—without which life is reduced to drudgery and hypocrisy, thus bondage. Kant in turn brought to a very high level the reflections on liberty and happiness as they can be understood within the framework of nature perceived as modern natural science perceived it, as a theater of necessity. Of course he could not be satisfied that a doctrine of liberty that was not also a doctrine of the will could suffice; nor could he accept the simple politicization of the pursuit of happiness, which left unrecognized the problematic status of happiness itself when reduced to calculation and not distinguished from obedience to duty as a goal of life.

Roughly through the time of Kant, the modern thinkers who contemplated modernity recognized that the troublesome implications of modernity for the quality of man's life were inseparable from the ruling conception of nature, that was also the ornament of modern understanding that criticism was not free to profane. With Hegel's discovery of the historical phenomenology of spirit, nature took its place among the moments of man's consciousness and, as the work of Nietzsche testifies, was in a measure replaced by history as the unassailable premise which both sustains and lowers upon human life and freedom.

The change of focus from nature to history produced no mitigation of modern man's dissatisfaction with the absence of any exaltation, vivacity, or high-heartedness from official political modernity as laid down by Hobbes and Locke and, incidentally, embodied in our parchment regime. On the contrary, it appears that the historicization of philosophy contributed to an intensification of that same dissatisfaction that broke out in Marxism and in what is now recognized as the proto-existentialism of Nietzsche. Marx expressed revulsion over the impoverishment of life that accompanied the generation of wealth under the auspices of privacy, and he denied that liberty was effectual or happiness distinguishable from gross satiety under the same auspices. Nietzsche found modern men so decayed in their spirit that by the light of his thought one may wonder whether any ennobling or inspiriting message could remind them of the very meaning of life, so possessed are they with mean impulses to stay alive, enjoy their liberty as guaranteed by liberal government, and pursue the futile gratifications that they absent-mindedly conceive to be happiness. Finally, Heidegger, in 1953, was repeating what he said in 1935 in praise of the "inner truth and greatness" of National Socialism, which consisted in "the encounter between global technology and modern man" (*An Introduction to Metaphysics*, trans. Ralph Manheim, p. 199). Men are alienated from their soil and their origins by a deadness to the meaning of their own being, a meaning that cannot fail to escape humans who are permeated by the calculating, planning, exploiting spirit of a technological age that thrives on using everything and that has come to the height of a long career in objectifying nature by discovering atomic energy. Gone is all tranquillity in the presence of things and gone also is the authenticity of the privacy we so vaunt ourselves upon. Life is trivialized, liberty is an illusion without authentic existence, and the pursuit of happiness is the pursuit of no such thing. Heidegger finds this equally true of the Soviets as of the Americans. It is a fact of modern life in general, and modern science, far from being the remedy, is part of the disorder, for it feeds the spirit of calculation. One might say that the seed planted by Kant has grown into the curious shrub of Heidegger—the rejection of calculation enlarged to encompass the criticism of that science that Kant would not abandon.

Even if modern natural science had not spontaneously become so conspicuous in the argument, it would have forced itself to the foreground by way of a question concerning the propriety of characterizing modernity so heavily in terms of the thought of the moral philosophers and meta-physicians. Heidegger himself quotes from the lecture on the history of philosophy in which Hegel says, "Only now do we in fact arrive at the philosophy of the modern world, and we begin it with Descartes. With him, we in fact enter into an independent philosophy which knows that it is the independent product of reason, and that the consciousness of self, self-consciousness, is an essential moment of truth" (*Hegel's Concept of Experience* [New York: Harper & Row, 1970], p. 27). Hegel's remark emphasizes this fact: modern science was understood by its archi-techts to have a human or moral meaning as well as a strictly technical power. Descartes especially brings together the moral fortitude or spirit-ual toughness that the way of science both demands and cultivates, and the promise that science holds out for prolonging life and emending souls, if only the spiritual physics or mechanics can be elaborated. At the fountain of scientific modernity, as at the sources of moral modernity, there is discernible the diremption of inspiriting and indulging that gener-ates the energy that has moved through modernity ever since.

Modernity has grown by consuming itself. Under the circumstances, it is not surprising that it has not abolished itself but has simply increased in concentration. Modernity could be said to consist of its own self-criticism, held together by the relative stability of the horizon within which the self-criticism takes place. Nietzsche and Heidegger can claim to look beyond that horizon; but it is unclear whether they have transcended or only perfected the historicism that is the hallmark of the most highly concentrated modernity.

That the discussion has moved away from the regime and our ways of life is defensible if the movement has been in the direction of the sources of that regime and those ways of life. We may begin to see that it has been so by reflecting on the opinion commonly found among us that our lives are excessively competitive. This is another way of saying that we are in the grip of invidiousness, the sign of egoism and thus of asociality. We are dissatisfied with ourselves because our regime and life are marked by private striving for the satisfaction of individual goals rather than seek-ing to attain our individual ends through the mediation of a perfectly social act of provision. Alienated from one another, we are alienated from ourselves, for it is contrary to the nature of humanity to live in a state of even latent uncooperativeness with the others. In brief, to provide for life in a way that divides a man from his fellows and within himself is to destroy life in the act of providing for it. Moreover, the liberty enjoyed by the mere egoist is illusory, for he must always be subject to his acquisitiveness and to those private men and private powers who either control or threaten to control his access to what sustains life. As for the pursuit of happiness, the term is deprived of its serious meaning by the impossibility of happiness for a being who is at odds with himself and his kind. The socialist element of our effectual regime, of which the foregoing is a simple reminder, is part of the modern world's self-criticism, selectively drawn not only from Hegel but from Rousseau, whence the moral impetus for it probably emanated.

No one can read Rousseau's moral and political writings, say especially *Emile,* and remain in doubt that Rousseau perceived a need to elevate men above the level of elementary self-interest and mere civil collaboration that Hobbes and Locke provided for. Rousseau speaks of happiness and of self-dependent fortitude, of resilience of spirit; and of course also of the tender sentiments. His strictures on invidiousness, on mean self-interest, on wealth in contradistinction to labor as the support of life, while evoking an antipathy to decadent opulence, do not point toward the social guarantees of welfare characteristic of communism but toward a moral renaissance to be embodied in the sturdy citizen-paterfamilias. The movement from Rousseau to Marxian socialism is not only a transition from righteous indignation to resentful hatred but a falling away from a doctrine of hardy self-dependence to one of socially secured preservation. Of course it is paradoxical that modern men should consider themselves to be fleeing from the preoccupation with mere life foisted on them by Hobbes and Locke when they turn to socialism.

As familiar as the socialist element in our ruling opinions is another set of beliefs that relate to authenticity, choice of one's own way, and the invalidity of the claim of reason to be the ultimate criterion of human choice and being. Through literature and many other media, we blame ourselves, by the light of those beliefs, for the decay of our individual personalities or selves. Thus we blame ourselves for a failure to experience life that rests on a failure to perceive that liberty means in fact a freedom of expression that does not stop at freedom of speech but takes in the whole range of moral and political choices which, if restrained by established institutions, are replaced by routine that is incompatible with the personal pursuit of happiness. Of course, when we blame ourselves for the decay of ourselves, we blame the established institutions that fashion us to be supine and that punish transgressions against conformity. This means that we blame the "regime," that which is taken as the established, and therewith as the self-repressing manifestation of other-than-selfhood. It goes without saying that this particular self-criticism looks toward existentialism, which descends from Nietzsche and Heidegger to the level of ordinary opinion on which we have been speaking of it. While Nietzsche spoke of the will to power, the overman, and the invitation to the eternal recurrence of the nauseous; and Heidegger proclaimed the authentic separation of *Dasein* from the dominance of the mass called "Them" or "They" (*der Man*) with an intention that was compatible with his own National Socialism, it cannot be doubted that the project of authentic existentialism is to harden—perhaps into petrification—the liberalized spirit of modern man and not to license it for petulant or hedonistic self-assertions. What exists among us now, as part of the extended regime that forms us and shapes our existence, is the ominous human discipline of high existentialism, passed through the medium of the liberalistic modernity it is intended to reform, and transformed by it into willfulness, consciousness-raising, and moral latitudinarianism. It would be morally wrong to pass from the subject of the vulgarization of existentialism without referring to the Nazism to which it lent itself, as well as to the attempts to turn it to the uses of communism that have an especial prestige in Europe.

Impossible to measure and impossible to overlook is the influence of psychoanalytic theory on the ways of our life. When Freud tried to present his work to the public in compact form (*An Outline of Psychoanalysis,* trans. J. Strachey), he began by discussing the mysterious but not for that reason deniable correspondence between body and mind ("the hypothesis of a psychical apparatus, extended in space") on which he erects the well-known structure of eros and destruction or death, part of a science that he assimilates to physics. As in the world described by physics, psychic events are not causeless and there is no evaporation of energies into nothing. On the contrary, there is a minute mechanics and dynamics in which no "error" is meaningless and no circumstance in principle unanalyzable, even though there is no possibility of reaching intelligible things in themselves. From this amalgam of elements more than reminiscent of ingredients in the thought of Spinoza and Descartes, Rousseau, and Kant, Freud constructs his famous account of man's psychic life, with a primary orientation upon therapy. He formulates in blunt language a radical generalization of the scope of sexual eroticism, develops a theory of the id, the ego, and the superego as psychic members of an economy presided over by the beleaguered ego, and proclaims the scientific infeasibility of a sharp distinction between the psychologically normal and abnormal. He discovers a therapy that depends on the liberation of repressed psychic material and its return to a place in the psychic economy where it can fortify the ego in its endless contest with the internal and external forces with which it must contend.

A spectator of psychoanalysis must be impressed by the difference between the authentic article and the popular impression of it. Striking is the transformation of repression from an act performed within the psyche by the conscious on the unconscious, to an act simply performed by the superego on the whole man, or, just as simplistically, by civilization as such on mankind. Taken in the latter vulgarized senses, it points toward a license to violate the rules, especially the rules governing sexual behavior, that emanate from civilized society. Moreover, Freud's reflections on the stress produced in a human being by the pressures of civilized life apparently were not part of a thought on his part that, as between civilization and surrender to the instincts, civilization—that is, restraints—must simply yield in the interest of mental health or happiness. On the contrary, he recognized a limit to the pursuit of happiness which is enforced by an irremovable destructiveness or aggressiveness in the human psyche that demands and presumably will forever demand the restraints of civilization, though according to rules he did not attempt to predict. Freud's psychoanalysis is a criticism of Hobbesian modernity as being unconcerned with the unconscious (thus of the realm of life, liberty, and happiness that politics as such is blind to); and it is a criticism of Rousseauan modernity as committed to the boundless malleability of man. Psychoanalysis shares the fate of the other strands of self-critical modernity in being received into the stream of modern life in the form of its own vulgarized hedonization. As always, the vulgarization is not without a basis in the primary thought: as existentialism might be seen as the criticism of modernity in the interest of spiritedness (crudely, "aggressiveness"), psychoanalysis is the criticism of civilization altogether, and therewith of modernity, in the interest of eros.

To this point I have attempted to indicate, by the use of a few conspicuous examples drawn from the atmosphere that we ourselves breathe, the basis for the assertion that we would not understand ourselves as a nation if we did not conceive our "regime" in the wide sense that includes not only our great political documents but the important influences on our way of life that emanate from unofficial thought. More specifically, I have tried to maintain that important, indeed decisive, elements of our "extended regime" consist of derivations from critical reflections on the classic modernity that informs our official or Constitutional regime. I have maintained further that those derivations typically have the character of distortions of the serious thought from which they are derived, and that the distortions have in general the quality of catering to our self-indulgence, even when the original thought had the opposite intention.

Perhaps this is to be explained as the revenge that is taken implacably on all subsequent criticisms by their target—the original principle of life, liberty, and the pursuit of happiness. It follows that the United States is the microcosm of modernity, repeating in its regime, on the level of popular consciousness, the major noetic events of the modern world. Our national self-dissatisfaction is the mirror of modernity's self-criticism. In our own way, we are mankind.

Of the preceding observations it must be said that at best they suffice only so far as they go. They neglect the bearing on what we are, and on what we can comprehend ourselves as standing for, of such immense moral influences as scriptural religion and natural science. These awesome forces, with their many manifestations, appear to stand toward each other in unrelieved antithesis. In fact they both presuppose a universe that is ultimately mysterious and in which the most important things can yet be known to man, especially the truth that there is a one or an absolute, the being of which dominates the whole. Scripture teaches that the absolute notices man as such while science conceives it as incapable of noticing anything. Scripture has therefore a clear moral meaning for all men: self-effacing obedience that must find expression, under the Christian dispensation, in love turned away from the body and in unshakeable conviction of faith. As one might say, eros has been immaterialized and spiritedness has been directed away from the moral goal of nobility praised by the pagans, toward the realm of truth and error, where in the worst case it appears as conscientious obstinacy. Like other great influences on humanity, it has a softening and a hardening aspect, a teaching about yielding to others and about urging one's own (even if one's own is borrowed.) Natural science does not have such a clear moral meaning for all men. As can be seen from the *Discourse on Method,* it has a moral meaning for scientists: resoluteness and privacy. Resoluteness is the virtue of the man who faces the unknown by choosing, even arbitrarily, a path (or better a direction) from which he does not swerve, on the model of a man lost in the wilderness. Resoluteness includes also the hardihood to be the chief and sole maker especially of one's greatest artifacts. Privacy is the necessary condition for scientific work. It means minding one's own business, sharing perhaps but not imposing, and generally abiding by the rule of live and let live, with "help live" emerging as a by-product. Resoluteness is the tacit criticism of guilty self-doubt and its consequent wavering in action. Privacy is the tacit criticism of dogmatic obstinacy. But the inspiriting lesson of modern science is much vitiated by the intimation that the resolute choice of a direction is a choice made in a wilderness—rather arbitrarily, for there is no final cause. Morally considered, objectivity without the object is hard to distinguish from subjectivity. The subjectivism that emerges from scientific resoluteness accords excellently with the mutual tolerance that emerges from scientific dedication to privacy. If natural science in the modern age has been thought of as the antidote to the hardness and softness peculiar to Christianity, the judgment would have to be scrutinized with strong reservations, not so much because the moral value of natural science had to pass down, from the scientists to the multitude, and thus undergo deformation, which it has, as because its moral value does not squarely confront the moral thrust of Christianity. Christian love, of which the present-day political equivalent is liberalism, marches in step with the beneficence of science, and with that tolerant subjectivism of science that now supports relativism. Moreover religion has, at least in the West, lost its dogmatic obstinacy, though it is true that science has at the same time become the source of notions that can exist in the minds of most human beings only on the strength of the authority of qualified experts. (In civilized countries, they are accepted voluntarily, and there are no civil penalties for rejecting or accepting a given theory of genetics, for example.) As scriptural religion has put itself in tutelage to science, and to many another worldly doctrine as well, it has converged on science in becoming more "erotic" and less inspiriting, if one may speak so; more mollifying and less fortifying of the human spirit; and the conscience that once made obstinate martyrs and pitiless torturers now makes, to our unheroic relief, constitutionally protected militants. More generally:—even or especially if modern natural science be considered part of the great critical reaction of modernity against the effeminating education spoken of by Machiavelli, the conclusion looms that the target and the weapon achieved a modus vivendi by which everything inspiriting has either been transformed into or been made ministerial to the mollifying or indolent.

If we return to the question, What is the status of scriptural religion and natural science as sources of our way of life or ingredients of our "regime"? we find that the answer runs in terms of a dialectic in the course of which the indulgent silently consumes the inspiriting. It would be absurd to make this a matter of reproach against troubled mankind, forever seeking to rid itself of the burdens and constraints without which it cannot live and with which it cannot be happy. Without any moralizing intent, however, one is justified in saying that not only has modernity constituted itself by criticizing and transforming itself, and concentrating its own principles by a process of self-indulgent distillation downward toward everyday life; but even on the plane of modernity's confrontation with pre-modernity, a similar process can be observed. The self-criticism of modernity is an episode of the continuous self-criticism of western man. Our self-dissatisfaction as a nation is our experience of that enormous comprehensive phenomenon. This, I take it, is the meaning of the

United States regime in its comprehensive sense, at the same time that it explains the meaning of our self-dissatisfaction.

Have we, with more pain than success, reinvented Hegel? I do not think so. Even if the whole dialectic of man's intellectual experience were precipitated only in our national existence, which I have not suggested, there is no reason to conclude either that we stand at the peak of a historic ascent or that attaining a perfection of self-consciousness—say understanding perfectly that man's life is encapsulated in us and we are therefore man's life—answers the question, What are we? If our "regime" and we ourselves are as I have tried to set them forth, then we are only one of a number of national microcosms of man's dialectical or self-critical noetic experience. Each nation apparently modifies and vulgarizes available thought according to a principle of selection and mutation that is, or is best articulated in, its own parchment regime, its Constitution, its guiding conception of justice and right. Politics originates nothing. Only if politics became philosophy or became united with philosophy, if practice united with theory, could politics, by dissolving itself, emancipate itself from its dependence on that over which it cannot gain control.

Yet politics, if dependent, is not inert, as is shown by the fact that the various nations resonate differently to the vibrations that flow over them as the stream of thought. Perhaps the highest task of political philosophy is to understand, as the highest task of statesmanship is to govern, the relation of political life to thought. The genius of the American regime assigns this highest task of statesmanship to the people themselves, and in so doing brings the nation to the outer limit of self-government rightly understood. This means that the character of the people is called on to stand in the place of wisdom. Our prospects in our third century appear to depend on the possibility that our moral resources will incline to fortify themselves at the spirited wells of modernity.

PPPPPPPPPPPPPPPPPPPPPPPPPPPPPPPPPPPPPP
PPPPPPPPPPPPPPPPPPPPPPPPPPPPPPPPPPPPPP
PPPPPPPPPPPPPPPPPPPPPPPPPPPPPPPPPPPPPP
PPPPPPPPPPPPPPPPPPPPPPPPPPPPPPPPPPPPPP
PPPPPPPPPPPPPPPPPPPPPPPPPPPPPPPPPPPPPP
PPPPPPPPPPPPPPPPPPPPPPPPPPPPPPPPPPPPPP
PPPPPPPPPPPPPPPPPPPPPPPPPPPPPPPPPPPPPP
PPPPPPPPPPPPPPPPPPPPPPPPPPPPPPPPPPPPPP
PPPPPPPPPPPPPPPPPPPPPPPPPPPPPPPPPPPPPP
PPPPPPPPPPPPPPPPPPPPPPPPPPPPPPPPPPPPPP
PPPPPPPPPPPPPPPPPPPPPPPPPPPPPPPPPPPPPP
PPPPPPPPPPPPPPPPPPPPPPPPPPPPPPPPPPPPPP
PPPPPPPPPPPPPPPPPPPPPPPPPPPPPPPPPPPPPP
PPPPPPPPPPPPPPPPPPPPP PPPPPPPPPPPPPPPP
PPPPPPPPPPPPPPPPPPPPP PPPPPPPPPPPPPPPP
PPPPPPPPPPPPPPPPPPPPP PP PPPPPPPPPPPP
PPPPPPP PP PPPPPPPP PP PPPPPPP PPPPP
PPPPPPP PP PPPPP PP PP PPP PPP PPPPP
PPP PPP PP PPPPPP PP PP PPP PPP PP PP
PPP PPP PP PP PPP PP PP PPP PPP PP PP
PPP P P PP PP PPP PP PP PPP P P PP P
PPP P P PP PP P P PP PP PPP P P PP P
P P P P P   PP P P PP PP P P P P   P
    P P P P   P   P P P   PP P P P P   P
    P P   P P   P   P   P P P   P   P
    P   P   P P   P   P P   P   P
    P   P P   P   P
                            P   P
                                                            P

Part One

What Is Welfare
Economics?

Reprinted from *Ethics* 65, no.
2 (January 1955). ©1955 by
The University of Chicago.

Contemporary welfare economics has drawn so heavily upon mathematics, psychology, and moral and political science that it can scarcely be understood without reference to the extra-economic premises and procedures to which it has bound itself. The purpose of this paper is to inquire into the meaning of the levy that economics has made upon the other disciplines, to try to state the characteristics of present-day welfare economics as the common terminus of three convergent lines of development—a mathematical, a psychological, and a moral-political.

I

What is the nature of the contribution made by mathematics to welfare economics? Most generally, mathematics provides welfare economics with an approach to the problem of heterogeneous assortments. That approach both implies and presupposes a theory of the natures of things and a theory of speculation concerning the natures of things. Let us consider briefly the wider meaning of the penetration of welfare economics by mathematics.

Professor Samuelson has shown the indispensability to welfare economics of certain value "assumptions," of which I take two to be pre-eminently important: First, that "individuals' preferences are to 'count.' " And second, "that more of any one output, other commodities or services being constant, is desirable; similarly, less input for the same outputs is desirable."[1] Together, these imply (a) that the state of welfare of a population is the composite level of gratification of all the idiosyncratic preferences of all the individuals in the group; and (b) that that level of gratification is affected by the relation between inputs and outputs. So far, the problem of welfare economics is one in the manipulation of heterogeneous assortments: how to make meaningful statements about a heterogeneity of men with their preferences confronting a heterogeneous output; and about that same congeries of outputs in juxtaposition to another congeries called inputs. What is necessary is a device adapted to the summary treatment of galaxies of micro-entities. Such a device is mathematical analysis, which can embrace as many individuals, and as many characteristics of as many individuals, as there are symbols; and the number of symbols is as large as the number of numbers.

To each individual, and to each relevant characteristic of each individual, a symbol is assigned. Equations must then be written in a number which depends upon the number of individuals in the assortment, for each individual, on being assigned a symbol, becomes a variable of the problem. Then a solution of the fundamental equation may be found, the principle of which will be this: no fewer variables in the solution than there are individuals in the original heterogeneity. Evidently, the act of mathematical aggregation is not also an act of classification, for the separate identity of each of the heterogeneous individuals is and must be preserved intact down into the conclusion of reasoning.

Thus the fundamental objects of discussion of (mathematical) welfare economics are not formed into classes but become the subjects of conclusions only as discrete individuals. It is therefore only in a manner of speaking that mathematics solves the problem of heterogeneity. Mathematical aggregation, in so far as it is also disintegrative of established classes, transcends methodology and enters directly into the substance of welfare economics in a problematic way.

What it implies is nothing less than a reconstruction of the two prime categories, man and goods. The reconstruction would individualize the species of man (i.e., reduce the species to, and replace it by, its individuals) and generalize the species of goods (i.e., dissolve the species of goods and replace them directly by their genus).

What are the grounds for this reconstruction and what precisely does it mean? It means, most generally, the rejection of the traditional taxonomy based upon the idea of the naturalness—hence irreducibility—of the species. "Man" is not a workable concept; only "men" are intelligible. The facts of humanity must be drawn out by the summation of idiosyncracies, not by abstraction from idiosyncracies. Classification is replaced by aggregation, and the species are replaced by heterogeneities. As for commodities, the specific differences among them too are obscured by their reduction to the plane of undifferentiated utility: not as shoes and apples but as sources of general "utility" are they made the subjects of theory.

What the mathematical reconstruction of the prime categories implies is not only a principle of taxonomy but necessarily, therefore, also a principle of definition, for each thing must be defined by reference to the class to which it belongs. The replacement of species by heterogeneities, i.e., of classes by individuals, renders the individual radically *sui generis*. He must be defined in terms of what differentiates him from others, not what likens him to others. This necessity falls upon welfare economics not in the area of men and goods, which the discipline does not attempt to define, but in the area of the definition of welfare itself, into which in one way or another the discipline does enter. We must consider two aspects of the definition of welfare, one mathematical and the other cast in the form, "Welfare is a state of consciousness." The latter will be discussed below; let us speak only of the former at this point.

The mathematical characterization of welfare takes the form of a functional expression: the welfare of a group is some function of an indefinite number of variables (written $W = W[a, b, c, . . .]$), the symbols representing all the factors that (1) may be expressed as quantities and (2) have an effect on the economic welfare of the group. Saying that welfare is a function of a, b, c, and so on, is a way of saying, at least in part, what welfare is. This way of saying what welfare is, is itself composed of parts: (1) welfare is a function; and (2) welfare is a function *of a, b, c, and so on.* To say that welfare is a function implies that welfare must be known by reference to what affects its amount, quantity, or size. But if welfare is a quality of a man, or of a population, or if it cannot for any other reason be reduced to quantities, the functional approach to the characterization of welfare would be at least misleading. Yet it is seized upon because it is an attractive alternative to the substantive definition of welfare with specific predicates. To say that welfare is a function of (is somehow related to the magnitudes of) a, b, and c is to say, of course, that a, b, and c must be replaced by nonsymbolic terms in any actual situation. By which nonsymbolic terms? This is the question that the mathematical characterizer of welfare is absolved from answering. He need only affirm the law of change in the amount of welfare regardless of what may be thought by this or that observer to bear upon it.

The virtue of such an approach to welfare is that it accords so well with the replacement of the human species by the human individual. The essential characteristic of individuals is their individuality. They differ infinitely as evaluators of welfare—as experiencers of it and hence as theorizers concerning it. Let everyone mean by a, b, and c whatever he sees fit to mean—*de gustibus non disputandum*. What is good for men is decided by their preferences, not by their specific natures—the inevitable by-product of the subversion of the species.

So far we have considered substantive implications of the incursion of mathematics into welfare economics. Does not mathematics have a right to be judged solely as an organon or method of pure reasoning? To a certain extent, the foregoing discussion implies that the mathematical method, like every method, has a supra-methodical meaning; every logic presupposes a metaphysic. This is eminently true of mathematics as a method of inquiry in welfare economics. To the extent to which mathematics makes it possible to discuss welfare economics *no matter what welfare is*, and thus necessarily by reference to the law of change in the amount of welfare rather than to its formal character, the employment of mathematics has this meaning: the truth about welfare is not embodied in substantive statements about welfare, which are conclusions deduced from true substantive premises; the premises must always remain "symbolic." Moreover, mathematical truth is indistinguishable from internal consistency in the process of reasoning: "truth" is the structure of the syllogism, not the verity of the proposition. What, then, becomes of the truth about economic welfare? The mathematical method implies that truth resides *in principle* in the *process* of reasoning about the *process* of change. In so far as the application of mathematical analysis to welfare economics either relies upon or itself creates the presumption that (1) knowledge of the flux of a thing is possible in the absence of knowledge of the nature of the thing; and (2) that truth resides in the process of reasoning rather than in the premises and conclusions as affirmations—to that extent the validity of the mathematical approach to welfare economics is problematical in value.

II

Professor Pigou has affirmed,[2] and welfare economists generally have not denied, that the elements of welfare are states of consciousness. This assertion raises two problems which are best described as psychological: First, in which of the states of consciousness is welfare included? Second, in what sense is it true that welfare consists of states of consciousness? Let us examine these in turn.

A. The distribution of man's psychic life between the conscious and the nonconscious continues to pose grave problems. In the presence of these, it is not likely that any categorization of the states of consciousness itself would gain unanimous approval. For the present purpose I shall use the safely extensive construction of consciousness that comprehends all of feeling and cognition, employing the term to include emotion or passion, imagination, memory, opinion, and knowledge. (Let us omit sense-perceptions by stipulating that welfare, as an "abstraction," cannot be a mere sensation, e.g., a sight, a sound, or a smell.) Of which of these is welfare composed?

Is feeling, emotion, or passion a state of the consciousness to which welfare might in principle belong? If so, a man's welfare would consist of his feeling of well-being. The problem then would be to identify the feeling or emotion of well-being. Actually there is none such. There are feelings of pity, anger, fear, and hunger, and of pleasure or gratification arising from many sources, but scarcely such a thing as the emotion of welfare. In other words, if welfare is to be reduced to a "feeling," it must be reduced to the undifferentiated feeling of "pleasure" from whatever source—and obviously there are many sources. This is unabashed hedonism. It is not probable that economists wish to be understood as meaning that a man is well off, "has welfare," whenever he experiences pleasure and in virtue of that experience.

We need not here rehearse the rebuttals of raw hedonism that have accumulated in a score of centuries. For our present purposes it suffices to point out that if welfare is an emotive state of consciousness, and if the consciousness can be in only one state or condition at a time, then the thinking man as thinking (i.e., as nonfeeling) cannot be possessed of welfare. There is no reason to take such a view of things seriously.

Is it possible that welfare partakes of imagination or of memory, i.e., of consciousness of what does not now, and possibly will never, correspond with reality? Is a man happy when he recalls his past happiness or dreams his dream of a situation in which he supposes he might be happy? The recollection of welfare is not welfare; neither is the recollection of a welfare-giving situation welfare. Surely the phantasm of welfare or of a welfare-giving situation is not itself welfare. If it were, we should have to look differently on the sale of narcotic drugs.

Then what of the opinionative state of consciousness? If welfare were to belong to opinion, men might believe themselves happy without actually being so, for anything subject to opinion is subject to wrong opinion. This is intrinsic to the nature of opinion and leads to the following contradiction: a man might opine himself happy, yet do so wrongly. Then he would be happy because he so opined himeself, yet he would not be happy because he wrongly so opined himself. The contradiction flows from the premises that welfare is the opinionative state of consciousness, and that opinion differs from knowledge (i.e., opinion may be right or wrong). The latter is scarcely questionable; it is the former which must be rejected as leading to an absurdity.

We have excluded as the possible elements of welfare all but one of the states of consciousness with which we began. Does welfare coincide with the remaining one, noetic awareness, knowledge, or thought simply? To say so would imply that a man's happiness consists in knowing himself to be happy—which cannot be true without qualification: He cannot know himself to be happy unless there is a happiness or welfare waiting to be known prior to his apprehension of it. The object of knowledge must at least in some sense antedate the knowledge itself. Yet surely it is true that the man who *knows* he has welfare truly has it, and his knowing it is indispensable to his fully having it. Does this mean that his welfare consists of a cognitive state of consciousness? Rather than that, it means that his welfare is completed by an act of cognition, but that the object of cognition, as indispensable to the act, is indispensable to his welfare.

B. Thus we are led to consider the second question proposed above, namely, in what sense is it true that welfare consists of states of consciousness. We may now say that consciousness necessarily implies an object of consciousness, a thing of which the conscious being is conscious. In our context that object must itself be either welfare or nonwelfare. If welfare consists of a consciousness of nonwelfare, welfare is reduced either to pleasure, a reduction which is untenable, or to the denial of welfare, as we saw when we considered opinion, memory, and imagination above. (Sense-perception as a form of consciousness would come under this precept too.) If welfare consists of a consciousness of welfare, then the very saying of the words proves that there is an objective aspect of welfare which is as much an element of man's well-being as is his consciousness of it. In brief, welfare is as much a state of being as it is a state of consciousness.

Only by ignoring this have welfare economists been able to discuss welfare "whatever it is," i.e., without reference to its objective conditions. Since welfare is actualized, realized, or completed by an act of knowing, or an apprehension of reality, an intelligible reality must stand as the material potentiality of welfare. It is hard to understand how a science of welfare can abstain from recognizing the existence of welfare itself, but so, it seems, modern welfare economics does when directly or by inference it proceeds as if welfare were "all in the mind."

Whatever is *all* in the mind is nowhere but in the mind—it is not part of the world of evident things. Each must be for himself the final judge and arbiter of whatever is radically inevident. Of such arbitration and judgment there can be no dispute; the individual is unassailable in his sovereignty. *Sui generis*, he cannot be classified. He can only be aggregated.

III

Present-day welfare economics has a crucial political characteristic which emerges pointedly in the fact that many of the discipline's most important conclusions can be stated exhaustively without reference to the institutional framework or regime that would serve to contain them. Those conclusions take the form of "purely economic welfare conditions" which, as purely economic, are suprapolitical, transcending polity and hence independent of polity in being equally binding upon all polities. Something similar to this seems to be present in the ideas of Professor A. P. Lerner when he writes that "liberalism and socialism can be reconciled in welfare economics."[3] I believe that Professor Lerner's thesis might be taken to mean that there are technical conditions of economic welfare which are related to political things as ends are related to means, surely not in any sense as means are related to ends. The technical conditions of welfare being once defined, liberalism, collectivism, or any efficient combination of the two may be employed to realize those conditions. Liberalism and collectivism may be expected to differ in eligibility for such employment only on grounds of efficiency, i.e., adaptability to the economic objective. Conversely, the economic objectives of a liberal and a collectivized society are indiscriminately the equalization of marginal social benefit and marginal social cost.[4] Only the mechanics of procuring the equality differ under the two orders.[5] Mr. I. M. D. Little affirms this in saying, "We may now sum up our discussion of the political implications of pure static welfare theory. We do not believe it can be reasonably and honestly used in defence of, or against, any particular political system."[6] Professor Samuelson's way of putting this is by saying, "the auxiliary constraints imposed upon the variables are not themselves the proper subject matter of welfare economics but must be taken as given,"[7] meaning by "the auxiliary constraints imposed upon the variables" such things as the political framework of society as it limits men's behavior in all senses.

This conception of the radical identity in aim of liberal and collectivized society is characteristic of those whose evaluation of collectivism and liberalism consists in inquiring how nearly they attain the same (economic) objective. For example, Barone finds that output, and hence presumably welfare, is maximized when costs are minimized and price equals cost. In his famous article on the Ministry of Production, he can be construed as concluding that collectivism is defective because collectivist planners cannot know certain technical variables except through empirical means—i.e., by, for all practical purposes, reproducing the essentially unplanable market.[8] Whatever else it means, Barone's conclusion means that the economic process is intransigent to differences of or changes in political institutions—every economy has the same formal end as every other—largely because the economic process is bound to technological conditions and to irreducible individual tastes. Economy, in other words, is supra-political or perhaps infra-political in that its requirements and conditions are entirely unresponsive to differences of time, place, and polity.[9] Putting this somewhat differently, Barone's conclusion may be taken to mean that one can discuss the best economy without reference to the best polity.[10] All polities have as their economic end the maximum gratification of desires with the minimum expenditure of effort. To understand the conditions under which satisfaction is maximized and effort minimized, it is necessary to solve an essentially mathematical problem—the comparison of the rates of change of two congeries.

The maximization objective is extrapolitical. It is, in other words, universal—equally ruling under freedom and tyranny, kingship, aristocracy, or democracy, barbarism and civilization. It is not subject to discretion any more than the principle of gravitation is subject to discretion. Its force proceeds from the irresistible power of the human phenomena from which it is derived: the primitive desires of mankind for pleasure and their aversion to pain and effort. It is irresistible because it is extra-rational or dependent upon the ubiquitous desires; and it is extra-political because it is universal in virtue of its being extra-rational. The full separation of polity and economy required the full separation of economy and reason, or the union of economy and passion in the radical sense.

The influence of this outlook upon welfare economics stands forth when we compare the present-day science with the form of it that existed, for example, in the writings of Adam Smith. No one will need to be convinced that Smith attached importance to the growth of wealth and to its widespread distribution. Yet in full appreciation of the contributions to output that could be made by the elaboration of the division of labor, Smith drew attention to the undesirable effects of industrialization upon the habits and mentality of the populace.[11] Equally cognizant of economic aspects of inequality in the distribution of wealth, neither he nor others of his age would have considered a discussion of this matter to be useful if it ignored the relation between inequality of wealth and what they called "subordination" in the political sense. Many similar examples could be given. In general, those early writers whom we think of as the political economists realized that the social apparatus designed to procure fulfilment of "purely economic welfare conditions" cannot fail at the same time to produce the most profound noneconomic consequences; and that those consequences cannot be omitted from the account except artificially and at the peril of arriving at conclusions which are useless or worse than useless. Hence an important difference arises between contemporary welfare economics and its predecessor science: When authors like Adam Smith advocated policies and institutions that promoted production and accumulation, they did so because the wealth-giving institutions had salutary noneconomic consequences of the highest importance.[12] Perhaps the last ones who took seriously the relation of economics to the whole were those proto-economists who antedated economics.

We might summarize this much of the argument by saying that, its explicit acknowledgments in the direction of noneconomic welfare notwithstanding, contemporary welfare economics, lacking the breadth of view that the science traditionally possessed, blinds itself to the largest bearing, which is the political or moral bearing, of institutions designed to implement the seemingly innocuous and incontrovertible maximization principle. In one way or another contemporary welfare economics has substituted the economy for the polity, or put the economy before the polity for the reason that requires the end always to be put before the means. The substitution of the economic for the politic, i.e., of the part for the whole, is a movement with deep and remote origins, into which it is here impossible to enter. We can, however, consider a brief and simple illustration of the effect that this movement has had upon the present constitution of welfare economics.

Present-day welfare economists regularly discuss the problem of the distribution of the national income. Not uncommonly, they refer to it as a moral and political problem—as somehow bound up with the problem of justice. Yet I believe that there does not exist in modern welfare economics a description of optimal distribution conditions based upon a reasoned conception of justice. The issue has eluded discussion in a variety of ways, of which perhaps the most interesting is the way reflected in the writing of some mathematical economists. Professor Samuelson's position among mathematical economists is such that one who seeks an example is not unjustified in turning to his works. I therefore recur to his *Foundations of Economic Analysis*. There, he infers the following "interpersonal optimal conditions"; "first, the marginal social utility (disutility) of the same good (service) must be equal for each individual; second, each factor of production must be divided among different possible uses so that its indirect, derived marginal social utility must be the same in every use and equal to its marginal social disutility."[13] One might comment on this passage either at great length or very briefly. Very briefly, without a precise understanding of marginal social utility and disutility, i.e., of how much of what is good for whom, or justice, the statement is quite void of meaning. By itself, it tells us no more than that where there is too much, something should be subtracted, and where there is too little, something should be added. That superfluity and insufficiency are destructive of welfare, of satisfaction, and of justice is not matter of dispute; it never was. We do not require higher mathematics to tell us that privation should be succored out of redundancy. What we require is to be told the nature of superfluity and of insufficiency, and to be instructed so that we may know when abundance and privation are salutary and deserved, when insalubrious and unjust and needful of rectification. The answers to these questions cannot be produced cybernetically, i.e., by inserting data into a formula or a formula-solving mechanism. The formula and the mechanism are nothing but embodiments of our notions, devices which can save time but can never save thought concerning the principles of things. Professor Samuelson's formulation inferentially defines the optimum as an "equality," albeit equality of marginal social utilities for every individual. What meaning can this have? Does it mean simply that if some are hungry while others are not, one possibility is to feed the hungry from the food of the prosperous? Or must we not inquire whether the hungry are so because they are depraved or indolent or unfortunate or exploited or gluttonous; and the rich because they are parsimonious, lucky, blessed, or unscrupulous? Moreover, is all poverty *poverty*, or is some of it austerity? Where does satisfaction become satiation? Wealth is the condition of satisfaction, but it also conveys power and responsibility. Who is fit to have how much of each? And how should we construe equality of marginal social utilities of goods for all persons? Is it to be taken before or after their education in the good things of life? And of what value is the principle before we know the distinction between the good and the bad things of life? We shall never know the answers to these questions from mathematical welfare economics as mathematical. These questions are alleged to be problems for "someone else." Perhaps they are. If so, the case for mathematical, indeed for all nonaxiological welfare economics, becomes, I believe, weaker, not stronger. For until these questions are answered, mathematical welfare economics is pumping in a vacuum. After they are solved, the important work is over. But mathematics can have no hand in their solution. Then what is the function of mathematics in welfare economics?

Professor Samuelson's principle is that welfare economics may make moral assumptions but does not deduce appropriate beliefs, i.e., moral conclusions. That is to say, the conclusions of (mathematical) welfare economics are as adaptable to unjust as to just decisions for the community: they are neutral with respect to justice. To which we must

subjoin our conviction that mathematical welfare economics has by this
very token brought forth a sterile progeny.

Conclusion

Our aim has been to say what welfare economics is, and to do so
especially by reference to the convergent mathematical, psychological,
and moral-political characteristics of the contemporary science. It now
remains to summarize the manner and the meaning of that convergence.
This may be done most concisely in terms of the answers to the question,
What is welfare? implicit in or presupposed by the mathematical,
psychological, and moral-political elements of contemporary welfare
economics. Mathematically, welfare is conceived as an aggregate of the
preferences of an unclassified human heterogeneity vis-à-vis an unclassified heterogeneity of goods and services. The mathematical characterization of welfare rests upon a far-reaching assumption as to the role and
meaning of species or natural differences among classes of things. In
effect it denies those natural specific differences, replacing them by genera
each of which is a spectrum of irreducible individuals. But genera not
composed of species ought to be called aggregations, or perhaps assortments. The mathematical view of welfare flows from a rearrangement of
natural things which is as much a de-ordering as a re-ordering.

Psychologically, welfare is conceived to be exclusively a state of
consciousness and not at all an object of consciousness. Therefore it
cannot be reduced to evidence, and hence it cannot be the subject of
argument, reason, or conviction. As a complete "subjectivism," each
man's welfare is what he takes it to be. He cannot be mistaken. Yet we saw
that the very idea of consciousness implies that he may well be mistaken,
for the consciousness of rational men is not of nonexistent things; and of
existent things there must be evidence.

Morally, welfare or the good is again conceived as, for every man,
unique. The political consequence of this idea is that the maximum
satisfaction of preferences takes precedence over the maximum satisfaction of the requirements of justice as the norm of the common good. The
practically decisive differences between polities are subordinated to their
common economic property: they must all serve to gratify in the highest
degree the arbitrary preferences of irreducible individuals.

The point upon which the psychological, moral, and mathematical
qualities of welfare economics converge is the axiom of the irreducibility of
the individual and hence the sovereignty of his passions. The short title of
this idea is Individualism. It is conceived of as the bulwark of Human
Dignity: what dignifies man's estate is the importance of each man as a

unique phenomenon. I believe that the mere statement of this idea suggests its dubiousness. The dignity of human beings proceeds from their common relation to nonhuman things at least as much as from their relations to each other. Their dignity is the attribute of their common nature, of what they possess jointly, not severally, and it inheres in what elevates them above nonhumanity rather than in what merely distinguishes them from each other. If this is so, the entire structure of modern welfare economics rests upon a sandy foundation. It would need reconstruction upon a plan the profoundest characteristic of which would be the affirmation of a human nature that transcends the feelings of individuals as such. That the transcendence of feelings is not a manifest impossibility or, worse, an outrage against conscience is proved by the importance which by universal consent is still attached to the concept of duty—something that transcends, ignores, and commonly overrides the feelings of individuals as such.

The extent of the truth in all the foregoing measures the extent to which, paradoxically, welfare economics has not yet begun to be: it measures the distance of the contemporary from the real. Of one thing we may be certain: the existence of welfare economics is no more proved by the presence of welfare economists than was the existence of medical science proved, in the second century, by the presence of physicians. It is not unimaginable that our science lies as much before us as theirs lay before them.

Notes

1. *Foundations of Economic Analysis* (Cambridge: Harvard University Press, 1947), p. 223.
2. *The Economics of Welfare* (4th ed.; London: Macmillan, 1932), p. 10.
3. *The Economics of Control* (New York: Macmillan, 1944), p. 4.
4. Ibid., p. 77.
5. But social cost and social benefit may be expected to have very different meanings in a liberal and a collectivist society, so that the reduction of the welfare conditions to equality of marginal social benefit and marginal social cost becomes practically of little help. The question which is crucial for welfare would still remain: By what scale of values would cost and benefit be assigned to goods and services in a collectivist and a liberal society, and what supra-economic ends would be sought and achieved through such assignments of cost and benefit? Of what use is the equation while we do not know how cost and benefit would be distributed between accumulation and consumption, variety and uniformity, industrialism and agrarianism, militarization and "civilianism," to suggest but a few of the likely problems.
6. *A Critique of Welfare Economics* (Oxford: Clarendon Press, 1950), p. 266.
7. *Foundations of Economic Analysis*, pp. 221–22.
8. E. Barone, "The Ministry of Production in the Collectivist State" in

Collectivist Economic Planning, ed. F. A. Hayek (London: G. Routledge & Sons, 1935).

9. Our approach to the problem of underdeveloped countries is quite consistent with this view.

10. I believe that Professor Samuelson's definition of the optimum conditions in the *Foundations of Economic Analysis,* pp. 233, 238-39, 246, brings him to a conclusion which in this respect agrees with that of Barone.

11. It seems that the dismissal of this entire matter from consideration is what is intended by Professor Samuelson when he concurs in the custom of hypothesizing "that production itself takes place in firms or industries which are distinct from the individuals, having no value in and of themselves." Ibid., p. 230. I assume that "value" here means "relevance to welfare."

12. I believe this can be proved, surely in the case of Adam Smith, although I can here do no more than simply to affirm it without proof.

13. *Foundations of Economic Analysis,* p. 246.

On the Relation of Political Science and Economics

Reprinted from the *American Political Science Review* 54, no. 1 (March 1960). ©1960 by The American Political Science Association.

That politics and economic life have much to do with each other is a remark matched in self-evidence only by the parallel observation that political science and economics are of mutual interest. All the more striking then is the difficulty one meets in attempting to state with precision how politics and economic life, or how political science and economics are related.

I

Consider for example the view that politics is the ceaseless competition of interested groups. Except under very rare conditions, as for instance the absence of division of labor, economic circumstances will preoccupy the waking hours of most men at most times. Their preoccupations will express themselves in the formation of organizations, or at least interested groups, with economic foundations. Politics, so far as "interest" means "economic interest" (which it does largely, but not exclusively), is the mutual adjustment of economic positions; and to that extent, the relation between politics and economic life seems to be that political activity grows out of economic activity. But the competition of the interests is, after all, an organized affair, carried out in accordance with rules called laws and constitutions. So perhaps the legal framework, the construction of which surely deserves to be called political, supervenes over the clashing of mere interests and even prescribes which interests may present themselves at the contest. Thus politics appears to be primary in its own right. But we are compelled to go a step further: Is not the legal framework itself a direct consequence of the rivalries of self-seekers, so that even the fundamental law or laws merely give expression to still more fundamental facts of life? We find ourselves at last asking whether politics is simply the extension of economic activity, as war was once said to be the extension of diplomacy; or whether, on the other hand, economic life is determined in its most important respects by acts of legislation irreducible to anything but a judgment of the general welfare.

But perhaps we have strayed in our reasoning, and the question whether political or economic activity is primary is not the right question. Perhaps instead we ought to begin by observing that there is political life and there is economic life. They are related in that they both occupy the same space, in a manner of speaking, a space loosely called society. There is a political aspect of society and there is an economic aspect. Questions of power are settled under the one, questions of wealth are settled under the other. Certainly, wealth may confer power and power may occasion wealth, but this does not diminish the difference between the two objects or between the activities by which they are sought and gained. If we pay attention for a moment to the social sciences that investigate these matters, namely political science and economics, we notice how little inclined each is to assert its "primacy" over the other. One studies society in its capacity as "state"; the other studies the identical society considered in its capacity as "economy." Society might also be studied as "culture," and perhaps in other capacities. The truth seems to be that men occupy themselves with numerous activities or kinds of behavior, in each of which the actors pursue something that appears to them worth while or necessary. The peaceful coexistence of the activities is reflected in the disinclination of the corresponding social sciences to invade each other with claims of precedence. Political and economic activity are related to each other, indeed, but in the sense that they are autonomous principalities, neither subject to the other, both contributory to society.

We could wish to be content with this explanation, if we were satisfied that the use it makes of the term "society" did not introduce a new difficulty. Society does not mean the universal concourse of all mankind. Invariably it means only some men, ordinarily those who live within a frontier fixed by conventions and under a common set of laws and institutions. If there were not laws and conventions, there would be no societies, or at any rate no societies in which the relation of politics and economics would be perceived as a problem. And how then is one to account for those legislative and political activities, or proto-political activities, which are the source of the law upon which society rests? Is such political activity in principle not merely a sophisticated device for securing life and property? We observe that the attempt to dispose of the problem of politics and economics by making use of "society" and "behavior" as primary only shows us more clearly how difficult it is to escape treating the relation of politics and economics as itself primary, in order to explain society.

When we think of the ground or foundation of society, we are reminded of the classic treatments of the theme, and of the differences that have existed among the ablest men who have applied themselves to the problem. Some, like Aristotle, have thought that the cultivation of property ("equipment") is the condition for the support of a good constitution. Others, like Locke, have taught that a good constitution is one that supports a sound system of property. And many men, before Aristotle and after Abraham Lincoln, have known that the very question of what may be held as property is decided by the law which gives its character to civil society—the very law which, some say, is framed by hands that hold or reach out toward property in every form. Again we are led to the problem of the relation between the political and the economic as a question of primacy or order.

II

Let us make a new beginning, restating the problem and its conditions. We should like to know, as exactly as we can, what relation exists between political science and economics. In order to proceed, we must have an idea of what is meant by a relation between sciences. In one respect, sciences can scarcely be said to be capable of having a relation with each other except in the trivial sense that, as bodies of knowledge, they may be lodged in the same mind, or in different minds. But sciences are not simply knowledge, for there is no such thing. Knowledge must be of something, and a science must have an object, which is the thing known or studied. Now it occasionally happens that one object is contributory or auxiliary to another in a simple and manifest way; as, for example, systems of waste and sewage disposal are contributory to comprehensive arrangements for safeguarding public health. In that case, the science of sanitary engineering would be contributory to the larger science of public health. It is generally true that sciences are related to each other as their respective objects are related, the sciences being, so to speak, the rarefied forms of their objects. If, then, we wish to investigate the relation of political science and economics, we ought to begin with their respective objects—what each one is about—and if possible determine the relation of those objects.

Political science is the science of government, or the science that has government as its object. As the object of political science, government is not the simple substantive which means *the* government; rather it is the transitive verbal noun which has "governing" as a near equivalent. Government must be by people and of people; some govern and many are governed. The instrument, by which those who are licensed to govern do their office, is law. The positive law, expressed, clarified, and executed by officers of government is the ligament between authority and citizenry, binding them together. Such law is in fact omnicompetent, and reaches or can reach, as history amply demonstrates, to every imaginable human act—with what right or what success we need not stop here to inquire. It is not to the purpose to enumerate the many human acts of which reckless or humane regimes take no cognizance; every act of nonintervention by the law is, as the words themselves say, an act of the law—a tacit or explicit act of abnegation. Thus it is by an act of the law, by which we mean an act of the lawmakers, that law is forbidden to interfere with worship and other things in this country. In brief, the distinction between public and private matters is itself a public matter, expressed in law by the makers of the law.[1] It is clear that the force of this observation is in no way diminished by the fact that, under the best circumstances, the governed consent to the acts of government, and may themselves be said to hold in their hands the ultimate authority that gives its sanction to the law. On these grounds it may be said that political science has as its object government, meaning by that the relation of governors and citizens, expressed in law, and comprehending, in principle if not in practice, all the deeds of all the men.

When we attempt next to understand what the object of economics is, we must begin by ignoring the fact that there is no such thing as economics in general, but rather socialist economics, free enterprise economics, the economics of slave systems, and so on. We may ignore these distinctions here for the reason that, in one important respect, the various kinds of economics overlap, since they all have their origin in the same circumstance, namely, human need. A certain exchange or transfer of matter must take place between men and their natural surroundings, and it must be effected by the use of objects which exceed the hands in hardness and other merely material qualities. In one sense there is no more fundamental fact about men: first of all, their nature demands matter, and the nature of what surrounds them also compels them to collect and utilize matter in order to stay alive.

It is a commonplace that a gap exists between matter as such and property. Matter is not automatically made property either by occupation or possession or prescription; for property is an extension of its owner, something physically external which is assimilated to him although it is not inseparable from his body. His appropriation to himself of what is external must therefore be recognized by others, or he will be parted from it by them at their convenience. Therefore the transformation of matter into property depends upon an act of convention or agreement by which each recognizes, and abstains from, the extended as well as the natural person of every other. We appear compelled to infer that the object of economics, namely, man's use of indispensable matter for the satisfying of his needs, is prior in principle to civil life and is indeed the root of law and civilization. This is what is implied by some of those who assert that the purpose of government is to guarantee property. In fact, however, the meaning of this reasoning is quite different. Although it appears to say that man's requirement of matter generates law, in fact it says that the transformation of matter into property requires law, or has law as its condition; and more precisely, it has not law simply as its condition, but law of a certain content and intention. For law that made each man the precarious beneficiary of the sovereign at the mere pleasure of the sovereign, as a child or servant is the beneficiary of the head of the household, would be undoubted law, but it would not be law that culminated in property.

We may notice now more exactly why there is not such a thing as economics simply, but rather as many varieties of economics as there are legal systems. The reason is that, what objects a man may hold as his property, saying of them that he needs them to live, is altogether a public or legal matter. The demand of self-preservation does not lead naturally to any particular institution of ownership, as a comparison of medieval natural law doctrine with capitalism amply demonstrates. It leads to a system of ownership only through certain acts of government. We know positively that the sense of the community, expressed in law, may permit the owning of a man or forbid the owning of the soil, permit the owning of engines of war or forbid the owning of a brocade cloak. Property, tangible as well as intangible, is the creature of the law, is subordinate to the law. What it is and who may have of it and what he may do with it is settled by acts of government.

But this does not quite conclusively establish the proposition that the object of economics is subordinate to the object of political science. For it has been known, since Plato's time at the least, that the rules with respect to property that come into force at the foundation of the community, or thereafter, have much to do with the subsequent development of the community as a political society. The truth of this follows from the meaning of property: property is an artificial elaboration of the man, the collection of objects which, when added to the man, form as a sum the civil person, a subject or citizen of a certain kind. He may be a formidable citizen if his person is greatly extended with objects, a negligible citizen if his person is destitute of every increment and he confronts his governors in his congenital nakedness, so to speak, or in his minimum scope, without addition.

That a man's powers may be expanded in other ways than by the increase of his "size" is obvious. But it must be said that the man wholly unexpanded in every way lacks the ground for that self-regard which distinguishes the citizen from the mere subject. To create a civil society of self-regarding men, which is to say men who confront government with a strong consciousness of their rights, the statesman should endow the people with those rights of self-enlargement which are the ground of larger rights. Liberal constitutions seem, according to the nature of things, to rest easily upon a base of economic freedom because of the ease with which political rights arise out of access to property. Conversely, authoritarian constitutions must circumscribe the acquisitiveness of subjects, or the subjects will grow beyond the power of the laws to hem them in. Regimes seem thus to derive their characters from the economic foundations that support them. There appears to be a strong reason for affirming the subordination of rule to property: rule is for the good of the governed, and the enlargement of property is equivalent to the enlargement of the man—the ground of his development as a human being and as a citizen.

We seem to have discovered that the economic arrangements are means contributory to political ends in a way so fundamental that it would be misleading to describe them as merely contributory; the means and the end seem in fact to lose their order and to disappear in each other. We have reached the point at which it is necessary to begin once again, for without a deeper principle than any to which we have thus far had recourse, we seem unable to break out of the endless alternation of the political and economic at what appear to be the foundations, each incontrovertibly determining the other and dependent on the other.

III

The clue to the solution of our problem is indicated by the history of the two sciences of political philosophy and economics. For twenty centuries there was but one social science, namely, political philosophy, and it had as its purpose to understand the nature of those who are to rule and of those who are to be ruled, and the nature or constitution of political society in the light of that understanding. The thinkers of classical antiquity, who impelled political philosophy in the direction in which it persisted for two millenia, understood the relation of rulers and ruled to be a natural relation in the literal sense that it arose directly out of observable and irreducible inequalities of human beings—inequalities in strength, to begin with, and other inequalities which became important in time. As Aristotle indicates in Book I of the *Politics,* pre-political society reflects the brute natural inequalities among human beings, while political society does or may reflect other inequalities. Under the best circumstances, the conventional or political order would reflect or incorporate or do justice to appropriate natural differences among human beings—including such differences as those between men and women, parents and children, and the aged and youthful, as well as between the exceptionally competent and those of meaner capacity. Political society is necessarily an articulation of unequals, and those concerned in it will be well off if their constructed or constitutional inequality harmonizes in the right way with the natural. The sovereign question is how that harmony may be achieved or approximated.

It is abundantly clear that Plato and Aristotle, who believed that the order of human inequality is natural, did not believe that nature was an engine for translating the appropriate natural order into the conventional order of human societies. In some respects, indeed, their teaching points to the urgent need of de-emphasizing the natural order of inequality in order to render political society possible or tolerable: the rule of the naturally strongest, the physically ablest, would or could be a rule of brutal barbarism. In other respects their doctrine implies indeed the friendliness of nature to civil society: nature furnishes the great quarry of matter out of which men may and can equip themselves for a social existence, and it furnishes them, if unequally, with that understanding of the meaning of inequality which men can translate into the description of an excellent political association. Only so far does the providence of nature extend. Nature provides the materials of political life, and it implies the form or outline of a proper political life, but it is not itself the efficient cause of the most desirable of political organizations, nor does it produce a general, much less an irresistible inclination toward them. On the contrary, the conventional or political order resists with a deep intransigence all efforts at converting it into the simply or naturally best order.

It is true that the political philosophy of classical Greece gives the impression of being dominated by the idea that nature is unqualifiedly or even providentially good for man, the direct source of the model of human perfection, private and political. From this famous ostensive teleology, it is easy to proceed to the conclusion that the ancients were fantastic optimists, nourishing a blind faith in a nature which appears plainly to us to be itself blind to man and his happiness. Yet it is quite clear, for example from Book I of Aristotle's *Politics,* that classical philosophy understood that nature is as much identified with the beginning as with the end, or that nature shows itself in the barbaric pre-political state as it does in the artificial condition of civil life. The bridge that connects the pre-political with the political condition is the activity of satisfying the needs that accompany man in all his states, i.e., the economic activity. An emphatically natural acquisitive activity is hunting, which Aristotle subsumes under war and connects with the seizing of men to make of them a property. The civil activity that has an "affinity" with hunting is exchange, which necessarily occasions commerce. The "growth" of civil peace, or civilization, or political life, is the transformation of the predation of war into the salutary predation of peace, the mercenary quest for increase and gain.

Aristotle saw at the same time that acquisitiveness was "natural," that it was deplorable, and that it was indispensable to civil peace. What is most conspicuous in his discussion is that he conceived it to be deplorable. Aristotle deplored retail trade, usury, and "acquisitiveness" in the name of virtue, a quality of man which is perpetually threatened by his nature as that shows itself in his necessitousness. And yet his virtue and all his manifest possibilities are unintelligible except in the light of his nature. The public or political function of political philosophy is to turn attention toward the meaning of nature as end and to divert attention from nature as the beginning; or to turn attention toward nature as provident and friendly to human excellence, and away from nature as polemic and divisive, which it is. The classics seem to have believed that excessive emphasis upon man's neediness would blind him to the reason for not becoming a self-regarding atom. But the self-regarding man is, as such, the opposite of the citizen, whose peculiar virtue is patriotism or regard for country and countrymen first and foremost—say institutionalized altruism. Without that quality, men cannot take their proper place among the ruled and assume their proper posture with respect to the rulers.

It is on this basis that the classical writers could simply comprehend the economic activity within or under the political, and discussion of the economic activities within the discussion of political life more generally. Successful political life depends upon a proper public emphasis upon those irenic elements of nature which are friendly to virtue and hence to political life, and the suppression or warding off of those polemic elements which are neutral or hostile toward the perfection of civil community. The instrument of that prudent emphasis is law, or convention, and its fruit is political society, which is an artifact, the product of provident men who are the great benefactors of their kind. They may be said to rise above nature through the breadth of their understanding of nature: perceiving that nature is in some ways friendly and in some ways indifferent to the perfection of political society, the classical writers declined to deduce political life from the simple laws of nature. Law must proceed from well-disposed intelligence, or from the wisdom of superior men. Law is a phenomenon of the relation between governing men and governed men, the political relation, the improved ectype of primary inequality. Political philosophy is the comprehensive social, not to say human, science, because it comprehends all the aspects of nature, the friendly, the indifferent, and even the hostile, under law that emanates from human discretion. It is based upon a narrow-eyed scrutiny of nature by discreet men who understood the precariousness with which political life is balanced upon its natural base.

It is a commonplace that the modern authors who found fault with classical doctrines did so because they conceived them to be founded upon a hopelessly sanguine estimate of the moral possibilities inherent in the natural order. Each thinker had his own way of articulating this belief, but we shall take up the view of Locke only, for Locke's formulation of the question was the one that brought property and economics most visibly into the foreground, and thus displayed most clearly the relation of political science and economics that is characteristic of the last few centuries.

IV

Locke's political teaching is famous for the great emphasis that it places on the historical progress of men out of the state of nature into civil society. Mankind are "but in an ill condition while they remain in [the state of nature], [and] are quickly driven into society."[2] It is noteworthy, however, that the state of nature, which men find intolerable, is said by Locke to be pervaded by the law of nature, and "the law of nature stands as an eternal rule to all men," a law the obligations of which "cease not in society but only in many cases are drawn closer."[3] The law of nature is indeed the law of the state of nature, but, as eternal and unchanging, like nature itself, it does not lose its force in the state of civil society; rather the opposite. The constant authority of the law of nature thus tends to diminish very much the difference in principle between the state of nature and the state of civil society: both states are utterly dominated by that "fundamental, sacred, and unalterable law of self-preservation for which [men] entered into society."[4] Men obey that law because it is an expression of, or inference from that "first and strongest desire God planted in men, and wrought into the very principles of their nature."[5] Obedience to the law of nature is indistinguishable from "pursuing that natural inclination [man has] to preserve his being,"[6] and, so doing, to avail himself of the means of comfortable living by a right which is discerned by natural reason. But unfortunately for the peace of mankind, obedience to the law of desire for preservation is not *eo ipso* obedience to a moral law;[7] on the contrary, a moral law, i.e., a law to which certain punishment is annexed, must be enacted in order to permit the law of desire for preservation to become a law of preservation proper.[8] The transition from the state of nature to the state of civil society is brought about in order to render the obligations of the law of nature operative for peace and comfort by having "known penalties annexed to them to enforce their observation."[9] More concretely, what is purposed by entering society is the preservation of property—life, liberty, and estate. But "property ... is for the benefit and sole advantage of the proprieter ... ," and it is to guarantee every man in the right to seek his particular good in the light of that maxim that the law of nature is made contributory to the *salus populi* by the laws of civil society.[10]

The immutable law of preservation is the sole ground of man's right to appropriate from nature what he needs to live comfortably. Men may appropriate directly from nature during those first ages when "want of people and money gave men no temptation to enlarge their possessions of land,"[11] but thereafter they are compelled to obtain their goods from other owners. Government exists in order to insure that no man will have to give up his goods except by his own consent, i.e., through sale or exchange, or lawful taxation. Government exists to preside over the orderly occupation and transfer of property, and thus to bring to its highest efficacy the sacred law of nature, the fundamental law of preservation. It exists for no other purpose.

In his remarkable papers on money and the rate of interest, Locke illustrates the orderly working of nature in civil society. The questions to which he addresses himself are the advisability of attempting to control the interest rate by positive legislation, and of attempting to halt an outflow of bullion by devaluing the coin—i.e., raising the nominal value of a given weight of silver. Locke concludes that it is not only inadvisable but impossible to produce the desired effects by the means proposed, because there are such things as "natural value" (we would say price) and "natural interest" which are determined by what he himself calls "laws of value." His application of those laws of value—essentially the law of supply and demand—shows them to be similar in their operation to that "settled law of nature," the law of gravitation.[12] Beginning with the natural motive— literally the source of motion—in the *amor habendi,* and adding to it the "right to make as much of [his] money as it is worth,"[13] the operation of the natural mechanism to which positive legislation must defer may then be deduced.

The science which is elaborated to deduce that operation is economics. Economics arose out of political philosophy as an autonomous social science, not in order to describe an "aspect" of society, but with the intention of clarifying the very ground of society as that ground is conceived by the modern doctrine of natural law, of which Locke's teaching is representative. Legislation, or the act of government, which is the object of political science, is decisively in the service of property, which is the object of economics. The autonomy of economics is in effect indistinguishable from the primacy of economics. According to the political science which culminates in this understanding, if the studiers of the law of nature succeed in their construction of the principle of nature, then nature can be viewed as providing the adequate efficient cause of civil society and therewith the effective guide for positive legislation. It appears that there is an optimism with respect to the efficient cause in modern natural law theory which is at least as great as the optimism about the final cause attributed to the classical political teaching. The optimism of Lockean doctrine is based upon the view that nature contains no end which is of higher standing than, or which is radically different in quality from, the beginning. He wrote, "The end of a commonwealth constituted can be supposed no other than what men in the constitution of, and entering into it proposed; and that could be nothing but protection from such injuries from other men, which they desiring to avoid, nothing but force could prevent or remedy...."[14]

The political benefits that have flowed from the acceptance of modern natural law principles have been so enormous that, at a time when they are threatened, we must reexamine their foundations in order to perpetuate them by strengthening those foundations wherever possible. The equating of the end with the beginning or with the primitive is a point at which there is a fault in the foundation, which might be divined from a wide range of human experiences. A ready illustration is the community of husband and wife. Men and women are drawn towards each other in their youth by a strong motive which may be called the efficient cause or beginning of their union. Human experience would not bear out the proposition that their community has no other end than that which might have been most manifest at the beginning. The beginning, by effecting the union, makes possible through that union a progress or maturing which raises their community to a different level from that on which it began, and gives it other reasons for growing than those which brought it into being. Connubial society can be but imperfectly understood in the sole light of the effective cause or motive of its coming into being. The attempt to understand political society primarily by that same light does not succeed better.

V

When we inquire into the relation of political science and economics, we are led back to the origin of economics in a certain act of political philosophy. By that act, political philosophy revised its understanding of its object and its content. So doing, it revised the view that it took of itself, for sciences are constituted by their content, and they define themselves in defining their content. Political philosophy chose at a certain point to account for political society as a mere mutation of the status of pre-political man. The self-limitation of political philosophy to the task of elaborating the primeval human purpose found expression in the modern doctrine of natural law. In confining itself to making explicit what is implicit in man's primitive state, political philosophy caused itself to be supplanted primarily by economics, the discipline that systematically enlarges upon the self-preserving motive of pre-civil man. Political science inherited as its content the ministerial questions pertaining to the support of the essentially economic order of society. In this way, and in the indicated order of rank, economics and political science arose out of the self-limitation of political philosophy.

The autonomy of economics rests upon an act of abdication by political philosophy. There is a question whether political philosophy did not, in that act of abdication, attempt to alienate what is unalienable. For what political philosophy in the seventeenth century proposed was to create a horizon for civil man by reconstructing the horizon of pre-civil man. But pre-civil man could have only the most imperfect grasp of the possibilities of political society; and he could have no grasp of the place occupied by political philosophy in political society. Yet our own political situation teaches us, if reflection would not, the need to inquire philosophically concerning economic and political things. Our circumstances strongly suggest the insufficiency of the horizon of pre-civil man by compelling us to recur to political philosophy. When we wish to understand the relation of political science and economics, we are compelled to undertake an act, however humble, of political philosophy. Our inquiry into the autonomy of economics leads us to discover the unalienable hegemony of political philosophy.

Notes

1. The general truth of this proposition is the ground for our ignoring nere the otherwise important differences among regimes.
2. *Second Treatise,* IX, 127.
3. Ibid., XI, 135.
4. Ibid., XIII, 149.
5. *First Treatise,* IX, 88.
6. Ibid., 86.
7. *Essay Concerning Human Understanding,* I, iii, 13.
8. Ibid., II, xxviii, 6.
9. *Second Treatise,* XI, 135.
10. *First Treatise,* IX, 92.
11. *Second Treatise,* VIII, 108.
12. *Elements of Natural Philosophy,* ch. I.
13. *Some Considerations of the Lowering of Interest,* 11th paragraph.
14. *A Third Letter for Toleration,* ch. II.

"Alienation" or Justice?

Reprinted from *Alienation: Plight of Modern Man?* edited by William C. Bier, S.J. (New York: Fordham University Press, 1972), where it appeared as "Response to Alienation from Political Science." ©1972 by Fordham University Press.

Alienation is a word of numerous meanings, many of which will not concern us. We will confine our attention to the state of otherness or apartness or the sense of being in a state of otherness or apartness, which the word commonly conveys. We must take note of the fact that alienation so understood is thought to be a problem, especially a problem with a political bearing. Our task will be to assess the view of it which sees it as a problem, and to judge of the aptness of the view which sees it as having a political bearing.

It must immediately appear strange that a man's sense of his otherness, of his distinctness from all those whom he must know to be "other," is regarded as a thing to be deplored and overcome; for one of the first things that any animal, and surely a man, must learn is where he ends and all else begins. Without such a consciousness of his own "otherness," he could have no sense of his own identity or boundedness. In the perfect confusion of himself and the All, he would, it is true, have no occasion to know hatred; but for the same reasons he would never experience love, except in its least attractive manifestation as self-love, and even that without consciousness of a determinate self.

Alienation Not Coeval with Civilization

However true any of this may be, one would be perverse in refusing to see that those who protest against the alienation of some or all modern men have a real if blurred perception of something massive in the lives of the millions. What is it that they claim to see?—not merely that men have a sense of their individual distinctness from other men and things, but that they have such a heightened and distorted sense of it that rivalry, invidious-ness, and the other blemishes of disharmony become dominant, giving to all of life its characteristic color. Men are kept from men, men and women are kept from each other, the generations, classes, and races are at odds, and the nations keep to themselves or worse. Far from any of this being arguable, it has been familiar for so many ages that one must ask why the contemporary complaint against it ascribes any of it to modernity or to modern politics rather than to the facts of human existence. There is an answer to this question: the defects in our relations with one another proceed from conventions and institutions—from human arrangements, not from the human condition metaphysically described as nature. Nature does not proscribe the love of men for men, of men and women for each other, and so on. Convention, sometimes called society or civilization, does that. Let us then turn away from convention or society and return to nature. How does one do this? By forming the most intimate relations with other individuals, groups, and nations—that is, by forming society or societies, indeed on a scale of breadth and intensity hitherto uncontemplated. When the reform of humanity through the deepest and widest association of human beings has been accomplished, mankind is constituted at last and alienation is overcome.

In reaching this point, we seem to have lost our way. We began by asking why the dividedness or alienation of men should be ascribed to the *modern* conditions, and we have replied as if the decisive modern condition is "convention," but with the implication that convention itself is singularly modern. Convention, which is to say the least very ancient, could be reasonably called peculiarly modern if modern convention is singularly or essentially convention: if it is convention simply. There is no proper reason for supposing that it is. There is, however, a way of understanding how middle-class or bourgeois convention can be confused with convention in itself. Suppose that the standards of the middle class are the cataclysmic abomination, the ultimate insult to mankind which will provoke the ultimate purification. Then, when the sham of "bourgeoisdom" is burned away, all falseness and hence dividedness will evaporate from among human beings. Because our society is the climactically defective one, the conventions or standards belonging to it are the uniquely corrupt ones, symbolizing if not precisely being the corruptness of convention itself. As we learn incidentally, "modern" should mean according to this construction "belonging to the capitalist period." Perhaps it is on the basis of some such suppositions that the rejection of middle-class convention is identified with the rejection of convention simply, though this is far from clear.

More clear is the psychological discovery that civilization as such is responsible for the social practices which keep men apart and in distressful frustration. By this understanding, alienation is probably coeval with civilization itself and precisely for the reason that civilization speaks with the voice of convention. To overcome alienation it would then be necessary to overcome civilization.

Proposed Antidotes to Alienation

There are, in brief, two influential views on alienation and its cure. One sees the source of it in bourgeois capitalism—that is, the political institution focused on property—and sees the cure of it in the overthrowing of that institution. The other sees the source of it in the subversion of human impulses which, unrepressed, themselves subvert humanity, and, re-pressed, bring on the diminution of joy and unity. Those who find men alienated by the conventions of property look forward to redemption when the higher civilization of communism has supervened and brought down those conventions. Those who found men alienated by the conventions of sexual morality were open to the thought that there is no perfect remedy within civilized life. Those of our contemporaries who find men alienated by the conventions of property and also by the conventions of sex are in danger of finding themselves in a state of contradiction which is itself one of the authentic conditions of alienation. It is not possible reasonably to assign the overcoming of alienation to both the peak and the collapse of civiliza-tion. Those who do so, however tacitly and unwittingly, believe themselves to be protesting against modernity. But so far as their protest is an apt or inept syncretism of contemporary communism and psychoanalysis, it in no way manages to escape from the circle of modernity in its inspection of modernity. In this respect too it is unaware of itself.

Perhaps there are imperfections in the thought of some alienationists. Nevertheless, they point to a problem which is genuine and deserves close attention, one which is close to the core of politics as such and pre-eminently to American politics: the problem of one and many or, as they are more likely to put it, the problem of one and other. To restate the issue: our lives are unhappy and our affairs are in disarray because of the distances in interest and sentiment which are opened up between each and all by the rules of society. Is it unfair to say that for the condition of distance between one and other there are two antidotes? One antidote is to overcome the distance by abolishing the difference between the one and the other, making a one out of two or more, which I call integration; the other antidote is to bring on a state of mind in one, such that it will cease to prefer itself to the other and might in the end prefer the other to itself, which I call altruism. Let us consider these in their political bearing.

According to its own self-understanding, the United States is a one which has been made out of many. No one could deny that there is and has always been an element of metaphor in this description of the federal union. For the moment, we are less interested in the question whether a perfect political integration is impossible than in the question (at least as old as Plato's *Republic*) whether such an integration is desirable. Is it of the essence of the political association that it contain elements irreducible to each other—bodies and souls, lower and higher, nobility and wisdom, to say nothing of male and female and young and old? If the political community is composed of such elements, as it surely is, then "integration" as the antidote to alienation must be understood merely figuratively. The one which is constructed of the many derives its unity from the fact that the diverse many are ordered and ranged in an articulated whole, composing a one in the way in which diverse fractions can add up to one. While it is easy to speak about such ordering and ranking, it is very hard to arrive at the principle of it, which is called justice. Apart from the difficulty of saying what justice concretely requires, the fact emerges that, when the radical remedy of integration is proposed for the disease of alienation, the disease itself is shown to have been wrongly diagnosed. The psychological formulation in terms of alienation replaces unserviceably the formulation in terms of justice, and deserves to be ejected by it.

What of altruism as the antidote to alienation? If altruism means a proper regard for the concerns of others, a rational abstention from making a special case of oneself, it is in itself wholly unexceptionable but is, like "integration," simply an aspect of justice and has nothing particular to do with alienation. If altruism must be given its more radical meaning—namely, a serious replacement of self-preference by preference for the other—then it is particularly important that it be examined by the light of claims which have been made on behalf of its contrary, namely, egoism.

There is, to begin with, a famous species of argument which appeals to preconventional nature in order to prove that the deepest and strongest drive in a man is toward the preservation of his life. When you see a man striving singlemindedly in his own interest, you see true man as he really is—undissembling, sincere, untinted by mere convention, undeflected by culture or society. Callicles, Hobbes, and Nietzsche have seen something along these lines. Is there not at least a likelihood that nature dictates egoism and is a stranger to altruism? If so, only by the most violent conventionalism could men be transformed into altruists—a prospect which can only repel the alienationists. This *démarche* is particularly awkward, for the political expression of sincere naturalism, unconfused by sham professions of care for others, proves to be familiar capitalism.

Thinkers who surveyed the egoistic tendencies of classic modern doctrine were sometimes offended by what they saw. The preservation of life in the easily understood sense was proving inimical to the true vitality of men: their enjoyment, their virtue, the keenness of their genuine self-life. Thus Rousseau in his way, Kierkegaard in his, Nietzsche in his, and all to some extent anticipated by Spinoza, pointed toward a heightened level of life based on a deeper understanding of "self-preservation" than the one which moves through the thought of Hobbes, Locke, and Adam Smith. In no case could this understanding be said to adopt radical altruism as a principle: rather the contrary. The doctrines of the self, in their early and, I believe, even in their derivative states, are primarily egoistic and exploit a relation with others for the sake of the happiness and vitality of the one, not of the other. A serious and by no means obviously base claim is thus raised on behalf of the individual man precisely in his contradistinction from others, a claim which deserves to be recognized as a reservation against radicalized altruism.

Arguments and claims which arise out of self-interest are rightly scrutinized with suspicion. We can do little more here than allude to the possibility that there are good men whose interests may rightfully be the basis of extensive claims and arguments. If worthy men advance their own measured claims, and the political society is organized to give those claims respectful and sympathetic attention, is the correct description of the regime "egoistical" or "just"? It is doubtful whether the alienationists are well equipped to give an impartial answer.

Basic Problem Not Alienation But Justice

We have been glancing at the proposed antidotes to alienation, and have found that something can be argued in support of the contraries to those antidotes. I wish to suggest now that there are reasons for doubting that alienation, or conscious "otherness," is simply and in itself the ultimate social evil. In the first place, as was already said, there could be no sense of being self without a sense of being other. Moreover, if there were no strong sense of barrier or gap, the human species would fall into the carnal chaos of unregulated herd-animals. Let us if necessary remind ourselves that the all-time illustration of man overcoming the generation gap is Oedipus. Akin to this thought is the popular wisdom that familiarity breeds contempt very often, and the insight that the ugliest work of art might well be a representation of beauty seen by a proximate eye. As it appears, both virtue and beauty demand distance.

We must be careful not to prove too much, not to seem to deny, for example, that a state is defective in some way if many of its citizens have the sense of being excluded from the community's life, with the result that they are lost equally to ambition and to shame. Still, common experience teaches that when a distance exists between two beings, including men, it is necessary to look impartially into the circumstances. A lamb which puts a distance between itself and a lion is not atrocious, nor is a man who separates himself from a snake or from a cannibal: the initiator of the distance may or may not be fair and reasonable. On the other hand, the one who feels himself kept at a distance might be under the influence of what is vulgarly called paranoia, or a pathologic sense of being rejected. If he correctly apprehends his rejection, what is the manly way for him to deal with it—in a spirit of envy, resentment, and vicious truculence; or with dignity, pride in neglected achievement, perhaps withdrawal to a fortified if invisible height? The answer evidently bears upon the justice or injustice with which the distance has been created. Of one thing we can be fairly certain: distance or "alienation" by itself is not a diagnosis. It is at most a symptom.

My aim has been to propose that, for purposes of understanding and discussing political life, "alienation" is partly unhelpful and partly misleading. It is not simply useless, but it has the decisive defect of distorting or obscuring the properly political issue, which is not whether a certain public act causes pain but whether it is just. These two criteria cannot be made to coincide except on the premise of gross hedonism— namely, that whatever gives pain is immoral and unjust because pleasure is the sovereign good. This premise does not necessarily conflict with the alienationist premise that love and intimate unity are the supreme goods, but it gives it a base or repulsive color, and I doubt that it is publicly or wittingly owned by the alienationists. None of the foregoing is meant to dispute the fact that a regime which engenders vulgarity, hurtfulness, mutual indifference, moral shiftiness, mendacity, or cruelty among its citizens is to that extent a failure. It is meant to argue that sounder progress is likely to result if we replace the question of "alienation" with the question "What is justice?"

PPPPPPPPPPPPPPPPPPPPPPPPPPPPPPPPPPPP
PPPPPPPPPPPPPPPPPPPPPPPPPPPPPPPPPPPP
PPPPPPPPPPPPPPPPPPPPPPPPPPPPPPPPPPPP
PPPPPPPPPPPPPPPPPPPPPPPPPPPPPPPPPPPP
PPPPPPPPPPPPPPPPPPPPPPPPPPPPPPPPPPPP
PPPPPPPPPPPPPPPPPPPPPPPPPPPPPPPPPPPP
PPPPPPPPPPPPPPPPPPPPPPPPPPPPPPPPPPPP
PPPPPPPPPPPPPPPPPPPPPPPPPPPPPPPPPPPP
PPPPPPPPPPPPPPPPPPPPPPPPPPPPPPPPPPPP
PPPPPPPPPPPPPPPPPPPPPPPPPPPPPPPPPPPP
PPPPPPPPPPPPPPPPPPPPPPPPPPPPPPPPPPPP
PPPPPPPPPPPPPPPPPPPPPPPPPPPPPPPPPPPP
PPPPPPPPPPPPPPPPPPPPPPPPPPPPPPPPPPPP
PPPPPPPPPPPPPPPPPPPPPP PPPPPPPPPPPPPPP
PPPPPPPPPPPPPPPPPPPPPP PPPPPPPPPPPPPPP
PPPPPPPPPPPPPPPPPPPPPP PP PPPPPPPPPPPPP
PPPPPPP PP PPPPPPPP PP PPPPPPP PPPPP
PPPPPPP PP PPPPPP PP PP PPP PPP PPPPP
PPP PPP PP PPPPPP PP PP PPP PPP PP PP
PPP PPP PP PP PPP PP PP PPP PPP PP PP
PPP P P PP PP PPP PP PP PPP P P PP P
PPP P P PP PP P P PP PP PPP P P PP P
P P P P P PP P P PP PP P P P P P P
  P P P P P P P P PP P P P P   P
  P P   P P P P   P P P   P   P
  P   P P   P   P P P   P
  P   P   P   P
           P   P
                     P

Part Two

"Capitalist" Liberalism

Reprinted from *History of Political Philosophy*, edited by Leo Strauss and Joseph Cropsey (Chicago: Rand McNally and Company, 1963), where it appeared as "Adam Smith, 1723–1790." © 1963, 1972 by Rand McNally College Publishing Company, Chicago.

The major writing of Adam Smith is contained in two books, *Theory of Moral Sentiments* (1759) and *An Inquiry into the Nature and Causes of the Wealth of Nations* (1776). His major professional employment was to serve, for thirteen years, as Professor of Moral Philosophy in the University of Glasgow. His fame now rests upon the foundation he laid for the science of economics. In all of this there is not much of political philosophy to be seen, even allowing for the inclusion of jurisprudence in the Morals course. Smith's contribution to economics, however, has the character of a description and advocacy of the system now called liberal capitalism; and the ligaments between the economic order and the political system, close under any circumstances, are exceptionally broad and strong in the world as seen and molded by Adam Smith. The close conjunction of economics and political philosophy, even or perhaps especially if tending toward the eclipse of the latter, is a powerful fact of political philosophy; the men, like Smith, who were responsible for it would have a place in the chronicle of political philosophy on that ground alone.

Smith is of interest for his share in the deflection of political philosophy toward economics and for his famous elaboration of the principles of free enterprise or liberal capitalism. By virtue of the latter, he has earned the right to be known as an architect of our present system of society. For that title, however, he has a rival in Locke, whose writing antedated his own by roughly a century. Our thesis will be that, although Smith follows in the tradition of which Locke is a great figure, yet a distinct and important change fell upon that tradition, a change that Smith helped bring about; that to understand modern capitalism adequately, it is necessary to grasp the "Smithian" change in the Lockean tradition; and that to understand the ground of engagement between capitalism and postcapitalistic doctrines—primarily the Marxian—one must grasp the issues of capitalism in the altered form they received from Adam Smith. To state the point in barest simplicity: Smith's teaching contains that formulation of capitalist doctrine in which many of the fundamental issues are recognizably those on which postcapitalism contests the field.

It would be vastly misleading to suggest that the initiative in modifying the classic modern doctrine was Smith's. To avoid that intimation, we must cover all of what follows with a single remark on the obligation of Smith to his senior friend and compatriot, David Hume. Smith's moral philosophy, as he in effect admits, is a refinement upon Hume's which differs from it in respects that, although very significant, are not decisive.[1] A thorough study of the relation between the doctrines of Smith and Hume would disclose in full the connection between liberal capitalism and the "skeptical" or "scientific" principles upon which Hume wished to found all philosophy. The broadest conclusions that would emerge from such a study can be deduced from an examination of Smith's doctrines alone, precisely because they do reflect so deeply the influence of Hume.

Many of Smith's fundamental reflections are contained in the *Theory of Moral Sentiments,* wherein he sets forth his important understanding of nature and human nature. He does this in the course of answering the following question: What is virtue, and what makes it eligible? The premise of his answer is that, whatever virtue may turn out to be, it must have very much in common with, perhaps it must simply coincide with, that by reason of which men or their actions deserve approbation. The question, What is virtue? is never distinct from the question, What deserves approbation? Approbation and disapprobation are bestowed upon actions. The spring of any action is the sentiment (or emotion, or affection, or passion—they are synonymous) which is the motive for committing the act. Approbation of any action must ascend to the passion which truly explains the action.

> The sentiment or affection of the heart from which any action proceeds, and upon which its whole virtue or vice must ultimately depend, may be considered under two different aspects, or in two different

relations; first, in relation to the cause which excites it, or the motive which gives occasion to it; and secondly, in relation to the end which it proposes, or the effect which it tends to produce.

In the suitableness or unsuitableness, in the proportion or disproportion which the affection seems to bear to the cause or object which excites it, consists the propriety or impropriety, the decency or ungracefulness of the consequent action.

In the beneficial or hurtful nature of the effects which the affection aims at, or tends to produce, consists the merit or demerit of the action, the qualities by which it is entitled to reward, or is deserving of punishment.[2]

Propriety and merit are thus the attributes of the passion behind each action that determine the virtuousness of the action. These bear a certain similarity to the "agreeable and useful" of Hume, but Smith believed his own doctrine to be original in that it avoids the final reduction of all approbation to utility, which Smith rejected on the Humean ground that "utility" is not as such recognizable by immediate sense and feeling, but only by a sort of calculation of reason. Smith believed he had been able to ground morality on a phenomenon of the passions alone, a belief to which the name of his book testifies. If sense and feeling are indeed immediate—unmediated in the sense that nothing is between them and the root of the fundamental self—then there is considerable value in bringing down the analysis of the virtues to its true bottom in the passions. In Smith's doctrine, the clue to that reduction is in the phenomenon of Sympathy, the criterion of propriety and merit.

Sympathy is a word used by Smith in its literal meaning, an etymological parallel of compassion: "feeling with," or a fellow feeling. It is a fact of which, perhaps, no further mechanical account can be given, that the passions of one human being are transferred to another by the force of imagination at work in the recipient. The man who sees or merely conceives the terror, hatred, benevolence, or gratitude of another must to some extent enter into that passion and experience it himself, for he must imagine himself in the other's circumstances, and therefrom everything follows. Of chief importance in the foregoing is the qualification "to some extent." If the impartial spectator, cognizant of what stimulated the terror, hatred, or other passion of the agent, feels in his own breast the same measure of that passion as moved the agent to his action, then the spectator literally sympathizes with the agent and approves his act as consistent with "propriety." The spectator experiences sympathetically the passion of the agent; and if he experiences it in the same degree, he further experiences the "sentiment of approbation" —for that, too, is a passion.

Propriety, however, is not the only ground of moral virtue. Not only the suitableness of the agent's passion to its cause, but the aim or tendency of that passion, its effect, has a bearing on the moral quality of the act in question. Smith refers to "the nature of the effects which the affection aims at, or tends to produce." The "or" is disjunctive, and we must later discuss the important difference between the effects that the sentiment aims at and those that the act it inspires actually tends to produce. For the present it is enough to note that when an action falls upon some human being, it will cause him to feel gratitude or resentment because it will be either beneficial or harmful, pleasurable or painful. If an impartial spectator, informed of all the circumstances, would sympathize with the gratitude felt by the object human being, then the spectator would judge the agent's act to be meritorious, and the second condition of moral virtue would have been met. In brief: if the actual or supposed impartial spectator should sympathize with the passion both of the agent (propriety) and of the patient (merit), then the agent's act may be pronounced virtuous on the basis of the spectator's feeling of approbation.

If Smith's elaboration of the sympathy mechanism did nothing more than show how a rather strict morality could be educed from the passions and the imagination alone, it would have a certain interest. In fact, it points toward a much wider circle of consequences. Sympathy cannot be separated, in Smith's formulation, from imagination. Together they define an undoubted natural sociality of man. By the exercise of two subrational capacities, sympathy and imagination, each man is by his nature led or compelled to transcend his very self and, without indeed being able to feel the other man's feeling, is able and is driven to imagine himself in the place of that other and to participate, how vicariously is a matter of indifference, in the feelings which are the fundamental phenomena of the other's existence. Smith, it will be recalled, wished to know not only what virtue is but what makes it eligible. Why—in principle—do men choose to be virtuous, when to be virtuous means to be deserving of approbation? Smith's answer is that it is of the nature of a human being to desire the approbation and love of his human congeners.[3] The first sentence of the *Theory of Moral Sentiments* intimates the withdrawal that is in progress from the doctrine of the war of all against all: "How selfish soever man may be supposed, there are evidently some principles in his nature, which interest him in the fortune of others, and render their happiness necessary to him, though he derives nothing from it except the pleasure of seeing it." The combination of imagination, sympathy, and the need for the love and approbation of other men is the ground for Smith's asseverations that nature formed man for society.[4]

Not only does Smith thus teach a natural sociality of man, but also the natural character of the moral law. He can with ease refer to "the natural principles of right and wrong,"[5] understanding by "right" not merely what benefits or avoids bringing harm to the agent. He can do so because the ground of moral action and perception is the inner constitution of human nature; not in the antique sense of man's highest possibilities, it is true, but in the sense of human psychology—the instincts, sentiments, mechanisms of sympathy that are the efficient causes of human behavior. These are perfectly natural, and the sentiments of approbation are equally so; hence the principles of right and wrong are incontestably natural.

Smith's version of natural right depends very heavily upon the construct of the "impartial spectator," the imaginary being who is supposed to represent all mankind in viewing and judging each individual's actions. Judgment rendered from such a point of view implies that no man may rightly prefer himself to the extent of making exceptions from the general rule in his own behalf. "As to love our neighbour as we love ourselves is the great law of Christianity, so it is the great precept of nature to love ourselves only as we love our neighbour, or what comes to the same thing, as our neighbour is found capable of loving us."[6] Recourse to the imagined judgment of general humanity at the same time directs conscience toward the imagined surveillance maintained over each man at all times by a supposed all-seeing humanity. The constructive standard of "universal mankind" is fundamental to the version of natural right and natural sociality taught by Smith. It is also a premonition of the postcapitalistic construct of "all mankind" as the focus of right and history.

It is true that Smith taught the natural sociality of man and the natural basis of the moral law, but this modification of the modern natural law doctrine did not mean a return to antiquity. It must be repeated that natural right for Smith rests upon the primacy of the subrational part of the soul, and that natural sociality as he understood it is not an irreducible principle of man but the product of a mechanism at work. Later on, Kant was to speak of the same phenomenon as man's asocial sociality. Natural sociality in this sense does not, as it did for Aristotle, point toward political society. It rather resembles gregariousness. It is a compassion with one's fellow species-members that has everything in common with the alleged unwillingness of horses to tread upon a living body (of any species) and the distress of all animals in passing by the cadavers of their like.[7] To claim on the basis of it that man is by nature a social animal is by no means to claim equally that he is a political animal. Man is tied to humanity by the bonds of immediate sense and feeling, but he is tied to his fellow citizens as such by the weaker, superinduced, bonds of calculation or reason, derivative from considerations of utility. As we have seen, the viewpoint of moral judgment for Smith is that of "man" or universal mankind, the homogeneous class of species-fellows. The moral law is natural in such a sense as to overleap the intermediate, artificial frontiers of political society and regard primarily the natural individual and the natural species. Under that law, the perfection of human nature is "to feel much for others and little for ourselves, ... to restrain our selfish, and to indulge our benevolent affections. ..."[8]

Political society, however, is not directed toward this humane perfection of human nature but toward the safeguard of justice very narrowly conceived. "Mere justice is, upon most occasions, but a negative virtue, and only hinders us from hurting our neighbour. The man who barely abstains from violating either the person, or the estate, or the reputation of his neighbours, has surely very little positive merit." Justice means to do "every thing which [one's] equals can with propriety force him to do, or which they can punish him for not doing."[9] Justice, in brief, closely resembles compliance with the law of nature as seen by Hobbes and Locke. Smith understood it so himself. He concluded the *Theory of Moral Sentiments* with a passage on natural jurisprudence, justice, and the rules of natural equity, meaning by all of them "a system of those principles which ought to run through, and be the foundation of the laws of all nations." (He closes by promising to take up this theme in a later work. His only other book is the *Wealth of Nations*.)

We shall not sufficiently understand Smith's version of man's natural sociality if we do not grasp thoroughly the difference between man conceived as a social animal and as a political animal.[10] It is helpful for this purpose to consider further the problem of justice, the singularly political virtue which might even be synonymous with obeying the positive law. Justice, in the context of Smith's moral theory, is a defective virtue. He prepares for the exceptional treatment of justice by dividing moral philosophy into two parts, ethics and jurisprudence, the subject of the latter being justice. The defense of justice means the punishment of injustice; and the punishment of injustice is based upon the unsocial passion of resentment, the desire to return evil for evil, the command of "the sacred and necessary law of retaliation" which "seems to be the great law which is dictated to us by Nature."[11] Political society is based upon a moralistic paradox, one of many we will encounter: sociality rests upon latent animosity, without which the state could not exist.

In the second place, justice, equal to rendering another no less (or more) than what is his due, does not command gratitude and therefore in Smith's system is not attended with merit—or with "very little." Considering both the nature of justice and the safeguard of it, it is a defective virtue in that it cannot, or almost cannot, deserve fullest approbation, on the grounds of merit as well as propriety.

In the third place, although there is a sense in which political society is natural, it is a weak sense. The national society is indeed the protector and the matrix of ourselves, our homes, our kin, our friends, and Smith does not for an instant dream of the withering away of the state. "It is by nature endeared to us." But "the love of our own nation often disposes us to view, with the most malignant jealousy and envy, the prosperity and aggrandisement of any other neighbouring nation."

The love of our own country seems not to be derived from the love of mankind. The former sentiment is altogether independent of the latter, and seems sometimes even to dispose us to act inconsistently with it. France may contain, perhaps, near three times the number of inhabitants which Great Britain contains. In the great society of mankind, therefore, the prosperity of France should appear to be an object of much greater importance than that of Great Britain. The British subject, however, who, upon that account, should prefer upon all occasions the prosperity of the former to that of the latter country, would not be thought a good citizen of Great Britain. We do not love our country merely as a part of the great society of mankind: we love it for its own sake, and independently of any such consideration.[12]

These reservations and qualifications upon political sociality deserve notice. They will appear in a swollen incarnation conjured by Marx a century later, when the replacement of political man by the species-animal reaches a climax.

It would be misleading to suggest that Smith's doctrine of man's sociality was a relapse into the Middle Ages or into antiquity. It would be more misleading to suggest that, in Smith's view, human nature is simply dominated by a natural sociality of any description. We have given attention to the mechanical or psychological bond of sympathy, at the basis of Smith's moral theory, in order to show the change in emphasis between the preparation of capitalism in Locke's doctrine and the elaboration of it in Smith's. But the theme of man's natural directedness toward preservation is not by any means made to languish by Smith. On the contrary: "self-preservation, and the propagation of the species, are the great ends which Nature seems to have proposed in the formation of all animals."[13] There is no reason to doubt that Smith meant this in all its force. We are able to gather, therefore, that if we use "altruism" and "egoism" in their literal sense, man can be described, according to Smith, as being by nature altruistic and egoistic—a species-member moved by love of self and fellow feeling with others.

It is one of the outstanding characteristics of Smith's system that sociality, withal of a certain description, and self-centered concentration upon preservation are shown as profoundly combined in a natural articulation of great strength; and this is achieved simultaneously with a rehabilitation of morality upon natural grounds: "Nature, indeed, seems to have so happily adjusted our sentiments of approbation and disapprobation, to the conveniency both of the individual and of the society, that after the strictest examination it will be found, I believe, that this is universally the case."[14] When it is borne in mind that Smith's teaching aims at the articulation of morality and preservation, and that the practical fruits of his doctrine are intended to be gathered by emancipating men, under mild government, to seek their happiness freely according to their individual desires, the accomplishment as a whole commands great respect. The reconciliation of the private good and the common good by the medium not of coercion but of freedom, on a basis of moral duty, had perhaps never been seen before.

In this wide and symmetrical edifice Smith perceived what appeared to him to be an irregularity or a class of irregularities. He observed that at certain points a disjunction develops between what man would by nature be led to approve as virtuous and what he is led by nature to approve as conducive to the preservation of society and the human species; and this notwithstanding the over-all truth of the passage quoted immediately above. It will be recalled that the elements of a virtuous act are propriety and merit, and that both rest upon a ground of sympathy. If men did not desire the sympathy of others, as well as respond to the impulse to sympathize with them, there would be no morality and no society. But the natural tendency of men is to sympathize especially with joy and good fortune; and it goes without saying that men not only desire to be sympathized with but to be sympathized with by reason of their prosperity, not their adversity. But the wish to be sympathized with on the grandest scale becomes, as a consequence, the foundation of ambition, which is the aspiration to be conspicuous, grand, and admired. To this aspiration the multitude of mankind lends itself, for it naturally sympathizes with eminence, that is, wealth and rank. But wealth and rank are not, as Smith occasionally said, necessarily conjoined with wisdom and virtue. He remarks, "This disposition to admire, and almost to worship, the rich and the powerful, and to despise or, at least, to neglect persons of poor and mean condition, though necessary both to establish and to maintain the distinction of ranks and the order of society, is, at the same time, the great and most universal cause of the corruption of our moral sentiments."[15]

Merit, we remember, is the quality of an act that the impartial spectator would pronounce worthy of gratitude. The decisive quality of such an act is the propriety of the agent's passion in committing it, his benevolent intent toward the patient, and the patient's pleasure in the benefit conferred, in consequence of which he desires to reciprocate a benefit to the agent. The conjunction is perhaps complicated, but through it all one condition stands out clearly: benefit must be conferred on the patient. Now Smith observes that there is a gap of sorts between the intention and the consummation. That gap is Chance. Because of mere chance good will miscarries, and the benevolent agent produces nothing or worse than nothing for his intended beneficiary. On other occasions the agent, intending nothing or possibly worse than nothing, happens to be the source of a benefit to the patient. Contrary to sound morality, the first agent's act goes without the approval of sympathy and the stamp of virtue while the second agent's act wins applause and gratitude. The universal tendency of men to regard the issue rather than the intention is said by Smith to be a "salutary and useful irregularity in human sentiments," for two reasons. In the first place, "to punish . . . for the affections of the heart only, where no crime has been committed, is the most insolent and barbarous tyranny." To try to live a common life while holding men culpable or laudable for their secret intentions would mean that "every court of judicature would become a real inquisition." In the second place, "Man was made for action, and to promote by the exertion of his faculties such changes in the external circumstances both of himself and others, as may seem most favorable to the happiness of all. He must not be satisfied with indolent benevolence, nor fancy himself the friend of mankind, because in his heart he wishes well to the prosperity of the world."[16] Smith goes on to speak of the utility to the world of the cognate inclination men have, to be troubled in spirit even when the ill they have wrought is wholly unintended, a subject that he illuminates with some healthy remarks upon the fallacious sense of guilt, illustrated by the "distress" of Oedipus. In sum, nature has wisely provided that our sentiments direct us toward the preservation of our kind where a conflict between preservation and either moral virtue or sound reason is brought on by the divergence of intent and issue.

Further in the same vein, Smith notes that when a man conquers fear and pain by the noble exertion of self-command, he is entitled to be compensated with a sense of his own virtue, in exchange for the relief and safety he might have had by giving way to his passions. But it is the wise provision of nature that he be only imperfectly compensated, lest he have no reason to listen to the call of fear and pain and to respond to their promptings. Fear and pain are instruments of preservation; a man or a species indifferent to them would die. The self-command that dominates them does not, as it ought not, bring with it a sense of self-esteem sufficient to outweigh the anguish of suppressing those violent passions.[17] Evidently moral virtue neither is nor ought to be simply its own reward; nor therefore can it be unqualifiedly eligible or eligible for its own sake. It must yield, according to the dictate of nature, a certain precedency to preservation.

In an important passage,[18] Smith unfolds further the paradoxy of natural morality as he conceives it. He is led to contrast "the natural course of things" with "the natural sentiments of mankind." It is in the natural course of things that industrious knaves should prosper while indolent men of honor starve, that great combinations of men should overweigh small ones, and finally that "violence and artifice prevail over sincerity and justice." The natural sentiments of man, however, are in rebellion against the natural course of things: sorrow, grief, rage, compassion for the oppressed, and at last despair of seeing the condign retribution of vice and injustice in this world—these are man's natural sentiments. The natural course of events, though, for all its offensiveness, has something weighty to recommend it. In allotting to each virtue, without favor or accommodation, the reward proper to it, nature has adopted the rule "useful and proper for rousing the industry and attention of mankind." Toil and moil happen to be indispensable to human survival, and the only way to draw them forth is by appropriate reward and punishment. The natural course of events supports the preservation of the race at the expense of precise morality; the natural sentiments of mankind are stirred by "the love of virtue, and by the abhorrence of vice and injustice." Nature is divided, but not equally divided against itself. The cause of unmitigated virtue can be heard only upon a change of venue to a jurisdiction in a world beyond nature.

Smith pursues his theme of the price in goodness and reason that must be paid to get the world's fundamental business done. He takes up the question, of much importance to his doctrine, whether the utility of actions is the basis of their being approved. If the answer were a simple affirmative, then it would follow that the principle of virtue (approbation) is rational: the calculation of usefulness. But we know that in his view the principle of virtue and approbation is not reason but sentiment and feeling, via sympathy. Yet it is evident that mankind exhibits a steady tendency toward those measures of labor and government which are the supports for the preservation of the race. Smith explains this by recurring to a delusion imposed upon men by nature, a delusion that does the work of reason better than reason could have done it. When we look upon the power or wealth in a man's possession, our minds are led in imagination to conceive the fitness of those objects to perform their respective functions. At the same time we sympathize with the imagined satisfaction of the possessors of those prizes. It is only a step from that to desiring ourselves to be happy in greatness, and thence to putting forth the immense exertions that eventuate in wealth and government. Upon consideration, it appears that we are led to pursue prosperity and power by a psychological motive, and thus to generate wealth and order among men as by-products of subjective "drives," as we would say. Moreover, and conjunctively, we act under the influence of the appetite for the means to gratification, not even for the gratification itself, when we seek after wealth and power. Both are desirable for the happiness they supposedly give their possessors. In fact, happiness is not at all or very little promoted by the possession of power and riches, those "enormous and operose machines contrived to produce a few trifling conveniencies to the body, consisting of springs the most nice and delicate, which must be kept in order with the most anxious attention, and which in spite of all our care are ready every moment to burst into pieces, and to crush in their ruins their unfortunate possessor."[19]

Smith's reason for depreciating distinction of wealth and place is of interest: "In what constitutes the real happiness of human life, [the poor and obscure] are in no respect inferior to those who would seem so much above them. In ease of the body and peace of the mind, all the different ranks of life are nearly upon a level, and the beggar, who suns himself by the side of the highway, possesses that security which kings are fighting for."[20] It is in this context that Smith announces, in the *Theory of Moral Sentiments,* the notion and the expression of the "invisible hand," very famous from its elaboration through the central argument of the *Wealth of Nations.* The passage deserves extensive quotation:

And it is well that nature imposes upon us in this manner. It is this deception which rouses and keeps in continual motion the industry of mankind. It is this which first prompted them to cultivate the ground, to build houses, to found cities and commonwealths, and to invent and improve all the sciences and arts, which ennoble and embellish human life; which have entirely changed the whole face of the globe, have turned the rude forests of nature into agreeable and fertile plains, and made the trackless and barren ocean a new fund of subsistence, and the great high road of communication to the different nations of the earth. The earth by these labours of mankind has been obliged to redouble her natural fertility, and to maintain a greater multitude of inhabitants. It is to no purpose, that the proud and unfeeling landlord views his extensive fields, and without a thought for the wants of his brethren, in imagination consumes himself the whole harvest that grows upon them. The homely and vulgar proverb, that the eye is larger than the belly, was never more fully verified than with regard to him. The capacity of his stomach bears no proportion to the immensity of his desires, and will receive no more than that of the meanest peasant. The rest he is obliged to distribute among those, who prepare, in the nicest manner, that little which he himself makes use of, among those who fit up the palace in which this little is to be consumed, among those who provide and keep in order all the different baubles and trinkets which are employed in the oeconomy of greatness; all of whom thus derive from his luxury and caprice, that share of the necessaries of life, which they would in vain have expected from his humanity or his justice. The produce of the soil maintains at all times nearly that number of inhabitants which it is capable of maintaining. The rich only select from the heap what is most precious and agreeable. They consume little more than the poor, and in spite of their natural selfishness and rapacity, though they mean only their own conveniency, though the sole end which they propose from the labours of all the thousands whom they employ, be the gratification of their own vain and insatiable desires, they divide with the poor the produce of all their improvements. They are led by an invisible hand to make nearly the same distribution of the necessaries of life which would have been made, had the earth been divided into equal portions among all its inhabitants, and thus without intending it, without knowing it, advance the interest of society, and afford means to the multiplication of the species.[21]

Beyond this there is no advantage in multiplying the evidence of Smith's belief that the dominant end of nature with respect to man, namely, the prosperity of the species as a whole, is achieved by mitigations of morality and reason. Since this is a point which postcapitalistic thought was to take up polemically and against which it was to bring its ultimate, most ambitious dialectic, it deserves to be examined with some attention.

That nature's end for man is advanced by the guidance of his sentiments rather than his reason follows from the premise that the passions are more governing than the mind, and every animal persistently desires its own uninterrupted being. A man's nature is more immediately reflected in what he feels than what he thinks; moreover, the difference between the two is not the profound one anciently conceived but is rather such as can be composed by their being both subsumed under "perceptions." Smith does not employ the language of "impressions and ideas" used by Hume in the enterprise by which the operation of the mind was given a unified appearance as the distinctions among sensation, emotion, and reason were blurred. If Smith had done so, he would more explicitly have concurred in Hume's definition of the self as "that succession of related ideas and impressions, of which we have an intimate memory" and of "ideas [as] the faint images of [impressions] in thinking and reason."[22] The reduction of the self, the ego or the real man, to his actuality or to the traces of what he has actually perceived rather than to his soul and its powers or "faculties" is part of the doctrine that rejected innate ideas and therewith all but the nominal essences. This doctrine, with its echoes of Hobbes and Locke, is interlaced with the view that the lines of force along which nature produces and communicates its motions penetrate him and govern him more through his passions than through his reason.[23]

In any event, Smith's formulation is that nature did not leave it to man's feeble reason to discover that and how he ought to preserve himself, but gave him sharp appetites for the means to his survival as well as for survival itself, thus insuring him in his preservation. But it is this same primacy of sentiment over reason, or at least the equal subsumption of them both under something like perception, that is the basis for the concessions which must be made against morality on behalf of preservation.

It will be recalled that Smith's moral doctrine begins with approbation: the virtuous is so because it is in fact or in principle approved by the sentiment of mankind. We now understand that a difficulty exists because nature teaches man to approve both what conduces to morality and what conduces to preservation. The instruction of nature is occasionally equivocal. Evidently the attempt to derive the Ought from the Is is vexed by the fact that, although what is virtuous is actually approved, it does not follow either that everything which is approved is virtuous or that everything which is virtuous is approved. It is from this circumstance that the "irregularities" or concessions previously mentioned have their origin. What, then, is to be gained by the psychological or "behavioral" derivation of a natural morality? It is that by this method, moral virtue may be deduced from the character of "man as man," i.e., in abstraction from his character as a political being and attentive only to his character as a "natural" one. Smith's moral philosophy aims at comprehending the basis of virtue as that basis may be said to exist in a fully actual state at every moment in "the bulk of mankind"[24] as such. That is to say, Smith's starting point is the natural equality of men in the sense elaborated by Hobbes. The contrast with classical antiquity throws light on the modern position. The famous scheme of Plato's *Republic* makes a high principle of the division of labor or distribution of functions in the political society because virtue in one social class could not well be measured by the same rule against which it must be measured in another class. Aristotle's *Politics* distinguishes the virtue of slaves, freemen, and men of excellence; the *Nicomachean Ethics* cannot be regarded as a manual of the excellence of the bulk of mankind. The ancient moralists coldly concentrated upon the distinction between the politically weighty people and the entire populace that dwelt within the frontiers. Only democracy has the merit of making possible the effacement of that distinction, and we are entitled to deem the "humanization" of moral virtue—its universalization or reference to what is actually present in "all men as men"—as the democratization of morality.

Democracy is the regime that minimizes the distinction between rulers and ruled, the fundamental political phenomenon; and in that sense it can be said that democracy or liberal democracy tends to replace political life by sociality (private lives lived in contiguity) at the same time that it diffuses political authority most widely. The abstraction of morality from the demands of political life proper is in a way impossible: political life has to be lived, and support for it must be provided in the form of economic organization, the use of force for suppressing crime and rebellion, the legitimation of conventional inequalities in the interest of order, and so on. Where morality is radically "human" or "natural" in the sense of those words that is opposed to political, the indispensable provision for political life will have the character of an inroad on morality, or an irregularity. It is not our contention that the moral basis of Smith's social doctrine is contrived to produce an abstraction from the conditions of political existence. It is rather, on the contrary, that in order to mitigate or forestall that abstraction, which his premises threaten to enforce, he must have recourse to "irregularities" of nature or exceptions to his premises.

There is hardly a better way of illustrating the elusive relation between rectitude and politics than by the following passage from Churchill's *Marlborough:*

> The second debate in the Lords . . . drew from Marlborough his most memorable Parliamentary performance. It is the more remarkable because, although he had made up his mind what ought to be done and what he meant to do, his handling of the debate was at once spontaneous, dissimulating, and entirely successful. As on the battlefield, he changed his course very quickly indeed and spread a web of manoeuvre before his opponents. He made candour serve the purpose of falsehood, and in the guise of reluctantly blurting out the whole truth threw his assailants into complete and baffling error. Under the impulse of an emotion which could not have been wholly assumed, he made a revelation of war policy which effectively misled not only the Opposition but the whole House, and which also played its part in misleading the foreign enemy, who were of course soon apprised of the public debate. He acted thus in the interests of right strategy and of the common cause as he conceived them. He was accustomed by the conditions under which he fought to be continually deceiving friends for their good and foes for their bane; but the speed and ease with which this particular manoeuvre was conceived and accomplished in the unfamiliar atmosphere of Parliamentary debate opens to us some of the secret depths of his artful yet benevolent mind.[25]

It is apparent that dissimulation cannot be made the principle of morals; it is also apparent that morality which makes no serviceable distinction between dissimulation in a noble cause and common mendacity will end either in the precisianism that condemns it all as vice or in the latitudinarianism that peers unsuccessfully for the line between vice and virtue. Ancient moral philosophy could in this respect be described as very politic.

It recognized in prudence a subtle virtue that animated the others from its seat in the mind. In palliation of the Odysseanism of the ancients' moralizing, it should be said that departure from the straitest morality was countenanced by them in the ultimate interest of something higher, for they did not conceive moral excellence to be the greatest of all excellences. The Smithian subtractions from morality cannot be in the interest of anything higher, for there is nothing higher: "The most sublime speculation of the contemplative philosopher can scarce compensate the neglect of the smallest active duty." "The man who acts solely from a regard to what is right and fit to be done, from a regard to what is the proper object of esteem and approbation, though these sentiments should never be bestowed upon him, acts from the most sublime and godlike motive which human nature is even capable of conceiving."[26] To state the case somewhat simplistically, the ancients and the moderns alike conceded something in mitigation of strict moral virtue, the ancients without repining because they had in view a higher excellence, Smith with mixed feelings because his aim could not exceed moral virtue in worth.

Smith's aim, a free reasonable, comfortable, and tolerant life for the whole species, found its hope, its basis, and its expression in the science of economics as he to a considerable extent launched it. Anything like a detailed account of Smith's economics would be far out of place here, and we shall confine ourselves to selected themes. His teaching in the *Wealth of Nations* is above all famous for its defense of free enterprise on a broad and simple line: The welfare of the nation cannot be separated from its wealth, which he conceives in the modern mode as the annual national product. But the annual product of the nation is the sum of the annual products of the individual inhabitants. Each inhabitant has an undying interest in maximizing his own product and will do everything possible to accomplish this if left in freedom. Thus all should be accorded this freedom, and they will simultaneously maximize the aggregate product and keep each other in check by the power of competition. His renowned attack on mercantilistic capitalism—the system of invidious preference for the merchant interest—is part of his argument that the common interest is served not by differential legislative stimulation of enterprises but by allowing nature automatically to convert the individual self-interest into the good of all:

> As every individual, therefore, endeavours as much as he can both to employ his capital in the support of domestic industry, and so to direct that industry that its produce may be of the greatest value; every individual necessarily labours to render the annual revenue of the society as great as he can. He generally, indeed, neither intends to promote the public interest, nor knows how much he is promoting it. By preferring the support of domestic to that of foreign industry, he intends only his own

security; and by directing that industry in such a manner as its produce may be of the greatest value, he intends only his own gain, and he is in this, as in many other cases, led by an invisible hand to promote an end which was no part of his intention. Nor is it always the worse for the society that it was no part of it. By pursuing his own interest he frequently promotes that of the society more effectually than when he really intends to promote it. I have never known much good done by those who affected to trade for the public good. It is an affectation, indeed, not very common among merchants, and very few words need be employed in dissuading them from it.[27]

We have no difficulty recognizing the natural reconciliation of the individual and common interest for which the *Theory of Moral Sentiments* has prepared us. Nor are we unprepared for the moral "irregularities" that Smith conceived to be incidental to that reconciliation. They fall under two or three main heads in the argument of the *Wealth of Nations*. In the first place, the prosperity of each and all cannot be disconnected from their productivity, and their productivity rests upon the division of labor. But the division of labor inevitably stultifies the working classes, much if not the bulk of mankind. The laborer's "dexterity at his own particular trade seems . . . to be acquired at the expense of his intellectual, social, and martial virtues. But in every improved and civilized society this is the state into which the labouring poor, that is, the great body of the people, must necessarily fall, unless government takes some pains to prevent it."[28] In his discussions he tries not to exaggerate the likelihood that the government will succeed.

In the second place, a large part if not the preponderant part of the economic life of the nation must come under the regulation of the class of merchants and manufacturers. His animadversions upon them as a body of men are sometimes shockingly severe. The burden of his objection against them is that their preoccupation with gain puts them in illiberal conflict with the other orders of society and with the nation as a whole—except by inadvertence.[29] The wisdom of government is necessary to prevent their mischief, i.e., their interested interference, and to give free rein only to their useful activities, i.e., their productiveness. Smith was not the dogmatist that some advocates of *laissez faire* were later to become.

In the third place, the annual addition to product is believed by Smith to be generated by labor. The "exchangeable value" or price of each commodity, once land has been made private property and capital has been accumulated, "resolves itself" into wages, rent, and profit. In this way, landowners and the employers of labor "share" in the produce of labor. Smith is at pains to argue that the profits of capital are not a wage for the "supposed labour of inspection and direction," which he said is often "committed to some principal clerk."[30] He was far from attempting to conceal the contribution to output that results from the accumulation of capital. On the contrary, he dwelt upon it; but he described it as taking effect by an "improvement in the productive powers of labour."[31] In the course of his investigations into what we now call national income account-ing, he certainly gave later generations some reason to regard him as holding a labor theory of value, with concomitant beliefs about distribu-tion. As for rent, that is "a monopoly price"[32] for the use of land, by the exaction of which the owner is enabled to share in the annual product of labor. We cannot fail to notice how little trouble Smith gave himself to justify this "sharing" and this "resolving." On the contrary, by a certain invidiousness of expression ("As soon as the land of any country has all become private property, the landlords, like all other men, love to reap where they never sowed, and demand a rent even for its natural pro-duce."[33]) he indicates a reserve as to its perfect propriety. He seems to think, it is true, that when the facts of distribution are recited, the intimation of possible inequities may be fully balanced by a statement of the broad, compensatory benefits: he speculates whether it might not be true "that the accommodation of an European prince does not always so much exceed that of an industrious and frugal peasant, as the accommoda-tion of the latter exceeds that of many an African king, the absolute master of the lives and liberties of ten thousand naked savages."[34] But Smith manifestly did not imagine himself to be addressing the multitude of laboring poor in detailed defense of capitalism, as Marx was to address them in detailed denunciation. Smith freely hinted at his notion that something like one of his moral "irregularities" lay around the root of the distributive order, but it was much outweighed by the correlative advan-tages for all—and he loathed the men of "system" who would be incapable of grasping such a simple computation.

Smith did not refer to the complex of free enterprise as "capitalism" but as "the system of natural liberty," or the condition in which "things were left to follow their natural course, where there was perfect liberty."[35] Nature meant for Smith the humanly unhindered or unobstructed, and this more amply means what is not confounded by the misplaced interventions of human reason: letting nature take its course, letting men do as they are instinctively prompted to do, as far as that is compatible with "the security of the whole society."[36] It is easy to conceive and to grant that natural is in distinction to artificial, human, or constrained to obey a forecontrived design. Thus freedom is all on the side of nature, as opposed to constraint on the side of human reason. At the same time, however, nothing in the world is so unyielding and hence constraining as the necessary dictate of deaf and dumb nature, while the source of man's freedom resides in his power of reason, the origin of his various contrivances.[37] Smith's manner of confronting this difficulty is in effect to declare for the freedom of reason harnessed in the service of the more binding freedom of nature: calculation at the command of passion. Smith's doctrine is pervaded by the consequences of the fact that the superordinate element, nature conceived as the free motive of passion, is the symbol of man's unfreedom, as Kant was to emphasize so elaborately.

It is a distinguishing characteristic of Smith's doctrine and of liberal capitalism at large that they do not conceive freedom to be important primarily because it is the condition for every man's existence as an individual moral being, the ground of his self-legislating will in action or of his humanity. Liberty continued to mean for Smith what it had meant to Locke, to Aristotle, and to the long tradition of political philosophy: the condition of men under lawful governors who respect the persons and property of the governed, the latter having to consent to the arrangement in one way or another. This view of liberty is primarily political and belongs to the libertarianism of Locke, not of Rousseau. The capitalistic project is not animated by a search for methods of institutionally liberating the inner drives of every man in the interest of the moral will. It is animated by a search for methods of institutionally liberating every man's natural instinct of self-preservation in the interest of external, politically intelligible freedom and peaceful prosperous life for mankind as a whole. Therefore Smith had no difficulty in conceiving man as free while both in thrall to nature and subject to forms of law which guarantee his external freedom but can scarcely aim to be the basis of his internal emancipation from that same nature.

Smith is thus at liberty to repose his trust in a wisdom of nature that shows itself even or especially in the folly and injustice of man: the moral hygiene that produces a multitude, in fact a race of self-legislators was not indispensable to his plan, nor was political life a species of psychotherapy for bringing on man's subpolitical emancipation. Smith was thus resigned to receive the benefits of civil society even if they must be mediated by certain undoubted ills, and he was prepared to do so indefinitely if the benefits are vast and the ills unavoidable. In this respect he anticipated the mechanisms of philosophy of history as it would emerge, but not its ends: good through ill and reason through folly, but no Elysium at a rainbow's end.

It is important for us to see more exactly what Smith's doctrine has in common with philosophy of history as that was later to develop. There is, to begin with, his belief in a "natural progress of things toward improvement"—animated by "the uniform, constant and uninterrupted effort of every man to better his condition," bettering his condition being understood in "the most vulgar" sense.[38] Smith illustrates this in an account of the progress of Europe from medieval disorder to the comparative regularity of modern times. The anarchy of old persisted because the great landed proprietors had troops of retainers who comprised, in fact, private armies. Nothing could produce order which did not dissolve those armies. The basis for their existence was the fact that the grandees had abundant income in kind which, under the primitive conditions of commerce then prevailing, they could not dispose of by exchange or sale. They accordingly were compelled to feed it to crowds of men who became their dependents and inevitably their soldiers. What brought down the entire system was the enlargement of trade, which enabled the magnates to convert their produce into money and thence into luxuries for their personal delectation instead of into the military basis of their political power.

> A revolution of the greatest importance to the public happiness, was in this manner brought about by two different orders of people, who had not the least intention to serve the public. To gratify the most childish vanity was the sole motive of the great proprietors. The merchants and artificers, much less ridiculous, acted merely from a view to their own interest, and in pursuit of their own pedlar principle of turning a penny wherever a penny was to be got. Neither of them had either knowledge or foresight of that great revolution which the folly of the one, and the industry of the other, was gradually bringing about.[39]

Smith speaks of the ascendancy of the Roman Church from the tenth through the thirteenth century. He regards it as signalized by the temporal power of the clergy, and that in turn as resting upon the influence of the clergy with the multitudes of men. The inferior ranks of people were bound to the clergy by ties of interest, the multitudes depending upon a charity which was bestowed freely because, once again, the clergy had no other means of disposing of an enormous produce from their lands. When such means presented themselves, the constitution of the Catholic Church underwent a profound alteration:

> Had this constitution been attacked by no other enemies but the feeble efforts of human reason, it must have endured for ever. But that immense and well-built fabric, which all the wisdom and virtue of man could never have shaken, much less overturned, was by the natural course of things, first weakened, and afterwards in part destroyed....
> The gradual improvements of arts, manufactures, and commerce, the same causes which destroyed the power of the great barons, destroyed in the same manner, through the greater part of Europe, the whole temporal power of the clergy.[40]

By these same instrumentalities, the species of mankind at large is drawn together, probably upward as well as onward. Smith regards the geographical discoveries as of unparalleled significance for the species: "The discovery of America, and that of a passage to the East Indies by the Cape of Good Hope, are the two greatest and most important events recorded in the history of mankind." The communication and commerce of the species as a whole was thereby in principle achieved for the first time in the memory of man, and with that epochal event came the supreme occasion for enabling all mankind reciprocally "to relieve one another's wants, to increase one another's enjoyments, and to encourage one another's industry."[41]

Smith believed that, to a large extent, nature speaks to history in the language of economics, and that the broad course of history so instructed is probably toward an easier, more cultivated, more rational and secure life for the generality of mankind. At the same time, he imagined that the advance of civilization was synchronous with the generation of a tremendous industrial mob, deprived of nearly every admirable human quality. Civilization is not an unqualified good, or more accurately, it comes at a price. This famous theme, of which Rousseau was the virtuoso, was developed by Smith with concern but without agitation. He proposed to palliate the ill with a wide system of almost gratis elementary schooling for the masses and with the encouragement of an unheard-of number of religious sects (as many as three thousand), each necessarily to be so small that every member of it would be conspicuous to the surveillance of his fellow communicants. All would maintain a vigil upon each other's morals that, far from being in any danger of flagging through lack of interest, would itself require to be moderated by febrifuges: courses of education in science and philosophy and artistic spectacles such as theater.[42] Smith repeatedly recommends the intellectual and moral state of much of industrial mankind to the most serious attention of government, not only out of philanthropy but for obvious reasons of state.

Our thesis, with a summary of which we shall now conclude, has been this: Within a short time of the completion of Locke's work, intelligent men began to reflect on and to draw out what would today be called the "moral implications" of his doctrine.[43] How far he had mitigated Hobbes's teaching of the natural ferocity of man and thereby turned political philosophy in the direction of economics has been shown above in the chapter on Locke.[44] But the chief teaching of the modern school of natural law was not thereby impaired: nature continued univocally to mean preservation, with the supporting rights to whatever pertains thereto. Now this came to be regarded as insufficient, and the reduction of man to his affections was thought to imply that man is affected not only toward himself but toward his species. Perhaps Locke was not given enough credit for the important mitigation mentioned above, which is in this direction, but in any event the theme was made emphatic by Smith (at about the time of Rousseau's *Second Discourse*). The reduction of human life to its emotional foundations was enlarged to become the ground of duties as well as rights. It cannot be denied that those duties were consciously made to revolve about the preservation of the species; but it cannot either be denied that duties are different from rights, and the two require somehow to be reconciled with one another. In the course of reconciling the duties of moral virtue with the rights of nature, which is to say preservation, Smith had recourse to the tension between nature and the moral order derived from it, leaving the reconciliation inevitably imperfect. From this germ grew the teaching as to the moral imperfection of the natural or best order of society—the free, prosperous, and tolerant civil society. In its self-understanding, capitalism thus anticipated the chief postcapitalistic criticism of capitalism: civil society is a defective solution of the human problem.

Our second point, inseparable from the first, is that the self-understanding of capitalism also anticipated an astonishing proportion of what was to be proposed by the nineteenth century as the alternative to capitalism. We have tried to show how the direction of capitalism was toward the construction of a universal mankind, both as the ground of duty (the universal spectator) and as the ultimate beneficiary of economic progress—thus as the ultimate society. The engine of that progress was the ignoble desires and strivings of man, channeled through the economic institutions of production and distribution that opened up to him from time to time. An expectation of good through evil, reason through unreason, progress, a belief in the tendency of the interest of mankind to supersede that of particular political society, in the preponderance of economic influence on human affairs, in the primacy of labor in the process of production, in the preoccupation of civil society with the defense of property, this and more which Marxism would trumpet was present to the doctrines of capitalism in one measure and form or another, as it has been our purpose to show. A strange light is cast on Marx's theory that capitalism contains the seed of its own negation. It might perhaps be said that according to its own self-understanding, the ground of capitalism coincides to a remarkable degree with the seed bed of its own negation; but the seed itself is an alien thing, namely, philosophy of history, something that was generated not by the working of any economic institutions but by an act of human speculation.

Perhaps Smith is to be blamed for not having extracted a metaphysic from that "wisdom of nature" which he believed to guide the human process and to which he so often recurs, a metaphysic that would historicize the consummation of the whole human career. Perhaps he ought to have perceived the potency in such a metaphor as the "wisdom" of nature and gone on to postulate still higher wisdoms by which the laws of nature itself might be brought under orders. He never reached that point, however, for he did not question the belief that there is an unchanging horizon within which all change takes place, that horizon or framework being Nature.

Regarding the philosophy of history we may observe for the present that when Rousseau's teaching of the malleability of human nature received its due cultivation and enlargement, it proved to be the little leaven that leavened the whole lump. The paradoxes and irregularities that liberal capitalism was willing to abide because of their origin in man's nature could not be tolerated by the nineteenth century since it no longer saw a need to tolerate them. The nature that gives rise to inconveniences must away, and itself submit to be superseded by the law of the change of nature, namely, History. It is this fissure, narrow but bottomless, that divides capitalism from communism.

Notes

1. *Theory of Moral Sentiments,* in *The Essays of Adam Smith* (London: Alexander Murray, 1869), part VII. sec. II. chap. iii *ad fin.,* p. 271. Comparison of such a representative passage from Hume as part V of *An Enquiry Concerning the Principles of Morals* with, for example, part I of *Theory of Moral Sentiments* will suggest the broad agreement between the two doctrines.

2. *Theory of Moral Sentiments,* I. I. iii. p. 18.

3. "The chief part of human happiness arises from the consciousness of being beloved." Ibid. I. II. v. p. 40.

4. For example, ibid., III. II. p. 105. Cf. Strauss and Cropsey, *History of Political Philsophy,* pp. 356–59, concerning Hobbes's denial of the natural sociality of man.

5. *Theory of Moral Sentiments,* V. II. p. 177.

6. Ibid., I. I. v. p. 24.

7. From Rousseau, *Discourse on the Origin of Inequality,* First Part. Readers of Rousseau's two *Discourses* will be struck by the similarity of themes and views between them and the *Theory of Moral Sentiments.* The division of human nature between self-love and compassion, and the qualified goodness of civil society are but instances.

8. *Theory of Moral Sentiments,* I. I. v. p. 24.

9. Ibid., II. II. i. p. 75.

10. The reader is urged to refer to the treatment of this subject in the chapter on Aristotle in Strauss and Cropsey, *History of Political Philosophy.*

11. *Theory of Moral Sentiments,* II. I. ii. p. 65; II. II. i. p. 75.

12. Ibid., VI. II. ii. pp. 202, 203–4.

13. Ibid., II. I. v. p. 71n.

14. Ibid., IV. ii. p. 166.

15. Ibid., I. III. iii. pp. 56–57.

16. Ibid., II. III. iii. pp. 96–98.

17. Ibid., III. iii. p. 129.

18. Ibid., III. v. pp. 147–49.

19. Ibid., IV. i. p. 161, and throughout the book.

20. Ibid., p. 163.

21. Ibid., pp. 162-63.

22. Hume, *A Treatise of Human Nature,* I. I. i and II. I. ii.

23. Hume's remark is characteristically uncompromising: "[the reason] can never oppose passion in the direction of the will." Ibid., II. III. Smith makes two remarks, in the form of allusions, which deny man's unique rationality: "mankind, as well as . . . all other rational creatures" (*Theory of Moral Sentiments,* III. v. p. 146) and "that great society of all sensible and intelligent beings" (ibid., VI. II. iii. p. 209.)

24. *Theory of Moral Sentiments,* III. v. p. 142.

25. Winston S. Churchill, *Marlborough: His Life and Times* (4 vols in 2 bks; London: Harrap, 1947), vol. III. bk II. p. 303. Reproduced by permission of Charles Scribner's Sons and George Harrap & Co., Ltd.

26. *Theory of Moral Sentiments,* VI. II. iii. p. 210; VII. II. iv. p. 275

27. *An Inquiry into the Nature and Causes of the Wealth of Nations* (New York: Modern Library, 1937), IV. II. p. 423.

28. Ibid., V. I. iii. 2. p. 735.

29. Ibid., e.g., I. conc. pp. 249-50; IV. III. ii. p. 460.

30. Ibid., I. VI. pp. 48-49.

31. Ibid., II. intro. p. 260. Also II. II. p. 271, etc.

32. Ibid., I. XI. p. 145.

33. Ibid., I. VI. p. 49.

34. Ibid., I. I. p. 12. Also, Introduction and Plan of the Work, p. lviii.

35. Ibid., IV. IX. p. 651; I. X. p. 99.

36. Ibid., II. II. p. 308.

37. Smith commonly juxtaposes "naturally" and "necessarily," the latter often used apparently as an intensified form of the former. Cf., e.g., ibid., pp. 8, 86, 357, 414, 421, 422, 591, 674, 723 and footnote, 754, 756.

38. Ibid., II. III. pp. 326, 325.

39. Ibid., III. IV. pp. 391-92.

40. Ibid., V. I. iii. 3. p. 755.

41. Ibid., III. VII. iii. p. 590; also IV. I. p. 416.

42. Ibid., V. I. iii. 2. pp. 736-38; V. I. iii. 3. pp. 747-48.

43. The reader's attention should be drawn to the work of Bernard Mandeville (c. 1670-1733) whose *The Fable of the Bees* (1714) had the subtitle "Private Vices, Public Benefits." Controversy raged around him, and Smith added his rebuke by dealing with him in a chapter "Of Licentious Systems" (*Theory of Moral Sentiments,* VII. ii. 4), at the same time admitting that Mandeville was not mistaken in all respects.

44. The reference is to the chapter on Locke in Strauss and Cropsey, *History of Political Philosophy.*

The Invisible Hand: Moral and Political Considerations

Presented as a Harry Girvetz Memorial Lecture on the bicentennial of *The Wealth of Nations*, 19 February 1976, at the University of California at Santa Barbara.

The bicentenary of *The Wealth of Nations* tends to be overshadowed by that of the United States. But the celebration of the country's past evokes inevitably reflections on its future, and to reflect on our future is to think of our institutions—of their stability and their prospects, thus the threats to them, and in turn the basis for those threats in the complaints so often voiced against commercial liberalism. The weightiest among those complaints, or the ones perhaps most often taken seriously, are moral: what are the rights and wrongs of commercial liberalism, what conception of justice does it elevate to authority, into what ways of life does it lead its participants? Evidently, speculation about our future draws heavily on thought about what we are, and thus about whence we are sprung. But our "whence" is, in some immeasurable degree, a past age's thoughts which have become our own conceptions and have become incarnated in our national ways and institutions. We are led from our political past through our actual present to our political prospect, and thence once more to the past, but this time to a past that lives in the pages of books. We find ourselves turning to *The Wealth of Nations* with a sense that reflection on the literary bicentenary is important not only in its own right but as the necessary preparation for investigating the issues evoked by the more splendid political anniversary.

It would be at the very least inconvenient to discuss *The Wealth of Nations* without reaching an early understanding about the name by which to call the social system that the book is famous for advocating. Inattention could encourage falling in with the common practice of referring to it as capitalism; but what that name presupposes differs materially from Smith's conception of the system's essence, and the term should therefore not be used freely in this context. The name "capitalism" suggests, and was employed by Marx in order to affirm, that the essence of this social and economic system is the generation of profit ("surplus value.") Everything important for the manner of life in this society follows from the employment of labor through the purchase of labor-power by possessors of "capital." To call the system of free commerce "capitalism" is thus to imply that the essential characteristic of the social order is the existence of the conditions that generate or enhance profit as such. These conditions are conceived to include preeminently the division of the people into what are loosely called classes, especially the classes of those who do and those who do not own the means of production. But classes in this sense have no legal status; they have only a speculative or dialectical definition. In this respect, they do not differ from the "classes" of people who live on opposite sides of a street, or of the even numbers between zero and eleven. Referring to such groupings as classes rather than sets obscures the fact that they are arbitrary or convenient—designated for the purpose of pursuing a certain line of argument or speculation. On the other hand, a legal definition goes beyond a speculative one in that it carries a positive imputation of right. Thus there was an imputation of right—however misguided is not now relevant—in the legal definition of the class of slaves, while there is no imputation of right in the ratiocinative definition of dwellers on one side of a street, or of a set of numbers. Evidently, a large problem is opened up by attributing to "classes" a decisive political importance in a society that ignores them legally, and that officially imputes no right to their existence or to membership in them.

However worthy of being pursued to a conclusion, this theme was introduced not for itself but in order to strengthen the argument for finding a name for Smith's system that is harmonious with his conception of that system. Fortunately, he in fact gave it a name, one with as heavy a freight of meaning as is borne by "capitalism": the "system of natural liberty" (IV. ix). As the name suggests, and as *The Wealth of Nations* maintains, the essence of Smith's system is consistency with the dictate or tendency of nature, not either the generation of an invidious distributive share or the friction of interests present in a society composed of functioning parts. Marx insists on presenting free commerce as though its essence were conflict; Smith presents it as though its essence is a kind of sociality or collaboration. Our immediate task is not to judge between Smith and Marx but to improve our understanding of Smith's doctrine, which we can begin to do by thinking about his phrase, "natural liberty."

Natural liberty is either a tautology or a paradox. Suppose for a moment that in his primary state (primary either in time or in principle), man is unrestrained by anything external to himself that hinders his moving or acting. Then the restraints that now do hinder him must have been imposed, as laws, conventions, practices, all have been imposed, by men on themselves. If the primary state is correctly called natural, then "natural" and "liberty" agree so well that the phrase resembles a tautology. Nature, or the primary, is the basis of freedom; artifice and convention are the grounds of constraint, and if freedom is accepted as the aim of society, then the effectual goal of society is to restore itself to nature, or to recapture nature through social institutions, or something to the same effect.

Simple or obvious as these notions might appear, they are full of difficulties. To begin with, the modification of society in the direction of nature—meaning by that the progressive weakening of the conventions and artifices that constrain—is tantamount to the weakening or even the dissolution of civil life. But the dissolution of civil life may well be equivalent to the dissolution of society itself, in which case the "naturalization" of society would be a misnomer for the dissolution of society. Then what began as a tautology would reveal itself as a contradiction: the attainment of society's essential goal, its naturalization and liberalization, would entail the dissolution of society. There is a way to avoid this outcome. Suppose that the modification of society in the direction of nature need not mean the weakening or discarding of conventions and artifices but rather the installation of "natural" conventions and artifices—human constructions that follow the indications of nature while still restraining men's movements. This suggestion will be intelligible if nature and artifice are mutually reconcilable—if man's making can be sufficiently guided by what man does not make. But why should not the products of two makers serve a single end, the end dictated by the one maker that comprehends the other? More concretely, suppose that the whole import of the artificial social construction is the recovery of natural liberty in the form of self-legislation. After all, the liberty of natural man consisted in a freedom to do whatever he desired to do, which appears to be the condition of a being that legislates for itself. Then the conventions of self-legislation would be those natural artifacts whose possibility we were questioning. Perhaps we could be satisfied with this if we were not conscious of a discord between doing what one desires to do and legislating for oneself. Doing what one desires means doing *whatever* one desires—now this and perhaps at another time something else; while self-legislation means to lay down laws that one obeys, and presumably always and steadily obeys, with the understanding that "obeys" carries with it not only constancy but the implication of an impulse that is to be overcome by obedience. But it is precisely the conquered impulse that comprises the "desire" in the expression, "to do as one desires." Self-legislation contradicts doing what one desires, and exists exactly in order to replace the rule of desire with the rule of something else, presumably something worthier, perhaps even something freer. It now appears that in progressing to the artifices that concur rather than conflict with nature, one reaches the point at which natural liberty again becomes confused: the institutions that follow those indications of nature which point to self-legislation clash with those indications of nature which consist in desire and in the impulse to act according to desire. Yet both sorts of institution or artifice can claim to give effect to freedom, indeed to natural freedom.

Perhaps we have reached confusion because we were not sufficiently precise in speaking of nature's indications, and of the sense in which man the artificer might be the agent of, or a fragment of nature, of the more comprehensive maker. More exactly, we have not faced the issue whether it is on the one hand responsiveness to desire or on the other hand self-legislation that nature sets forth as true "natural liberty." It is clear that nature cannot well teach both if self-legislation is the expression of man's freedom in a voluntary act to confine his desires.

If self-legislation is natural freedom, then obedience to the desires or instincts is natural bondage. Moreover, if self-legislation is natural freedom, then man's primary condition or natural state is bondage and not freedom, for subjection to (self-legislated) law presupposes a prior condition that calls for law. But in any case, why speak of obedience to desires or instincts as bondage? Because the desires and instincts move us as if, or perhaps literally, mechanically. Acting under mechanical impulsion or necessity is acting without intention or volition, thus acting without being the prime cause of one's acts. It is acting for causes that cannot be traced to one's own will. But as long as it remains unclear that a being that exists in the order of nature, as man does, *can* separate itself from the chain of natural causes sufficiently to act under the causation of its "will" alone, so long will the suspicion linger that the will is simply a construction or hypothesis, something hypostasised in order to underlie "freedom," as the soul might be called something hypostasised in order to underlie the motion and thought of otherwise inert body. On the assumption that every act (indeed every event) must have a cause, but that "freedom" requires that there be acts which are not caused in the usual sense, one posits a Will that is capable of causing acts in such a way that the odium of necessity does not cling to the acts and thereby deprive them, as mere responses to externality, of their possible morality. One could imagine that a settled determination to purge action of the moral contamination of simple causation might lead a thinker to conceive a weakening of the authority of the ordinary process of causation rather than to superimpose on that process an extraordinary, higher, cause unlike any that operates wholly within the order of nature. In other words, one might expect a Hume to arise who would argue that causation is mysterious rather than absolute and unshakable, instead of expecting a Kant to arise who would introduce freedom of the will and the immortality of the soul as correctives outside the causal chain of natural necessity. Reflections on Hume and Kant at this point are not a luxury but rather are indicated because of the degree to which Hume's thought impinged on Smith's and some of Smith's understandings recommended themselves to Kant. In order to avoid leaving the impression that the questions of natural liberty, desire, and the action of the will need be discussed only in terms of the simple alternatives already presented, we should notice that Nietzsche, not an advocate for liberal commerce, rehabilitates instinct by *uniting it with the will*, and ascends to a freedom so intimately affiliated with creativity as to be within the reach of humanity on a plane beyond the grasp of society or of politics.

In this conspectus of possibilities, we must recognize one more before we turn thematically to Adam Smith, his system of natural liberty, and the invisible hand. It might be crucial to distinguish among the desires and passions when ascribing to nature certain unwilled causes of human action. According to a famous notion of Smith's contemporary, Rousseau, most of what we now possess as passion has been generated within society and does not belong to our pristine nature. Consequently, to gain ascendancy over hatred, envy, greed, or pride is not simply to master nature, or to acquire control over a process of natural causation in an unqualified sense, but is rather to find a means within the order of natural causes whereby to bring the powers of nature to bear upon or against one another for a moral, human end. But precisely if the present ensemble of human motivations that we think of as our natural apparatus had a genesis or history, the system of rewards, penalties, and incentives that we devise to govern our impulses is partly "natural" and partly only historical: "human nature"—what now is—is emphatically not coeval either with nature or with man. So far as Rousseau contemplates the adjustment of human nature as it now is to some more authoritative—more primitive, more free—natural norm, he does look for a norm "outside nature," outside what we now know to be, and what is for every practical purpose, our nature. But the prospect for finding a standpoint unequivocally and consciously outside nature in order to enable mankind to master nature in the interest of freedom and morality began with Kant, who elaborated for the purpose a metaphysics and a moral philosophy that stand or fall with the possibility that a realm of freedom, outside the realm of natural necessity, exists and is the scene of the action of the human will.

These remarks are prompted by the occurrence of the term "natural liberty" in the name that Smith applied to his system. They are intended to suggest that Smith's system should be regarded in its relation to a great structure of modern reflection on man's moral condition. That reflection had been brought on by the apprehension that a perfectly mechanized nature, of which humanity forms an integral part, will be graspable by man's mind exactly in proportion to the rule of regularity, predictability, or necessity in that nature. But the more necessary and knowable the natural world, the less free are the human ingredients of it, and the more painful the predicament of modern men, who see their science and their freedom as so grounded that each is a mortal threat to the other.

It is understandable that modern men should be especially afflicted with these apprehensions, for the modern age is emphatically the time of the flowering of natural science, which is a human consciousness of nature as a mechanism; and that consciousness has proved capable of becoming the consciousness not only of the whole chain of natural causes, but of man's place in that chain. Does consciousness of his place in the overwhelming chain of necessity enslave man; or does his higher self-consciousness, his consciousness of *his* consciousness of nature, emancipate him by elevating him above his condition? It is very hard to be sure whether a perfectly clear view of one's entanglement seals one's bondage or rather dissolves it; but it is easier to see that a slave who does not know himself to be one is not simply enslaved. The human being for whom natural science does not exist as the intimation of an infinite chain of causes is not aware of himself as integrated in such a chain. He is not aware that nature poses or constitutes a threat to his freedom; he is necessarily even less aware that his consciousness of his plight is (i.e., would be) *eo ipso* emancipation from his enslavement. He is unaware of these things because he is not a philosopher but a citizen—a fact that remains decisive until it is shown that the deepest thoughts available to an age seep into the average consciousness as *Zeitgeist*. In such a case, average men would have a feeling, perhaps a vague sense of unhappiness or detachment, but certainly not the clear and distinct understanding of their situation which is prerequisite to their enslavement, nor the clear consciousness of their own consciousness that is the condition for their emancipation from the bonds of nature. Failing a theoretical perception of the nature of things, what remains to a man is life within his horizons as these appear to him through his everyday existence. So far as the issue is freedom and bondage, those horizons are the horizons of the citizen, who as such thinks of his freedom and bondage in direct and immediate terms, which are political: is he or is he not in thrall to men who wield the state's power. But even if, or rather especially if there seeped into the average consciousness an unhappiness that reflects a philosophic conception of man as enthralled to nature, it would be folly or wickedness to represent that unhappiness as the product of political formations. Further, it would be absurd to hold out hope of emancipation at all unless there were means, which would have to be other than those of contemplation, for giving the mass of mankind an existence on a plane "outside of nature." But those means do not exist, and every nostrum offered under such a guise proves to be one kind or another of state organization, or political regime. Thus the folly and wickedness are compounded, for the means of emancipation that are offered, being political, are represented to be effective against a bondage that has no political foundation at all but arises from man's inclusion in the infinite chain of natural causes.

The claims and offers that appear so problematical have indeed been made, and with great practical effect. They are directed, of course, against the system of thought and life engendered by Adam Smith. For the moment, we do not know how vulnerable Smith is to the attack. We have seen that he uses the term "natural liberty" with an innocence that is either thoughtless or farseeing, maintaining as it does a total silence about any possible tension between natural necessity and human freedom. In revolving that issue, I have tried to show that there is a sense in which there is no problem, and also a sense in which there would be no solution if there were a problem. There would be no problem, and if a problem no solution, if the problem and the solution would have to be political or practical rather than philosophic or contemplative. But Smith, in proceeding so directly to the compatibility of nature and liberty, appears to adopt what I have called the average man's posture or the horizon of the citizen. In doing so, has he avoided a spurious issue that has bemused much of modern thought, or has he overlooked a crucial condition that has vitiated much of modern life? If the former, his stature has never been properly acknowledged. If the latter, we can understand only too well the basis for those complaints against our institutions that disturb the celebration of our political bicentennial. Against the background of the issues so delineated, we turn to Smith's formula of the invisible hand.

Smith makes reference to the invisible hand in two places, in *Theory of Moral Sentiments* (1759), and in *Wealth of Nations* (1776). Let us look at the two passages.

The produce of the soil maintains at all times nearly that number of inhabitants which it is capable of maintaining. The rich only select

from the heap what is most precious and agreeable. They consume little
more than the poor, and in spite of their natural selfishness and
rapacity, though they mean only their own conveniency, though the sole
end which they propose from the labors of all the thousands whom they
employ, be the gratification of their own vain and insatiable desires,
they divide with the poor the produce of all their improvements. They
are led by an invisible hand to make nearly the same distribution of the
necessaries of life, which would have been made, had the earth been
divided into equal portions among all its inhabitants, and thus without
intending it, without knowing it, advance the interest of the society,
and afford means to the multiplication of the species. (*TMS* IV,
i. 1. 10)

As every individual, therefore, [naturally] endeavours as much as he
can . . . to employ his capital in the support of domestic industry,
and [necessarily] so to direct that industry that its produce may be of
the greatest value; every individual necessarily labours to render the
annual revenue of the society as great as he can. He generally, indeed,
neither intends to promote the public interest, nor knows how much he
is promoting it. By preferring the support of domestic to that of foreign
industry, he intends only his own security; and by directing that industry in such a manner as its produce may be of the greatest value, he
intends only his own gain, and he is in this, as in many other cases, led by
an invisible hand to promote an end which was no part of his intention.
(*WN* IV, ii)

It is clear that the invisible hand is not a metaphor for a power by which
nature compels men to perform any acts. The invisible hand is a metaphor
that certainly presupposes that men are compelled to respond in act to
their natural selfishness and rapacity. It presupposes that men may be
described as being in bondage to the compulsions of nature. But in
contradistinction to what it presupposes, what it says is that something
called nature transforms the ugliness and bondage of man into a true
human good. Whatever else can be said, it seems obvious that Smith
begins by conceding that man is a passive object, governed by and immersed in an overwhelming environing force, that he is part of a great
chain of causes; and then Smith must find a way to extricate humanity
from a desperate slavery that, in destroying freedom, threatens morality
(what morality has an automaton?) The way that Smith finds for achieving these ends is the discovery of nature in its expanded amplitude. Nature
is to begin with the inescapable causes of human actions. It then proves to
be also the power that prescribes the remote ends of those actions and in
addition causes those ends to materialize in fact, according to an intention
that must be said to belong to it, nature, and not to the human actors.
There is scarcely any way for us to avoid a deep sense of uneasiness

brought on by the suspicion that Smith's nature is only too literally just that—Smith's construction: a rationalized wish.

Smith's vision of nature might be defective, but it does not differ from others in being a construction. No one has ever seen nature; what we see is the world, and from it we go on to arrive at nature, which is an explanation of the world. There can be no such thing as an account of the world as *nature* that does not go beyond the mere description of the phenomena as phenomena. But what is the philosopher free to add? Only what makes the world intelligible. And what can that mean? May Ideas be added to the phenomena? May God be added to the world, as if nature, the explanation, is itself a thing to be explained? Does this perplexity not reveal that the world to be explained might have to be seen as the sum of the phenomena and the explanations of the phenomena, with the consequence that not only the intelligibility of the world but the goodness of the comprehensive explanation for man, i.e., the goodness of the natural philosophy for man, becomes the criterion that governs the question, what is the philosopher free to add to the phenomena in order to arrive at nature? Whatever might be the answer to this question in general, with regard to Adam Smith it may be said confidently that he added compulsion and benevolent purpose to the world in order to arrive at nature. Man in nature is the subject of a benevolent despotism; nature is the benevolent despotism that, added to the world, makes it intelligible and, incidentally, good. I have come close to suggesting that natural philosophy can resemble high mythologizing. And I have come close to suggesting that Smith locates within the world, in order to constitute nature, what Biblical theology locates outside the world in order to explain what came to be called nature. Smith makes it unnecessary to look beyond nature—to a divine will above it, as Scripture teaches, or to a human will alongside it, as Kant teaches. What Smith achieves is the transposition of an ancient understanding that nature is exhaustive into the theoretical arena in which nature is thought to be wholly mechanical. When I say that Smith achieved this transposition, I do not mean to imply that he was the first to envision exhaustive mechanical nature. On the contrary, the clarity with which Spinoza, for example, perceived both the vision and the threat contained in it to freedom and morality, typifies the reason for modernity's insecurity in the embrace of nature. What I do mean to imply is that Smith's achievement gives us the decisive clue to the discovery of the decisive question for his system: what does it tell us about the status of man in nature supposed both exhaustive and mechanical?

The figure of the invisible hand brings to light the fact that, along with human bondage in nature goes the reconciliation of the selfish impulses with the good of many or all. If the individual and society and the species are fully integrated in comprehensive nature, then nature could be said to be taking care of her own in exploiting greed for the common advantage. But in so doing, nature appears to release every human being from a conscious concern with the happiness or good opinion of the rest of mankind. Certainly it is the intention of much of Smith's work to show the contrary. The invisible hand goes no further than to argue that, in matters of preservation—the production and distribution of the means of life— the repellent egoism of men is mechanically converted into actions useful to society and species. But Smith believed that he understood how, in important affairs of life that are not reducible to mere preservation, nature leavens the self-regard of men and converts it into virtue. In making what looks like an act of arbitrary distinction between matters of preservation and matters of morality, has he in his own way recognized the distinction between what were once called external goods and goods of the soul; and in so doing, found a means for reconciling mechanical nature with both preservation and morality? It is to the *Theory of Moral Sentiments* that one must turn for an answer. The metaphor of the invisible hand serves its chief theoretical purpose, I believe, in bringing to light a problem for which the solution must be sought in a different context, as I shall now attempt to show.

   A leading question of the *Theory of Moral Sentiments* is, What is virtue? Smith makes it clear from the outset that he is in fact interested in the question, what are the grounds of the distinction between right and wrong, what accounts for the human recognition of this distinction and what accounts for the large measure of practical respect enjoyed by the distinction? He begins his discussion—in the first sentence of the book— by announcing a premise that will bear the weight of much of what follows: "How selfish soever man may be supposed, there are evidently some principles in his nature which interest him in the fortune of others, and render their happiness necessary to him, though he derives nothing from it but the pleasure of seeing it." This is simply a matter of fact. But Smith notes the further fact that there is no way by which one human being can feel the feelings of another, although our responding to those feelings plays so large a part in our lives. The link that proves to join one sentient being to another is imagination. We are forever having vicarious experiences because we are able, indeed because we are unable not to imagine ourselves in the other man's position. On the fact that men so to speak exchange themselves in imagination with one another depends the fact and the force of morality. One observes a human act and one puts oneself, in imagination, in the place of the agent, and, if there is a patient, then in his place too. Then one considers whether there is a harmony between the strength of the passion that moved the actor to act and what one oneself could have felt in the same case. One judges by the same means whether the gratitude or resentment of the patient was suitable to the good or ill received. Thus human beings come to know approbation and disapprobation; but only because, through imagination, the feelings of one man are transferred to another. The natural mechanism that produces this transfer is responsible, therefore, for what is called Sympathy—a term that Smith insists be understood in the technical sense of fellow-feeling ("com-passion") rather than in the special sense of kindliness or benevolence: it applies to all the sentiments, gentle or angry.

The mere operation of the sympathy mechanism does not of itself explain morality, although it explains the approbation that underlies morality. In order to arrive at a norm that is undistorted by idiosyncrasy in bestowing and withholding approbation, Smith applies the construct of the Impartial Spectator, an imaginary bearer of the judgment of universal mankind which is infallible because of its impartiality as distinguished from its possible wisdom or virtue. If it be asked how any man can divine the judgment of the Impartial Spectator, the answer is that the Impartial Spectator is really none other than that "reason, principle, conscience, the inhabitant of the breast, the man within, the great judge and arbiter of our conduct" (*TMS* III, iii). We can easily enough find the way to duty by the use of natural common sense in conjunction with an honest desire to do right (*TMS* III, vi). A man who forms his behavior on such lines will find by repeated experience that he gains the approbation not only of an imagined Impartial Spectator but of his living fellow men. He will find at the same time that he has discovered morality, for virtue is precisely what deserves the impartial approbation of humanity.

Smith sets it forth that men by nature desire or need the approbation of their fellows. We have by nature the strongest desire for the love, the gratitude, the admiration of mankind (*TMS* III, iv). From this irresistible inclination proceed not only the general rules of morality but their strong grip on our behavior. Smith does not neglect the demands of preservation and utility; but he persistently denies that moral criteria or incentives can be derived from or reduced to considerations of mere advantage. Nature apparently does two things for mankind: it implants a powerful instinct of survival in the individual, even a tendency to gross and repellent selfishness; and it endows him with the imagination and gregariousness that unite the species mechanically through Sympathy. With the use of an invisible hand, it cajoles and compels us to society and virtue, to prosperity and humanity.

Smith's work demonstrates that, if one takes nature quite seriously and receives it altogether in its modern acceptation as mechanism encompassing mankind, one need not reject as a premise the impulsive sociality of man, or jeopardize morality, abandon mankind to deductions from self-preservation, or jettison the virtues as such. Obviously it must be asked whether an author may reasonably load or overload nature with this philanthropic freight. We cannot reach that sovereign question in this discussion, but must confine ourselves to the meaning of Smith's project as a project.

Smith's thought is an impressive effort to solve, within the limits of mechanical nature alone, the problem of morality: the source and the ground of the distinction between right and wrong, virtue and vice. It is a peculiarity of Smith's doctrine that it resolves the central moral questions faithfully to the tacit presupposition that nature is indeed the *comprehensive* mechanism. Smith reasons by abstraction from the question of man's freedom within the grip of that mechanism. Of course he perceives that men are free to do well or ill, to heed or to ignore the call of conscience. But that fact does not respond to the much more radical question of freedom within nature, as is clear from a formulation of the issue that directly addresses Smith's own argument: Is the man who fulfills all the requirements of virtue as the sympathy mechanism defines virtue preeminently free or preeminently a slave to the strong need that men have for the approbation of their fellows? Evidently, Smith does not regard this as a crucial question. If one had to guess why he did not attach the importance to it that, for example, Kant did, one might conjecture that he regarded the difficulty as artificial or superfluous. For if one speaks literally of nature as comprehensive, as all-inclusive; and of man as absolutely articulated in the chain of natural mechanism, then one ought not to speak of man's bondage to or in nature, for bondage is a relation between a one and some other which is capable of being "over against" the first. Two things may both be conceived as included in some larger One that comprehends them; and then either might be "over against" in relation to the other. But so far as the one is contained in the other as a part is in some whole, "bondage" is a misleading figure for characterizing the status of the part, for there is no "over against" in their relation. A wheel in a clock is not in bondage to the clock any more than the clock is in bondage to the wheel. Thus the question of man's "freedom" in the order of nature (under the stated assumptions of comprehensiveness and mechanism) does not arise spontaneously, i.e., without stimulation from presuppositions. It expresses the notion that to be part of *the* Whole is not different in principle from being part of any limited whole like a family or a city; and in seeing inclusion as assimilated to domination, it appears to envision subjection of the will of the part to the will of the whole. But precisely if the principle of the whole (nature, in this case) is mechanism— say the motion of lifeless matter according to mere laws of physics—then will can enter only as a confusing metaphor, and the issue of freedom is a gratuitous intrusion in the context. It is in a sense such as this that the difficulty could be regarded as artificial or superfluous. I freely grant that Smith's references to the intention of nature appear to expose him to the charge that he imputes a will to nature. Those references would have to be shown very precisely to point to some characteristic of nature that differs decisively from volition, in order for Smith's abstraction from the question of freedom vis-à-vis nature to be adequately covered by the suggested reasoning. For the immediate purpose, I am assuming, but cannot discuss the assumption, that a purely mechanical principle such as that of evolution through natural selection is compatible with a teleology of nature but does not presuppose a will in nature.

Superfluously to raise the question of man's bondage to nature has effects that go beyond the theoretical. It either prepares the way for despair: there is no escape from the absolutely comprehensive and equally tyrannical grip of the natural All; or it compels men to find, which probably means invent, an enclave inside or a platform outside nature in the form of a state of the consciousness or the will, by which in spirit man will elevate himself to freedom in a sense most elusive. (I speak profanely, of course, and without respect to what may be hoped for through the enlightenment of revelation.)

Articulating man entirely within nature, yet declining to see a question of man's freedom vis-à-vis nature, Smith has adopted an ancient simplicity: man's integration in the order of nature is beneficial rather than threatening to humanity, and is concordant with man's sociality and his virtue. Smith's project for liberal commercial society is part of his wider project for accommodating man's sociality and morality to the environment of mechanistic nature, although the traditional setting for that conception of man in nature is the older and teleological vision of nature. Evaluations of commercial liberalism that do not consider this fact are, I believe, to that extent defective. And they deprive one, moreover, of access to a most interesting reflection: modern society, like modern natural science, might be more reconcilable with the moral benefits that we tend to connect with "the tradition" than we sometimes permit ourselves to perceive.

Perhaps the time has come to remind ourselves of the twin bicentennial with which we began. Through reflection on the issues that surround the concept of the invisible hand, we are enabled to see what justifies Smith in restricting the sense of the term "liberty" to contexts that must be called social or political, and thus what allows him to use such an expression as "natural liberty" without internal contradiction. If we see so much, we may see also the superfluousness of the vast and popular constructions that presuppose the bondage of man in nature, and deduce on that foundation ambitious projects for an imaginary human emancipation that have carried great masses of mankind into very palpable political servitude. Finally, we may see the sense in which the *Wealth of Nations* illuminates the liberal commercial polity of the United States, vindicating it at least in part against those moral complaints that arise from insufficient thought about freedom in and out of nature.

Modern Communism

Reprinted from *History of
Political Philosophy,* edited
by Leo Strauss and Joseph
Cropsey (Chicago: Rand
McNally and Company, 1963),
where it appeared as "Karl
Marx, 1818–1883." ©1963,
1972 by Rand McNally Col-
lege Publishing Company,
Chicago.

Marxism presents itself as a comprehensive account of human life, and
not only of human life but of nature as well. It offers an account of man's
present, and of his past and future, educing its teaching from the premise
that a full and final account of things is impossible except as an account of
the transitoriness or endless flux of things. The definitive description of
the present is given in Marx's economic writings, i.e., in his critical
analysis of capitalism. The account of past and future, or of the evolution
of society, is given in Marx's writings on the theory of history and the
relation of history to a certain notion of metaphysics. Marx's political
philosophy consists of his teaching on economics and his teaching on
history and metaphysics—on the present society and on the coming into
being and passing away of all societies including the present.

The reader might wonder whether an economic analysis of capitalism is
the same as a full account of the modern time (ignoring for the present the
existence of communist countries). It is Marx's contention that the
economy is the living kernel of the society, and therefore to grasp the truth
about the modern economy is to understand the most potent facts about

modern society. But the reader might also wonder whether a full account of society is equivalent to a full account of human life. Marxism takes the two, if society is rightly understood, to be equivalent. Marxism can thus present itself as a comprehensive explanation of the past, present, and future of man. It claims to have discovered that the economy is the true ground of society and therewith of human life. Marx's analysis of the present, i.e., of capitalistic economy, is based upon his labor theory of value. His account of the transition from past to future, i.e., of history, depends on his doctrine of dialectical materialism. Our description of Marx's political philosophy will therefore have this outline: (1) Dialectical materialism, or Marx's theory of history and of the priority of the economic conditions; (2) the labor theory of value and Marx's account of the capitalistic present; (3) the convergence of dialectical materialism and the labor theory of value.

In what follows we shall speak of "Marxism" and the doctrines of Marx. It should be understood that from 1844 on, Marx had as his collaborator Friedrich Engels, who gracefully and without doubt justly declared that Marx's was the genius of the movement, although he, Engels, had made his contributions to it. We shall not try in every case, even were it possible, to distinguish Engels' work from Marx's.

Marx repeatedly asserts that the study of man must concern itself with "real" men, not with men as imagined or hoped for or believed to be. Marx means by this that the foundation of social science is not a notion of some wished-for human good, or some reconstruction of pristine "natural" man, but rather empirical man as anyone could at any time observe him. Empirical man is primarily a living organism consuming food, clothing, shelter, fuel, and so on, and compelled to find or to produce those things. Men might once upon a time have survived by using materials which they simply found and gathered, but the increase in population at some point forced them to produce their necessities and thereby to become distinguished from the beasts. The singular sign of humanity is conscious production—not rationality, or political life, or the power of laughter, for example, as some have maintained. There is, to be sure, an element of unclarity in Marx's teaching on this point, since he concedes that human production differs from "production" by beasts in that the human being plans or conceives in advance the completed object of his labor while the bee or insect toils by mere instinct. In other words, only human production is characterized by rational intention, and human production could thus be said to be unique because it is the doing of the rational animal. Then, however, it would be more exact to assert that man's singular characteristic is rationality rather than productiveness; but Marx is prevented from saying so because the implications of that assertion would interfere with his materialism, which argues that man's rationality or rather "consciousness" is not fundamental but derivative. The Marxist doctrine of the primacy of production in human life rests upon the belief that it was the pressure of his needs that first forced man upward into his humanity and then continues to press him onward and upward; and that the content of his reason must be determined by conditions external to his reason, conditions which are strictly material.

In what ways, more exactly, do the material conditions determine life and thought, according to Marx? He begins by observing that, in every epoch, men have access to certain productive forces, which they apply by making use of the objects—animals, tools, machines, and so on—in which those forces are embodied. But the forces of production—say, roughly, the bare technology—compel men to adapt themselves and their institutions to the requirements of the technology. Nomads, for example, who suddenly gained access to steam power and mechanically drawn agricultural implements would be forced to give up their nomadism and to adopt instead the sedentary habits, division of labor, trading practices, and property institutions which are determined by factory production, and also to take up the practices and institutions correlate to agriculture. That this is true in a general sense is self-evident; it surely was well understood in Greek antiquity. As stated above, however, it is insufficiently comprehensive to express Marx's meaning. Marx asserts repeatedly that to a given set of forces of production there corresponds a certain "mode of production," such as the Asiatic, the ancient, the feudal, and the modern bourgeois or capitalist. According to the feudal mode of production, for example, the possessors of the means of production and the men who labored with or upon those means were connected by a personal relation of mutual responsibility; under the capitalist mode, employers and employees are, as the terms imply, users and used, free of duty to each other, with only the payment of money connecting them. With each such mode of production, there goes, as an effect, one form of social organization. A compact formulation of this view is given by Marx in his letter to P. V. Annenkov, December 28, 1846: "What is society, whatever its form may be? The product of men's reciprocal action. Are men free to choose this or that form of society for themselves? By no means. Assume a particular state of development in the productive forces of man and you will get a particular form of commerce and consumption. Assume particular stages of development in production, commerce and consumption and you will have a corresponding social structure, a corresponding organization of the family, of orders or of classes, in a word, a corresponding civil society. Presuppose a particular civil society and you will get particular political conditions which are only the official expression of civil society." This he compresses further, in *The Poverty of Philosophy* in the remark, "The hand-mill gives you society with the feudal lord; the steam-mill, society with the industrial capitalist."[1]

The conditions of production determine the prevailing property relations, meaning by the latter not the abstract definition of property, but rather who in the particular situation has access to property and who is prevented from acquiring it. Under feudalism, there were lords who possessed land and had rights to other property, and serfs who could accumulate no property. Similarly under the other social circumstances: under capitalism, employers own and accumulate, employees struggle along on the verge of destitution, owning nothing, separated from the means of production. This doctrine is directly connected with the Marxian belief that the conditions of production control distribution of income and consumption of output. They also govern exchange: if production is organized around a commonly occupied arable, for example, there will not even be exchange of the produce of the soil, only sharing. It follows also that money will be in use or not depending on the mode of production: money is not, in its present meaning or use, intrinsic to every economic situation or to economic life as such.

Marx asserts, therefore, that it is a mistake to treat consumption, distribution, exchange, money, and so on as eternal categories having an abstract, permanent content, relevance, or validity. It is one of the defects of the science of political economy, "bourgeois" economics, that it views these purely historical phenomena as fixed categories, having an objective, essential, "natural" character—things that can be understood once and for all because they exist once and for all. Not only are the "categories" historical products, but the science of those categories, namely economics, proves itself to be merely historical or transitory by mistaking the transitory for the eternally true, i.e., by believing itself to consist of laws founded in a changeless nature. Marx denounces Edmund Burke, but through Burke all economists, for his assertion that "the laws of commerce ... are the laws of Nature, and consequently the laws of God."[2] Actually, according to Marx, the economic science of the capitalist period is given its "categories" (wages, interest, exchange, profit, and so on) by the practices prevalent under capitalistic production, and it takes up these categories without recognizing their genesis in the historical conditions. Failing to treat its material as historical and bound to pass away, it of course condemns itself to pass away when its material does so.

Marx's doctrine of the dependence of theories on the historic conditions of production takes in far more than economic theory. He asserts that all morality, philosophy, religion, and politics are the result of the conditioning of men by their environment—their manmade environment which is the expression of the mode of production. The opposite view, that man has an independent intelligence by the light of which he fashions his institutions and forms his convictions, is rejected as ideology, the Marxist term for the doctrine that thought has an independent status.[3]

Marx's materialism has been presented thus far as asserting simply that the conditions of production determine the concrete character of human life, which exists as a "superstructure" on the foundation of the more truly real material conditions. Nothing has been said, however, about the goodness or badness of the actual superstructures that have in fact arisen on the hitherto existing material foundations. Such a judgment is intrinsic to Marx's materialism, however, and to it we now turn.

All historic modes of production have had one feature in common, and that feature has in turn affected all the corresponding societies: control of the means of production has not been shared by all men, but in each age some have been owners or possessors while many more have had to give of themselves, i.e., of their capacity for work (having nothing else to give), in order to have access to the instruments of production, to gain a livelihood. Thus in all previous history the act of production has brought many men into dependence upon the few. The masses have been deprived of the opportunity to become free and self-respecting men because they have always been forced into the position of cringing dependents—slaves, serfs, or proletarians—subject to men who, although private citizens or subjects like themselves, could yet arbitrarily deprive them of their living by cutting off their connection with the means of production. The dehumanization inevitably resulting from such servile dependence has been compounded by the poverty imposed upon the many by their exploiters.

Furthermore, the process of production, from its inception, had a character that Marx calls "natural" in the sense that certain natural differences among men (of physique, talent, and so on) determined the allotment of special tasks to individuals, and the relations of production were therefore determined, imposed, or involuntary, thus natural in the sense of not resulting from human choice. The prototype of all such allotments is the division of function between male and female in continuing the race. This grew into the more general form of division of labor incorporated in the family. As the forces of production were developed, the division of labor became increasingly elaborated, and the particular occupations became correspondingly restricted. As men are compelled by the conditions of production to become shepherds, plumbers, or violinists, they are deprived of the opportunity to develop to the full their human capacities by turning their minds freely in all directions. They are made into fragments of men, prevented by the stultifying division of labor from growing into whole men for whom labor would become a source of satisfaction rather than pain.

While this parcellation is going on within each man, the same process is being repeated among the men. The community comes to be composed of weavers who are set in opposition to bakers, farmers pitted against merchants, townsfolk versus country people, hand workers against brain workers—a war of all against all, fought on the field of material interest, the terms of struggle dictated by the mode of production. Finally, the fracture of society is completed by the coalescence into a class or group of classes of the few who control the means of production, and the parallel coalescence of the many dispossessed into the class or classes that work at the means of production.

The fracturing of social life may be epitomized in the existence of civil society or bourgeois society. (The German term used by Marx is *bürgerliche Gesellschaft*, which may be translated as either civil or bourgeois society.) The breakdown of the integrity of human life is symptomatized and presupposed by the split in our common existence between the political and the economic and social: "Where the political state has attained its true development, the individual leads not only in thought, in consciousness, but in reality, a double life, a heavenly and an earthly life, a life in the political community, wherein he counts as a member of the community, and a life in bourgeois society, wherein he is active as a private person, regarding other men as a means, degrading himself into a means and becoming a plaything of alien powers."[4] Civil society means for Marx an individualistic enclave in society, the realm of privacy as against community, with the understanding that community finds its corrupt expression in political society under now-prevailing conditions. Civil society, far from being synonymous with political society for Marx, is the infrapolitical cognate of political society that is an inevitable part of the capitalistic order. A simple equivalent of "civil society" in this sense is "the economy" of a capitalistic state, or even "the market." Civil society is the stratum of common life that is given its essential character by the self-assertiveness of men, one against the other, in the name of their inalienable, irreducible rights. The sanctity of those rights, thought by writers like Locke to be the ground for guaranteeing the freedom and thus the humanity of men, is rejected by Marx because he views the assertion of those rights as the source of, surely the expression of man's dehumanization. The war of Marxism against the ruling principles of Western constitutionalism must never be mistaken for a mere skirmish.

It is evident, according to Marx, that the many-sided factual negation of all community of interest under capitalism results from the private ownership of the productive resources. Production, a social act in the sense of being by and for all men, cannot be carried on humanely and rationally if the institutions of production are private, particular, and hence antisocial.

The modes of production and institutions of property that have existed hitherto have caused fragmentation and conflict within and among men. What has kept the fragments of society from flying apart? Or, more pertinently, what has prevented the many from summarily ridding themselves of the impositions of the few? According to Marx, the state power is precisely the agency devised by the oppressive few to keep the many in order. The state is the organ of class coercion, made necessary by the dividedness of society that is engendered in turn by the private control of the means of production. It goes without saying that the government does not appear in this light to the multitude of men. Marx allows that all classes collaborate in sustaining government by respecting it and its power of coercion; but this means no more than that men, because of the imperfection of their material conditions, are prepared and compelled to erect over themselves their own tyrant, their own creature that must, as it does, assert itself against them.

It was Marx's belief that while men remain in the state of constraint, of subjection to want and to one another via the process of production, they will be unable to lead fully human lives; for full humanity would require perfect emancipation from bonds of every sort. If Marx had ever used the term "state of nature" in his own name, he would have meant by it the state of man's incomplete domination of nature, the alternative to the state of freedom. While men are in bonds, as they have been under government and "civil society," they experience as part of their bondage a constraint that compels them to contribute to their own dehumanization through institutions of their own devising.

We may conclude this summary of Marx's materialism by explaining the foregoing remark, and at the same time showing how Marx conceives the state of need and the state of political society to coexist as the state of human bondage or what he calls man's alienation. Without a grasp of this element of Marxism it would be impossible to form a sufficient judgment of Marx's political philosophy as a whole.

Returning to our point of departure, we note Marx's primary observation that man is a needing being. Each man is condemned to dependence upon external things, say nature, and upon other men to help supply his needs. But in addition to being essentially needy, man is what Marx calls a species being or a social being, which does not mean simply that man must live and act in common with other men, but that man cannot realize his human possibilities except by acting upon and being acted upon by other human beings. That man knows his fellow-men to constitute a whole of which he is a part, and that he therefore associates himself with them in thought in a way which is ruled out for all subhuman animals, is part also of Marx's rather diffuse notion of man as a species-being. At any rate, it was Marx's belief that man's essential activity, production, has in all previous societies been carried on under institutions that compel men to look upon each other and upon nature itself as alien things, objects, mere means to the end of satisfying the individual's needs. Productive labor itself has always been regarded as a painful necessity because of the conditions under which it has been performed. Thus men's environment and their fellow-men have been objects of predation, and the acting men themselves, and their very own essential life-activities, have been merely instrumental, means to ends without the intrinsic worth they must have if man is to be fully human, to be at one with himself, or to overcome his "estrangement" from nature, from himself, and from the fruits of his labor. Marx's contention is no less sweeping than this: until every man simply merges himself in the whole of humanity, producing only because production is the release and cultivation of human energy, and not because production is a way of obtaining subsistence directly or through exchange by exploiting other men's neediness—not until then will men be perfectly free and the perfect, final articulation of man, society, and nature be achieved. Until that time, men will distort each other's natures by treating each other as objects, each being made thus to grow up at odds with his species, even regarding nature itself, incidentally, not in its beauty and splendor but as a source of gain. The arrangement of the process of production within the institution of common ownership of productive resources, under the formula "From each according to his ability, to each according to his needs," is thought by Marx to be the condition for causing the absolute translation of human life onto a basis which is in the most literal sense unprecedented. Men have lived hitherto in civil society, i.e., under institutions that have presupposed or positively cultivated self-interest as the principle of productive life and life itself. Marxian materialism leads up to the supersession of all civil society and its replacement by the human species as a universal brotherhood. Marxian materialism, which begins by insisting upon the need to consider empirical man, paradoxically ends in a social prescription with no empirical foundation or precedent.

It was stated above that, from the point of view of Marxism, economics or political economy is defective in that it gives an account of economic life in terms of prices, wages, costs, profit, capital, and so on as if these were transhistoric "categories," or eternal elements intrinsic to economic life under all circumstances. The now common definition of economics as the science of the allocation of scarce resources among alternative uses is a better example of what Marx objected to than most economic notions that existed in his own day. This definition implies that there is something that can be called the economic problem for all men in all stages of civilization and technology, and that the rational solution of that problem requires either genuine or simulated markets to produce certain equilibria between commodity and discommodity—a universal law resembling the generalizations of physics. Marx's denial of the truth of political economy was not only a denial that the economists had given an accurate description of free enterprise. It was a denial that the description of a particular economic arrangement was a timelessly true description of the essence of economic life. This in turn is part of Marx's broad doctrine that in general there are no timeless essences and therefore no eternal truths which are not either trivial or purely formal. Marx's political philosophy is mingled with a theory about the nature of all things; indeed his political philosophy is to a certain extent governed by a universal scheme or "system," a doctrine that things neither have essences nor do they, as fixed things, have existences, but they have histories or careers. Becoming, according to the formula, takes the place of being.

Marx followed Hegel in fact, if not in expression, in rejecting as "metaphysical" the view that there are finished "things" or "objects" which have a fixed, given, straightforward constitution. He asserted on the contrary that everything is affected by both change and relation. Thus the various species are forever evolving and the individuals come into being, grow, and then decline. The inanimate things are thrown up by natural processes and then erode, oxidize, or otherwise decay, while internally, they are, like the living beings, constantly in motion. Moreover, each thing is affected, indeed constituted, by the relation in which it stands to other things. For example, a man who is a servant is a servant only in virtue of his relation to another being who is the opposite of a servant, namely a master. The nature of a servant is not intelligible by exclusive reference to the servant himself, just as one could not understand "employee" if there were not "employers." In addition, there is an element of contradictoriness that is introduced into the constitution of perfectly motionless, unchanging things independently of their relations with other things: a curved line, everywhere curved, is nevertheless straight between two points infinitesimally separated. The best example of this paradox is given not by Marx and Engels but by Democritus: "If a cone were cut by a plane parallel to the base, what ought one to think of the surfaces resulting from the section: are they equal or unequal?"[5] The easy answer is "both."

Further, the lines of distinction between classes of things are not sharp, for there are individuals at the margins that are as much of one class as of another ("plant-animals" and "sensitive plants"); and even life itself is not simply distinguishable from nonlife. The transition from life to death is not instantaneous (e.g., the nails and hair continue to grow after "death"), and life proper consists of a process by which the living thing continually dies and renews itself through excretion and nutrition, so that life is inseparable from a continuous dying. It goes without saying that if life and death were in no way distinguishable, it would be impossible to distinguish living from dead material, or to say of life that it implied or presupposed or even required death; yet the Marxist position is that life as a process is not simply life, but it is also necessarily and at the same time death. Life exists as a process in virtue of a contradiction: life is both life and death. And so it is with the other "things."

All things are in flux, as Marxism asserts following Heraclitus, and all flux is motion. To understand the character of all things, it is necessary to grasp the universal law of motion, the law governing nature, human history, and thought. That law is derived from the Marxist doctrine of the essential contradictoriness of motion itself. Since the time of Zeno the Eleatic, a "proof" has existed that motion is impossible: every moving body is at each instant in one and only one place—which is the definition of being at rest. To be in motion is thus to be at rest and also not to be at rest. Each thing is, therefore, by analogy with a body in motion, equally what it "is" instantaneously and what it "is" historically, not in spite of, but in virtue of the fact that the two are contradictory.

Contradiction is fundamental to development, i.e., to historical change, when change is assimilated to physical motion. Change is generated by contradiction through the mutual opposition of the two contradictory elements present in the thing in question. Consider an example given by Engels: a grain of cereal is planted, and it is annihilated as a grain while the plant grows up. As the plant develops to its own extinction, it produces many grains like the one from which it sprang. The grain is the affirmation (or "thesis"), the plant the negation (or "antithesis"), and the many grains the negation of the negation (or "synthesis"). Let us consider one more example: select any algebraic quantity, a, as the affirmation. Negate it by multiplying it by -1, to form $-a$. Negate the negation by multiplying it by itself and the product is a^2, the affirmation on a higher level. The sequence of affirmation, negation, and negation of the negation is called the dialectic, and it is this that Marxism believes to be the universal law of nature, history, and thought. All development occurs on this pattern.

In the special case of human history and thought, a cause is assigned to the unfolding of the dialectical process. That cause is the mode of production and its mutations. Because the primary phenomenon is the material conditions of production, the Marxist doctrine of history is called dialectical materialism, to distinguish it from the idealist dialectic of Hegel which asserted the primary phenomenon to be self-dependent reason as the source of historical change. As a theory of human life, dialectical materialism asserts that the ground of all development in society and understanding is contradiction in the order of production. The most massive of such contradictions is the conflict between classes in society. By subsuming the opposition of class interests under the apparatus of the dialectic, Marxism seeks to show that the conflict cannot be resolved through compromises or mutual accommodations but only by a "negation of the negation," i.e., by revolutionary changes in which the existing classes are annihilated and replaced by a synthesis "on a higher level."

An important element of Marx's political philosophy is his reconstruction of history for the purpose of showing that history has in fact been governed by the materialist dialectic. According to that reconstruction, each epoch inherits a mode of production and a complex of relations among men that is peculiarly fitted to that mode of production. Eventually a change takes place in the mode of production, brought on perhaps by a change in needs that could have been engendered by that very mode of production, and, more immediately, brought on by a fundamental discovery or invention stimulated by those needs. The new mode of production comes into being while the relations among the human beings are still those generated by the previous mode of production. The contradiction between existent social relations and the emergent mode of production, i.e., the clash between the established and the embryonic dominant classes, is the source of "all collisions in history."

Marx and Engels cite a number of historical developments as evidence of this hypothesis, the most amply treated being the transition from feudal to capitalistic society, and the evolution toward postcapitalism. The former is explained by recurring to the rise of machine manufacture in the Middle Ages, first in the textile industry and then more generally. The spread of machine production broke down the structure of guildmasters with journeyman and apprentice labor, replacing it by a relation of bourgeois employers and wage-earning employees between whom no ties existed but that of the wage payment. The manufacturing mode of production was the vehicle by which the most fortunate and most active escaped serfs rose to displace the guild-masters as the owners of the new means of production, and to become the progenitors of a new class, the bourgeoisie. Opposed to them, at the same time indispensable to them, were the proletarian laborers having nothing to live by but the wages from the sale of their labor power. As industry and commerce expanded, the scale of production increased enormously, and as it did, the relations between the owning and nonowning classes underwent a further change, an aggravation. The clash of interests between capitalists and wage-earners inevitably sharpened, for the proletarians' condition had to deteriorate because of the contradictions that are intrinsic to capitalism, contradictions that will appear when we consider Marx's critique of capitalist production. For the present it suffices to say that, according to Marx, the full development of machine production (under private ownership) requires the absolute pauperization and dehumanization of the wage-earners because of the pressures of capitalist competition. At last the wretchedness of the masses will become unbearable, and the conflict of the classes will break forth into a decisive combat—decisive because the victory of the proletariat will usher in a new age of man.

The proletarians have neither the wealth nor the wish to become the owners of the means of production *as a class*. Unlike every other insurgent class in the past, their purpose is not to take the place of their oppressors but to put an end to oppression. The means of achieving this end is to abolish the private ownership of the means of production and thus to abolish the distinction between owners and nonowners thereof, the distinction which is the condition for the division of human society into classes. Upon the dissolution of classes will necessarily ensue the end of the class struggle and the beginning of strictly human history. When that has occurred, the relations among men will have caught up with the latest great development in the mode of production; the conditions of oppression disappearing, the need for coercion will disappear as well, and the state will wither away to be replaced by the universal brotherhood of man.

Marx was well aware that his prognosis for mankind was necessarily linked to a diagnosis of prevailing conditions. He realized that he must investigate the contemporary (European) world in its essentials, which is to say in its economic character, in order to satisfy himself and others that the dialectic of materialism is actually operative in the decisive period, namely the present. It was necessary for him to demonstrate that the law of the nature of capitalism is the law of the transformation of capitalism into something radically different. His enterprise incidentally required him to show that no explanation of capitalism other than his own had grasped the essential character of capitalism, and therefore no other account, at least no other then known, could be made the basis of a prognosis for mankind. This means that ordinary political economy, which did not come to the conclusion that capitalism is self-vitiating, is in various respects unsatisfactory even as a description of how capitalism works. Marx's own economics is almost wholly "critical," devoted not to the explanation of how a socialist economy should or would be constituted but to a detailed representation of the self-contradictoriness and transitoriness of capitalist institutions, and to the inadequacy of political economy as known. The inseparability of the two criticisms is implicit in the subtitle of *Capital: A Critique of Political Economy.*

Marx's general criticism of political economy has already been mentioned. We must take up here his critical analysis of capitalism proper, and with it his more specific reflections on political economy. The title of his major economic work, *Capital,* indicates what seemed to him to be the central economic problem. Capital, according to Marx, does not mean simply the artificial means of production—equally a stone axe in the hand of the primitive, a bow in the hand of a Grecian hunter, or a power loom in nineteenth-century England. Capital is productive wealth in the peculiar form that generates profit. The prevailing system is called capitalism because the means of production, privately owned, are a source of profit to their owners the capitalists. It is very important to understand the nature of profit with perfect precision, for profit is at the heart of the prevailing social and economic order. Profit is not simply any economic surplus, such as might arise in primitive or feudal economies, any more than capital is simply productive wealth. Profit and capital are uniquely, mutually complementary.

Profit appears directly as a part of the price of a commodity, a part which the owner of the means of production, the capitalist (as Marx was not the first to call him) is able to claim. What exactly does his share consist of? How does it originate and by what right does the capitalist lay claim to it? Classical political economy had provided a certain answer, which was the point of departure for Marx's own analysis. Classical political economy had begun with the assertion that labor is the source of value, that the amount of labor embodied in a good is thus related to the amount of value in the good, and that the relative values of two goods must be in proportion to the relative amounts of labor embodied in them. The accompanying presumption is that the one who has created the value by pouring his labor into the object has the right to be the owner of his product. The classical economists agreed that, when production was carried on by individuals for themselves, using their own hands and the implements fashioned by them or owned by them, each man could claim for himself whatever he produced. But that condition ceased when, in order to carry on production, men required access to land and instruments belonging to others. Thereafter, those others had a right to share in the product. Evidently, profit (to leave aside the problem of rent) is coeval with the accumulation of productive property by some members of society.

There was, according to the classic view, a period of human life when every man could "produce" independently; and then there was—and still is—a period in which land was made subject to appropriation, and the accumulation of durable property was made feasible. In the earlier period of human life, the labor theory of value applied in its simple and direct form. In the latter period, the product of labor is shared with capitalists and landlords. Readers of the doctrines of Hobbes and Locke, but especially the latter, will be reminded of the division of all human history between a period in the state of nature and a period in the state of civil society. We are now prepared to understand more fully Marx's asseveration that classical political economy assigns to the institutions of capitalism the status of prospectively timeless, natural conditions. Classical political economy and the political philosophy to which it was linked regarded as absolutely epochal the progress of man from the prepolitical to the political condition. That same crucial change was perfected or consummated with the replacement of absolute monarchy by constitutional government, for between a subject and an arbitrary master there is only the law of nature. That crucial change in the human state was connected by classical political economy with the accumulation and protection of property in the means of production. The institutions of property thus come to parallel, and to have the same status as, civil society or civilization—political life—itself. Neither Hobbes and Locke nor the classical political economists looked beyond civil society for a further radical melioration of man's estate. It was left for Rousseau to raise the broad question of the goodness of both civil society and property, and thus to open the way for his successors to search for a horizon beyond that of civil society. Marx, in rejecting the view that property and civil society, or say political life, were the absolute condition for decent human existence in peace and prosperity, denied the natural and permanent status of "the laws of commerce." He rejected the implication of classical political economy that profit and the private ownership of the means of production are here to stay, as much as and for the same reasons that political society is here to stay.

Surely Marx did not concede that the transition from the state of nature to the state of political society was the absolutely epochal change in human life. Neither did he concede that the parallel change from the pure to the diluted application of the labor theory of value was epochal or even that it provided a valid ground for understanding the prevailing economic institutions. That a difficulty indeed existed in that mode of explanation was noticed by Ricardo as he examined Adam Smith's theory of value and wages. Ricardo pointed out that if it were true in a simple sense that a commodity which required a day's labor for its production should be said to contain a day's-labor-worth of value, then when that commodity is exchanged for labor, it should purchase its equal in value, namely a day's labor. The brief formulation would be, labor embodied equals labor commanded, for any commodity.[6] In other words there would be no profit: a workman could be hired for a week only if his product for the week (or the full value of it) were paid him as his wage. The fact that the wage is not equal to the whole product compelled Ricardo (and Smith, incidentally) to find an alternative formulation, one that ascribed value-productivity to capital as congealed labor. Marx rejected the Ricardian and other classical explanations of profit, wages, and value because those explanations, in accounting for the difference between the labor embodied in and the labor commanded by a commodity, did not lead up to a condemnation of profit as resting upon exploitation, which Marx believed it to do. We must now consider his alternative explanation.

Marx begins by noting a problem that arises out of the exchange of goods: when one commodity is exchanged for another, a common ground is indicated between two things which appear to have nothing at all in common. Suppose a pair of shoes to be exchanged for three shirts. The shoes and the shirts are so perfectly unlike as to be incommensurable. How can the ratio of three for one, or any other ratio, ever be arrived at? To deal with the problem of commensurability, Marx recurs to, but modifies, a distinction which was traditional in political economy, the distinction between value in use and value in exchange. For the distinction use value–exchange value, regarded by political economy as fundamental, Marx substitutes use value–value. The reason for this is that he does not regard exchange as a permanent, natural institution but rather as a historic and transitory one. But exchange value is derivative from value proper, and in order to understand capitalism it is necessary to understand exchange value and therefore value simply. Returning now to the two commodities, we notice that they are absolutely unlike so far as we consider their value in use or their qualitative character, each good being designed for a certain purpose that the other could not serve. Now a shoe comes to be a shoe in virtue of having been produced by the peculiar labor of a shoemaker. A shirt is a shirt because it is the product of shirtmaking labor. The difference between shoemaking and shirtmaking labor is the source of the qualitative difference between shoes and shirts. Marx goes on to assert that, just as the two commodities can, indeed must, be looked at as if they are not only dissimilar but also have commensurable values, so the labor that produced them must be capable of being looked at not only as qualitatively differentiated labor. It must also be seen as homogeneous or undifferentiated human labor, as the generation of a certain amount of motion in a certain mass by a certain expenditure of human energy. As skills, therefore, the kinds of human labor are simply different; but as toil, all labor is the same, and is measurable in units of time, according to the length of its duration. Upon this latter fact depends the mensurability and commensurability of values. The summary formula would be, differentiated human labor produces use values and qualitative differences among commodities, while undifferentiated human labor produces value simply and quantitative commensurability among the commodities. Thus it is in their character as products of undifferentiated human labor, not as products of specific labor aimed at satisfying specific wants, that commodities have commensurable values and can enter into exchange.

It should be pointed out that the assignment of labor alone as the source of value is not demonstrated by Marx, but is asserted by him as something self-evident.[7]

The foregoing account of value provides support for Marx's definition and elaboration of the notion of a commodity. By a commodity Marx means a good which is privately produced for the sake of exchange (or sale, i.e., exchange against money). Capitalism could thus be described as a system of commodity production and, as such, based upon confusion and distortion. Rationally, the sum of all the individual labor-powers in the community is the aggregate of labor-power available to the society for the satisfaction of all its wants. If men were to live without distortion in their affairs, their labor-power would be directly applied to the satisfaction of their wants rather than to production for exchange. Because the means of production are privately owned, however, production is carried on not directly for its true purpose—the satisfaction of wants—but for the special advantage of the owners of the means of production. The social character of labor is thus mediated and distorted by the mode of production. What Adam Smith regarded as a peculiar virtue of private enterprise, namely, the voluntary performance of a social function under the influence of a desire for private advantage, is regarded by Marx as the ground of the iniquity and instability in the prevailing system. Why he did so conclude can be understood if we look further at the capitalistic mode of production as Marx interpreted it.

Indispensable to capitalism are the private ownership of the means of production and the existence of a body of men who both do not own any means of production and are perfectly free, in the sense of being unbound to the owners of the means of production by any personal ties of duty or rights. In order to live, the unpropertied must therefore engage themselves to labor at the machines and on the land of the propertied. The propertyless in effect sell to the propertied a commodity called labor-power—not labor. Labor-power means the ability to labor for a given period; labor means the actual duration of the labor. For Marx the distinction is crucial. Labor-power is a commodity, under capitalism, and that means that it is something produced for sale and having a value determined by the amount of labor congealed or incorporated in it. But what could be meant by the amount of labor incorporated in the capacity of a laborer to work for eight hours? The answer is, that amount of labor that was required to produce the necessities that must be available to the man furnishing the labor-power in question. Somewhat more broadly, the value of a day's labor-power is determined by the amount of labor necessary to produce the subsistence for the laborer and his family in order to maintain the supply of labor-power at its level, not only from day to day but from generation to generation.

Let us suppose that in order to provide all the materials of subsistence necessary to support a labor-power of eight hours, six hours of labor must be performed. Then the value of a labor-power of eight hours would be equal to the value of six hours' output. One would then obtain the output of eight hours by giving for it the output of six hours. The value generated by the employed labor-power during the two hours of its application while it is "not paid for" is called by Marx "surplus value"; it is the basis of profit. Profit exists only because a portion of the workingman's labor-power results in an output for which he is not paid. Yet he is not being cheated, in a certain sense. Marx is at pains to point out that the labor-power is bought at its full value, its value understood as being rigidly subject to the labor theory of the value of all commodities including labor-power itself. Thus the man is paid in full for his labor-power but not for his labor. By this formulation Marx believed he had solved the problem that classical political economy had failed to clarify with consistency, the problem caused by the inequality of the labor embodied in a product and the labor commanded by it. His solution depends on the distinction between labor and labor-power. By this radicalization of the labor theory of value that applies it to labor-power itself, Marx was enabled to argue that a serious hidden contradiction of capitalism was brought to light: the relation between employer and employee is at one and the same time both cheating and not cheating. In the sense that it is not cheating, no one can individually be blamed: the buying and selling of labor-power are done at full value according to the rules of the market. So far as it is cheating, however, it requires rectification. Marx's conclusion is that the abuse demands the abolition of the system rather than a change of the rules within the system: "reform" could never suffice, because no mere reform could terminate the buying and selling of labor-power.

This contradiction is but the ground for many more. For example, from the proposition that profit originates in the consumption of labor-power by the capitalist, it follows that profit can be made to increase either by consuming more labor-power or by increasing the amount of labor that is produced by a given labor-power (say, approximately, increasing the output per working day). But the increase in output per day (increase in productivity) is achieved by increasing the use of machinery. Increasing the use of machinery opposes the increase in consumption of labor-power. In order to prevent the introduction of machinery from suppressing the profitable consumption of labor-power, the working day must be lengthened. Marx thus arrives at the conclusion that the introduction of machinery leads and will lead to the lengthening of the working day and to the formation of a large population of the chronically, technologically unemployed.[8] Here and elsewhere, Marx's economic analysis led him to make certain grossly incorrect predictions as to conditions in a matured capitalistic economy. Not because his power of prediction is in itself of great interest, but because so much of his revolutionary animus is vindicated by the horrors he professes to foresee in the flowering of capitalism, his mistakes of prediction come to have a singular effect on the credibility of the analysis on which they rest.

To continue. The restless struggle for profit causes the capitalistic economy and society to be in a state of endless flux. Under the lash of competition, which tends to reduce profits, capitalists must constantly revolutionize the process of production in order to cheapen it. Old skills are rendered obsolete and the average level of skill required in the work force is reduced as the motions of the artisan's hands are analyzed and copied in machinery. Since the fundamental condition of capitalist economic life is a free, propertyless work force toward which the propertied have no duty, the whole burden of technological change falls upon the wage-earners in the form of unemployment and poverty. But technological change as such is not peculiar to capitalism; only under capitalism does it become a source of misery. In a dialectical manner, Marx argues that in its abuses, capitalism serves to expose a transcapitalistic human problem that can be resolved only by the transcending of capitalism:

> ... Modern Industry ... through its catastrophes imposes the necessity of recognizing, as a fundamental law of production, variation of work, consequently fitness of the labourer for varied work, consequently the greatest possible development of his varied aptitudes. It becomes a question of life and death for society to adapt the mode of production to the normal functioning of this law, Modern Industry, indeed, compels society, under penalty of death, to replace the detail-worker of to-day, crippled by lifelong repetition of one and the same trivial operation, and thus reduced to the mere fragment of a man, by the fully developed individual, fit for a variety of labours, ready to face any change of production, and to whom the different social functions he performs are but so many modes of giving free scope to his own natural and acquired powers. [9]

It must be pointed out that the tendency of technological change has not in fact been to reduce the average level of skill in the work force or to lead to falling real wages and a growing "industrial reserve army of the unemployed." Nor is there any evidence anywhere in the world that modern technology can be made compatible with institutionalized jack-of-all-tradeism.

Marx takes up many more aspects of capitalistic economic life than we can deal with here. His single-minded purpose throughout is to show that in virtue of what capitalism is, in virtue of its being intrinsically contradictory, its development must be its dissolution: the more it fulfills itself and approaches its peak, the more it destroys itself and approaches its fall. He provides a remarkable summary of his understanding of the case, late in Volume I of *Capital:*

We saw in Part IV., when analysing the production of relative surplus-value: within the capitalist system all methods for raising the social productiveness of labour are brought about at the cost of the individual labourer; all means for the development of production transform themselves into means of domination over, and exploitation of, the producers; they mutilate the labourer into a fragment of a man, degrade him to the level of an appendage of a machine, destroy every remnant of charm in his work and turn it into a hated toil; they estrange him from the intellectual potentialities of the labour-process in the same proportion as science is incorporated in it as an independent power; they distort the conditions under which he works, subject him during the labour-process to a despotism the more hateful for its meanness; they transform his life-time into working-time, and drag his wife and child beneath the wheels of the Juggernaut of capital. But all methods for the production of surplus value are at the same time methods of accumulation; and every extension of accumulation becomes again a means for the development of those methods. It follows therefore that in proportion as capital accumulates, the lot of the labourer, be his payment high or low, must grow worse. The law, finally, that always equilibrates the relative surplus-population, or industrial reserve army, to the extent and energy of accumulation, this law rivets the labourer to capital more firmly than the wedges of Vulcan did Prometheus to the rock. It establishes an accumulation of misery, corresponding with accumulation of capital. Accumulation of wealth at one pole is, therefore, at the same time accumulation of misery, agony of toil, slavery, ignorance, brutality, mental degradation, at the opposite pole, i.e., on the side of the class that produces its own product in the form of capital. [10]

Marx believed that when, at last, the bourgeoisie had been reduced for the most part to proletarianism by savage competition, and the proletariat had been reduced to stark poverty by the laws of accumulation and profiteering, then the uprising would occur and mankind would stand on the eve of history. [11] It is not going too far to assert that Marx's economics consists of the attempt to show how that fateful transformation is implicit in the labor theory of value as concretized in the practices of capitalism.

Whether or how far these doctrines of Marx are sound is a question of more than ordinary interest to the world. It arises in two parts: whether what Marx regarded as inevitable is so; and whether the premises of his system are acceptable. These questions we must now take up.

Marx's predictions are on two subjects—the fate of capitalism and the character of socialist society. On the former he is at great length, as we have seen, and to a large extent he predicts incorrectly. A century after he came to his conclusions, it is fair to deny that the introduction of machinery must lead to lengthening of the working day, that there must be massive, growing, technological unemployment, that the bourgeoisie

must be proletarianized and the proletariat pauperized, and that socialism is the culmination of capitalism. Marx's predictions were based
upon the belief that an economic order has a life and being of its own, that
it resembles the articulation of inert parts, and that when it is somehow or
other launched on its way, it functions mechanically, as little subject to
change of direction as a bullet shot from a gun. Marx had a certain
loathing for utilitarianism, but he was as prone as any utilitarian
doctrinaire to liken social life to a syllogism. Logic is supremely universal,
everywhere and at all times the same. It is expressive of reason, but it has
nothing to learn from prudence. Marx made concessions, but absolutely
insufficient ones, to such simple and undialectical influences as laws—
laws to limit the length of the working day, laws to encourage or compel
collective bargaining, to enact workmen's compensation, progressive
income taxation, unemployment insurance, old-age benefits, laws to
regulate securities exchanges, to promote full employment, to protect
competition, to control the money supply, to support agriculture, to
relieve the sick, to suppress the adulteration of food, to compel the young
to submit to be educated, to insure savings, and a thousand other laws,
not the least of which is the law that puts lawmaking under the influence
of the reigning multitudes that he mistook for a pauperized proletariat.
Marx was an astute journalistic observer of political things, but in his
teaching he conceded nothing significant to politics, i.e., to discretion,
which he discounted as mere "reform." He postulated the economic man
with as much narrow assurance as any political economist, if with a more
brilliant rhetoric.

Marx's predictions are not only of the baleful kind. Occasionally he
alludes to the character of life in the postcapitalistic epoch and gives brief
sketches of the communist world. There is no way to test empirically his
visions of socialism, because all existing socialist societies claim to be in a
state of transition toward communism proper, and every disparity between
the expectation and the reality is explained as temporary. Whether all
such disparities are in truth temporary, or how many could be temporary,
depends upon the soundness of the ground upon which Marx's expectations rested. We turn to that question in conclusion.

The ruling principle of Marxian socialist society is, "From each
according to his ability, to each according to his needs." This is a maxim
fit to serve as the fundamental law among loyal, wise, and incorruptible
friends, devoted to one another with an absolutely unselfish benevolence.
Among such friends, not only would no individual seek his advantage at
the expense of others, but the thought of doing so would never occur to
him. In this sense, duty as duty would be transcended: what the mere
sense of duty dictates to a man capable of selfishness would be the most
spontaneous desire of a man as member of the friendly society. His duty

would not appear to him as duty. Marxian society would be a society of billions of friends warmly joined in the rarest and most sensitive union of amity.

It is imaginable that there would be a great concourse of men living together without any threat of coercion to restrain them from offending each other, but that their uncoerced sociality would reflect not goodness but utter indifference, the extinction of every animating impulse. Marx emphatically does not have this in mind: his socialists would be alive at the peak of all their powers, each abundantly active. His vision of life for the generality of mankind is what the ancient thinkers conceived as the highest possibility open to the wisest and the best—the mutual love of a few noble spirits, elevated above every petty desire, free from every trace of envy or worldly ambition, willingly sharing that invaluable good which does not pass away from its possessor when he bestows it upon another and which is multiplied when it is divided, that good being wisdom. The notion of the quintessence of justice materializing among the wise is intelligible, for wisdom excites the admiration that generates love, and wisdom is a good for which men cannot contend invidiously but only harmoniously. The conditions for rational benevolence would be fully met among the few who desire a good the pursuit of which cannot corrupt. The perfect society is the society, then, in which philosophy as the rule of life would become indistinguishable from justice, which also is the rule of life. In the perfect society, justice would administer itself, and it would therefore be perfectly pure because untainted by the need to coerce, to punish, or to deceive. The disappearance of justice into philosophy might be said to be equivalent to the disappearance of the political in the philosophic.

The perfect society could not be described except on the premise that there is such a thing as philosophy, that a few men take it to be the greatest good, that more than a few never can or will take it to be so, and that therefore it is in the nature of things that justice and political society or government will not dissolve into philosophy. Marxism dreams of the disappearance of justice and political society—not in philosophy, it goes without saying, but in rational economics, and therefore for the mass of humanity, not merely for the infinitesimal few.

The economic system that would be approved as rational by Marx would of course not be the liberal economy in which the "economic man" finds free scope for his "rationality." That rationality, which is in fact only self-interested calculation, is thought by Marx to be infected with contradiction. A self-contradicting rationality would appropriately serve as the spring of action in a system that seeks prosperity through poverty, freedom through subordination, and the common good through the emancipation of self-preference.

Pre-Marxian, or at any rate pre-Hegelian, political philosophy, both ancient and modern, was characterized by a certain moderation that allowed it to approve regimes which achieve reason through myth, freedom through coercion, or sociality through selfishness. Wayward and unreflective as men are, they may still be made amenable to social life if they can be brought under the guidance either of well-disposed men or of cunning institutions that play men's lower motives off against each other to a salutary outcome. In either case the end or outcome was conceived to be of utmost importance, apart from such considerations as whether the end is given by nature, or whether it justifies the means. How far Marx was affected by the tendency of Kant to depreciate the mere ends we cannot here consider; but it is certain that Marx repudiated the willingness of the ancient and the eagerness of the modern traditions to make peace with, though not to surrender to the weaknesses of human nature, and to be content with society consisting of men as they are. Marx dreamed of that human condition in which good ends would be sought by good men using only good means and responding to (because possessing) only good motives. The basis or presupposition of his dream was the generation of a new man, or the regeneration of man—and the instrument of regeneration would be the rational economy rightly understood.

Unexpectedly, we now see coming into view a ground of agreement between ancients and pre-Marxian moderns on this most important point: political life rests upon the imperfection of man and continues to exist because human nature rules out the elevation of all men to the level of excellence. The connection between civil government and man's imperfection is expressed by Rousseau, for example, in the form of the distinction between state and society: men can be social while uncorrupted, but in political community they prey upon and are preyed upon by one another.[12] At the beginning of *Common Sense,* Thomas Paine wrote, "Society is produced by our wants, and government by our wickedness; the former promotes our happiness *positively* by uniting our affections, the latter *negatively* by restraining our vices.... The first is a patron, the last a punisher."

Rousseau may be said to have suggested, via the doctrine of the perfectibility of man, that government may be more and more replaced by society: in the perfect freedom of self-government, coercion loses most of its sting. But Rousseau did not at all suppose the utter collapse of government into society, for he did not suppose that all men would become philosophic, nor that there is any perfect substitute for the full rationality of men that would render coercion and rhetoric of all kinds, i.e., political life, dispensable. He did not, in brief, expect ordinary selfishness simply to disappear from among the generality of men.

What in Rousseau was a limited suggestion, although an emphatic one, came to be the dogmatic core of a confident prognosis, a strident propaganda, and a revolutionary incitation in Marx: the state or political order will wholly wither away, and homogeneous mankind will live socially under the rule of absolute benevolence—from each according to his ability, to each according to his needs. No longer will duty be performed incidentally to the pursuit of selfish interest. The link between duty and interest, which is to say the subordination of duty to interest, will be broken for once and all by the abolition of the categories "duty" and "interest." They will be abolished by the revision of the property relations, by the inauguration of a new economics which will bring on the full perfection of human nature via the transcendence of production for exchange.

In barest outline, Marx's radicalization of Rousseau can be said to rest upon the supersession of philosophic reason by historic reason. Philosophic reason, the intelligence of individual human beings, being unequally present among men, political society with coercion and rhetoric cannot be dispensed with if calamity is to be avoided. So the philosophic tradition believed. Marx's teaching is that there is a reason inherent in the course of history: History abhors a contradiction as profoundly as nature was ever thought to abhor a vacuum. Whether a contradiction means more than a clash of interests, we are not told. In any case, the unviability of every individual contradiction is transformed by the philosophy of history into the unviability of contradiction simply. The philosophy of history tries to communicate its confidence that contradiction must wipe itself out, working through the discontents of men afflicted with the symptoms of the contradictions that exist in society. The progressive resolution of contradictions, and the movement of man toward the condition free of contradiction deserves to be called the expression of historic reason. It supersedes or overcomes the philosophic reason, or the intelligence of individual men, not only in the obvious sense that, through the historic evolution of human nature, the unequal distribution of intelligence will cease to have political relevance. When the new breed of man is generated by the common ownership of the means of production, all the old (natural) categories of right will fall before the logic of history, and subphilosophic men will live in uncoerced and myth-free (i.e., perfectly rational) society, as only the rarest of men were thought to be able to do, but even more emancipatedly than the rarest, who never had the benefit of the perfect environment. The multitudes of men will be conditioned to reach the heights by abundance of goods produced and distributed without any opposition of interest. Marx appears to believe that, if men are divided by scarcity, they would be united by abundance. We would be readier to be convinced of this if there were reason to believe that men will some day be indistinguishable from the grazing herbivores.

Marxism is famous for looking forward to the end not only of political life but also of religion. Religion is the belief in the existence of a realm of the whole where there is a rectification for every defect in the terrestrial world. Here there is death, there life. Here iniquity goes unseen or unpunished, there it is recorded and retributed; or if it is beyond human punishment, it receives divine punishment even here below. The goodness that is ignored or mocked on earth is accounted and honored in heaven. The belief that the whole is or tends to be good can be maintained even if the visible part of the whole is imperfect, by arguing that the invisible part perfectly makes up the deficiencies present to our view. We would be led far out of our way if we attempted to compare the teachings of the theological and the philosophic traditions with respect to this question; but we may observe that the ancient philosophic tradition also taught that nature as a whole is good. Yet it is not so unequivocally good as to render superfluous the coercion and rhetoric that support political life; thus the goodness of nature as a whole does not permeate all of human life. On this fundamental point there is a ground of agreement between ancient philosophy and revealed religion: for all practical purposes, the goodness of the whole, whether the whole is the sum of the natural and the supernatural, or the complex of form and matter in nature itself, cannot be translated or transformed into the goodness of man's common life. In the case of modern political philosophy, the goodness of nature as a whole was characteristically not asserted; teleology was of course rejected, and the wretchedness of the state of nature strongly argued. Nature required to be rectified, or rather to be governed; and the clue to the government of nature was to be found in the laws of nature—the laws of science and the laws of politics and economics. The belief in the possibility of conquering or governing nature perhaps opened the way to the Marxian notion that the perfection of human life is possible, and not only possible but foreseeable, in the classless society. But as has been seen, that consummation was not explicit in the teaching of pre-Marxian modern political philosophy. Not before Marx asserted the historicity of nature itself,[13] the absolute perfectibility of human nature under the influence of economic conditions, was it supposed that political life and religion must vanish and be replaced by uncoerced, rational society.

We are led, through the doctrines of Marxism, to reconsider some commonly held views. One is that there is a deep hostility between philosophy and political society because philosophy, by its unconfined questioning, eventually exposes the polity itself to the blasts of skepticism;

while the body politic, suspicious of theories and prone to Philistinism, always threatens the thinking sort of men with contempt or worse. But however well-founded the mutual suspicions might be, we observe that philosophy, certainly classical political philosophy, argues that man is by his nature political and that political society is the truly human society taking into view the characteristics of men generally. Philosophy has been thought to threaten politics; we see that in fact it defended politics, and that the anticipation of the end of political life had to await the supersession of philosophy by history—that is, by the doctrine of the emendation of Nature.

Another opinion brought under revision is that between philosophy and religion there is in principle war to the death, the one asserting the supremacy of reason, the other of faith. We have seen that philosophy can have, and did for ages have, a certain common ground with religion; both had views of nature that did not lead to the expectation of perfect society within the natural order. The theoretical discountenancing of religion in the name of an aspiration toward perfect society had to await the supersession of philosophy by history.

We might summarize by saying that the replacement of philosophy by history was the condition for the replacement of politics and religion by society and economics. This is the kernel of Marxism.

Marxism is not simply another political system, or one more ideology. It proposes nothing less than the end of the West—of political life, philosophy, and religion—as the foregoing summary indicates. Perhaps we should look forward with eager anticipation to the end of the West—but we cannot know whether we should without rationally examining the project for strangling philosophy. That rational examination is part of the philosophic quest itself. We cannot free ourselves of philosophy, if only because we must philosophize to pass judgment on philosophy. We begin to suspect the soundness of the antiphilosophic historicism of Marx. Observing its weakness prepares us to concede that history can make room for spiritually impoverished societies: the viability of Marxist nations is a sign not of the soundness of Marx's prophecy but of the unsoundness of the sanguine historicism on which he based it. We have every right to conclude that history is the opiate of the masses.

Notes

1. Karl Marx, *The Poverty of Philosophy,* ii. 1. 2nd observation.

2. *Capital* (New York: Modern Library, n.d.), I, 834, n.1. Copyright by the Modern Library. Pagination is the same in the edition published by Charles H. Kerr & Co. The reference is to Burke's "Thoughts and Details on Scarcity."

3. Cf. Engels' *Herr Eugen Dühring's Revolution in Science [Anti-Dühring],* x.

1: "... ideology, the deduction of reality not from itself but from its mental image."
Also Engels' *Ludwig Feuerbach,* iv. 7th par. from the end: "... ideology, that is,
occupation with thoughts as with independent entities."

4. "On the Jewish Question," in *Selected Essays by Karl Marx,* trans. H. J.
Stenning (New York: International Publishers, 1926), pp. 55-56.

5. From K. Freeman, *Ancilla to the Pre-Socratic Philosophers* (Cambridge:
Harvard University Press, 1957).

6. David Ricardo, *Principles of Political Economy and Taxation,* i. 1.

7. See, for example, *Capital,* i (p. 45).

8. Ibid., IV. xv. 3 (p. 445).

9. Ibid., 9 (p. 534).

10. Ibid., xv. 4 (pp. 708-9).

11. See ibid., xxxii.

12. Cf. the sentence with which Montesquieu begins I. iii of *The Spirit of the
Laws.*

13. See above, p. 98.

Readings

A. Marx, Karl, and Engels, Friedrich. *The Communist Manifesto.*

Marx, Karl, and Engels, Friedrich. *The German Ideology.* Ed. R. Pascal. New
York: International Publishers, 1939. Part I.

Marx, Karl. *Theses on Feuerbach.*

Marx, Karl. *Capital.* New York: Modern Library, n.d. Bk I, part I, chap. i,
secs 1, 2, 4.

B. Engels, Friedrich. *Ludwig Feuerbach and the Outcome of German Classical
Philosophy.* Ed. C. P. Dutt. New York: International Publishers, n.d. Chap. iv
"Dialectical Materialism."

Engels, Friedrich. *Herr Eugen Dühring's Revolution in Science (Anti-Dühring).*
Trans. E. Burns. Ed. C. P. Dutt. New York: International Publishers, 1935.
Part I "Philosophy."

Conservatism and Liberalism

Reprinted from *Left, Right, and Center,* edited by Robert A. Goldwin (Chicago: Rand McNally and Company, 1965). © 1965 by The Public Affairs Conference Center, The University of Chicago.

Political life in the United States is energized by the action upon each other of the two major political parties. It is sometimes said, however, that the difference between the two parties is less fundamental than the difference between conservatism and liberalism, with which the difference between the two parties does not sufficiently correspond. The conclusion has sometimes been drawn that our political life would be improved if the distinction between the parties were made to conform to what is rightly or wrongly conceived as the truly fundamental difference of opinion prevailing in this country. There is at least plausibility in the argument that administration under either party, as things now are, must be vitiated and made incoherent to the extent that each party is both conservative and liberal, at odds with itself and thus in danger of rendering the national policy ineffectual on important occasions.

Incoherence or self-contradictoriness is one defect that vitiates policies and administrations; another is orientation upon narrow or ill-conceived ends, however consistently pursued. Therefore, before giving careful attention to the meaning of conservatism and liberalism, one cannot know whether to wish for a national policy compounded of elements drawn from both of these clashing opinions or for a policy dominated by only one. The question of the organization of political life gives rise immediately to the questions of political principle, in the present case to the issues that turn upon the meaning of conservatism and liberalism. To the investigation of these we now proceed.

I

Although conservatism and liberalism confront each other directly as movements, their names appear not to take notice of each other. "Conservatism" stands for conserving the inheritance, "liberalism" for devotion to liberty. The tension between movements appropriately called by these names should disappear if the inheritance is liberty. In the United States the inheritance is indeed liberty yet the tension is real and persistent. This is an indication of the fact that the names describe imperfectly the phenomena to which they are attached: conservatism is in its own way fully as dedicated to liberty as liberalism is. It appears therefore that liberalism is not propertly differentiated or characterized by the literal meaning of its name. It is necessary to begin with a more specific or peculiar characteristic of liberalism, namely, its inclination toward reform or change, in order to progress in examining the disjunction of conservatism and liberalism. We shall begin therefore by saying that conservatism respects the received while liberalism respects the improved.

Each generation that is guided by what it receives defers to the judgment of preceding generations, just as each individual who is guided by the rules he receives submits thereby to be ruled by other men's opinions and wishes. Generations and individuals who respect the received abdicate judgment and supinely accept as authoritative what is agreeable to other men, or what other or earlier men have agreed or consented to. They accept convention as more authoritative than their own reason or their own judgments, if any. Conservatism implies deference to the authority of convention: conservatives are "conventional." The conventional is antithetical to the natural in the way that a standard of conduct founded only on the agreement of men is contrary in its essence to a standard that would arise out of the nature of men and things independently of human agreements. The standards that men establish by agreement are of course artificial. Thus it happens that to respect the conventional is also to respect the artificial. It is also to respect whatever be the deep and powerful motives, such as the passions of men, that guide the formation of those agreements or conventions. If conservatism is respectful of the conventional, the artificial, and the traditional, it may be said to that extent to abjure nature and reason. Perhaps the tension between conservatism and liberalism reflects or is even constituted by the antithesis of the conventional and the natural.

Generations and individuals who respect the improved or who incline toward reform defer to no reason but their own. The conclusions that their reason brings forth may be profound or preposterous and their motives may be earnest or vain; but their desire to be free in mind and self-subsistent is recognizable clearly. They wish to examine each age and situation as it is, that is to say, as it differs from other ages and situations; and they wish to prescribe for the age and situation by the light of what they understand for themselves, by acts of reason, rather than by the light of other men's agreement as to the good. To refuse the authority of conventions, and to investigate the nature of each thing—each age and situation—by the light of reason seems congenial to the spirit of reform and thus to the spirit of liberalism. It therefore appears that the tension between conservatism and liberalism repeats the antithesis of convention and nature: conservatism accepts the yoke of convention, liberalism craves the freedom of nature.

There is a measure of truth in this, but it is not conclusive. The argument is weakened by the consequences of the fact that some conventions grow up imperceptibly, such as the manners, morals, and customs that prevail among a people, while others are more deliberately contrived, namely, the artificial conventions such as constitutions and laws. Men who defer to convention in the former sense acknowledge the authority of what comes into being in a quasi-natural way, by imperceptible growth. Men who incline toward reform, on the other hand, acknowledge their dependence upon human contrivance or upon what is artificial rather than natural. On these grounds it is conservatism that is close to nature, liberalism to convention. Also, the appeal to an unchanging human nature as a check on the spirit of reform is characteristically conservative. Moreover, reform necessarily implies a difference between things as they are and things as they should be. The liberal standard by which this difference can be understood is not nature or any natural end, good, or goal. Also, it is a mistake to conceive nature as partaking of freedom and not of necessity or constraint. The liberal appeal from conventionality is evidently not as such a proper appeal to nature. It is more nearly an appeal to freedom conceived as being incompatible with formality, or nature misunderstood as identical or coextensive with freedom.

The failure of the disjunction between liberalism and conservatism to repeat the antithesis of nature and convention is further shown by the extent to which the liberal appeal from convention ignores the fact that convention is by nature intrinsic to political life. In their families, men are generally bound to a decent common life by the ties of natural affection. When they must live together in large numbers and without the natural affinities to rectify their conduct, their nature requires that they replace those natural affinities with formalities or conventions that are the ground of political as distinguished from domestic society. In this way nature demands convention. A political opinion that appeals incontinently from convention cannot then, paradoxical though it may seem, properly be said to appeal to nature. It is important for us to know this as we try to grasp and weigh conservatism and liberalism, for if either could properly maintain a claim to have established politics upon nature, it would obtain an immense ascendancy.

The reservations of liberalism against convention are not limited to political matters in the narrow sense, however, and cannot be dismissed before they are considered in their wider intention. Those reservations manifest themselves in the *mores,* the manners, customs and, one is tempted to say, the conventions that govern speech, dress, education, the arts, literature, and many other things. The objection to being bound by the rules or conventions in these various activities is stated on behalf of self-expression, the activation of those abundant powers said to be latent in every human being, those powers loosely called "creative" which are present in men as the gift of nature and the development of which is freedom in a high, transpolitical sense.

The appeal from convention on behalf of self-expression cannot be decisively rejected on the ground that self-expression brings forth inanity or worse in the overwhelming majority of cases, for the worth of self-expression is not thought to be measurable by the worth of its external product but by the benefit conferred on the acting man himself through the use of his powers. This liberal notion is reminiscent of and must be compared with the much older thought according to which the performance of certain acts is humanizing because to be human in the truest sense means to be active in the employment of the most human powers.

Those who entertained that thought conceived the act of thinking to be good in itself and without respect to any external product that it might bring forth. Indeed the act of thought and the thought itself are one and the same, and are good for the acting man. They humanize him. The liberal view has some similarity to this, but differs from it essentially. Unreconciled to the inference from the fact that sustained and fruitful thought is not a possibility for a great many, liberalism may be said to have egalitarianized and thus democratized the humanizing act by finding it in the free expression of all powers, unbound by conventions and unjudged by the confining criteria of truth or accomplishment. The humanizing act is not the measured act of reason but the act of freedom, or the act of the self not perfected in reason. The guiding thought is that it is healthier to be oneself than to be right, perhaps because being right has no meaning beyond being oneself. Whether egoism of this kind is tantamount to putting pride above truth, and whether the ego can ever attain to a sense of self-subsistence while it is aware that it puts its self-subsistence above the truth are questions that we will not pursue. At any rate, by popularizing and politicizing it, liberalism has uttered a distorted and transformed echo of the ennobling truth that man is perfected by his action; but the distortion and transformation were in the interest of a benevolent intention guided by a vast, and hence vastly dangerous, optimism. The optimism lay in the belief that nature confers, as it would in the best of all worlds, all good things at once: liberty together with equality and fraternity. Great confusion is latent in the existence of this belief in the minds of men side by side with the belief that nature is simultaneously good and also normless, endless, or irrelevant to the difference between good and bad. The attempt to unite the contradictories of crude optimism and impoverished positivism has proved damaging to liberalism as a theory, although it has not hindered liberalism as a political movement. It is instructive to note how wide is the gap between theoretical sufficiency and political efficacy.

II

The reservation of liberalism against convention corresponds to an appeal to nature in a manner of speaking, withal to nature understood as in direct support of the liberty, equality, and fraternity of all men. Yet the disjunction of liberalism and conservatism is not equivalent to the antithesis of nature and convention, not only for the reasons already given but also because conservatism too, regardful as it may be of convention, is itself dependent upon a distinct conception of nature from which it is to some extent derived and to which it must make a constant if tacit appeal. The character of that conception of nature is most discernible in the aspect of present-day conservatism that is especially conspicuous, namely, its stand concerning property and economic life.

Conservatism leans emphatically toward capitalism or free enterprise, which was called by Adam Smith "the system of natural liberty," in which every man is "left perfectly free to pursue his own interest his own way."[1] The language of leaving men perfectly free expresses the thought that they were originally or naturally perfectly free. This notion is not peculiar to or the invention of capitalism or conservatism but is rather the inheritance bequeathed by the classic modern political philosophy of the seventeenth century and shared by capitalism and conservatism with liberalism, as has been seen. According to the familiar view, men are by nature absolutely needy, or driven above all by the desire and need to preserve themselves.

Also, they are wholly free to do whatever they see fit to reach this supreme end. Men are by nature free, and equal in their freedom, but driven apart from each other by the very condition that makes them both free and equal, namely, their neediness. It is the nature of men as it is the nature of all things to seek their private or individual good, or to be selfish. As Adam Smith noted in a famous passage, "It is not from the benevolence of the butcher, the brewer, or the baker, that we expect our dinner, but from their regard to their own interest."[2]

In their leaning toward capitalism, conservatives of the present time evince their belief in a nature that is in direct support of the liberty and equality, but not fraternity of men. A group of free and equal rational beings who are not naturally social must wish to find some means of preserving their freedom and equality, as far as possible, while counteracting their natural asociality. Capitalism is the institution by which men have solved the problem of preservation or need on a basis of freedom and equality in opportunity, without aspiring to transcend their alleged natural asociality but only to counteract it. In an ingenious way, that very asociality has been exploited to the end of reconciling duty and interest, as the quotation from Adam Smith indicates. It is noteworthy that the capitalistic reconciliation of duty and interest is novel, for it does not operate through legal coercion or punishment for dereliction of duty so much as "freely" or "naturally" through gain or reward for compliance. The principle appealed to is pleasure rather than pain, desire rather than aversion, the "toward-which" rather than the "away-from-which," as it would be in a theological system that dwelt on heaven and scarcely mentioned hell.

It is a practical supposition of this system that the moral imperfections that spring from man's natural asociality can produce, when correctly managed, the same public effects as do the moral virtues themselves, but more reliably: tradesmen will do their duty out of selfishness more dependably than out of good will. There is no way of measuring the risk in thus depending upon means and measures to produce their own opposites, as selfishness is expected to produce the good of others; nevertheless, from the premise that man is naturally directed toward his preservation and not toward his excellence, it follows that institutions should be sought which transform selfish acts into socially beneficial ones. Such institutions would be harmonious with nature in the sense that they would not frustrate man's natural selfishness and further in that they conduce to the preservation of the species as a whole, which is the natural end.

Capitalism, and thus present-day conservatism, adheres to a view of nature according to which duty is reconciled with interest in such a manner as to become absorbed or obliterated by interest. The peculiarity of the conservative appeal to nature is that it leads to the collapse of morality into Utilitarianism. At this point the conservative appeal to nature comes into conflict with the conservative inclination toward the old, the old-fashioned, the conventional, the received, and the notion of the traditional as good. Conservatism as a movement of political opinion in the United States is divided against itself exactly for the reason that one of its branches is dominated by an inclination toward free enterprise while another branch is dominated by a reminiscence of traditional morality as conducted into the modern time either by religion or by a recollection of classic antiquity. Some part of the theoretical poverty or self-contra- dictoriness of conservatism at the present time can be traced to this circumstance. Conservatism, like liberalism, is afflicted with a desire to have the best of several worlds. The wish in both cases is for freedom based upon a morally normless nature. The consequences of the attain- ment of that wish proving to be unsatisfactory, liberalism adds the hope that freedom will generate human excellence and conservatism adds a discordant recollection of moral virtue rooted in the teleological under- standing of nature that has been rejected by modern conservatism almost as widely as by modernity in general.

The disjunction between liberalism and conservatism does not cor- respond to the antithesis of nature and convention. Both liberalism and conservatism appeal to and depend upon conceptions of nature. The difference between the two political opinions is illuminated by the difference between the two conceptions of nature to which they respec- tively recur. That difference may for the immediate purpose be reduced to the point that liberalism envisions the natural fraternity of mankind and conservatism concedes no more than the "asocial sociality" of man. The liberal view is that man's nature prepares him to live uncoerced in society. This opinion coheres with the belief, now quite old, that the convention of property is the chief dissolver of the natural bond that joins men in communities and all mankind as a species. The liberal animus against coercion (for example, in favor of therapy rather than punishment for crime, and *a fortiori* against capital punishment) is thus related to the liberal animus against property ("property rights" are subordinate to "human rights"), property being divisive or contributory to invidiousness or "competitiveness." The wicked love of possession lies near the root of coercion, inequality, and invidiousness, respectively the negations of that liberty, equality, and fraternity directly supported by nature.

III

Conservatism supposes that there is a development from man's asociality to his property; liberalism believes that the development is from his property to his asociality. This division on a theoretical plane brings us to a confrontation of the two movements of opinion on the political plane. As experience and doctrine have taught, men making a constitution must assign the final authority in the political community either to one man or to several or to the people as a whole. The purest reason for assigning it to one man is his superiority to all the rest. Minority rule can be justified only by the pre-eminence of a group or class with respect to capacity for government or to wealth. Where liberty in the radical sense is the ruling consideration, the highest authority is left in the hands of the mass of the citizens. No more than any other men could the authors of the United States Constitution assign the highest authority at the same time to the wealthy and to all, for many were poor. They constructed a framework of popular government with ample safeguards for property, which means for the owners of property. It is clear that to exalt the few because of their virtues is to elevate them with an eye to what they can contribute to the common life; while to protect the rich as such is to show a concern for the interest of property as such and to defend it against laziness, malicious envy, or any other turbulent or tyrannous distemper. The United States Constitution is an instrument which not only mediates the claims and interests of the propertied and the unpropertied but also assimilates those claims and interests to one another and generalizes them, sheltering life and liberty beside property under due process of law. The Constitution takes no notice of, and certainly accords no political advantage to, the propertied as a class. By its protection of property it translates the fragile natural right to life and liberty into a substantial civil right to that which sustains life and liberty. Critics of property have argued that property is of merely civil or conventional rather than natural origin, and that what has been created by convention can through the same agency be limited or withdrawn. This proposition is a sound premise for the argument that begins with noting the status of property as a merely civil right and draws the conclusion that therefore it is not "absolute" but can be granted and must be exercised only in the degree compatible with the civil convenience. It provides no basis at all for the conclusion that property as a merely civil right can be curtailed at will without jeopardy to the natural rights, that is, the liberties, of which it forms the civil support. Each human being constitutes a petty monarchy within the borders of the political community. Unequipped, he is naked. With his adjunct property, his monarchy is a defensible sanctuary into which he can retire and from which he can sally forth in the presence of tyrannical neighbors or encroaching government, supported by the inviolability of a private sphere of life. It is true that there are two pinnacles of liberty or self-sufficiency, one which is reached by way of property and the other, still higher, by way of indifference to and even some privation of external goods. The latter, however, is not of the sort contemplated either by the Constitution or by the liberal critics of property, and emphatically not by its conservative defenders. Restricting ourselves to the theme of the liberty of citizens in a modern republic, we must conclude that carelessness of property is to be counted among the offenses against civil rights directly, and against natural rights eventually. We have returned to the notion that property is an ingredient in the rectification of man's asociality.

IV

The liberal reservations against property express themselves only partly in the form of partisanship for the poor as against the propertied, or as reservations against property simply. This is understandable in the light of the progress of equality and the vast surge of abundance during the last quarter- or half-century and more. Those reservations are far more likely to appear in the form of a doubt as to the decency of business enterprise or of the gainful use of property in business and especially in big business. That doubt is reflected in a solicitude for the employees of business, expressed in sympathy for the labor movement, and in a solicitude for the customers of business, expressed in sympathy for the consumer movement. The root cause of that doubt is the fact, not only not denied but emphatically asserted by the authors of capitalism, that business enterprise is animated by selfishness. Acts animated by selfishness are instantly suspect. This ground of the liberal view of business property is entirely understandable, and we must now return to it in order to complete the discussion of the opposition between conservatism and liberalism in respect of property.

The liberal belief that actions proceeding from selfishness are tainted by the human poverty of that motive is not new. Pagan antiquity blamed narrow selfishness as ignoble and derogatory to the common good. Religion condemned it as vain, hence impudent in the face of God. Modern thinkers have denounced interestedness as incompatible with morality, which they conceive as based upon the sense of duty and not upon any calculation of benefit. These positions are tenable, respectively, by those who recognize the intelligibility and the value of both nobility and the common good; those who have an earnest faith; and those who enter into the austerity as well as the presuppositions of Kant's doctrine as a whole. Liberalism does none of these things. Its revulsion from selfishness grows out of its view that self-interestedness is inimical to the equality and fraternity, and ultimately to the liberty, of men. Liberalism wishes simultaneously for the cultivation of men's idiosyncratic freedom and their coalescence into social community united by the intimate bonds of their natural brotherhood under the skin. Liberalism therefore wittingly or otherwise envisions that social state in which men would wish to benefit themselves only in ways that are beneficial or at least not harmful to others. In that state men's perfect integration into community would be indistinguishable from their perfect freedom to do as they please. This states the character of liberalism's reconciliation of duty and interest, so different from that of conservatism. The liberal reconciliation of duty and interest envisions the collapse of the distinction itself in a social state of liberty, equality, and fraternity directly prepared by nature. At the same time it is of the greatest importance to bear in mind that liberalism is egregiously open to the suggestion that nature cannot mean anything more than "human possibilities" or "experiences" or "change," as in the pragmatist teaching. It may properly be said that liberalism has adapted to its peculiar dream about nature the preliberal thought that man is by nature social.

The perfection of plurality supporting the consummation of unity may permit or require the cultivation and expression of all idiosyncratic differences; but it could not tolerate differences of an invidious character. At least two classes of differences are invidious: differences of opinion as to good and bad, right and wrong, or just and unjust; and differences of interest. These are the deeply divisive differences. Whether a liberal society would be in fact a free society, and if not, whether the oppressions would conduce to the highest good, are grave questions unknown to liberalism and outside our present scope. We must notice, however, that for the sake of avoiding a reliance upon notions of the common good, liberalism recurs to the theory of interest groups; while in order to avoid the interested fragmentation of fraternal community, liberalism looks beyond propertied selfishness. The theoretical inadequacy of this position need not be drawn out.

V

If the conservative conception of nature is discernible in the conservative stand on property, the liberal conception of nature is indicated in some of its aspects in the liberal stand on patriotism. As liberal thought inclines away from the divisiveness of certain institutions of property, so it inclines even more noticeably away from the dividedness of men grouped according to their nations, which seems to be an arbitrary division very much to the detriment of peace. Liberalism certainly looks beyond the love of country to the love of mankind. Patriotism is unavoidably discriminatory, becoming akin to preferring one's own as such and, in the vulgar extreme, degenerating into the simple dislike or hatred of foreigners. Repelled by the selfish and unreasoning love of self as by the ignorant and truculent hatred of the alien, liberalism aspires to the transcending of the nation, if only through the union of the nations. Its sentiment is humane and its peaceableness is a salve to mankind. It utterly ignores, along the way, the solid ground for self-preference that exists among the citizens of a well-constituted nation. Rightly repelled by vain self-love, it is dogmatically blinded to self-respect and conceitedly captivated by a priggish self-depreciation. It also ignores that irreducible element of variety that must be present in the conceptions of men as they grope for the good in order to govern themselves by its light. Liberalism, which makes a by-word of pluralism and recoils from "absolutes" however misunderstood, should welcome the diversity of nations, and their sovereign security upon which that diversity rests, as a valuable guarantee of the freedom of men to go their separate ways in the quest for justice or for the truth about justice. It must be conceded, however, that the highest good known to liberalism is not truth or even liberty itself, but fraternity and its *alter ego*, equality. Politically speaking, this has come to mean that the highest good known to liberalism is peace, or self-preservation.

If it is true that patriotism, known and called by that name, is more a conservative than a liberal virtue, the reason is that the conservative derivation of the social good from the working of individual self-preservation has not extinguished, but has been mitigated in its selfish tendency by, the sentiment that old ways are good, that one's own is good and that, if it is narrower, it is also more human, surely more civil, to love what is near and similar, as such, than what is remote and strange, as such. It might appear that there is a natural contradiction between love of the household or care for its prosperity on the one hand and love of country on the other. Yet it is a matter of experience that love of country need not be extinguished by the most animated concern for the household, while it must infallibly be extinguished by the doctrine that exhibits it as offensive to peace, as an ignorant expression of ethnocentric bias, the neurosis of aggressive personality types, the posturing of the fatuous for the edification of the gullible, or the delusion of innocents seduced by schemers after wealth and power.

The tendency of liberalism to depreciate the polemic preference for one's fellow citizens in favor of the irenic love of one's fellow men, and thus to weaken the force of patriotism in favor of the cause of peace, is parallel in its effects to the liberal belief that it is wrong to demand of men that they show themselves to be trustworthy before one trusts them but that on the contrary one must trust or affect to trust them precisely in order to regenerate them and render them good, hence peaceable, thus trustworthy. This belief grows generally out of the notion that institutions have rational or intended functions and also psychological or adventitious side-effects. Very properly, liberalism demands that all the effects be considered. Swept on by its overriding vice, liberalism concentrates from time to time on the supposed psychological effects of the working of public institutions, such as schools, and ignores the function intrinsic to the institution itself. But the belief in question grows more specifically out of the notion that, among nations, there are no genuine issues but only attitudes or states of mind which, if they are inconducive to peace, can be removed by the methods of conflict resolution, or exorcism of mass delusion and neurosis. It is evident that the maintenance of constitutions and regimes would tend to lose its status as a sovereign concern or even as a genuine issue under the influence of this view. The theoretical inadequacy of liberalism reasserts itself at this point, at which it becomes clear that the libertarianism of the liberal view and the psycho-pacifism of that view would come into contradiction whenever a free country would find itself compelled to make war in order to preserve its free constitution.

The belief that trust or the feigning of it should precede trustworthiness is not in itself a delusion. It is part of a truth drawn from experience: in order to inculcate the virtues, it might be prudent for a mentor to feign the belief that his ward already has them, in the hope that a sense of responsibility, an instinct of decency, a modest respect for authority, and a wish to please will collaborate to generate the anticipated habits. If these motives are overridden by a deep-seated opposition of interest, sentiment, or intention between mentor and ward, and *a fortiori* if the two parties do not at all stand to each other as mentor and ward, and the one thus has no certain means of disciplining the other should trust prove to have been misplaced, then this mode of moral education is particularly unpromising, partaking as it does of the aggravation of vice by burdening the weak with temptation to transgress; while as a principle of policy it could be impartially described as irresponsible.

The liberal view is consistent with itself in applying to domestic as well as to foreign affairs the dictum that trust edifies, and absolute trust tends to edify absolutely. Without the support of this dictum, it would be more difficult to sustain the liberal belief that political participation qualifies the citizen rather than that his qualifications are prerequisite to his participation in political life. There is a considerable measure of truth in the liberal view that ought not to be overlooked. To the extent, however, that this belief is tantmount to the expectation that, through the (psychological) conditioning of the electorate by "participation," the difference between the rule of many and the rule of excellence will tend to vanish, the view is based upon a mere hope, for participation in a politics from which the invidiousness of human standards has by intention been expelled, in the interest of "conditioning," cannot serve as an education in civic right.

Liberalism is inclined toward trust, which is compounded of faith and hope, and it is also inclined toward love and peace. It seems to be the carrier in the present time of Christian conceptions born in ages past, a circumstance made singular by the fact that liberalism, positivistic in its outlook on divinity, assists at the replacement of religion by culture. The faith and hope of liberalism together comprise a faith in the hoped-for regeneration of man, a trust based on the thought that the evil in man is his impulse, generated by desire, to have things for himself of which he must, in gaining them, deprive others, or, failing to gain them, suffer frustration and succumb to resentment or disturbance. Want, or wanting, is the root of evil, and the self-centeredness or antisociality of want-satisfying man is the evil itself. Satiety through technology will be the Paradise Regained in which man will eat of the fruit of the tree of science, expel want, and dwell in the house of concord forever, in the brotherhood of man without the fatherhood of God.

It is no less singular that conservatism inclines toward belief both in divine providence and in man's perfect dependence on his own providence. One branch of conservatism reaches out toward religion and another reaches out toward laissez-faire. The branch that reaches out toward religion is informed by the human disposition to have faith in the old, in what is prescribed and certified by ages past, and what is at the same time one's own by inheritance. The branch that reaches out toward acquisitiveness is informed by the two varieties of selfishness, one of the body and the other of the spirit. The former seeks the external goods that sustain the good of the body, and it is not different from acquisitiveness or self-preservation; the latter aims at self-dependence, in a manifestation which, humble as it may be, is of the same genus as the virtues itself. It seems paradoxical that conservatism should join the acquisitive to the moral, and it would in truth be simply paradoxical were it not that virtue is itself so deeply self-regarding. Moral virtue is animated by a self-regarding disdain of those actions which expose a man's dependence, or the degree to which he falls short of mastery—of things and of himself and of other men. What is quite paradoxical is that the common man's aspiration to be self-sufficient is condemned to be expressed in an undisguised and even perspiring pursuit of wealth, hence an undissembled confession of dependence. Nevertheless, the point can as properly be made that the effort and discipline of satisfying want contribute to the goodness of men as can the contrary argument that the effort corrupts man and community. It is in the context of these considerations that one must reflect on the strange fact that conservative opinion embraces both the supremacy of self-preservation as the mainspring of life working its way pitilessly through the market and also the doctrine, echoing old teachings, that moral virtue in its aspect of hardy self-dependence is good.

It may be granted, as Rousseau proclaimed, that it would be desirable to transform men into beings who could be selfish in the elevated sense that is equivalent to self-esteem without being selfish in the ordinary sense that is inseparable from invidiousness. That it is possible to produce such a disjunction in the mass is a thought that has kindled the faith of liberals and the irritated incredulity of conservatives. At any rate, liberalism emerges as the vehicle of reason emancipated from tradition, of positivism, and of Christian virtues to be inculcated by the conditioning effect of the works of science; and conservatism emerges as the champion of religion and of the worldly or politic virtues distorted and shrunken to conform with the conditions prevailing in a community dominated by the teaching of indefeasible natural rights and of the indistinguishability of virtue and vice in the natural condition of man.

As now appears, the common notion that liberalism appeals to reason and conservatism to tradition, or to prescription, or to the ancestral, is insufficient. In appealing to natural science, liberalism appeals indeed to a vast knowledge, but it is a knowledge about things the first principles of whose being are left veiled in darkness or in mere belief; and in its anticipations of man transformed by his standard of living and by the social conditionings of education, political participation, housing, and so forth, liberalism appeals to faith and hope unalloyed. For its part, conservatism rests upon a faith or opinion that the good is the respectable, the conventional, and perhaps the merely old; while in its character as the party of laissez-faire, it is the heir of Hobbes' teaching of the supremacy of natural reason, as that reason has been made impotent, after the manner of science, to ascend to the principles or nature of its objects. Liberalism and conservatism depend upon faith or opinion, each in its own way. Liberalism does so in the way characteristic of the prevalent science of nonhuman things, that is, by abstention from examination of the first principles upon which all else rests—not because these principles are too sacred to be unveiled but because their existence is denied. Conservatism depends upon faith or opinion in the way characteristic of political practice, that is, through the intuitive disinclination to dissolve in speculation the ingrained habits and beliefs that are the fiber of political community.

VI

Conservatism and liberalism are movements of opinion, residues to some extent of political philosophy but not themselves political philosophy. They are constructed of discordant elements, as has been our purpose to show, that cohere in equilibria that are from the theoretical point of view precarious although perhaps pragmatically feasible enough. Each is not only beset by a certain internal tension but is, in addition, partial with respect to the truth. On the themes of property and country, liberalism draws attention to the natural unity, conservatism to the natural dividedness of man. With respect to the question of the function of reason, as for example in the realms of science, religion, and history, the liberal understanding rests upon faith in one sense, the conservative understanding rests upon faith in other senses, as we have seen. Political opinion in our time is related to political wisdom as dreaming is related to thinking.

A philosophic understanding might be free of these shortcomings, for it would make the necessary concessions to the jangling truths which are undoubtedly in the possession of both conservatism and liberalism. This fact cannot be transformed into the premise of an argument to the effect that American public life should be given a philosophic basis. On the contrary, the dictate of reason is rather that the political truth be approximated by the equilibrium of the imperfect movements of opinion. For this to take place, these movements must be so moderated and controlled that the tension between them does not result in the annihilation of either—not for the sake of diversity, but for the frustration of dogmatism of the right or left. The danger of a collapse of the Constitution into the doctrines of either party would increase if liberalism or conservatism could command unmixed, hence unrestrained and eventually agitated, majorities in the electorate. In a curious way, the last resort of political reason now proves to be the temperate equilibrium of error.

Notes

1. Adam Smith, *The Wealth of Nations* (New York: The Modern Library, 1937), p. 651 (Book IV, Ch. IX).
2. Ibid., p. 14 (Book I, Ch. II).

Political Morality and
Liberalism

Paper presented as "Political
Morality" at the Center for
Constructive Alternatives,
Hillsdale College, Hillsdale,
Michigan, 10 September 1973.

The decisive question concerning political morality is, What is it? By referring to *political* morality, one seems to suggest that political morality differs from morality simply. But whether it truly does so is in fact the decisive question: what political morality is, and whether it differs from morality simply, should come to light at the same time. Therefore, instead of proceeding by trying to show how political morality differs from morality, I shall begin by taking as a premise an assertion that will, I hope, not prejudge the issue but that will be acceptable as a starting point. The premise is this: men who live in political society are, by virtue of that very fact, in such a position that at least some of their acts touch the life or well-being of that political society. For the present purpose it is unnecessary to investigate the meaning of "political." I shall, it is true, be thinking of entities like "the United States" and "the Soviet Union" rather than corporations and families when referring to political society, but I believe that what follows will show that the exact meaning of political society does not affect the outcome. We might almost—though by no means entirely—replace the word "political" with the word "public" or perhaps "communal" in the phrase "political morality," for the present purpose.

I am presupposing that men live in political societies as those are ordinarily recognized, and that some of those men's actions are certainly relevant to the life of their political societies while some of their actions are totally private. I recognize the need, for some important purposes, to state precisely the basis for distinguishing a publicly relevant from a purely private act. I recognize also that the definition of that distinction is itself an act of political society, and that this fact would have to be clarified in an exhaustive treatment of our theme. But for the present purpose, no more is needed than the formal distinction between public and private acts in the foregoing loose sense.

We may now address the qestion, What are the kinds of acts that bear on the well-being of the political society as such? and from there go on to consider the norms that govern those acts and that permit of judgments on the morality of the men who perform those acts. There are in the first place the acts performed by rulers, governors, and all other officials—men who are authorized to discharge a public duty. In the second place, there are the acts performed by private men but directed toward the public as such, or performed with a view to having a public consequence. Lastly there are the acts performed by private men and directed only toward other private men which nevertheless have a public bearing or importance. Our task is now to take up these three classes of acts in turn and consider the moral problems related to them.

The criteria for regulating and judging the deeds of public officials with a view to their morality seem to be obvious and few. Officials should practice honesty, courage, truthfulness, and all other virtues in performing their political acts. They should act in unswerving obedience to the laws. And they should scrupulously distinguish between themselves in their private existence and in their public capacity, never regarding their private interest or prejudices while they act as political officers. Let us consider these apparently obvious rules one by one.

Conceive to begin with a military commander leading his country's troops. The soldiery, far from home, are at large among a helpless population whom they tend to abuse. The commander has always enjoyed a reputation for mildness and now, in order to preserve that reputation, abstains from the severities he would have to practice on his army. In brief, he prefers gentleness (or perhaps popularity) to cruelty. This famous example, drawn from *The Prince,* barely introduces the complexity of the case but it unmistakably suggests a reason for doubting that the practice of a moral virtue by a public man is in every case advantageous to the political society. One could multiply examples at length (See *Khrushchev*

Remembers, introd. Edward Cranshaw, trans. and ed. Strobe Talbott [Boston: Little, Brown & Co., 1970] pp. 220–23). Is it well to be truthful and open when one is charged with the public's secrets? Should one practice dissimulation in order to extract an enemy's secrets of state? The point of general interest that begins to emerge is this: that mere advantage, survival, or prosperity is so close to being the good for a political society while so far from being the whole good for a man, that the pursuit by a public man of his individual good or excellence may, if it have nothing to contribute to the good of the whole, be compelled to recede from sight. Logic if not decency would prevent us from leaping to the conclusion that therefore private vices are the source of public benefits. This is a proposition that might be maintained, but not on the basis of what has emerged thus far in the argument.

Let us consider further the leading assertion, which is that public men should practice the moral virtues in their conduct of public business. During the great Stalinist purges of the thirties, it was common for public officials in Russia to make both denunciatory and self-accusing statements known by all parties to be false. While their reasons for doing so are complex, and include torture, there is reason to believe that "party loyalty" was believed by the accused revolutionaries to take precedence of the truth, of the so-called "objective truth." Now it appears that each regime might especially prize and encourage moral qualities that reflect its own nature rather than the nature and goodness of humanity as such. Loyalty to one's comrades and one's party is on the whole meritorious, but like many a virtue, preeminently courage, it can be put in the service of dubious ends. It is not obvious that in every case the rule of right conduct for a public man as such is the dictate of a moral virtue. We have seen so far that political society in itself, and then the particular kinds of political society or regimes, appear to put demands on political officers that can differ from the obligations of unqualified moral virtue.

Turning now to the second of the maxims for officials that seemed so evident, we wonder if there is anything in the nature of things that would intrude on the absolute obligation of a public officer to obey the laws of his country. Here our task is made easy by the horrendous events of recent history: certainly an official of Nazi Germany might and indeed should have thought twice about obeying the laws and lawful commands that came to him. But is it necessary to turn to a perverted and despotic regime to find signs of the problem? It is well known that Abraham Lincoln too had to give thought to the question whether exceeding the laws and even the basic law in the interest of the law's own intention is not incumbent on a statesman in unusual circumstances. Thus it appears that there are at least two kinds of reasons that a public official's actions might deviate from strict legality: pressure from a standard higher than that of the law; and the interest of the law itself, or, more exactly, of the regime to which the law is ministerial.

One cannot refer to the authority of a law higher than the positive law of the state without acknowledging the existence of Hobbes's famous denial that such authority can overrule the force of civil legislation. A discussion of the soundness of Hobbes's position would not be relevant to our present concern. It is sufficient to note that men have always found and no doubt will always find means to withdraw themselves far enough from the claims of their citizenship to gain a view of their regime that is independent of its legal authority over them. Since this withdrawal is, in its highest manifestation, philosophy, we cannot condemn it absolutely without some sympathetic reflection. But since in its lowest manifestation it is fanaticism or sheer criminality, we cannot forbear to scrutinize it with suspicious attention.

The third of the obvious rules for public men was that they segregate strictly their interest and prejudices as individuals from their functioning as public officials so that they do not exploit their public positions for private advantage. There is a sense in which this rule is indeed self-evident and unexceptionable, and ought not to be involved with sophistications. But there is another sense that is not without interest. If a man conducts the business of his political office by performing deeds that are of an unquestionable probity, and of advantage to the public, but he performs them with a view to his own distant interest accurately discerned from afar, has he violated the rule that an official's public deeds should be performed selflessly? The answer is not obvious. It is clear that an official who uses his office to enrich himself, even if he never steals a penny of public money to do so, is reprehensible in a way that an official who toils for the public in order to protect his tenure of office is not. Is nothing more at stake than that greed is more objectionable than ambition? That is, should the rule be revised to read, officials should keep their private interests separate from their performance of public duties so as to be sure never to acquire wealth through their occupation of a public office? This would narrow the issue, and would obscure the important moral consideration: if a moral act is one done out of a moral disposition, or out of virtue, then it is hypocrisy or ignorance to ascribe political morality to acts committed by public officers in accordance with the spirit of the United States Constitution itself; for it is known that the Founders sought—and discovered—means to induce officials to behave properly as officials out of calculation rather than moral excellence. On the other hand, if a moral act is one that outwardly resembles an act having an origin in virtue while in fact it has its source in any good or bad motive whatever, and if the public has no means of discovering nor indeed any interest in discovering a man's motive for acting advantageously to the state, then "morality" in the strictest sense as a criterion for approving an official's action would be put in extreme jeopardy.

Every reader of the *Nicomachean Ethics* will know that the gap between a moral man and a moral act is not of recent discovery. That disjunction acquires a special pertinence in a regime that makes a point of replacing the moral disposition of a particular human being with the publicly advantageous outcome of an act, in the sphere of official administration. For as a result of that replacement, political morality in the sense that identifies it with the virtue of individual officers of state is abolished in favor either of legality or *raison d'état;* the most authoritative norm that can be applied to an official's act is either the law of the land or the act's favorable outcome from the point of view of the state. To press a claim on the part of virtue in the strict sense under those circumstances is to thwart the regime's principle of administration and perhaps its principle of conduct generally. It is important to know that the particular regime not only encourages some and represses other human traits and virtues, but that it also has something to say about the status of moral virtue altogether. The purpose of this remark is to point to the empirical respect in which moral virtue may be said to be dependent on political life, to balance the widely-acknowledged fact that political life is guided by moral considerations.

Some of the preceding arguments must now be brought together. So far as the Constitution deliberately dispenses with the moral virtue of officials as qualifications for office and as criteria for judging their acts, it tends, among other things, to replace morality with legality as the norm by which "political morality" is to be discriminated. But we had earlier reminded ourselves of well-known reasons for hanging back from the position that the law of the land is the absolute criterion of the praiseworthiness of public or, for that matter, private acts. If, or to the extent that, the principles of the constitution produce an impasse between the arguments for and against absolute legality, the surviving effectual, or unencumbered criterion of political morality would be *raison d'état.*

As a subordinate rule under the general maxim that political morality demands of an official that he segregate his private interest from his conduct of public business, I have suggested that it demands also that he refrain from intruding his private prejudices or convictions into the grounds on which he bases his public acts. A legislator must not insinuate his prejudices into his legislative decisions; a judge is expected to keep his anger and his ideology, no less than his greed, out of his judgments. Speaking more affirmatively, a public official's morality in this regard consists in suppressing whatever springs from himself as particular or private and acting solely as the voice or instrument of the public. (It is troubling to remember that a man's moral virtues might be included among the things that pertain to him as a private being.) The will of the public is recorded in the laws. Then it seems clear that political morality (for officials) consists in obedience to the law. But we have seen the restrictions to which that conclusion is subject, and are aware that *raison d'état* offers itself readily as an alternative to legality. Yet how unlikely it is that men will accept *raison d'état*, the general interest or advantage of the political society, as the final touchstone of political morality as the term applies to public officials.

The foregoing, which has dealt with political morality in relation to the acts of official men, leads to the conclusion that moral virtue, legality, and *raison d'état* all enter into political morality but do not exhaust or simply define it. The judgment that draws upon each of those in the proper degree and on the right occasion, which judgment in its most authoritative manifestation is statesmanship, is the true kernel of the political morality of ruling men.

We turn next to the acts of private men who, though private, can direct their acts toward the public as such, or toward the political society, with a view to producing a political consequence. The largest and least striking class of such acts includes such law-abiding deeds as paying taxes, doing jury duty, performing military service when called upon, and doing the other services which ordinary citizens must contribute if political society is to survive. It is clear that the primary criterion of political morality applicable to these acts is simple legality: no more is demanded of citizens than that they obey the laws. They are honored for exceeding the call of duty, but the direction beyond duty is defined by the laws that prescribe the duty itself. The innumerable acts of obedience to the laws can be understood as so many expressions of concurrence in the aims and acceptance of the forms of the particular political society. (For the present purpose it does not matter how much of that concurrence and that acceptance is rational, or voluntary, or the opposite.)

More spectacular are the acts that are not animated by sympathy with the regime and by a desire to obey its laws. These acts proceed from the private judgments of private men as such, or from "conscience." We have already acknowledged sufficiently that political morality cannot be simply equated with legality, and that private judgments and so-called conscience can make a serious claim to be heard. Equally familiar and equally solemn is the argument that it is impossible to receive into political respectability the notion that private conscience may overrule the law, because that dictum is a threat not merely to a particular regime but to political life in principle. To this the upholders of conscience might reply that there is more to valid political life and indeed to proper political morality than what can be received into public respectability. If this were absolutely true, it would indeed cover the serious reformer as well as the traitor and the fanatic with the palladium of political morality; but it would arm simultaneously and equally with the same weapon those public officers for whom the relation of political morality and legality is a grave problem too, as we have seen, equipping them to act conscientiously with utmost energy against those who resist the law in the name of conscience. On the plane of political morality, in abstraction from the goodness and badness of particular regimes, it appears that there is an equilibrium between the weight of official prerogative in controlling the acts of private men and the solidity of private men's claims to act toward the regime out of a disaffected detachment. When opposed grounds of action are equally well supported in reason, what arbiter is there to appeal to except force? Evidently, if there were a way to ascend from the plane of political morality to some truth about the goodness of the regime in question, the issue might still be resolved by force but we would have at least the satisfaction of knowing that in principle the force employed on one side is rightfully or righteously used. To state this point somewhat differently, fully rational political life would be based upon the transcendence of morality by knowledge of the good, i.e., the good regime, as the decisive political influence. But political life is in the service of morality. Something seems to stand in the way of fully rational political life. It is not proper to say these things without mentioning the name of Plato and his *Republic*.

We now pass on to consider the third class of acts, those performed by private men and directed toward other private men but having nevertheless a bearing on the life of the political society. This defines a large class of acts—those performed by all those men whose functions have not been preempted or appropriated by the public itself. The content of that class will vary from regime to regime, and its details, though crucially important for other purposes, do not concern us here. I shall assume the definition that fits the United States at the present time, which means that the class includes the acts of businessmen, many teachers, many writers and journalists, clergymen, some lawyers, a host of artists and musicians, and doubtless many others. These are responsible for supplying, employing, educating, informing, edifying, defending, and bemusing us; and the success with which they perform their functions has a good deal to do with the success of the particular political society of which they are a part. The question to which I wish to draw attention is, What standards are there by which the politically important acts of such men—the acts important to the political society—can be judged? My assumption is that political morality rightly understood encompasses those standards because the acts in question bear materially on the character and quality of life in political society. That assumption is fundamental to the argument of this paper.

If one begins with the acts of businessmen as such, and supposes that the source and criterion of those acts is "virtue," one runs immediately into the contrary, authoritative understanding of Adam Smith: not goodness (or "benevolence") but self-interest controls the actions of market men. This is a fact not of nature alone but of nature fortified by law. In any event, speaking particularly of our own regime, the political morality of market men appears to consist in legality above all else. Can one think of another force that could obstruct the traffic in obscene, defamatory, or insalubrious products? Certainly it is in principle possible to answer yes to this question: earnest confidence in the validity of moral principles, belief in divine behests, unfaltering taste for beauty, and other guiding impulses. But how do these guiding elements of the human beings' constitution enter them, and what causes them to depart? Is this coming and going not to a high degree the doing of private men in their dealing with other private men—of teachers, writers, clergymen, lawyers, artists, all going about their affairs, forming and training us according to their various lights?

Is there no standard of political morality by which the acts of these formers and reformers should be measured? Unfortunately there are at least two—one, legality or the conservation of the regime; and the other, the true, good, and beautiful as they are in themselves. An astounding characteristic of the most liberal regimes is that they legally renounce the authority to impose legality, or the conservation of the regime, on private men as the standard of some of those men's most powerful acts. Then it would appear as if those regimes, looking beyond legality with infinite daring or infinite confidence, depend upon the true, good, and beautiful to assert themselves and to consecrate the regime, unassisted by the law acting on its own behalf. Alternatively, it would appear that the unfettered activity of private men is as such, and apart from the character of its private and public effects, the good for which there is no standard beyond its own self, not even in the true, good, or beautiful.

It is not within our present scope to consider the immense question whether the ultimate basis of the political morality of citizens is legality, the good, or freedom. We have assumed the more limited task of considering that question in relation to our own regime or one like it. Speaking very generally, the United States has remained true to its original dedication to liberty; but whether the exercise of that liberty is officially conceived as somehow under the guidance of a supervising rationality or is itself the only rationality there is, is a national enigma. In the former case, democracy would be expected to winnow out and reject the false and evil and to bring to light and admire truth and good men. In the latter case, liberal democracy would be without any standard of political morality that is not offensive to another equally authoritative standard: because the free regime is the source of freedom, it is good and its preservation is good and legality is therefore a norm of political morality. But so far as freedom is conceived as frustrated by legality, and the strictly private sphere of action is more and more enlarged and fortified against the legal, as for example in the area of "expression," the preservation of the regime itself decays as a norm of political virtue. In a special, emphatic, and somewhat repellent sense, such a regime includes in its principle the seed of its own destruction, for its does not express that minimum ingredient of the goodness of anything, namely, an animus or disposition favorable to its own continued being. I believe it is fair to go so far as to question how far anything that is defective in this respect deserves to be called by the name of the class of things that it resembles. More concretely, how far is a regime truly a regime if its principle of constitution lacks the unambiguous animus to persist in existence?

In the light of these considerations, I suggest that an urgent need of our political society at present is for a clearer perception of the respect in which the political morality of private men in their private actions consists in legality, i.e., law-abidingness plus an acknowledgment of the broad scope of law in private life. This is all the more desirable in view of the degree to which our polity emphasizes legality as the principle of public men's political morality while it depreciates legality as the great rule of private men's political morality. If it is in any way true that a return to consciousness of the extent to which justice means legality is a great and pressing need, then whatever other conclusion we may be entitled to arrive at, we seem justified in hoping that the country will be spared "creative jurisprudence."

Radicalism

Reprinted from *Public Policy*
18, no. 3 (Spring 1970), where
it appeared as "Radicalism
and Its Roots." © 1970 by the
President and Fellows of Harvard College.

The radicalism that is the subject of this paper is a phenomenon of the mid-twentieth-century United States. It has connections with radicalisms of other places and times, and some of those connections will emerge, but to establish them is not my chief purpose. The elucidation of Radicalism —in the locally and temporally narrowed sense—is made difficult by the fact that it is a thing without an acknowledged parent or a maker; it is not the product of any designing mind. It is visible in its parts and in the motions of its parts, but it is obscure in its principle and therefore in its provenance. Our chief task is the discovery of its principle. In pursuing it, we are compelled to begin with what is at hand—the sayings and doings of people who claim to be or who can without partiality be described as being Radicals. We are therefore in the exposed position of trying to extract the definition of Radicalism from the behavior of its partisans, who of course cannot be reliably identified as such while Radicalism itself remains undefined. In this all-too-familiar situation, there is hardly an alternative to beginning by appealing to the most elementary fact which will gain reasonable consent, namely, the literal meaning of "radical."

Radical means pertaining to the root. Radicals—of all times and places—are so called in that they aim to lay the axe to the root of their object. It follows directly that the notion of radicalism (which we now derive from radicals as their characteristic) furnishes a criterion for the judgment of radicalism: The accuracy and the depth of understanding that it displays in conceiving the root of its object are the test of the radicalism itself. If there were a perfect radicalism, it would consist of a perfect understanding of its object and therewith of that object's root; and of an undistractable animus to destroy that object at its root. A "radicalism" possessing only the former would be wisdom; only the latter, fanaticism; some of both, a more or less dangerous nuisance or scourge of the constitution.

There are people who affirm a desire to lay the axe to the root of the prevailing social arrangement. It is sometimes charged against them that they are vague in their minds, betraying a disqualifying cloudiness of thought when they inveigh against "the system" or "the establishment" or other nebulosities impossible to locate. This charge may or may not prove valid in detail; it is not only invalid but broadly misleading, so far as it implies the worthlessness of an objection against a social arrangement as a whole. The social arrangement as a whole means the economic, political, moral, cultural, and social dispositions of the nation, or in brief the regime; and although there are grave questions as to the manner in which the regime should be subjected to scrutiny, there is no question as to the importance of scrutinizing it. Radicalism is a mode of scrutinizing the regime, a willingness and even eagerness to thrust investigating fingers anywhere in order to turn over every stone while testing the foundations.

It is evident that the definition of Radicalism presupposes the critique of Radicalism: Precisely what mode of scrutiny of the regime it is depends upon whether it can or cannot, does or does not understand the regime and upon whether the criteria for judging the regime that it brings to its task are sound criteria. If Radicalism comprehends its object and judges it by sound criteria, then it participates in the genus of knowledge, or rational apprehension. If it misunderstands its object and judges it moreover by confused criteria, but persists nevertheless in desiring to lay the axe to the root of the regime, then it belongs in the genus of attitudes or of mere animus. Only by surveying the content of Radicalism through the sayings and doings of those whose objection is to the regime at large can we discover what class of things Radicalism falls in and in so doing make our judgment of it and its partisans.

The Manifestations of Radicalism

The most conspicuous manifestation of Radicalism is the assertiveness, vehemence, or even violence with which the claims and desires of Radicals are expressed and their projects published and sometimes prosecuted. There is another manifestation of Radicalism, however, that is thought to be contradictory of the first, namely, withdrawal from the world of interests, conflict, and exertion, and retirement to sequestered places, either rural or urban, to serve peace, love, and other desiderata. These modes of Radicalism are doubtless in a state of tension; it is not yet obvious that they are in a state of mutual contradiction. On the face of it, the aggressive Radicalism might be no less than the prerequisite to a human condition as purified of violent projects as is the branch of Radicalism that has already entered upon its musings.

To reconcile the Radicalism of hostility with the Radicalism of love and images as means are reconciled with ends would be, however, to obscure much that is of importance in the meaning of both and of interest in their relation to each other. It is useful rather to begin with their promulgated common hostility to the life of the middle class—anglicization of bourgeoisie—and to the regime vaguely described as dominated by that class. (I say "vaguely" because Radical writers are among those who refer to a power elite consisting of an oligarchy highly placed and widely connected, who are or who dominate the "establishment." If such people belong to the middle class, then the middle includes the upper extreme of society. At the same time, Radical writers denounce the vulgarity and backwardness of middle-class taste and morality, which undoubtedly are characteristic of much of the subbourgeoisie as well. So far as "middle class" is represented as including what is both higher and lower than itself, there is a confusion in the Radical conception of the social problem as located in the middle class.) Hostility to the bourgeoisie was, of course, the animus of the Old or communist Left before the appearance of that New Left which is related lineally if not always obviously to Marxist radicalism.

The animus against the middle expresses itself concretely as objection against the economic institution which converts self-interest into helpfulness through the mediation of desire for gain; against the monogamous matrimonial morality supported in the main by male labor outside the home; and against what may be called the bourgeois esthetic, the level and variety of sensation and fantasy fostered or tolerated in a regime in which restraint is meant to take precedence of "experience."

Beyond these shared objections to the life of the middle class there are others which cannot be understood to be directed against bourgeois society *qua* bourgeois, as is indicated by the fact that they arise also in communist countries: against "bureaucracy," but to some extent against governing authority altogether, as appears explicitly in the anarchist zones of Radicalism. There is a particular resentment against government, entertained by the young as such and taking the form of an insistence upon the capacity, and the right, to self-governing participation in governments otherwise thought to rest properly in the hands of older people or of lawful authorities; but it is obvious that that resentment and this insistence do not belong exclusively to students or to young people as such.

The Radical Beliefs

What of a positive character underlies the negative or critical edifice of Radicalism just sketched? First it is to be noticed that the themes around which the objections group themselves are wealth, sex, the image-life of man or in a wide sense his poetry, and rule. These are also the great preliminary preoccupations of Plato's *Republic,* where they conduce to the investigation of justice and philosophy. Radicalism might be defined allusively as an attitude critical of the prevailing regime's dispositions with respect to wealth, sex, poetry, and rule but prevented from setting out on its projects with a respect for philosophy (or even for reason) and consequently with a capacity for comprehending that nature to which it seems to wish to return.

Economy

More specifically, the Radical objections against the bourgeois economy are largely repetitions of Marx's objections: It is exploitive, eventually unsuccessful, war-making, and dehumanizing or "alienating." Without restating Marx's doctrines, we may note as relevant to the present purpose that those doctrines critical of the capitalist economy fall into two classes: those, pre-eminently belonging to *Capital,* which elaborate the labor theory of value; and those, developed notably in the "early writings," which pursue the theme of alienation. The former argue the injustice of capitalism in the narrow sense that equal is not given for equal in the compensation of labor, although Marx tries, with much success, to avoid presenting the issue as one of justice in favor of presenting it through a relation of quantities that resembles a human physics or social science. The latter argues the injustice of capitalism in the wider sense that men's lives are distorted by it and men themselves made unhappy in the peculiar ways implied by the cant-word "alienation": undergoing the supreme damage of partition or being made separate in some sense or from some things, a riving of man from man, from his product, perhaps even from himself, although this last is hard to understand because there is no clear doctrine of what substantive thing in a man undergoes the partition and what substantive parts remain, mutilated yet viable.

The Radical objections against the bourgeois economy that grow out of the labor theory of value need not be examined in detail here. Whatever their merits and defects, they possess an implausibility that has left wage-earning America indifferent to them. Considering only that Marx's economics and its acolytes announce the pauperization of a working class which does not find itself impoverished, and the reduction to misery and impotence of a middle class whose wealth and power the critics simultaneously denounce, one can perceive reasons for a mistrust of the theoreticians responsible. At any rate, such objections appear to be more prominent in the notions of the aggressive Radicalism, and the objections on grounds of alienation appear more prominent in the notions of the withdrawn Radicalism. It would be wrong to regard the two groups of objections to capitalist economy as mutually contradictory, and the two modes of Radicalism as therefore mutually inconsistent, for the human meaning of the objection derived from the labor theory of value is translatable without distortion into the language of alienation: The hardship imposed by middle-class economy constricts and stultifies the life of the multitudes, so reducing the scope and quality of their animate experience (psychic life) as to part them from everything with which they must be united in order to be human—their fellow men, their products, environing nature, perhaps even themselves, if that thought can be made intelligible. In brief, they are deprived of the power to exercise the basic human right freely to have Experiences. But to have Experiences is to live. The right in question is therefore the right to life, but not to mere life; rather to felt, quickened, or actual and hence enjoyed life: life amply understood as inclusive of happiness. It is at the same time the right to liberty amply understood: the freeing of the consciousness in full or at least growing sensitivity to itself, reaching at last and at best the height of self-consciousness that is the consummation of freedom.

The retiring Radicalism recoils from whatever in capitalism lies behind the use of money, that incarnation of the rule of *quid pro quo.* Money is the instrument of exchange as opposed to gift, and of purchased, hence constrained, labor as opposed to freely-proffered, helpful work. The constraint reaches also to the narrowing of the work-activity according to familiar criticisms of the division of labor. Thus the human impulse freely to produce whole and varied things, for which impulse the cant-word is creativity, is subverted. The constraint implicit in the use of money thus defeats simultaneously freedom, love, and creativity; the bourgeois economy is the locus of the denial to men of the highest good and the highest experiences open to them.

The place of these objections against the capitalist economy in the larger construction of Radicalism is not yet clear, and will not be clear until more of the Radical complaint has come to light. One fact emerges, however: Radicalism is a passion to uproot the present society because that society is believed to reduce the general level of vitality and of sentiment—if those two differ—and in particular to interfere with the sentiment of love. The aggressive and the retiring branches of Radicalism do not clash on the plane of that passion to uproot. As will appear, the stresses arise along another plane, that of the so-called Self in conflict with itself.

Morality

Radicalism is critical of middle-class morality, in the narrow sense of sexual propriety and in the wider and more precise sense of the norms of conduct at large. Let us confine ourselves to one example of the issue in the narrow sense and one in the wider sense, because those will suffice to disclose the crucial point.

There is, in the first place, a Radical dissatisfaction with the legal and tacit stricture against all sexual union except that between husband and wife. That stricture is sometimes called middle-class and sometimes Puritanical, implying a class or a Christian basis. (We neglect for the present the view that identifies the class basis with the Christian basis.) Whether it has either basis, or some other, such as psychoanalysis, for example, might suggest, the Radical notion of it is that sexual union is the concern only of the adults whose voluntary act it is; and since adulthood tends to be defined in terms of the maturing of the body (consider the common saying, "Old enough to fight, old enough to vote"), the emerging thought seems to be that the capacity for sexual union is itself the sign of rightful freedom to decide to unite sexually.

Supporting this thought is the notion that love is good (Radicals, often young, do not linger over the transition from sexual union to love), pleasure is good, and human interference with either is not good. Without human interference, human beings would presumably never have become an enclave in the kingdom of nature, denying themselves what all other animals, lacking even the means of conceiving a question as to the rightness of their behavior, enjoy as a matter of course. The interference with love and pleasure is artificial. It corrupts in one way those who acknowledge and submit to it, and in another way those who acknowledge but circumvent it: The penalty for frustrating or attempting to frustrate nature with artificialities is either frigid desiccation or dishonesty.

As to sexual union, Radicalism can be said to criticize the prevailing morality on the ground that it controverts nature. In this regard, however, the prevailing morality only bears the character of morality as such, which cannot fail to demand conduct different from that dictated by the mere impulses of nature. So far as the Radical desire is for a regime possessing a moral order purged of human interference with the freedom of natural impulse, even in the name of sincerity and warmth, Radicalism is a rejection not of middle-class or any other particular morality but of morality simply. This does not imply the impossibility of a Radical code of behavior; it implies that such a code would be profoundly impulsive or "free," in the sense equivalent to immoral.

There is, however, the further Radical dissatisfaction with prevailing morality as being grossly partial to the male over the female. A sign of this bias is the division of labor that assigns domestic tasks to the female and extramural employment to the male. It is hard to say whether the fact that the housewife's labor is unsalaried, whereas extramural employment brings a money reward, contributes anything to the judgment that domestic activity is inferior to a career; but that judgment is certainly in the immediate background of Radical feminism, which maintains that the assignment of some activities to men and some to women is not rooted in any essential difference between men and women, but is merely a human, historical, or "cultural" phenomenon that unjustly works to exclude women from the superior activities.

The kernel of this Radical position ought perhaps to be stated as follows: Traditional morality is unduly impressed by the difference between male and female, of which the most conspicuous and the least controversial, but not necessarily the most relevant signs, are merely somatic. History, convention, and culture have given undue recognition to the natural-somatic, thus becoming preoccupied with the differences between male and female, while declining to recognize sufficiently the natural-psychic, the realm in which the similarities between male and female predominate. The Unisex pattern offers itself as a counterpoise against this distortion, weakened in its effect, however, by the tendency toward beardedness, which moves in a direction in which few women are prepared to follow.

The two points of the Radical objection against received morality have the following character. The first, in the interest of sexual emancipation, makes the case for sincere recognition of mankind's subjection to the natural impulse toward union of the bodies—joyful capitulation to nature as somatic, and candid veneration of sexual union, normally the human act that more expressly presupposes and draws attention to the difference between male and female than any other. The second point of Radical objection against received morality, in the interest of equal opportunity, requires the repression of emphasis upon the somatic nature in males and females and therewith an aversion of the attention from the respects in which they differ. The basis of the relation between male and female is conceived in one way when pleasure is at stake and in the contrary way when equality as to the way of life is at stake.

It is clear that Radicalism is unwilling to accept behaviorism of the cultural-relativist school, which would mollify Radicals with the observation that some cultures practice sex discrimination and some do not, but every cultural practice must be judged by the norms of its own tradition and development and not by norms imposed by a skeptic's mind upon the native practices. It is also clear that Radicalism (except Marxist Radicalism) is not prepared to call upon a law of Historical Rationality, nor upon a doctrine of natural teleology, in elaborating the norms with which it would like to replace the liberal but unprogressive ones of mere cultural status quo. There is a question whether Radicalism has any independent resources to draw on in its need.

"Music"

The art—literature, music, drama, and the other arts—of Radicalism discusses explicitly the themes of war, poverty, sex, and so on, and to that extent simply speaks for itself. But Radical art has also a tacit character, a view of which proves helpful in understanding Radicalism itself. Beginning again with what everyone knows, absurdity is said to play a crucial part in the most influential and original artistic assertions concerning life and being, assertions with a Radical intent.

If Radicalism means a deep objection to the *prevailing* conditions of life, then Radical-absurd art must teach that life dominated by the bourgeoisie is indeed absurd but not that life as such is absurd. For if Radical art expressed the belief that life is a scene in a madhouse under all social conditions, Radicalism would stand self-convicted not merely of absurdity but of viciousness in agitating for profound and painful social change. Perhaps aggressive Radicalism inclines to the view, compatible vaguely with Marxism, that only bourgeois life is absurd, whereas the withdrawn Radicalism inclines to believe, on the contrary, that existence itself is absurd—a notion deeply inconsistent with the former, but vaguely compatible with vulgarized existentialism. As to Radical art, however, its premise and its message to the effect that life in general is without intelligible foundations in nature or reason are of interest to us and merit consideration. This notion appears in at least two artistic manifestations. First is the art that consists of the arbitrary re-ordering of the parts of a natural entity such as a human form or face, to produce a novel image as real as the natural one but more authentic because expressive of artistic vibrancy and choice. Second is the kaleidoscopic art, of which there is also a musical variety, which attempts to make visible and audible the play within the mind of the fleeting subintelligibles, the experiences which are in the realm of consciousness without being in the realm of intelligence or showing a connection with the realm of intelligence. In this they differ from the material of the unconscious as investigated by Freud, whose thought was precisely that knowledge of that material is indispensable to adequate knowledge of the "rational" activity of man. Paradoxically, the "kaleidoscopic" experiences referred to are more remote from the intelligible than is the unconscious, while they yet belong to the conscious as images belong to it. The relation of the art expressive of those experiences to the self-inducing of hallucinatory sensations is evident: Hallucination is the psychic state of which kaleidoscopic Radical art is the imperfect representation. The psychic state in question is perhaps that in which the subject is as far from contact with every object as he can be except in dreamless sleep which, if it exists, is psychic death and not an act of the mind. The state in question is the state of those who have for the time being isolated the mind from its government as well as from its objects. Psychoanalysis has investigated the unconscious in its healthy or troubled articulation with the government of the man. The Radical esthetic (or music in the oldest sense) has a very different interest or root: precisely the discovery and enjoyment to the fullest extent possible of that level of experience on which the mind is disjoined from the government of objects and of the mind itself. Marxism, it is to be noted, does not imagine or desire emancipation of the spirit from objective reality. Psychoanalysis does not suppose or seek the emancipation of the mind and therewith of the man from the government of the mind, withal unconscious. The departure of Radicalism in a new direction of deep anarchy suggests that the quarrel of Radicalism is not with middle-class society but with every manifestation of rule by which human life is directed: rule by the nature of objects and rule by the government of the mind or some part of the mind.

Rule

We come thus to the last of the four themes of Radical criticism, the theme of authority or rule. Presumably, men have always shown resistance to being ruled; and also have always been moved to give themselves supinely to their leaders. These natural tendencies, which might be called psychological, precisely so far as they belong to all men do not belong to Radicals as Radicals but do belong to them as they are men. The point is worth considering because the exchanges between Radicals and their critics on the psychologizing of substantive issues makes it pertinent in the context as well as in itself. The following remarks should be viewed as a parenthesis to prepare for considering whether the Radical reactions against authority are reactions against authority as such or against authority as wielded by prevailing governments.

It is probably fair to say that the immediate initiative in psychologizing the substantive issues lay with Radicals who, preponderantly young, affected to dismiss as unreachable everyone over the age of thirty, thus injecting into the discussion the notion of a generation gap. This psychological approach was not the invention of the Radicals, who had before them, among other examples, the example of the Old Left, which routinely described the security activities of the United States (though not always of its opponents) as originating in hysteria and paranoia, vulgarly understood. This was in doctrinal contradiction to the Old Left's stated belief in the class explanation of bourgeois militarism, but we cannot now take up the complicated interpenetration of socialism and psychoanalysis in the formation of Left opinion. In any case, observers of Radicalism began to take note of the extraordinary behaviors of its partisans, who explained themselves as being in a state of rebellion. The behaviors and the accompanying explanation gave rise to accounts of Radicalism that were based on Radicalism's own report of itself as young and rebellious, i.e., accounts in terms of the rebelliousness of the young. It is true that Radicals also tried to explain why they were in a state of rebellion, but they immediately suffered the effects of the prevailing disposition, shared by themselves, to explain men's doings by reference to causes which the agents do not recognize as causes—class affiliation, culturation, libido, history, and so on. In addition, the behavior of Radicals was guided occasionally by theories of the absurdity or irrationality of the human condition altogether, a conception which, reinforced by the stresses of feeling simultaneously a diffuse hatred ("anger") toward the environment and a need to love all mankind universally, while also undergoing the shocks of drug use, led to conduct capable of being supposed clinical. Observers of Radicals then began giving it as their opinion that some Radicals or perhaps typical Radicals showed symptoms of known disorders such as paranoia, technically understood. At this point, Radicals retorted upon their observers that the issues should be considered on their merits and without reference to the (psychological) characteristics of the people involved, a reasonable demand that will, if accepted generally, help dispel misconceptions as to the generation gap. In any case, it is unclear whether the Radical retort is intended as a demurrer, granting the allegations of dementia for the sake of the argument and then seeking to show that the implied defectiveness of Radicalism would have no intelligible connection with the supposed infirmity of Radicals; or whether it is a denial of the disorder as alleged. Strictly, if the Radical position were to be of general interest rather than serving merely to clear individuals of an imputation, it should have the character of a demurrer. As Tocqueville has intimated in his *Recollections,* there is nothing to prevent even clinically frantic men from having prominent places in important revolutionary movements. It is worth observing, though, that there is a difference between a revolution that can tolerate or that perhaps even requires occasional madness in its directorate and one that, according to the implication of the critics' diagnoses of Radicals, rests on a basis of abnormality. Without claiming to judge the facts of the dispute between Radicals and their psychological critics, one can say that the Radicals are right in asking that the issues be examined on their merits, i.e., as if there is reason and rational discourse which together are decisively important (in a world otherwise described by Radicals as decisively irrational). At the same time, it should be admitted that there is a proper if subordinate place for psychological observations on political phenomena. If a political doctrine is erroneous and cannot claim assent through reason, but it nevertheless has adherents, one might explain that fact on subrational grounds: passion, prejudgment, or some cause of which the agent himself is unconscious. Or if a doctrine is sound but its adherents adhere to it for reasons other than its soundness, psychological explanations might serve. In the former case, it would be not only scientifically correct but perhaps also politically desirable to show by psychological reasonings that the mass of support sustaining the view in question is no sign of its merit: People who support the position for irrelevant reasons might be induced to abandon it for other irrelevant reasons. In general: Explanations in terms of subrational causes are appropriate when the thing to be explained is itself subrational, always leaving room in the subrational for ordinary error and mere ignorance. The first duty of the psychologizer is to show the irrationality of the thing to be explained. So far as this is what Radicalism requires of its critics, Radicalism is clearly in the right.

We return now to the Radical objections against the exercise of authority, intending to consider those objections without unnecessary speculation as to Radical youth's subconscious reasons for rejecting all authority. We will not try to ascend higher than the prevalent view that government has an obligation to freedom, a formal and even vague proposition that has sustained the practice not only of liberal democracy but of communist dictatorship in our time. The democratic and the communist regimes have arisen in obedience to the dictate of freedom, variously understood; and now both regimes are under criticism, each in a way appropriate to its character, in the name of freedom. Some of those criticisms are being delivered by Radicalism, and they constitute the Radical attack on concrete authorities rather than against authority in the abstract. We turn to those criticisms now.

Modernity has converted the thought that self-government is good into the political judgment that democracy is good. But it has been held against the great liberal democracies that, within them, not all men are enabled to practice self-government fully or even equally: Some people do not have that access to the political process which is the supposed condition for self-rule because of inequalities that have entered or been preserved in the regime. The most conspicuous inequality of that kind proceeds from the existence of classes, notably the middle class, and consists of the exclusion of whole segments of the citizen body who have taken their places in the disparaged classes. In addition, almost all men in the democracies lack free contact with the political system because their contact with the ruling power is mediated by bureaucracies. This means that individuals, often petty-minded, have a decisive effect on the rules they administer by the manner in which they administer them: Individuals as such, because they are also functionaries of the government, exercise rule over others, official democracy notwithstanding. In addition, the bureaucracy is the very locus of dehumanization and unreason ("absurdity") in mass government; it is a thing huge and shapeless, slothful yet impulsive, cunning, unwise, and heartless. (A question arises again whether it is not unacceptably absurd to proclaim absurdity as a world principle and also to be repelled by its manifestations.) As can be seen, the class defect and the bureaucratic defect of democracy collapse into a single defect: A significant portion of rule is taken away from the public as the whole political body and is appropriated by groups or individuals acting in pursuit of special—i.e., particular—interests. Not only is freedom curtailed, through interference with self-government, but the distribution of good and bad things is distorted to the advantage of those who can participate effectively in political life.

It is noteworthy that the counterpart of western Radicalism in the European communist nations objects against the regimes there prevailing that "new classes" have grown up in the ostensibly classless societies, and that a bureaucracy with all the shortcomings enumerated is interfering with the people's happiness, or freedom.

To summarize: There is a right of self-government based upon the goodness of freedom and of reason (with an indeterminate reservation in the interest of "absurdity"). The exercise of that right is not protected by democracy as now practiced. Self-rule requires the radicalization of democracy by direct action ("participation") of all, and emphatically of those in whom the operation of the prevailing system has engendered the most acute ignorance, hatred, and detachment from political life ("alienation"). In this way the injustices of class distinction and the dehumanizations of bureaucratic officiousness will be removed, as the effects of administration are minimized: "All power in the hands of the people." All must share actively in governing.

But there is another line of Radical objection against the prevailing system, or perhaps of recommendation for improving it: In the world as the scene of moral and thus political action, there is no firmer ground than the goodness of commitment or engagement. (We cannot take up the question whether it is possible to reconcile the opinion that commitment is the good with the opinion that freedom is the good, or either of these with the opinion that love is the good; but the question is genuine.) In an "absurd" world, it is imperative that every individual make his commitment to "values" and to courses of action in order to complete his moral life (although it is unclear why, in an absurd world, completing one's moral life is better than leaving it uncompleted) and thus to perform the essential act of self-government. It is true that obstinacy is thus capable of being transformed into virtue, but only if affiliated with arbitrariness. There has perhaps never been so forthright a teaching to the effect that a notion or an aspiration is good for the sole reason that it is one's very own, nor therefore a teaching so polemic in its nature as distinguished from its self-understanding. But in any case, it is clear that every man has a duty of self-government, a duty so powerfully animated by idiosyncrasy that the translation of this duty into a basis for social life demands the most improbable suppositions, as for example that men will be so reconstituted that their self-assertions will be mutually harmonious; and that the harmony of idiosyncrasies will not itself destroy the moral worth of self-assertion, which requires an antithesis lest it evaporate into conformism.

The duty of self-government thus can scarcely be conceived as conducing to that participation in civil government which is seen as the result of giving effect to the right of self-government. Performance of the duty of self-government, as described, implies renunciation of the right of self-government, as described. Performance of the duty in question presupposes the elaboration of administration through the defection of the citizens from participation in government, a participation inconceivable on the part of multitudes of men whose individual virtue consists of aggressive singularity. The right of self-rule implies the replacement of bureaucracy by direct self-government; but the duty of self-rule, equally based on Radical premises, implies the replacement of government by administration or bureaucracy, the consummation desired by the old radicalism under the name of the withering away of the state. Perhaps we have returned to the disjunction between aggressive Radicalism preoccupied with the right, and withdrawn Radicalism preoccupied with the conflicting duty, of self-rule.

Conclusion

It should now be clear that there is no truth in the common assertion that Radicalism does not propose anything positive. There is a single theme that dominates the Radical criticisms of the prevailing institutions of wealth, sex, poetry, and rule, a theme with a positive intention, and that theme is the keen experience of life. Capitalism, monogamy, the received arts, and democracy itself are rejected in turn as being repressive of the full and free experience of life; but life, liberty, and the pursuit of happiness are precisely what the prevailing regime was called into being to enhance. An important fact emerges: Radicalism is not so much the antithesis of the prevailing regime as the intensification or radicalization of that regime. Radicalism, presenting itself as the negation of the middle-class order, misunderstands both itself and the middle-class order, as the offspring misunderstands both itself and its parents when it regards them as strangers rather than as progenitors; and when, in ignorant dialectic, it goes on to live by slaying its ancestry in one mode and uniting with it in another, the doom of all, presaged in the original ignorance, supervenes, as the tale of Oedipus displays. The prevailing order, with foundations laid down by such men as Machiavelli, Hobbes, Descartes, and Locke, prescribes the regime that is dedicated to life vouchsafed on earth in abundance, peace, and liberty. As has appeared, Radicalism expresses a dissatisfaction with the stultification of the multitude produced by the manner in which the abundance is procured, the peace maintained, and the liberty (which is merely political) either routinized or unjustly contracted. What it proposes is the reanimation of human life, the galvanization of mankind to a pitch of vitality not hitherto known, but to hedonic ends differing from those familiar to bourgeois morality only in degree and impudicity. More concretely, it proposes the full animation of man as individual and also as species: the emancipation of men to exploit for their individual satisfaction the difference between the body of male and of female, and also the subsumption of the difference between male and female under the category of humanity—recalling for the moment only one illustration meant to be representative from among the themes presented above. The one animation is a man's assertive glorying in his own life triumphant, the other is his withdrawn glorying in surrender to the overwhelming flood of the mass of humanity. As a backward look reveals, there are indeed two sources of morality, or two directions in which spiritual fulfillment may be sought—the triumphant assertion of the man's ascendancy in and over a world which he accepts; and the willing surrender of the man to the world and its denizens, a losing himself in it and a submergence of himself among them, calling his defeat a victory because the beating was partly of his own administration. That there is an ethic of pride and an ethic of humility is not a recent discovery; and that the contradiction between them may be conceived as overcome by the thought that defeat in this world prepares for individual glory in another is very familiar. But that there can be a political regime which enables a multitude to glory in the assertion of each self to its utmost of animation, and which will also achieve the abnegation of each in the all, is a thing to be believed only on a showing of reasons and of wisdom by careful men.

Radicalism is unable to make such a showing. It begins as an expression of modern man's distress over the impoverishment of life brought on by the great reformation of science and politics that defines the modern time. In its casting about for relief, it demonstrates its fidelity to its ancestry by repeating in its own premises these discordant principles of classical modernity: Man and his ego are central to the world; yet the assertive pride of men is their own natural enemy. Adhering to its inherited notions, Radicalism examines the doctrines of which it can permit itself to take cognizance. What emerges is no one mind's product but a melange of Marxism, psychology affected by psychoanalysis, and existentialism adapted to the general understanding. In addition, Radicals look, as men for thousands of years have looked, to the East, hoping to retrace the steps that brought mankind into the world and out of repose. But the East is in turmoil, the scene of the demolition by occidental communism and technology of that tranquil edifice deafeningly celebrated by the Radical muse. Radicals have no difficulty in joining their respect for Marxism-Leninism, in the modes of Ho and Mao, with their appreciation for Buddha to form a saprophytic anomaly compelled to thrive on the corpses of Marxian historicism and oriental quietism. Burdened by inconsistency and shallowness, the daring of Radical projections takes on the color of irresponsibility rather than of genius.

We are a few steps closer to being able to say what Radicalism is and to form some judgment of it. Radicalism is an unreasoned but not un-founded revulsion produced in modern men by modern life, and an unfounded revulsion produced in modern men by human life as men must live it. Characteristically, Radicalism proposes to cure modernity by intensifying it, and to banish the ills of life by a universal vivification based upon a sense of death and void. It finds man in fragments and proposes to make him whole by calling him a Self—a thousand planets conjured to become a cosmos through spontaneous creativity: "choice." It appears incapable of distinguishing its one revulsion from the other, since it is incapable of distinguishing the transitory from the enduring: Requiring a knowledge of nature as a ground on which to stand and build, it does not possess and it prevents itself from acquiring that ground by alienating itself from philosophy, that skepsis that looks beyond the horizon of modernity. It has more in common with ignorance than with vice, with folly than with malice, although hatred, meanness, self-righteousness, and perversity are its outriders as it converses with compassion in the headlong carriage. It is probably a fit; but an episode in a protracted ague.

```
PPPPPPPPPPPPPPPPPPPPPPPPPPPPPPPPPPPPPPP
PPPPPPPPPPPPPPPPPPPPPPPPPPPPPPPPPPPPPPP
PPPPPPPPPPPPPPPPPPPPPPPPPPPPPPPPPPPPPPP
PPPPPPPPPPPPPPPPPPPPPPPPPPPPPPPPPPPPPPP
PPPPPPPPPPPPPPPPPPPPPPPPPPPPPPPPPPPPPPP
PPPPPPPPPPPPPPPPPPPPPPPPPPPPPPPPPPPPPPP
PPPPPPPPPPPPPPPPPPPPPPPPPPPPPPPPPPPPPPP
PPPPPPPPPPPPPPPPPPPPPPPPPPPPPPPPPPPPPPP
PPPPPPPPPPPPPPPPPPPPPPPPPPPPPPPPPPPPPPP
PPPPPPPPPPPPPPPPPPPPPPPPPPPPPPPPPPPPPPP
PPPPPPPPPPPPPPPPPPPPPPPPPPPPPPPPPPPPPPP
PPPPPPPPPPPPPPPPPPPPPPPPPPPPPPPPPPPPPPP
PPPPPPPPPPPPPPPPPPPPPPPP PPPPPPPPPPPPPPP
PPPPPPPPPPPPPPPPPPPPPPPP PPPPPPPPPPPPPPP
PPPPPPPPPPPPPPPPPPPPPPPP PP PPPPPPPPPPPPP
PPPPPPP PP PPPPPPPP PP PPPPPPP PPPPP
PPPPPPP PP PPPPPP PP PP PPP PPP PPPPP
PPP PPP PP PPPPPP PP PP PPP PPP PP PP
PPP PPP PP PP PPP PP PP PPP PPP PP PP
PPP P P PP PP PPP PP PP PPP P P PP P
PPP P P PP PP P P PP PP PPP P P PP P
P P P P P PP P P PP PP P P P P P P
 P P P P P P P P PP P P P P        P
  P P    P  P  P    P   P P P     P    P
   P       P  P       P    P  P        P
   P                       P  P        P
                           P
                           P
                           P
```

Part Three

Modernization: United States Policy and the Meaning of Modernity

Reprinted from *American Foreign Policy and Revolutionary Change,* edited by Jack B. Gabbert (Pullman: Washington State University Press, 1968), where it appeared as "United States Policy and the Meaning of Modernity."

I

It is a commonplace of our day that this is a time of revolution. Domestic movements as well as various currents and agitations abroad are freely described as revolutionary. The two articulated branches of United States policy, domestic and foreign, are accordingly conceived to be directed toward essentially revolutionary conditions. Since it is indispensable to the soundness of any policy that its end be clearly understood, we might pause at the outset to consider the character of revolution, and then of the revolutions, that apparently define the ends of United States policy and produce the environment in which that policy is executed.

Revolution means primarily a turning in the sense of a re-turning, a coming back to a position occupied previously or a closed motion performed in relation to something that is itself relatively motionless. Revolution thus has the primary meaning of motion within a horizon of rest. Whether the primary meaning of revolution should or to any extent does survive in the derived political meaning is at this point not an appropriate question. It does seem to be true that the meaning of revolution has itself undergone a radical change in passing from its primary to its derivative, political sense. Thus our contemporaries generally conceive revolution as a radical or essential over-turning rather than a re-turning, a movement producing the largest possible departure from what went before; although there is nothing to prevent revolutionists from claiming to restore an older order that has suffered corruption or decay through some defect of a ruling element. During the period in which the Marxist doctrine of revolution has been the most conspicuous and perhaps the most influential one, revolution has been widely taken to mean the production of an absolutely new situation rather than a returning to abandoned principles. How far this understanding itself conflicts with the Marxist notion of history as a spiral progress—a motion with respect to an unmoving axis if not to an unmoving point—is outside our present concern.

"Revolution" is also used in another sense—more figurative, less political, but equally suggestive of radical change. We speak of the Industrial Revolution in what is perhaps the most famous example of the use of the word to mean a great innovation that has its origin in some theoretical or technological development not deliberately aimed at over-turning a political arrangement. Although a revolution in this sense does not aim at destroying a regime, it can certainly produce a far-reaching or decisive overturning, such as, for example, the mere political effect of industrialization of some of the newly formed African countries.

Without going any further into the meaning of revolution in general, but concentrating on the implication it is thought to have for the overturning of what is established, we recognize a fundamental question as to United States policy in a world situation described as revolutionary. Should our policy be friendly to any or all of the alleged revolutions, or should it oppose all or some of them? And, since the question as to opposing revolution implies but only implies the possibility of opposing revolution, the question whether revolution can be resisted effectually must be raised and faced explicitly.

The United States has a leading position in the established world order, an order that stands to be overturned by revolutionary action against it. It is obvious that the United States should to that extent have a counter-revolutionary policy. But there is an opinion that identifies "counter-revolutionary" with "blindly unprogressive," on the premise that revolution is progressive and counter-revolution is therefore unprogressive. It is of course fallacious to argue from the premise that revolution is progressive to the conclusion that counter-revolution is unprogressive, unless one means to claim both that all revolution is progressive and nothing but revolution is progressive. Otherwise, the most that can be concluded is that counter-revolution obstructs the peculiar variety of progress, if any, connected with a particular revolution. If that progress should be simply another name for the obliteration of our regime, we have not only a right but even a kind of duty to react against such a revolution as vigorously as need be.

Whether revolutions, all or some, are progressive cannot be known except if the meaning of progress be known. Whatever progress, or change for the better, may prove to mean, we may be certain that there is one thing it cannot mean: progress cannot be defined as the transition to the most recently produced state of things, without violence to logic and to morality. Logic is offended when, to the question "What testifies to the progressiveness of the revolution?" the answer returned is "The fact that the revolution produced (or will produce) the newest state of affairs," which is to say that a revolution is a revolution. Morality is offended when, to the question "What is the criterion of a progress or improvement in the condition of men?" the answer returned is "A change is to be regarded as an improvement if the new condition effectually abolishes the old." This criterion for understanding morality is fatally exposed to two diametrically opposed objections. Either it proceeds from the unacceptable pragmatism that identifies the good with whatever can force itself onto the human scene; or it proceeds from the unfounded optimism that sees the world as a place in which nothing can survive if it is not good.

These matters deserve consideration because the revolutionary bias in favor of revolution must be disposed of before a basis for United States policy can be established in a world situation described as revolutionary. For this purpose it is not enough to show that revolution might not be progressive in the sense of "bringing improvement." Revolution may be progressive in the sense of being that stormy wave on which the future rides and by which the present, or what is called the status quo, is washed away. So considered, revolution is the instrument of History. Leaving aside all questions as to any upward trend of History, statesmen might well pause before embarking on courses that ignore the Historical wave of the future. Once having paused, however, they face a question that could prove paralyzing: how can a revolution be distinguished from a mere political project, or an experiment on a scale however vast—in brief, a phenomenon that might be large but not necessarily connected with anything foreordained or irresistible? The answer to this question is that for practical purposes, that is to say, for the purposes of policy formation, statesmen do not know because they cannot know when they are in the presence of History. They can, sometimes with great difficulty, determine that they are in the presence of some force that they cannot resist or some object that they do not have the power to remove; but in all important cases, statesmen are compelled to resist a force to the maximum of their power before they can determine that it is irresistible, and they have no alternative to using every ounce of their strength against an object before allowing themselves to be convinced that it is immovable. In the great confrontations, too much is at stake for any responsible statesman to accept speculative answers to what are in principle empirical questions, namely, is a given force irresistible and is a given object immovable. The only way to find out is to try. The cost of trying might well be excessive, in which case it ought to be understood that the information that became available was not that the force was irresistible or the object immovable but that no one was willing to bear the burden of determining whether they were so, which is a very different kind of truth.

If it is so exceedingly difficult to judge of the possible and impossible concerning ponderables like power and its objects, how much more difficult must it be to recognize the metaphysical entity History itself, together with its offspring, the Inevitable and the Impossible. The problem that faces statesmen in a revolutionary world is, however, sometimes thought to be precisely to discover the Historical meaning of current revolutionary events in order to be ruled by that meaning and to avoid at all cost coming into conflict with History. Thus, to live by this rule, as was said, a statesman would have to be able to recognize the Inevitable and the Impossible. What can this mean?

The Inevitable is what is absolutely necessary. Necessary, as applied to some event in the future, describes a thing that clearly exists as a potentiality in the present or that is latent in the present. One would not speak of it as inevitable if it existed actually at present, so it is clear that the Historically Invevitable is that which has perhaps never existed actually but which absolutely must exist in the future.

The Impossible on the other hand is what by virtue of its definition cannot be because its being (if that can be conceived) would contradict the definition of reality or would conflict with the meaning of being itself. What things are impossible? According to a widely held view about History, one cannot turn the clock back. This means that it is impossible to bring back to life a dead state of affairs or a dead epoch. The existence in the future of something that had an existence in the past is thus an example of an Impossible.

If we put together the Historically Inevitable and the Historically Impossible, we discover that some things which never actually were must be; while some things which actually were cannot be. We are puzzled, because the fact that something once existed—say feudalism—is a decisive proof that nothing in its definition contradicted the very definition of being. The fact that feudalism vanished is a decisive proof that something in its definition conflicted with continuous eternal being; but we would know that much about many things without recourse to a doctrine of the Historically Impossible. How can something that has demonstrated its capacity to be by actually being now prove to be absolutely incapable of being? It would seem that the being with which feudalism did not collide has been replaced by a new being with which feudalism must collide and by which feudalism must be prevented from having an actual—or even a potential—existence. But if the meaning of being or the ground of being itself changes from time to time, what meaning can there be in the view that something has a real being in potentiality at one time and preserves that being into its maturation as actual a long time later? Without painful contortions of tautology ("a historical epoch is the period during which the meaning or the ground of being stands still, as we know from the actualization of the potential within that period of time"), it is impossible to maintain at the same time the transience of being and the doctrine of the Historically Inevitable.

This doctrine of the mutability of being or something of the kind is the premise of the view of History which in turn sustains the conceptions of revolution and progress by which statesmen are sometimes expected to guide themselves. But progressive revolution means a transition from one historical state to another under conditions that enable one to say of the later that it represents progress over the earlier. Such a comparison would be impossible if there were not some permanent ground underlying the two states, something unchanging that furnishes the measure of historical change. What does not change is precisely that core of being, that framework of existence that we call nature, which is at the same time denied by the Historically Impossible, required by the Historically Inevitable, and presupposed by the notion of Historically progressive revolution. Perhaps it is true that the notion of revolution must include an ingredient of re-turning to what is fixed and unchangeable.

As we examine the prevailing concept of revolution and its supporting and surrounding doctrines, we are impressed by how little help they give to statesmen whose duty is to deliberate on the forming of policy rather than to prognosticate their country's ineluctable fate. It is quite true that statesmen ought not to lead their countries into attempting the impossible, but it is equally true that they will never be able to recognize the impossible by aplying the touchstone of History or of Revolution. Indeed, if History and Revolution teach submission to a fate, they not only fail to enlighten policy but render it meaningless because futile.

It is sometimes said that we cannot escape History, meaning that we cannot escape our past or our future. According to this view, the past is alive beyond our power to kill it and dead beyond our power to resurrect it. I have tried to show that if United States policy is conceived as confronted by world revolution, revolution cannot in turn be conceived as the instrument of History without bringing on the paralysis of that policy and without committing theoretical mistakes. I shall also try to show that the view of revolution that is to be avoided on the foregoing grounds is moreover in a state of tension with the founding principles of the United States regime. I hope, therefore, partly to have shown and partly yet to show that American policy in a revolutionary world must proceed from a skepticism as to whether the world is in a state of revolution.

II

An antirevolutionary policy on the part of the United States might be neither impossible nor reactionary. What is to be considered is whether it would be right and sound. We turn to this question by reflecting on the meaning of the various modernizing revolutions that United States policy is being called upon to grip. These appear to be three in number.

The earliest of them is the revolution of Marxian Communism, which qualifies as a modernizing revolution because, although at least a century old, it presents itself as the avenue to advanced modernity, the means for correcting the proto-modernity that came forth in the sixteenth and seventeenth centuries. That proto-modernity replaced vestigial medieval feudalism by establishing the urban middle class with its characteristic proclivities and functions and putting it in a dominant position. The Marxian modernizing revolution appears as a war against the middle class, and presents itself as showing the way to a modernity from which the middle class has been eliminated. We shall have to consider why this is thought to be necessary or desirable with a view to the advancement of modernity.

The second modernizing revolution which the United States must confront is domestic to this country, although not without counterparts elsewhere. It consists of a confused and confusing composite of theoretical and practical movements, some having an academic, some having a literary, and some having a scientific origin, some related to peculiarly American conditions and some not, but all tending toward an as yet vaguely discerned innovation of manners, morals, and quality of life. Again, the bourgeois world as such is the visible target. We shall look briefly at this domestic revolution later.

The third revolution to be noticed by policy is the revolution that aims at the modernization of the so-called Third World. This revolution is not one but at least two movements, one technical and the other political. How the United States should view it depends upon whether the technical movement is or can be independent of the political, and whether the political movement is on the whole capable of being judged beneficial. These questions will now be taken up in order.

It might appear strange that the middle class should be the human target of a potent revolution (namely, the Marxian) for the ascendancy of the middle class was traditionally seen as the means of avoiding the dominance of either the aristocratic or the penurious, and thus of avoiding the inevitable conflict between the extremes. But with the disappearance of the aristocracy, the middle class became exposed to two superficially opposed criticisms: one, that it had inherited the uppermost place in the social order, climbing from its mediocre station to the odious eminence vacated by the aristocracy; and the other criticism, that it suffers by comparison with the class it replaced in ways that are painfully illuminated by the ambiguity of the very word "mediocre." According to the first criticism, the middle class has acquired the appetite for oppression or exploitation that finds readiest expression among the most powerful; and sole ownership of the means of production gives of course great power. According to the second criticism, the bourgeois is a mean being of crass desires, and of low cunning in devising the means to gratify those desires. In the somewhat altered terms of an ancient Greek analysis, the two criticisms of the bourgeois explain him by reference to greedy appetite, animosity, and calculating desire.

Marxism is, of course, in revolt not so much against the bourgeoisie as against the manner of life that has evolved in modern society presided over by the bourgeoisie. That manner of life is stigmatized as being impoverished through the release of man's self-interestedness in a most repellent form. The Marxist revolution on behalf of high modernity is guided by the thought that emancipation of the self as self-preserving produces an enslavement and stultification of the self as self-fulfilling. The Marxian modernization appears to remind of the distinction between living and living well. At any rate, the emancipation is what we call "individualism and individual freedom." The enslavement and stultification are what Marx called "alienation." What we regard as the pursuit of happiness he believes to be the descent into misery. This deserves to be considered.

In its project for overcoming the proto-modern malaise, the Marxian revolution aims at a version of modernity peopled by men purged of possessiveness, animosity, and calculating desire. These comprise so large a part of the fundamental human appetite that Marxism can be taken to desire a world peopled by men largely purged of appetite. Why should one of the major revolutionary movements confronting us consider it desirable and possible so to reform the human condition? It considers it desirable because it thinks it knows that the best for man is the depreciation of or even abstraction from the bodily separateness of each from the others, and the depreciation of that natural otherness by the conjunction of the bodies in perfect sociality. The dialectic utilized by Marx is the continuous and necessary decay of specific othernesses, a movement in the direction of the completed One. The genuine socialization of the human kind would be impossible while human beings are animated by divisive appetite, which must therefore be eliminated.

The Marxian revolution aims also at the perfection of the individual human selves as such at the same time that those selves are perfectly immersed in society. It is thought that they not only can be perfected while being immersed but that they must be immersed or submerged in order to be perfected. A self divided from others by divergence of interest, appetite, and function ends by being a fragment not only of the human kind but of the whole man that he himself might otherwise have been. Marxism seeks to show that the perfection of the vital, productive, and irenic self (as distinguished from the polemic and basely selfish self) requires mainly the removal of constraints. The two great sources of constraints are nature and man, which produce, respectively, scarcity and punitive law. Science will abolish scarcity; History armed with revolution will abolish property and therewith the condition for punitive law. The perfect One is to be composed of the perfectly free Many.

Marxism appears to yearn for that nearly passionless condition of man said by Rousseau to prevail in the state of nature. It yearns also for the ascendancy of innocent selfishness over aggressive selfishness, and for the vibrant vitality of the multitude of individuals in a state of freedom approached through a radical correction of the property relation, thus deepening the reminiscence of Rousseau.

The aspiration of the Marxian revolution toward a political solution based on utter sociality and perfect idionomy raises the gravest doubts as to the soundness of the thought on which that revolution is based. From those doubts arises the question, crucial to United States policy, whether the Communist revolution is not the pursuit of a chimera, and thus to be opposed as a blandishment leading humanity to a leap into the unknown. This question concerns us because a United States policy based exclusively on the fact that Communism threatens us in our present state would command only unquestioning loyalty. We wish to know whether such a policy deserves also the loyalty of those who question, that is, those for whom the soundness of Marxism is still an open question. For this reason we turn to the issue of the relation between the ill of bourgeois society as Marxism understands it and the remedy that Marxism proposes.

Marxism describes itself as materialism, teaching that the modes of need-satisfying production are decisive of the level and quality of human life. This aspect of Marxism represents an important concession to the spirit of Hobbes, withal a concession in the form of a radicalization. Hobbes' emphasis on self-preservation led, through Locke, to capitalism. Marxism is in this respect a radicalization of that principle of modernity from which flow the characteristics of modern life regarded by Marxism itself as particularly odious. But Hobbes' thought as to the primacy of preservation is linked with a broad rejection of natural teleology, a rejection of the understanding that the species, their boundaries and their perfection, are constituents of a timeless natural order. This too is not only conceded by Marx but radicalized in his doctrine to the effect that the fundamental propositions of life, thought, and being are not "true" but are at best Historically valid. However, while such authors as Machiavelli and Hobbes apparently adhered to the view that there is an abiding human nature, evidenced powerfully in the passions, Marx implies the historicity of the constitution of man when he looks forward to the time when perfectly free human beings will desire to do exactly what they ought to do without the mediation of a selfish motive.

In referring to the historicity of man's constitution, one appears to touch on a deep disagreement between classic and revolutionary modernity as to the agency by which nature is replaced. Machiavelli, Descartes, and Hobbes taught that man himself has the task of making and remaking the edifice of life and thought. Marxism, as a theory of dialectical Historicism, appears to replace human agency with History, which is said to have an efficient and final causality of overwhelming power. When, however, one considers the Marxist thesis that the task of man is not to interpret the world but to reform it, and when one tries unsuccessfully to think of an important respect in which the Marxian revolutionaries would have acted differently on the world stage if they had possessed no doctrine of History, one realizes that for all important practical purposes, Marxism too depends upon the skill and activity of men and not upon a mystical History to work out the destinies of mankind. With respect to the historicity of man's constitution and the shaping of his social life, the Marxian revolution has the character of a radicalized version of classical modernity.

In attempting to show how Marxism is an intensified form of the proto-modern understanding I have not been leading up to the conclusion that Marxism is not a radical innovation. I wish rather to draw attention to the following consideration bearing on American policy toward the Marxian revolution. If the Western world is in distress for the reasons alleged by Marxism, it is in distress because it lives along the lines laid down (whether before or after the fact is not our present concern) in the thought of the great sixteenth- and seventeenth-century architects of modernity. Are we to understand from Marxism that our distress is caused by our living according to principles which are corrupt because they have outlasted their vitality, or that our distress is caused by our living according to principles which are corrupting only because they have not been driven to their most radical conclusions? Marxism as it sees itself, namely, as the historically detached criticism of capitalism and bourgeois society, implies the former. Marxism as the cure of modernity through the intensification of modernity implies the latter. So far as it implies the latter, it implies the vitality of those principles and not their Historical moribundity, for it appropriates them for the purpose of radicalizing them. Moreover it implies that the cure for a disorder is an intensified application of the cause that brought it on. There is all too much reason for saying that if the Marxian modernization movement is correct in its diagnosis it is wrong in its therapy; while if it is wrong in its diagnosis, we are of course not interested in its therapy.

Marxism confronts the Western world and especially the United States with a program and a threat that stimulate us to reflect on the disorders of our social life. We are asked to choose between giving ourselves over to a radical version and adhering to a moderate version of what we believe is the source of our difficulties. The United States policy of resistance to the expansion of Communism has the meaning of a national decision to adhere to moderate proto-modernity.

We turn next to the second of the modernizing revolutions, the vaguely defined movement said to be in protest against the established norms and authorities in public and private life. It can be discussed only in general terms for it possesses no articulated doctrine coming from any single mind capable of being compared with that of Marx. Of its many aspects, one of the most revealing is its view on authenticity, the defect of which quality is perhaps the chief fault charged against the middle class. The praise of authenticity is the obverse of the blame of hypocrisy. Hypocrisy means publicly pretending to respect the virtues while privately offending against them. The blame of hypocrisy could therefore be expected to introduce a demand that the virtues be respected not only in public pretense but sincerely and in private. The contemporary revolution of morals is better known for teaching that authenticity means publicly owning the hitherto private deviations rather than sincerely adjusting the private conduct to the respectable public profession. It is a short step from revealing vice to denying that there is any vice at all—except concealing it.

What is the root of this extraordinary impulse toward self-revelation, toward a notion of truth as self-revelation, or toward a morality which presupposes that there is no truth except the truth in self-revelation? Its apparent kinship with the public nudity of decadence as distinguished from the nakedness of innocence gives rise to the suspicion that the fundamental force at work here is hedonism—pleasure of the senses is the true natural good. One can believe that a license to enjoy shamelessly what have hitherto been forbidden pleasures might not be recklessly rejected, if offered to an entire generation. But so much of what comes under the protection of this moral innovation is in no sense pleasurable that hedonism by itself can hardly explain the revolution as a whole. For comprehended in this movement of revelation are a literature of defeat, hostility, and self-destruction; a music and art of stress, shock, and studied incoherence; and a cult of hallucination with votaries from the slums to the campuses. The common channel in which these currents flow is defined by the thought that there is an authentic truth about man which lies hidden under layers of consciousness, opinion, knowledge, reason, convention, prejudice, and, comprehensively, of civilization. Alternatively, there is an abyss into which a man must look, soundlessly screaming, in order thereafter to live a true life. Emancipation depends upon facing what lives in the depths. We are reminded at this time that deep means low as well as profound.

It is one thing to say that the relief of spiritually distressed individuals requires a laying bare of the lowest strata of their psychic life in order to locate the disorder. It is another thing to say that civil society must be transformed into an environment meant to be hospitable to that substratum of the soul which is the eternal repository of what resists civilization. The publicizing of the private in this radical sense is not merely offensive to taste and manners but would be politically absurd.

This antisocial revolution speaks of love, but unintelligibly. Love is a genus containing many species, some of them incapable of amity with others. Some love is sensuous, some intellectual; some is predatory, some self-sacrificing; some is violent, some tranquil; some wise and some foolish. Nothing known about the moral revolution gives reason to believe that when it declares for love, it does so out of sober care for the requirements of civil life. The love that pours out of minds indoctrinated with the sovereignty of the unfathomable and uncontrollable self will have more in common with white-hot anger than with a modest devotion to the common good.

Certainly there are great differences between the Marxian revolution, with its depreciation of the natural individual and his unsocial appetites, and the moral revolution, which would absolutize the near-void in every man, apotheosizing the lunatic carnival of unquiet things that dwell therein. But in spite of the manifold differences, both the moral revolution and the Marxian appear as radicalizations of the proto-modern teaching that nature, far from abhorring a vacuum, is or approaches one. In important respects, nature is a moral void and rather an opportunity for the mind of man than a preceptor to it. The rebellion against civil society and hence against civilization can be said to find a parent in Hobbes, of all people, for it was he who taught so explicitly that man's natural state is morally chaotic, and Locke made even clearer the thought that we are never far from a disorderly resumption of our whole natural liberty. A great act of imagination on Rousseau's part enabled him to see that the criticism of civil society latent in the formulation of Hobbes and Locke—namely, that civilization grates upon our nature—could be the starting point in envisioning a civil society that does not offend against nature. Ever since his time, men have dreamed of obtaining, simultaneously, the conveniences of society and the stimulations of a psychic life unspoiled by oppressive social strictures, not for rare spirits but for the generality of men. The moral revolution appears as the latest attempt to solve a problem of modernity by giving an extreme expression to a thought that lies near the root of modernity.

On the basis of the limited evidence afforded by the two modernizing revolutions discussed so far, one might say that the progress of modernity has consisted of a succession of self-criticisms, the stages of which comprise rejections or modifications of certain premises of proto-modernity and the compensatory intensification or radicalization of some others. One might speculate on the prospect for modernity while it remains confined within its own horizon, conceiving no remedies for its ills except remedies that are themselves congeneric with those same ills. If such self-limitation were not merely accidental but were essential to modern thought—perhaps through its susceptibility to Historical notions of progress—the crisis of modernity could be severe indeed. That crisis would be rooted in the death of philosophy, or an incapacity to consider all possible answers to all possible questions. This is a speculation that we cannot now pursue.

The moral revolution appears to be a movement with origins so deep as to be intractable to public policy, and thus to be or to resemble a revolution in that Historically overwhelming sense described earlier in this paper. It might well prove to be so, though after all it is not literally or metaphysically impossible but only most unlikely that we will be governed by a succession of statesman who, by example, policy, and speech can stem the tide. This point is by no means without its practical importance, as can be seen through considering the effect of this moral radicalization on the capacity of America to confront the Marxian revolution. Even modernity must acknowledge the transhistoric truth that a nation's foreign policy and its domestic policy are but two aspects of the same thing, namely, the spirit of the nation. It is not yet known whether our character as a nation will support the policies that our place at the head of the free world requires us to adopt.

The third of the modernizing revolutions affecting United States policy is the one occurring in what is called the Third World. The Third World is so called because it belongs neither to the Communist world nor to the free world. Its revolution might be supposed therefore to be directed neither against Communism nor against capitalistic constitutionalism, but rather against some condition or conditions that now prevail in the Third World regions. For brevity's sake those conditions will be brought together in the one word "undeveloped." The modernizing revolution in the Third World is a movement that understands "modernization" as synonymous with "development," and "development" in turn as meaning the acquisition of the technical skills of production and administration now available in the leading nations. Of course those skills cannot be acquired or retained without the support of an appropriate structure of education, morale, and investment, so the preparation of the infrastructure is also included in the modernization process. Finally, since a number of the places in which these developments are occurring were at one time parts of colonial empires, the process of modernization often includes the foundation of a new nation, or giving expression to nationalism.

I have been maintaining that modernity is a human epoch in which men's thoughts and hopes have run in certain recognizable channels; and that out of those thoughts and hopes have sprung the movements of change which, for reasons stated, deserve to be called modernizing. Whether sound or unsound, those thoughts and hopes have tried to keep in view the issues that lie near the core of life rather than on its industrial substratum or at its administrative periphery. The use of the word "modernization" to mean acquisition of techniques and the establishment of nations without reference to the human ends being sought through technique and nationhood represents a decisive weakening of the meaning of modernization. In its new sense, modernization abstracts from the most imortant political fact now threatening to unhinge the world, namely, the confrontation of the two gigantic systems of modernity, the champions of which are contending for hegemony over the unexpired portion of the modern time. Under the circumstances it is not only pretentious but misleading for the so-called revolution of modernization in the Third World to claim so comprehensive a name.

The Third World revolution presents a face of neutrality to the most exigent political crisis of the day. On consideration, this modernizing revolution looks more like a hanging back from the principles of modernity than an eager movement to embrace them. Such a position might prove untenable but it is easily understandable. Why should not the semiformed or antiquated countries desire the fruits of modernity without desiring also to embrace either of its principles when both have been so effectively flayed by each other? Why should developing nations, with their overburden of difficulties, not wish to avoid those entangling alliances with either party which must rule out help from or expose to the reprisals of the other party? The same detachment which generates sympathetic understanding of the plight of neutrals will generate, however, sympathetic understanding of the even more critical plight of antagonists. Why should United States policy gaze benignly on what stares back indifferently? The task of United States policy is the relatively simple one of distinguishing its Third World friends from its Third World enemies; as far as possible, increasing the number of friends while making no enemies. United States policy has sometimes been criticized as inept or worse in having taken so many neutral revolutionaries for enemies, treated them as such and irrevocably alienated them. The critics have not explained how a neutral revolutionary who wishes to preserve the good will of a great power could fail to find ways of letting that fact be known. The ineptness of a small power that allows itself to be mistaken for an enemy by a great potential benefactor is immensely greater than any ineptness chargeable to the State Department.

III

Thus far this statement has considered some of the objects to which United States policy must address itself. In conclusion I should like to consider the bearing of modernity on policy itself as such, not from the point of view of what it addresses but regarding it as a product of the men, the nation, and the times that generate it.

Policy is an informed plan for action. Actions aim at producing results which are thought to be good because they serve some human end conceived at the very beginning or at the founding of the nation to be good. This prior conception is what "informs" policy. Policy is thus the continuous penetration of the changing present by the unchanging beginning. Policy expresses a continuing return to the principles of the nation. As metaphysicians would say, the principle which is decisive for the coming into being remains decisive continuously for the preservation of the being. Less abstractly put, the preservation of the nation means first of all the preservation of its constituting thought.

That constituting thought or judgment as to the human good serves the nation as such in the same way as the great organizing hypotheses of natural science are said to serve man through their lending intelligibility to what is in itself unintelligible. A constitution gives the nation a world view which is and must be its own world view. Contrary to the opinion of social science, rational "ethnocentrism" is not a mere vice of political life but is indispensable to it or at least inseparable from it. This will continue to be true as long as political life remains distinguishable from philosophy, that is, as long as each form or specimen of political life will proceed from some compromise between wisdom and man's inability to live by wisdom alone. The number of defensible compromises will never collapse into unity.

From this contingency of all regimes, if from nothing else, follows the impermanence of all regimes. But it is instructive to contemplate the impermanence of modern regimes in particular, not only for the practical but also for the theoretical lessons that may be learned. That impermanence can be traced to a teaching that reflects the modern view of the whole. I shall try to illustrate this remark by referring to two of the founders of the modern age, Machiavelli and Descartes.

Machiavelli gives what appear to be conflicting precepts when he teaches that nations must recur continually to their founding principles and also that what is presented to statesmen by the unfolding times is decisive with respect to distinguishing good and bad. Assuming that he meant both counsels equally, we see that they need not contradict each other if the founding principle is itself an expression of the need always to respect the flux in the nature of things. Descartes taught that the natural whole is by no means the organized cosmos that tradition said it was, but that great acts of human making or founding are indispensable to rendering it similar to a cosmos. Again we observe the superimposition of an artificial stability on a natural flux.

The political life of the United States, and therewith the sources of United States policy, bear the marks of having originated in the thought of classic modernity. We have a constitution which, while not the product of a Machiavellian Moses or Romulus, nor the plan of a Cartesian architect, is the work of a collective intelligence working in commission as nearly as possible as if it were a single human mind. It expresses the thought that the human good is the restless pursuit of one end after another ceasing only in death. The firm structure made by man can rest only upon the flux, if not void, with which nature provides us as the human opportunity, the occasion that enables men to achieve greatness.

United States policy towards the Marxian revolution expresses this nation's determination to perpetuate the firm structure of artifact that gives shape to our political existence. That artifact is the Constitution. But the principle incarnated unchangingly in the Constitution is a principle of moral flux. That principle of moral flux, of the dubiousness of the moral criteria, is the animating force behind the moral revolution taking place domestically. The moral revolution jeopardizes the policy of this nation toward the Marxian revolution. It could not be clearer that our prospects as a people and the fate of our policies are inseparably bound up with the meaning of modernity.

The Moral Basis of
International Action

Reprinted from *America
Armed,* edited by Robert A.
Goldwin (Chicago: Rand
McNally and Company, 1963).
©1961, 1963 by The Public
Affairs Conference Center,
The University of Chicago.

The power of nations to inflict pain, destruction, and death in warfare has been brought to such a peak that men feel themselves compelled as never before to find means for preventing that power from being used. The instruments of mutilation and devastation are tremendous and their action comprehensive to such a degree that their employment would produce effects that shock the mind, for they reach perhaps to the impairment of the human race as a whole. It is by no means easy to obtain agreement as to the essence of moral offense in general; but it is transcendently easy to obtain agreement that it would be monstrous, and if monstrous then immoral, for men to burn up the moiety of mankind and to denature the loins of those who survive.

We have not yet said what is meant by moral; but skill at definitions is not a prerequisite for concluding that every man and group of men has a duty to abstain from destroying mankind. One could go further. The enormity of exposing the world to nuclear blasts is so absolute that an absolute moral obligation is created to abjure the weapons themselves:

they must not be allowed to exist, for their existence is the potentiality of
the absolute evil.

It therefore appears that each nation is by duty bound to practice a
voluntary restraint, to limit its own action and power of action in the
interest of some good which is not its obvious, immediate self-benefit. For
the sake of fulfilling a duty to the rest of mankind, each nation should to
some extent deprive itself of the means to supremacy or even of defense.
As we reflect on this duty, we notice how well it corresponds with what
appears as the notion of morality at large. Morality is a standard of
conduct which guides men to recognize and show concern for others, and
to act out of some larger motive than the convenience, safety and
well-being of themselves.

The demand of morality may be said to be in the direction of deliberate
self-incapacitation. So far as this is true, morality is in apparent conflict
with policy, or in other words with calculation in the interest of the actor.
This is admitted both by the friends of morality, who see it as moderating
the brutal egotism of life, and by the cynics, who see it as the delusion by
which the strong are seduced to abstain from benefiting from their
strength. In either case, solicitude for another is put ahead of or at least
alongside concern for the actor's own advantage. It is easy to imagine why
the claim of morality is sometimes thought to be very tenuous.

The common violation of morality suggests that something fundamental in human nature is outraged by the demand that the interest of another
be made the measure of a man's or nation's action. The demand of
morality appears to conflict with natural self-love and with the power of
calculation that supports it. Nevertheless, to think only of oneself is
perhaps more an offense against rationality than against decency. Other
men and other nations have a concrete, objective existence which cannot
sensibly be ignored, not merely because they will protest and retaliate, but
because, from an impartial point of view, their being and their interest are
equal in importance to the actor's. If one avoids the plain folly of picking
himself out of the whole human race and making a special case of
himself, he will easily be led to grant that he has no right to live by one set
of rules and to expect everyone else to live by another. He must keep the
others in mind when he seeks to form the rules of his own behavior. He will
see that the fundamental likeness of all human beings in their humanity
leads to the fundamental equality of all human beings in their rights.
Morality means to act with consideration for the rights of others.
Necessarily we must curb ourselves in action out of respect for the
objective equality of the others who exist around us. We must do so not
out of any mere sentiment of sympathy, or even fear of retaliation, but out
of a rational perception that mankind is a whole, while each individual is

but a part and must content himself with only so much advantage as one among equals can sensibly claim.

Thus it would appear that morality as self-limitation is the dictate of reason, based upon a rational being's power of seeing his relation to others with an impartial, objective eye. Knowing his own demands and desires, he immediately knows the demands and desires of other men, for in the relevant respects the other men are exactly like himself. The intensity of his wish to live, to be free, and to set his own goals is the measure of the same wish in others. Not any moral sense, or even conscience, but bare objectivity extorts from him the concession of the equal right of every other man to the same goods that are important to him. And since his wish for the good things of life, the same wish on the part of others, and his power of understanding the equal right of those others all exist by nature, why should one not say that the moral duty of self-limitation is a natural obligation and thus binds all human beings equally?

The more we prove that the moral law is binding, the more we are obliged to explain why it is so commonly ignored in practice. Evidently, "binding" is ambiguous, meaning both "ought because it is right" and "must because it is compulsory." There is a difference between what makes justice good and what makes it obeyed. Where the two influences have little to do with each other, or even conflict, the moral system in question is defective. We must evidently look further into the sense in which a moral obligation is binding. To do this, we shall have to think further about the basis of the moral order, that basis we have been calling "objective" or rational. We are led to carry the inquiry in this direction because the standard of morality has been said to be rational and therefore binding, yet there is a gap between this rational standard and the standards of behavior actually obeyed by the rational animal.

We may begin by noticing that the moral problem is peculiar to man, in the sense that only the actions of men are subject to moral restriction. The misconduct of things and beasts is not called immorality. The reason for this is that men have a unique power to control or govern themselves. A beast can be trained, indeed, and it will show signs of apprehension when it breaks a rule, but there is no reason to suppose that it experiences anything but a fear of consequences when it does so. When it behaves well, it does so out of mere obedience. Men, however, do not merely obey; they are capable of themselves positively willing to do what is also required of them externally. They are thus unique in the whole world as willing, self-controlling, rational beings. This is a most important fact, for as a result of it, men have an overriding absolute worth or, as is often said, a dignity. The dignity of man is absolute; men therefore have an absolute moral obligation to one another, and incidentally, corresponding absolute moral claims on one another.

The word "absolute" is used in a literal sense to describe the mutual moral obligations and claims of men. The worth of man is so great that our duty to each other cannot be based upon any calculation of interest. To base our actions toward each other upon some calculation of interest leads to the contamination of every seemingly good deed: we would be truthful only to preserve our credit, kind only to preserve ourselves from retaliation, grateful only to encourage benefactions, and so on. Actions so performed would not express any recognition of man's dignity; all of them on the contrary would imply the treatment of other men as things to be manipulated, by cunning appearances, for the benefit of the actor—who would deserve to be so called for more than one reason.

It is clear that this conception of moral duty, resting upon the premise of man's capacity for willing, really rests upon the premise of man's capacity for willing freely—or, in brief, upon man's radical freedom. Now if there is a moral teaching based upon the belief in man's freedom and dignity, we are compelled to take it seriously because we regard our own political system as itself based upon man's freedom and dignity. To be true to ourselves, we might have to adopt as our own the absolute standard of morality which veers away from interest and toward uncompromising obligation, a standard that jeopardizes diplomacy or even foreign policy as we know it.

The notion of an absolute moral duty to all mankind certainly implies a solemn obligation—to our allies and to neutrals, and to our enemies no less, as human beings with an absolute worth. In brief, it seems to point toward unilateral disarmament if necessary, thus toward our voluntary extinction as a nation, as the purchase price for human lives. It seems to require of us that we remove ourselves from the path of History and submit without resistance to be overrun by the course of events, in the interest of mankind. I shall try to show that such a notion of an absolute moral obligation rests upon error and cannot be the guide to action; it does not oblige because it cannot and ought not oblige in practice.

1. The rule of absolute moral obligation is derived from a generalization about all mankind, and it pretends to oblige every man toward all of mankind. It claims a status similar to that of a law of nature. But it is a fact, as objective as any moral metaphysic, that men live not under the moral laws of nature but as members of nations under positive laws. The existence of bodies politic with different legal systems is the sovereign practical fact. The inference from this fact is that homogeneous mankind is superseded in practice by politically differentiated mankind; that laws obliging all mankind must be mediated by the legislation of the nations. The fundamental condition for the translation of absolute moral duty into political practice therefore does not exist in the world. Absolute moral duty to mankind is without a clear meaning so long as the most compre-

hensive active unit of the human kind is the national body politic and not the human race. When we confront other human beings, it is not simply as men but as fellow citizens, or as Frenchmen, Britons, or Russians. We recognize thus that humanity is radically divided, and the division is along lines of the divergent moral understandings and legal constitutions that inform the several political bodies. From the variety of moral foundations beneath the several political societies, two things follow: the duty of each society toward every other is affected by the character of the one toward which action is to be directed, just as our moral duty to act toward parsons and pickpockets, bearing in mind their common humanity, does not eventuate in the same conduct toward both. And second, since not all societies (and perhaps no societies) subscribe in their constituting principles to the view that there is an absolute moral duty of man to man, any nation that derived its practice from such a view would involve itself in the difficulties described next.

2. If absolute moral duty as described is to be the guide of any nation's practice, it would have to be recognized by mankind generally, that is, by all the nations or by the important nations, as the guide to their actions. If it were not, then obedience to the moral law would inevitably entail suicide, or if not suicide, then disgrace. Coincidentally, obedience to the moral law would guarantee the triumph of the immoral, of those who feel little need to obey the moral law. A moral law that brings the obedient to death and shame and guarantees the success of its violators is not fit to be discussed at length by men with practical responsibilities.

3. The absolute moral law claims to oblige us in the name of duty alone, apart from every consideration of interest or benefit, and to speak in the name of human dignity and freedom only. But we notice that to obey the absolute moral law would under present circumstances remove the last practical defense of human dignity and freedom, as will be argued. Moreover the absolute moral law is not, as it claims to be, mindful only of pure duty and oblivious of ends and consequences. It rationally regards human survival, freedom, and dignity as goods worth pursuing; its absoluteness dissolves before the higher worth of the good it aims at. If obedience to that law imperils the very goods the law is based upon and must seek to preserve, then obedience to the law is an absurdity, and the law obliges no one, although it is a very objective law.

Our first general conclusion is that moral laws are not "absolute" in their force but must be obeyed in such a way that the result of obeying them is consistent with morality or simple decency. Morality uninformed by sound judgment is theoretically, let alone practically, null. This means that we must and do believe that deceitfulness is immoral, yet espionage is not to be eschewed; homicide is baneful, yet we must be ready to destroy the enemy; intervention in foreign sovereignties is reprehensible, yet we may not hang back from it.

Historically, the belief in a rational and objective ground of morality has led to views of mutual obligation quite different from the principle of absolute duty just examined. If rational and objective mean founded on common observations that anyone can make and verify at any time, then there is no more rational and objective foundation for morality than this: that all men, like all living things, have an overpowering preference for themselves, each one devoted to his own interest more than to anything in the world, with "interest" subject to some latitude of definition but not very much. But in that case it is both impractical and theoretically unsound to argue that man's duty to man must be understood as abstracted from every consideration of interest and consequences. Human nature would rule that out. Recurring to the remark made earlier to the effect that morality is inseparable from self-restraint out of regard for others, this powerful fact of invincible self-love makes a most unpromising foundation for morality, unless in some way the law of the jungle can transform itself into a moral law.

In fact, precisely this or something like it is thought to happen; for it is clear that belligerent selfishness gives rise to conflict and mutual injury, and thus defeats itself, since it ends in destruction among the selfish parties. It was noticed long ago that the ends of self-interest are best promoted by strictly enforceable agreements to live and let live, agreements by which each binds himself to abstain from the goods and persons of the others in order himself to be immune from destruction. It goes without saying that such agreements would be not useless but dangerous to those who entered into them if there were not effective arbitrators to enforce them, and to punish violations; otherwise, faithless contractors would exploit the simple who honor their engagements.

On this view of the human situation, morality may be said to grow out of, or to be replaced by, or to be identical with rational selfishness. Selfishness dictates that each individual respect the absolute right of others, and that he and the others ratify the tenders of their mutual consideration by submitting to be ruled by laws with penalties attached. Let us call this the condition of institutionalized mutual regard.

What does this notion have to contribute to our understanding of the moral ground underlying international action, military or other? What is the character of the moral obligation that nations have toward one another? It is no other than an obligation to live by the laws that are enforced between the nations for the preservation of each and all of them, and to submit to the punishments impartially inflicted for disobedience.

But what are those laws, and where are the authorities that punish the infractions? Evidently there are none of either.

If morality means to follow the dictate of survival under legal restraints in the interest of everybody's equal right to follow the same dictate, but among the nations there are no legal restraints of any significance, then plainly the nations' moral obligation dissolves into the right of naked power wielded by each country in its own behalf. Violations by one nation of another's right to survive can easily be recognized, but there is no judge to reprobate those violations and to order and execute retribution except the injured nation itself and its allies. The only mutual consideration that exists or can exist among the nations is what they extort from one another by the fear of consequences, that is, by force.

It is disturbing to reflect that if one begins with the rational and objective natural rights of men to life and security, one ends with the reduction of international morality to violence or threats of violence, and nothing more. This conclusion is unacceptable for, if admitted, it would render us incapable of judging the moral quality of Hitler's acts to strengthen the Third Reich and Churchill's acts to strengthen Great Britain. But the need and the possibility of making that discrimination are facts as rational and objective as the common impulse toward self-preservation. We therefore have not arrived at a satisfactory understanding of the moral basis of international action; where the oppugnancy of justice and interest is resolved by the reduction of the former to the latter, the moral system in question is imperfect.

In presenting the two moral extremes, the one of absolute duty to all men as men and the other of simple calculation in the interest of the agent, we have run into these difficulties: either the moral action of the one party exposes him to ruin at the hands of an immoral antagonist (with the consequence that morality leads invariably to the triumph of evil); or the possibility of moral discrimination disappears entirely, leaving as the only criterion of action the submoral criterion of success in survival. In either case, what begins as morality ends as immorality.

With this behind us, we can set down the requirements of a moral ground for international action, military and other. And if it turns out that no moral system can without self-contradiction meet these requirements, then we may conclude that morality is irrelevant to the conduct of nations, and all is just in hate and lust. The requirements for such a moral order are these: (1) That a nation be able to abide by the rules of right conduct without harm to itself even if every other nation in the world ignore or violate them. (2) That notwithstanding the full compatibility of the moral order with survival and victory, the rule of morality not simply dissolve into the right of the stronger, that is, the criterion of success.

Beginning again, we recur to the simplest and most generally admitted notion as to the meaning of morality: morality is self-restraint. Hitherto, we have taken self-restraint to mean a voluntary holding back either from violating an abstract precept of duty or from injuring others. The implicit supposition has been that the overriding problem to which morality addresses itself is how to define the duties or rights of men, the extreme solutions to the problem being either duty apart from calculation or calculation apart from duty. But there is no need for morality to mean either the one or the other so exclusively. This becomes clear to us when we consult the normal human understanding of what conduct deserves blame and what deserves praise. We blame people who deceive, defraud, plunder, attack, and murder; but curiously we also blame those who are vacillating, miserly, gluttonous, lewd, or craven, although it is not possible to say, for example, "gluttonous toward others." These latter defects are not primarily the sources of injury to other men. They are rather flaws of weakness, for example, the weakness of being unrestrainedly fond of some external good, or of being incapable of exercizing that amount of self-control that enables a man to come to a conclusion or to suppress cruel, effete, or otherwise disgusting passions. We might note at the same time that a man overcome with the sense of duty, who plunged incontinently, that is, unrestrainedly into every situation where good needed to be done, would come under deserved censure as a dangerous meddler, especially if the only good accomplished was the salving of his conscience. There is a path between morality in the service of preservation and morality in the service of duty, abstractly considered; and that path is the one indicated by the general understanding of mankind. It follows the rule that self-restraint is not confined to the agent's acts against others but touches his character more comprehensively.

The first rule of morality is indeed self-restraint, and the first rule of self-restraint is to avoid falling under condign hatred, shame, or contempt. The corollary of this rule is that morality rests upon sober judgment of circumstances, men, and things, so that the agent will avoid the disesteem earned by folly; and that it culminates in a justified sense of self-respect. Morality, thus, is not intelligible as an abstract or formal principle but only as the sum of concrete characteristics, the possession of which enables the agent to deserve praise and respect. Morality without virtues is vanity.

What are those praiseworthy characteristics, and what does any of this have to do with the international action of the United States? The answer to the first will be tantamount to the answer to the second. Neither a nation nor a man can avoid shame if it is craven, heedless, self-indulgent, wanton in ease, irresolute in deliberation, wastrel in pleasure, squeamish in contest, faint in adversity. Virtue is etymologically related to manliness; but the relation is evidently more than etymological. What course is then open to the United States other than that dictated by the moral law undistorted by doctrinairism?

I believe that if we test this rule of morality, which rises more or less directly out of common human experience, we will find that it meets the two conditions laid down earlier as being indispensable if the moral criterion is to be applicable to the nation's action. We are at no disadvantage if all the world but us behave brutally, foolishly, agressively, deceitfully, and in every other way immorally. Prudence and decency demand of us that we make every effort to withstand every attempt that can be made against us; to do less would be contemptible and thus immoral. To do as much would be to work toward safety through morality. It goes without saying that morality so conceived utterly excludes those avoidable deeds of massive violence that can be defended only on the premise that success justifies everything. Certainly success is not the touchstone of morality as naturally understood, and it is not sensible to infer righteousness from survival, nor vice from failure. It is indeed possible to be respectable in defeat and contemptible in victory; but it is not possible to be respectable in defeat if defeat is the result of sloth, decadence, or a failure of nerve.

By this view, war and therefore the preparation for war are, in themselves, neither morally good nor morally bad, any more than homicide is morally good or bad. The homicide of a police officer upon a fleeing criminal is morally good, the homicide of a fleeing criminal upon a police officer morally bad. War is dreadful, and the preparation for it painful; but a theory that defines the painful as the immoral is nothing but hedonism or an encouragement to hedonism, no matter what appeals it may make to sentiment, conscience, or a show of rights. War is bad but it is not bad in the way that a supine indifference to disgrace and slavery are bad, for the latter comes from moral corruption and the former only from a fearful necessity that some men cannot, because of the vice of others, avoid.

War is bad because pain and death are bad, and death worse than pain. But we must reflect on the order of things, and recognize the difference between the death of men and the death of nations. Individuals die, but those remaining make up the loss. Cities are reduced to material chaos, but in an amazingly short time the destruction is repaired. The resurrection of a regime, however, is a thing rarely seen. The Constitution subverted, liberty disappears, and the human flotsam remaining suffer the ultimate demoralization, which is not death but subjection to the unlimited will of a master. Those who would investigate war and peace as part of the moral problem may never stray out of sight of the fact that the necessary condition for all morality is freedom, and the condition for freedom is the absolute integrity of the body politic—guaranteed by the power and willingness to make war.

It is evident that morality can retain its connection with self-restraint without collapsing into self-incapacitation. On the contrary, the demands of morality, seen in their relation to freedom and honor, are more energizing than they are paralyzing. Then the question arises whether there is anything at all that could contribute to the greatness and safety of the nation for which a justification could not be found by appealing to honor. The answer to this is surely No if the appeal to honor is a specious pretext, and as surely Yes if the appeal to honor is itself honorable. But assuming for the moment that the appeal to honor is not hypocritical, what sort of act would a nation be compelled to deny itself for purely moral reasons, contrary to its urgent interest?. Is there something dishonorable, for example, in espionage? In deceitful counterintelligence? In the apprehension of a rebel by means of a ruse? In the subversion of a foreign government with which we are not at war? Not one of these questions can be answered except with knowledge of concrete circumstances. The most relevant circumstance is the character of the nation doing the deed in question, and the character of the men or nation to which it is done. What should one answer to the question, Ought one to spy on his neighbors? To enter a strange house in the absence of its owner? To detain another man by force? There is no answer in the abstract, but only in the light of the character of the agent, the one to whom the deed was done, and the circumstances.

Obviously the question arises, Which nation is to be the judge of all these things? The answer is that we must judge for ourselves, both of ourselves and others, and trust that history will vindicate us when our reasons are known and our intentions are proved by the event to have been reasonable and humane. Those who raise the question, Who shall judge? do so, very often, in the belief that it is self-evidently absurd for us to be judge of our own morality. In truth it is no less, and perhaps far more absurd to hope that a reliable judgment on our morality will be brought by a poll of the nations, many of which are moved by animosity and envy, and more by ignorance. We must go forward to preparation for war, the neutralization of enemies, the adaptation of foreign regimes, and all other things needful, doing right as it is given to us to see the right, and trusting to the only judgment fully informed of our intentions, namely, our own. In another world a more schematic or precise answer could perhaps be given to this question; and if we were a petty nation in the hinterland of Africa, the question would not practically arise for us. But in this world, morality must paddle its own boat with whatever implement comes to hand; and the problem is ours because the United States is where it is and not in central Africa. The teaching of morality may be reduced to this: we must do everything that needs to be done to insure the survival of ourselves, our friends, and our free principles, indulging neither ourselves nor others, avoiding sentimentality no less than brutality, and mindful that if we weakly hang back, we will ignominiously hang alone. Those who desire to see this wisdom reduced to a punched-tape program must await their translation to another, better universe; likewise those who wish to see it purged of all severity.

It will surely be objected that to imperil the human race on the point of honor is to inflate Quixotism from an eccentricity to a calamity. We must therefore try to keep separate in our minds these two principles of action: the one, that it is wrong and dishonorable weakly to submit to domination; and the second, quite different, that what deserves to be defended should be defended, and what deserves to be resisted should be resisted, but that it is not sober to make a virtue out of defense and resistance regardless of the worth of the things to be defended and resisted. In other words, the appeal to honor alone is defective, and must be perfected by a showing that honor is aroused in a good cause; otherwise it is suspected of being a euphemism for truculence or ferocious obstinacy. Do we have any reason for believing that the sovietization of the world is an evil commensurate with the peril created by opposing it? that it is the menace to dignity and freedom it was earlier said to be? To answer this question fully would require a full statement of the character of communism; here we can provide only the barest intimation.

Marxism begins with materialism and ends with the homogeneity of mankind. Marxist materialism differs from traditional materialism in attaching fundamental importance to the process of production, that is, to self-preservation by means of "technology," primitive or complex. The problem of preservation is primarily a technological, not a political problem for Marx. Indeed the complete solution of the problem of preservation is radically nonpolitical: when the means of production are commonly owned and production is made a wholly social process, politics, or ruling and being ruled, will cease among men. The aspiration of communism is a total solution of the economic problem by means that would reduce all mankind to a single classless, that is, homogeneous mass: a huge herd of sheep safely grazing. Human distinction is the source of the human problem, and therefore distinction must be terminated. The "heroes" will be "heroes of the shovel" and "heroes of the loom": heroes of social production. This could be called the ultimate vulgarization of humanity, or the final indignity. We see it foreshadowed in the substitution of the shoe for the gavel in council, and the hairy chest for the clean collar in diplomacy. Because dignity is inseparable from distinction, the resistance to sovietization was said to be in the interest of human dignity.

What of freedom? Communism aims at life without the state, or without formal government. We are not interested for the present in the empirical question of whether the state can wither away. We observe simply that Marxism makes no provision for the form of government, for constitutional guarantees and so on, all such being impermanent and beneath its serious noncritical notice. The governments that have arisen in socialist states have therefore had to be improvised to administer the proletarian ascendancy during the revolutionary phase of world communism. They are governments singularly adapted to the stringencies of revolution—autocracies. But it may be asked, what of the postrevolutionary times, if any? No man can know the answer to this; we can only discern a presumptive answer, or a likelihood. The formlessness of the herd without distinction exposes it perpetually to the highest concentration of irresponsible authority—wielded for the noble end of administration, all other problems having vanished. More simply, a flock demands a shepherd.

The bias of Marxism toward matter and in opposition to form bears fruit in an unprecedented threat to human dignity and freedom. Honorable resistance to sovietization is thus more than merely honorable.

Readers may be pardoned for failing to see in the Soviet Union now a population of grazing sheep. Far from a fat and torpid flock, they are an active, patriotic, spirited community, exhilarated by their hard-won achievements, conscious of greatness and lusting for its gratifications. That they are all these things is a vindication, not a contradiction of what was said above: finding their revolution confronted by hindrances, they compel themselves to rise to formidable heights of exertion. They are in the irrational condition of heroically laboring to destroy the possibility of any future heroic labor, while congratulating themselves on their own heroism. It is not the self-contradiction but the menace in their doings that is our present concern, and how we must respond to it.

We are in the position of respecting and praising the sense of honor, and of discerning it well-developed in our enemy. We will prove his right to rule us if we do not prevent him from exercising it; and we can maintain our right to be free only by being in a position to exercise it. In plain language, to his irresistible force we must oppose an immovable obstacle. If we do so, we appear to increase the possibility of global depopulation, to scant our duty not to contribute to the death of mankind. Two questions then arise: Do we in fact increase the possibility of destroying mankind? Is it our duty, if the answer is Yes, to surrender to the Soviet Union in the interest of human survival?

As to the first question, the issue is in doubt, depending entirely on what happens when the engineer of an irresistible force knows himself to be opposed by an immovable obstacle. There is not one iota of preponderance on the side of the view that the activator of the great force will choose to dash it against an absolute resistance. But if he entertains any reasonable doubt that our response will be absolute and remorseless, he will have less reason to keep the peace. This means that at a certain moment we must harden ourselves to look at the beauties of peace and prepare to see in their stead a contaminated chaos peopled with human carrion. If we cannot stand this thought, we are not ready to fight and will therefore be compelled to do so—or to truckle and prostrate ourselves.

On one condition would the sacrifice of ruin not be excessive: if we triumphed and the enemy were in the end destroyed. It is absurd to say that there are no victors in war. The one who survives in freedom is the victor; the one who must humble himself and surrender his ways and institutions at the dictate of his enemy is vanquished—as much now as when men fought with clubs. Victory is as much better than defeat now as when David smote Goliath. Nuclear physics in its great productivity has changed many things, but it has not yet brought forth a palatable isotope of humiliation.

Perhaps it will be said that there can be no victory where there are no survivors. This is true enough, but inconclusive. The question is, What follows from it? The most obvious conclusion is that we must do our utmost to insure that plenty of us will survive, so that the nation can go on, in the enjoyment of victory. But it might be argued that no one could possibly survive the next war, which must come to an end with the apocalyptic death of the human race. Let us for the present accept this assumption as empirically correct. Then there must not be a next war. To argue so is plausible, but again inconclusive, for the argument tells us nothing about the form in which the cost of avoiding war must be paid. It might be that we pay for peace by abject surrender. That is unthinkable. It is unthinkable because the argument in favor of doing so is based upon the premise that, morally and politically, nothing matters—nothing, that is, except survival. The proper name for this position is not philanthropic morality but nihilism without intestines. The fortified species of nihilism also argues that nothing matters—except success. We have lost contact with the human spirit if we can no longer sense the repulsiveness of nihilism and the depravity of it in its emasculated form. If nothing matters, then human life does not matter. (Who would mourn it?) If anything matters, it is the decency of life and the possible self-respect of men. Still, where there is life there is hope for some amendment of any evil. We agree, and recommend the thought to our enemy; it deserves his consideration no less than ours. In brief, there is one cost of avoiding war which is more than we can afford: subhuman self-abasement.

Then we must pay for peace by making such a preparation for war that apprehensions for the safety of mankind will for once begin to influence the calculations of the enemy. If he is beyond or beneath a care for man's preservation, he is the manifest enemy of the race, fit to be hedged in or destroyed, certainly requiring to be diligently guarded against. If he is capable of such a care, then we need not, as truly we ought not assume the whole burden of providence, devoting our progeny as it may be to Moloch. Effectually bringing home his duty to our adversary is a far more defensible method of discharging our own moral duty to mankind than would be giving over the world to a moral enigma; for we would then be performing a sort of missionary work, animating a solicitude for human survival in places where it has been hitherto unknown or without effect.

It is a paradoxical and fearful fact that the only way we might have peace is by opening our minds to war. That way lies the presumption of safety—in war if it comes, through peace if it does not. It is not necessary to say that there is no guarantee that mankind will not be decimated and irradiated. Nature itself does not vouchsafe his survival to man: the instruments of general destruction of which we now stand in dread are inferences from principles implicit in nature, principles which have lain in darkness from eternity, waiting to be grasped and put in execution by man. We happen to be the climactic generation, in whose time the combination of man and nature seems to be achieving the critical mass. We cannot avoid our fate, but we need not be craven in confronting it. On the contrary, the ways of danger and moral decay are one. Life itself hangs by the thread of honor.

We seem to have concluded that the dictate of morality coincides with the interest of men and nations whose purposes are compatible with freedom and high-mindedness. This conclusion was the one intended.

In the course of our attempt to clarify the moral basis of international action, we have been led to take up two extreme but not unrepresentative examples of moral doctrine and a third which avoids the extremes. To simplify, the three could be said to turn, respectively, on Duty, Rights, and Honor. The conclusion has been that the first two are, for the purposes of guiding international action, imperfect, and the third is to be preferred. Supposing this for the moment to be true, of what practical value is the conclusion? Is it possible for a nation simply to adopt the moral principle of its choice for application to its international business? There is reason to doubt that this can be done with complete ease or freedom. The reason is that each nation is given its character by the elaborate set of moral judgments already embodied in its system of laws and practices. Implicit in the laws and customs is a notion of what action is just, what is proper and decent, what is worthy of esteem—in brief, of morality. As an example, we could contrast the famous system of the ancient Spartans with that of our own country now. No one would argue that we could simply "adopt" for international purposes the morality of Sparta, while our constitution as a nation rests on a radically different moral basis. If all our notions of tolerable conduct are fashioned by one system of judgments, can we act externally on another? We shall consider in the remainder of this paper the relation between the municipal morality of a nation and the demands of existence in a world of nations.

The problem is made especially severe by the kinship that exists between our general moral outlook as a community and the two moral dispensations described above as the "extremes." When we go back to the Declaration of Independence, for example, we read of man's inalienable rights—which are the same natural rights that we noticed earlier in the discussion—all derivative from the natural right of all men to self-preservation. The Declaration enumerates the inalienable rights to life, liberty, and the pursuit of happiness; the Constitution speaks of life, liberty, and property. The replacement made by the Constitution is not of the nature of a revision but a clarification: the rights to life, liberty, and property are inseparably connected with happiness, in our moral and political understanding as a nation. It is only when each man is guaranteed in his person that his property is secure, and only when he is safeguarded in his property that his person is inviolate. Our political system makes provision for translating those natural rights into a meaningful ground of civil life by wedding the institutions of capitalism to those of constitutional government. Political freedom is possible on various bases; in the Western world it exists on the foundation of certain economic institutions, and the concurrence of capitalism and modern democracy is by no means a coincidence. Liberty and prosperity, the aims of our order, are provided for at one and the same time by a principle that authorizes the individuals to act in their own behalf under the protection of a government to whose rule they give their consent so long as it defends them in their freedom to act in their own behalf. The essence of acting in one's own behalf is calculation. This is the basis for the remark made at the head of this paragraph, to the effect that deep in our own moral and political foundations there is a kinship with the extreme moral principle named after "Rights," leading to undiluted calculation.

But the assertion was also made that as a nation we have an affinity for the opposite moral extreme as well, the one called by the name of "absolute Duty." Long ago, the reduction of morality to the rules of calculation was seen to be open to various objections. One line of objection was to the effect that when morality collapses into mere calculation, patriotism or love of the common good tends to languish or to disappear. This view when broadened or exaggerated becomes the criticism that, under the reign of private calculation or institutionalized egotism, care for the absolute worth or dignity of man as man vanishes, and life deteriorates accordingly in the moral respect. Those who hold this view feel a need to oppose "human rights" to "property rights." The objection on behalf of patriotism or civic virtue found a certain expression in the yearning for republican, agrarian simplicity often voiced in our earlier history. The criticism on behalf of man as man is more characteristic of the reforming or Liberal tendency as it now is among us. What began as solicitude for a sort of virtue that can become patriotism has been replaced by a solicitude for humanity or Society, a care that need not eventuate in patriotism.

Thus our moral life as a nation vibrates between the poles of calculation and a radicalized alternative to it, the former polarizing on Property, the latter on hostility to it and on radical, undiscriminating Equality. The former is at the heart of our national conservatism, the latter epitomizes contemporary Liberalism. Neither is in its nature oriented upon the sovereign good or the good of the country as men's profound concern: neither pays heed above all to honor, the sober mean somewhere between calculation and duty.

There is indeed a lack of perfect congruity between our ruling moral predilections and the preferred moral basis of international action. But if we must act on the strength of what we are rather than what we might wish to be, there is little doubt as to the course we ought to follow. One of the two poles of our moral world stands as an encouragement to men to love their theory of homogeneous mankind more than they love their country and their countrymen, where the demands of the two come in competition. The other pole, grounded on the perhaps low but surely solid principle of calculation, is not out of contact with the intermediate moral ground of decent self-regard or honor. Husbanding our strength, gathering our allies, and preparing to avoid the supreme disaster of servility and disgrace, we at least avoid the imprudence of opposing armed brutality with impotent dogma. Our enemey is abundantly furnished with dogma, but his action is notably unobstructed by it. His moral ground contains two elements, as does our own. One of them, if made the spring of his action, would bring down his regime and his empire in instant ruin. It is no less than the replacement of political life as known on earth by an absolute morality, to be inculcated among men by the economic institutions of communism. The other is Revolution—its necessity, its goodness, its inevitability. They are respectively his end and his means. The first is never allowed to get in the way of the second, which is the ruling element of his moral nature. It behooves us to remain in touch with our adversary on this simple level in order to oppose him—undistracted by sentimental dogma which he mocks, game theory which he ignores, and all other sophistications that are wasted upon a political intelligence which rightly or wrongly regards coercion as the ultimate rationality. Under the circumstances, we may allow ourselves to be led by calculation where perhaps we cannot be taught to soar by honor.

We began by thinking of man's duty to mankind. Reflecting on morality in its connection with the deeds of nations, we could not avoid the themes of honor and nobility, or more largely of human excellence. Human excellence, as if finds its expression among the masses of men ranked in their nations, is called civilization. Whatever reminds us of civilization reminds us at the same time of our duty to civilization, which means in practice to civilized men. What begins as a reflection on duty to man ends, under the influence of a glimpse at human superiority, as a reflection on duty to civilized man and to civilized nations. The way to discharge our duty to civilization is to sustain it where it exists before trying to inspire it where it never has been. Upon this point, remote from doctrinairism, the morality of calculation and the morality of honor come within sight of one another. The resulting gain in strategic competence brings them within earshot of one another. We must not despair if they never join hands.

The Right of Foreign Aid

Reprinted from *Why Foreign
Aid?* edited by Robert A.
Goldwin (Chicago: Rand
McNally and Company, 1963).
©1962, 1963 by The Public
Affairs Conference Center,
The University of Chicago.

This essay addresses a question which can be stated with complete
simplicity, but which, contrary to opinion, cannot be answered except
with some difficulty. The question is whether a wealthy nation, say the
United States, has a moral duty to extend aid to the undeveloped
countries. Throughout, the attempt will be made to observe the distinction
between duty and interest as strictly as possible. Whether it is to our
interest to strengthen the economy or the military establishment of an
undeveloped country is in large measure an empirical question, to be
resolved by noting whether the recipient nations are in fact strengthened
by our help, whether they become well affected toward us as a result of
being helped by us, and so on. Whether, on the other hand, we have a
duty to extend such aid is not an empirical question; one cannot point to
facts and let them speak for themselves, prescribing our obligations to us.
We can progress toward the answer only by reflection.

The question whether we have a duty to extend foreign aid is of special
concern precisely because mere duty and interest, as different as another's
benefit is from one's own, can easily conflict. We can never rest easy, nor

be united in our policies, if the suspicion exists that what we do for others we do out of duty but against our interest. Moreover, not all men will be satisfied with policies that aim at our advantage but which appear at the same time to violate a duty to benefit other human beings. Because of the possibility that duty and interest will conflict, the grounds of each must be investigated in the light of the distinction.

In this paper, it will be assumed that if foreign aid should be contrary to our interest, there is a very strong presumption against giving it; and if it turns out to be to our advantage, there is an equally strong presumption in favor of giving it. We shall not take up the question whether it is in fact beneficial or contrary to our interest. In either case it is necessary for us to know whether there is a duty to extend it—a duty which is perhaps so compelling that we could be justly convicted of selfishness and hypocrisy if we withheld it, notwithstanding the very strong presumption against giving it if it is contrary to our interest.

The discussion that follows consists of four parts. The first three parts take up, in turn, the three principles which are commonly appealed to, tacitly or openly, by those who speak of our duty, or our moral duty, to give freely to the undeveloped populations. The first of these principles or grounds for giving is the sentiment of fellow-feeling with others in their sufferings. It is a fact that men are compassionate of the sufferings of other sentient beings, and that they feel an impulse to be charitable. Our first task is to take up the question whether the inclination to compassion or charity is rooted in our human nature in such a way as to oblige us with the force of duty.

In the second place, we must consider whether the meaning of the modern scientific project—the conquest of nature—does not imply an obligation on the part of the advanced nations to mitigate the miseries of the backward.

Thirdly, we must inquire whether our democratic principles impose upon us, by virtue of their appeal to the rights of man, a duty to all humanity whose cause is proclaimed in the Declaration of Independence.

In the fourth part a resolution of the question is presented in the form of a statement of the ground of our national duty, somewhat different from those enumerated.

The question of policy before us is in some measure a theoretical one, and though this may be deplored it cannot be helped. The practical issues are in fact questions of what it is right and prudent to do in crucial conjunctures. Right and prudent always have opposites. It is the task of high authority to discriminate between the one course to be followed and the many courses to be avoided, by ascending as far as need be to the truths that illuminate experience and transform it into understanding. It is self-evident that age brings experience without fail, but understanding only in some cases. If facts do not speak for themselves, we must put a pressure upon them. They stand in relation to us as patients, passive things or things acted upon; and we are the agents, the acting beings who operate with them. There is no other way to understanding. This truth does not stand in need of apology; but we must allow ourselves to be reminded that theoretical inquiry, like a proud servant, will not do its office where it is not made welcome.

I

Wretchedness and poverty so far preponderate over well-being in the world that it is surely more feasible to count the comfortable than to measure the world's destitution. It is very fitting that the prosperous should give a thought to the miserable, and reflect on how the matter stands between them—what are the duties of affluence and what are the rightful claims of privation. As citizens in a wealthy nation, we learn something from the contempt in which men of means are held who take no pity on the worthy poor that come in their way. Further, among the wealthy we make a distinction. We do not admire, but we can concede something to the reasoning of the niggard who starts from his own frugality and concludes with a certain indifference to the privations of others. But how can we exculpate those who surfeit themselves, while under their feet the children of poverty learn the way of brutes in the school of starvation? We gratuitously insult the suffering as well as the opinion of mankind if we gormandize while a parent anywhere must stop his ears against the cries of his unfed young. Hunger accuses satiety, and comfort seems to owe an expiation to wretchedness.

The natural compassion of man reaches down to the faceless insects themselves. Darwin wrote of the pity he felt for a wasp struggling for life in the strands of a spider's net. The sympathy that we feel for the members of our race is only part of a sentiment we are capable of feeling for any sentient thing. Apparently there is a law of our nature that bids us relieve the sufferings of all things able to suffer, and certainly of our fellow-men wherever they may be. We appear to incline toward a universal charity.

If that inclination were sufficiently powerful in us, it would have as much the force of duty as our inclination and duty to multiply. The inclination toward a universal charity would confirm us in what we believe, apart from inclination or sentiment, to be our duty: we owe something to the other members of our species because of the similarity they bear to us. Like naturally goes together with like. Our care for others is part of our care for ourselves.

The scope of man's duty to man would appear thus to extend to the horizon. It is all-inclusive, comprehending everything that, like ourselves, can suffer. As soon as we say so, we are troubled by the failure of that rule to accord with many of the common practices of mankind which could not to a healthy mind appear objectionable. No one, for example, objects to the extinction of malaria-bearing mosquitoes or plague-ridden rats, although it is true that many men would be squeamish about themselves destroying the vermin which they know must be eliminated, just as they might be converted to vegetarianism if they had to slaughter the animals on whose flesh they gladly nourish themselves. It is clear that the sentiment of compassion a man can feel for the brutes' sufferings cannot be directly translated into a duty to the brutes on the mere ground of their being sentient things as we are. Our feeling about their feeling is in need of a rational correction, as we demonstrate by our use of them.

It is true that the brutes resemble us in being sentient; yet by our acts we evince our understanding that sentience does not put them upon such a level with us that we may not do with them as we see fit, even to taking away their lives for our bare convenience or pleasure. It is not their sentience or capacity to suffer pain and to fear death that determines our use of the brutes, but something else, perhaps reason, which is the basis of so profound a distinction between them and us that an assertion of their rights against us is unthinkable. If duties are the correlate of rights, then it is clear that as the brutes have no rights against their superiors in the order of nature, so men have no duties to them, notwithstanding their capacity for terror and pain. In the same sense in which a superhuman being could not be said to have a duty to man, man cannot be said to have a duty to the subhuman beings.

Certainly a man is to be blamed who cruelly abuses his brutes. Brutality is the name given to his offense; and by committing it he will arouse the indignation of a humane society. As the words brutal and humane imply, those who stand higher in the order of nature forfeit their station when they deal with the lower simply according to the way of the lower. It is amazing but true that if we did not begin by recognizing the inferiority of the brutes, we would not have the contempt for brutal men which becomes the ground for humane treatment of the brutes. It is important that this be understood, for it is a refutation of the belief that considerate behavior flows only from a duty in the agent which is correlative with rights in the patient; and that, rights existing only among equals, wherever there is to be considerate behavior, it is necessary to postulate the fundamental equality of the actor and the one acted upon—say, in that both have a strong love of life, or are equally capable of similar sentiments.

Our sympathy evidently reaches to myriad places in animate nature where we have no duties founded upon the rights of the sentient things that are acted upon. Moreover, bare sympathy or fellow-feeling is an imperfect guide to obligation for other reasons than those which are revealed by reflecting upon the status of dumb animals. For example, men compelled to observe the execution of a condemned criminal would certainly do so with some feeling; yet apart from any question as to the rightness of the verdict or the justice of the sentence, they would not feel a sense of duty to help him avoid his fate. The agitation engendered in a witness by the paroxysms of a strangling convict may be tantamount to an impulse to save him; but sympathy with the condemned man is over-weighed by sympathy for his victim and other considerations, and the criminal is left to perish. Reason must arbitrate among the sentiments, or else actions become arbitrary—based ultimately on the pleasure and brute strength of the most violent men.

The suffering criminal exemplifies the human being whose pains are brought upon him by his guilt. But the suffering of the destitute may be brought upon them by misfortune rather than by anything for which they or anyone else could be responsible. What if not chance causes a blameless child to grow into a blameless but bad man in the midst of a natural waste? The land is poor and hunger is his portion, but through no one's fault: no one is responsible, not he nor any other human being. In truth, no one is responsible for the sufferings of men whose pains have their source in simple misfortune or chance. We would have a duty to the purely unfortunate at the other end of the world if duty were wholly unconnected with responsibility. To be responsible means literally to be answerable. He who is answerable for the ill is answerable for the remedy; but he who has only looked on intervenes to relieve the sufferer gratuitously, not out of duty. The intervention of the benefactor might make us love him; his indifference might make us loathe him; but his intervention cannot be demanded of him as a moral duty that is correlative with a right belonging to the one in misery.

This conclusion seems offensive to what ordinary humanity requires us to answer when we ask, Am I my brother's keeper? It is, however, not so obviously offensive to it as at first appears: for men conceive a care and affection for their brothers which they do not and cannot feel for unknown beings on remote continents. A man at the other end of the world cannot and ought not presume to claim what a parent, a brother, or a child might reasonably expect. That a man should keep his brother from harm is not to say that he is guilty as long as a human being anywhere exists who is poorer than himself. On the contrary, to acknowledge a duty of universal charity would be to enslave the rational and industrious to the rest. Worse than that, it would make an odious concession to the mere desire of the poor for comfort and wealth. The mere desire for prosperity, so far from deserving to be encouraged with alms, is in itself scarcely respectable, but is rendered more so by the industry and discipline that it brings on in those who labor to satisfy it. The desire for wealth which is not accompanied by the impulse to generate it through labor and forethought may be dismissed as a form of vulgar envy, made uglier by laziness. We conclude that a duty to relieve the suffering of our fellow human beings, for example through foreign aid, may not be deduced from the injunction of a sentiment of universal charity.

II

We could thus leave the backward nations to extricate themselves from their difficulties as well as they can except so far as it benefits us to help them, if the duty of universal brotherhood meant simply the duty of universal almsgiving. But we are told occasionally that it means something far more than charity so narrowly understood. When we consider how man stands in relation to the whole of external nature, we appreciate how tight is the bond that draws into unison the members of our rational species. All together, we face external nature as a dual adversary: it is the enigma in which are wrapped the mysteries of our origins and our ends; and it is the inhospitable quarry from which we must gain the materials of survival and the equipment for a civilized life. Nature is both a riddle to the mind and a reluctant harvest in a stony field. We draw our theories and our subsistence from her grasp with almost equal difficulty. It has been said that the highest task of man, of mankind as a whole, is to establish its intellectual and technical supremacy in the world by conquering nature—discovering her secrets and turning her matter to human use. It is not a part but all of humanity that is bewildered and confined in the matrix of nature; it is the task, indeed the humanizing mission of man to emancipate himself from nature entirely. Only when he has penetrated to every significant truth—about matter, life, and disease, for example—and learned how to do whatever seems good to him—even to sowing human life on other globes in the outer spaces, and to remaking human nature itself—only then will man dominate his cosmic antagonist and dissolve the natural matrix that contains him. The freedom of mankind as a whole is imperfect as long as we are compelled to admit that there are things unknown to us and other things impossible.

The unity of mankind evidently need not be made to rest upon a vague and self-contradicting sentimentality, but rather can be inferred, it seems, from our status as a species in the order of nature. The function of man is to make use of his innate powers in order to realize his perfect freedom from bondage to nature. Perfect mastery of nature as the highest human possibility is the life-activity of the human species: it is our business on earth or beyond earth. In this task we participate as a species, for only a rational animal could conceive or execute such a plan, and all men participate in the rational nature of their species. On this ground the whole of mankind can be said to be one, and united in the contest with nature.

When science will have won its final victory, the argument for the universal responsibility of all men for all men will no longer be vulnerable to the rejoinder that only he who is answerable for the ill is answerable for the remedy. The blameless child who grows into the bad but blameless man in a barren waste will be relieved by science, which will abolish barren wastes, turning every desert into a garden, overcoming the mischances of individuals: chance will claim no more victims. The common human enterprise will bear fruit in a universal abundance which will bring relief to every human being, and every human being will be entitled to demand relief as his right because the mastery of nature is the work of humanity at large.

Swept on by the catholic benevolence of science, we are in danger of forgetting why we are engaged in discussing science. The reason is that the human kind is divided between the advanced and the backward. The backward are so, with respect to the standard of living surely, to say nothing of political influence, because science is an exotic among them. It belongs to and has its home among only some of the nations. No one knows where it may one day become domesticated; everyone knows that it now flourishes in the minor fraction of the human race. Science might be the human project in the sense described above only if it were the universal human project equally distributed among the peoples of the world.

Evidently a grave objection exists against beginning with the scientific project and ending, as if by inference from it, with universal benevolence in the form of a duty to extend foreign aid. The excellence of science and its essential human-ness are, as was said, intimately connected. If the emphatically human activity is science, then men stand higher in the order of humanity if they are more scientific, lower if they are less so. Alternatively, a more scientific nation is more civilized than a less scientific one. Science is not in fact the project of the whole human kind but of some parts of it more than others. The existence and the power of science do not point to a duty of the advanced and scientific peoples to relieve the backward; the existence and power of science simply raise again in another connection the question whether there is a duty of the more advanced to the less, based upon a genuine right of the less advanced. The elevation of science to the hope and the principle of humanity causes such a qualitative gap to open between the scientific and the subscientific parts of mankind that the subscientific portion's claim to consideration *as a right* is proportionally weakened.

The scientific project is not, as such, the basis for a duty of the developed to the undeveloped. Nothing intrinsic to science requires the scientist to benefit the non-scientist rather than simply to benefit himself and his society—for his society is host to his laboratory—and to relieve his own estate to the utmost. If it be argued that the underprivileged will look on in a mood of deepening envy and resentment until they are ready to erupt in plunder, then the answer is, either repel them by the power of science under arms, or mollify them with whatever is needed to distract their restlessness. Such policies are intelligible and could easily be defended; but like the argument to which they are a reply, they have to do not with duty but with interest.

As it happens, there is a deeper reason for doubting that the scientific project points toward universal benevolence. That reason is the essentially qualified goodness of the scientific project itself, that is, of the absolute subversion of nature by man in the name of an unimaginable, trans-democratic because transpolitical freedom. Let us reconsider the meaning of the scientific conquest of nature, thinking first of the relation in which man and nature stand to one another. By nature we shall mean "the way all things are which men have not made," whether we can explain how or why they came to be so or not. Included in nature is also "the way men are," for certainly we are not our own creatures. Then nature, including human nature, is something that stands over against us, that has a way of its own, different from how we would have it if we had the making of it according to our own plan. The things we make we control, fashioning them to achieve some purpose or good of ours; but the unyielding things that exist according to a scheme not our own compel us to accommodate ourselves to them. We must plan our acts so that we do not dash ourselves against the intransigence of an uncompromising world.

As long, therefore, as man must take account of an unyielding "other," something which exists by a plan that is not his own and which refuses to lend itself to the purposes of his good pleasure; and which in fact will wound him or destroy him if he flaunts its tendencies—as long as man is opposed by such an "other," there is at least one firm criterion for judging the goodness of his own doings: he does well when, at the very least, he does not violate the conditions of existence laid down by that "other" with which he must coexist. And when that "other" is no less than nature itself, meaning the way man himself is and the way the universe external to man is, then the criterion of his well-doing is very comprehensive indeed. He is, so to speak, formed by the opposition of an unyielding "other" in the way that iron is formed against the anvil. The intractable "other" provides a frame of reference for judging of human actions by constituting the conditions within which all human action must occur.

As men we have the visible shape that we do because the inflexibility of the skeleton imparts it to us. In other ways our life is as it is because, for example, we cannot control the weather, the climate, and the sex of babies, to say nothing of the manner of our coming into being and the inevitability of our passing away. We are in thrall to nature, and our servitude is at the same time the fundamental condition of our lives and the background for judging whether we act ill or well. But the project of science is to throw off the bondage of nature, and to emancipate man by giving him autonomy in nature, with the understanding that autonomy in nature must mean rule over nature and nothing less. Perfect autonomy would mean the state of being absolutely unconditioned.

It is beside the point to rejoin that science seeks to discover the laws of nature and therefore aims at a more perfect obedience rather than at sovereignty. The nearest analogy to the case would be the discovery by a subject of the whole fundamental law of his king's behavior. Who can doubt that that subject would then be able to rule the king? He who masters the law of the lawgiver can master the lawgiver and take his place. There is no higher rule than that which governs the legislator.

When this is understood, we may perceive why in principle science cannot dictate a moral duty to relieve the backward. The meaning of science is given by its intention, not by the feasibility of that intention; and the intention of science is to liberate man utterly from the alien framework that controls, informs, and guides him. But an absolutely uncontrolled, uninformed, unguided being has no relation of obligation to any "other." And now it is of supreme importance to recollect that science is not the possession of all men but only of the scientists. Not mankind but those in possession of science would become the absolutely unconditioned beings. The profundity of the chasm between the scientific and subscientific people becomes obvious when we remember that the scientific conquest of nature includes the conquest, that is the reformation, of human nature. Those men who know how to remake man would have the power to transform the subscientific human beings into docile slaves as well as into scientists or whole human beings. It is impossible to persuade the scientist that he ought to elect to make every man a free, full-flowering, active, self-expressing savant except on the ground that every man should be enabled to give full expression to his natural faculties, actual or only possible. But that argument above all is without merit for the purpose because it presupposes human nature and the flowering of human nature as we know it, while the scientist lives for the transcendence of that nature and is in fact necessarily indecisive as to what sort of nature he ought to implant in man in place of that which now exists.

To determine whether natural science implies a standard of moral obligation is not a school exercise but a matter of grave political concern; and whether it implies a moral obligation in the greater toward the less is precisely one of the points on which we must satisfy ourselves if we are to have any confidence that our programs of foreign aid are neither marred by stinginess nor founded on weak sentimentality. Science, which has had so much to do with shaping our times, has as its principle and epitome, Knowledge is Power. No generation has had clearer ocular evidence than ours has to show that there is nothing in science itself that tends to limit the direction or extent of its own development. Surely no one will undertake to say what miracles will have been performed, barring catastrophes, in a century; and in a millennium, the Creation replicated. Nothing intrinsic to science or power limits or prescribes the use to which power is put, as we can prove to ourselves if we consider the standing of an agent made omnicompetent by his omnisapience.

Toward whom could the omnicompetent re-creator of nature be thought to have a duty, and what would be the ground for the existence of a duty binding such a being? He could be imagined to have a duty to his prospective creatures, that is, to the whole of human and non-human being about to take shape under his hands. We see how problematic the existence of such a duty is when we try to understand what the omnicompetent agent would be bound to perform, and why or how, being omnicompetent, he could be bound. As to the first part of the question, it might be thought that the Agent has a duty to make a good world, consisting of good men and a proper inanimate environment to support or encourage their goodness. We shall not stop to try to understand what could be meant by a good world. It is hard enough to understand the goodness of parts, which can be judged by how well they are articulated to form a whole; but to judge the whole, we have perhaps nothing to fall back on but existence itself: the whole is good if it exists, that is, if it is not destroyed by internal contradictions. Since it is not open to human scientists to bring the whole into being, their project for the perfect conquest of nature is perhaps not to be construed absolutely or literally. Still, the question of the standard of goodness for the beings they can re-form persists. We shall not try to answer it; our problem is, does the omnicompetent agent have a duty to make his objects one way rather than another—say, free rather than servile—or to put them into one state of being rather than another, for their advantage.

Duty as moral obligation is a bond upon those for whom there exists an "other" that matters. Why does the "other" matter? Either by prescription of law laid down by a greater power; or because of a calculation of the benefit of the one acting; or gratuitously out of the desire of the one acting. But a duty of the omnicompetent scientist to his objects cannot follow from the legislation of a greater power than omnicompetence as such, for there is none. Nor can the dictate of the agent's benefit be called a ground of duty; the proper name for that motive is calculation. Nor is the gratuitous desire of the powerful agent the ground of his duty; on the contrary, what is done gratuitously is by that very fact not done out of the right of the patient or out of any duty binding the agent.

Thus it follows that if science means the conquest of nature, and knowledge is the power of conquering nature, then the possession of scientific knowledge as such carries with it no *duty* to improve man's condition but only a possibility of doing so. Their possession of science does not impose a duty upon the advanced nations to assist the others. This is not to say that the powerful and prosperous ought not to succor the weak and wretched, but that the latter have no right growing out of a duty in the former, imposed upon them by their power and prosperity, to benefit the backward.

III

Fortunately for the cause of philanthropy, the fact that there is not implicit in the power of science a restraining duty to the unscientific need not mean that the power of science is restrained by nothing at all. On the contrary, precisely because the power of science is presumed (by science) to reach indefinitely far in all directions, it does not reach in one direction rather than another. Since the improvement of man's condition is a meaningless phrase unless it rests upon clear notions of the difference between making conditions better and making them worse, the power to make the human condition better must be guided by men who possess knowledge of the difference between better and worse for human beings. But that knowledge is of the sort needed by men who direct other men's actions; it is the knowledge needed by legislators. Scientists as such must, as in practice they do, come under law, under human law, under human legislators, and thus under political authority. Scientists or the ministers of supreme physical power are under the jurisdiction of political authority; science itself is or may be brought under that authority, for science is an activity of human beings. Therefore the possibility exists that out of the ascendancy of politics over science, as of the human over the subhuman, a duty arises that causes the power over nature to activate an engine of beneficence.

We cannot here take up in its own right the question how far science can or must be brought under political prudence. But we are entitled to make this purely deductive remark: All those who refuse to live with the conclusion that science leads to no duty of benevolence, and who then turn to the ascendancy of political judgment over scientific power, must then recognize that they have conceded the insufficiency of the broad scientific project as it conceives itself; and that they have done so because science provides powerful means but gives no humane guidance as to ends. Liberal-minded men who find themselves dissatisfied with the scientific outlook are in fact dissatisfied with the moral neutrality of science. It may be assumed that they are a fortiori dissatisfied with that scientization of social science that deprives even political science of the moral content appropriate to it, more emphatically than science proper is so deprived.

Instead of the general question, Does the political control of science imply that the monopolists of science have a duty to relieve the estate of the backward, we will confine ourselves to the more limited question of United States policy, in the following form: Is there something in the nature of democracy that imposes a duty of universal beneficence upon a democratic nation?

The answer seems implicit in the words of the Declaration of Independence: "We hold these truths to be self-evident, that all men are created equal, that they are endowed by their Creator with certain inalienable Rights, that among these are Life, Liberty, and the pursuit of Happiness." We govern ourselves, only a part of mankind, by the light of a principle that we assert to be true of all mankind. We appeal to nature and the nature of man and to the laws of nature, and by that same appeal we appeal to the single humanity of men everywhere. The bond of equality among all men is made the bond of equality among Americans. If the natural equality of all men is the constituting principle of democracy, then perhaps it is wrong for us to enjoy prosperity while others, our equals, are in adversity, to be well fed while others are hungry, to live out our three score years and ten while others are destined at birth to perish before the prime of life. The ruling principle of democracy encompasses all humanity; men may be excused for supposing that the ruling principle of democracy imposes upon democrats a duty to all humanity.

It must be allowed that the great Declaration does not dwell upon moral duties, nor does it emphasize the transcendent unity of mankind in opposition to the dividedness of mankind into nations. The Declaration is a statement of rights, not of duties; the only duty mentioned is the duty that men have to enforce their natural rights when other men violate them. And assuredly the Declaration is an announcement of political independence, of emphatic distinctness from the rest of mankind: "separate and equal" is the language of the Declaration to describe the station of Americans among the nations. The equality of all men in their natural rights is of no practical effect until there is political society to put those rights in steady execution: "to secure these Rights, Governments are instituted among Men." Democracy is a form of government, it emphatically presupposes political life and therewith the division of the world into nations. It does not view man directly as a natural being, a member of a species, over the barriers so to speak of conventional distinction. Democracy recognizes, as it could not exist without recognizing, the difference between fellow-citizens and aliens. Thus wherever the Constitution pronounces that certain things may or shall not be done, it means they may or shall not be done where the Constitution has authority; it lays down the law primarily to Americans as such. Democracy, in brief, is a form of government, a political regime predicated upon the belief that the enjoyment of the natural or universal rights depends on the conventional, political particularization of mankind into separate, viable bodies, namely, nations, under government. Democracy is not a basis for the amalgamation of the human kind into one mass and it neither depends upon nor leads up to a fundamental moral duty.

Whether or not it is paradoxical, it is yet true that the democratic teaching of the Declaration begins with natural equality but does so in order to conserve conventional inequality, for example, inequality of wealth and inequality of political authority, which is what is meant by government. The democratic teaching of the Declaration and the Constitution contains nothing that is intended to afflict the conscience of wealth or power lawfully obtained and employed. True as this is in the relations of fellow-citizens one with another, it is a fortiori true in respect of the rest of the world.

If we were compelled to speculate on the reason that our democratic principles are so free from the taint of misdirected egalitarianism, we might look for the answer in some writings of the draftsman of the Declaration. In his *Notes on the State of Virginia* (toward the end of Query XIV), Jefferson describes a scheme for the competitive, progressively selective education of the young. His plan would operate by passing the students upward through a school system that sifted them and reduced their numbers drastically as they moved from one stage to the next higher. By means of these dismissals, "the best geniuses will be raked from the rubbish annually." Jefferson speaks freely of boys (not boys and girls) of "superior parts" and "superior genius." The natural equality that is intrinsic to our democratic principles is not all-inclusive. It coexists with natural inequalities of the sort that Jefferson knew and that we know will assert themselves in every classroom. The fundamental principles of democracy do not contemplate an undifferentiated humanity. It is impossible to infer from the classic democracy of the Declaration of Independence and the Constitution of the United States a duty to mankind, partly because it is impossible to infer from that democracy a limitless egalitarianism. Our fundamental democratic principles depreciate neither certain natural nor certain conventional inequalities. In other words our democratic equalitarianism is political, not universalistic.

It is not to be supposed that every group or nation constituted by a universal principle (such as that all men are created equal) is obliged by the universality of its principle as if by a moral duty to all men. This becomes clear when we consider our moral duty to beings who are undoubtedly men, but who are not ruled by our universal principle, or who indeed are ruled by an antithetic universal principle. It is evident that we do not have a moral duty to extend foreign aid to Red China, and the reason is that their universal principle would destroy ours. In the same way, churches do not always take seriously the argument that, because they teach the fatherhood of God and the brotherhood of man, they have a duty to comfort pagans, heretics, or even schismatics as such. The reason for this is not obscure: the goodness or truth of each universal principle implies the goodness of the practical influence of that principle upon living, acting men. It is not possible rationally to believe in the goodness of democracy and at the same time to interpret democracy as if it implies a duty that is destructive of democracy by being antithetic to the existence of democratic nations as such. If democracy implies a moral duty of any kind, it is to cultivate those qualities suited to keep democracies alive, which is as much as to say, it obliges us to preserve ourselves.

A very small nation may be constituted by a very large principle. Ancient Israel was petty as a nation; its constitution was vastly comprehensive. It is wrong and dangerous to suppose that the universality of our democratic principle obliges or even entitles us to act toward other men as if our universal principle had universal applicability. In order to make it possible for us to act toward all men as if our universal principle were in force or had authority among all men, it would be necessary for us to extend our rule over all men or at least to propagate democracy among them universally. What duty that might spring from the goodness of democracy could exceed in vitality the duty to spread the source of that goodness, democracy itself, to every corner of the earth? The danger and the infeasibility of such imperialism in the name of a theory is proved through the conduct of our adversaries, who also subscribe to certain universal propositions, assertions about all men, and who wish to act upon those principles toward all men. Inevitably we and others resist. Resistance is inevitable because there are many—how many is hard to say—universal propositions, assertions about all men, that can be maintained and that might even be true. That all men are created equal is one universal principle; that they incline toward the good is another; and that they are determined in their natures by their material conditions is a third. If political life and therewith national "duties" are to be founded upon each nation's extension in practice of its own universal theory, there will be no alternative but for diplomacy to turn into dialectic or war. The former is impossible, the latter undesirable. The conclusion is that we must be content to cultivate our own democratic vineyard and to sit in the shade of our constitutional doctrines without imagining that, because the Thirteenth Amendment follows from a truth about all men, it is *ipso facto* the guide to our action upon all men. It is not and cannot be so; it does and is meant to govern the conduct of Americans toward other Americans, of men who owe allegiance to the Constitution. It has literally no meaning if read in any other sense.

This is not to say that the nation must not act in defense of its life principle. On the contrary, it must so act; the Declaration teaches this as a duty. But there is no such thing as a duty implicit in democracy to act democratically in defense of democracy. Therefore the government's actions in defense of democracy have the essential character of deeds done in the interest of living democracy, that is, of democratic nations; they do not in principle have the character of deeds done out of a universal duty inferred from the universal principle that lies at the heart of democracy.

The foregoing has been intended to show that the democracy of the great Declaration and of the Constitution does not imply or presuppose the radical unity of the human race in such a sense as to impose duties of beneficence upon the prosperous. Neither its substantive teaching as to equality nor the formal universality of that teaching makes it possible to deduce from our democratic principle such a duty as would convert science into an engine of universal beneficence under the tutelage of democracy.

IV

It is very difficult to demonstrate, either from the sentiment of charity, or from the significance of the scientific project for the melioration of man's estate, or from the principles of democracy itself, that there is a duty to relieve the wretched, or that adversity has a moral right to be succored by prosperity. It is even more difficult to obliterate from the human heart a fellow-feeling with fellow-men, a sense of compassion for the pains of other beings and, indeed, even of sympathy with their pleasures to some extent. Certainly compassion for the pains of others can be explained as the result of our putting ourselves in the place of the sufferers, of our imagining pain and then weakly experiencing it in some form. To explain compassion in this way is to imply that what we do to relieve the sufferer we do in order to remove a cause of pain in ourselves. Acting so is to obey something different from the dictate of moral duty. Nevertheless, however human sympathy may be explained or explained away, men who lack it are doubtless capable of the most extreme brutality, for they feel nothing for their victims and can therefore give way to the cruelest passions. At the very least, compassion acts as a bond among men, heightened when the beautiful, the well-endowed, or the eminent suffer; stimulated by the sights and sounds of agony but soothed by an aversion of the eyes and a stopping of the ears; weakened by the competition of self-interest; diminished to nothing by long habituation as in sport arenas, in abattoirs, at the scaffold, on fields of battle, or even in hospitals of mercy; and capable of being distracted and turned into its opposite by indignation or the appetite for revenge.

Compassion is not itself the basis for the unity of the human race, but it reminds us of the fact of that unity. Our question whether there is a duty to extend aid abroad cannot be answered unless we can give an account of that unity, determining at last whether we are all one in such a sense that, in principle, the blessings of the few belong in part to the unblessed many, or whether we are one in some other sense. Now it is self-evident that the human race is a unity that consists of parts or elements, and it is evident from our having to discuss foreign aid that some parts are in a condition to which the others aspire, but not vice versa. Whether one civilization more truly deserves the name than does another is surely a difficult question, one that we need not answer here; but we cannot abstain from noting that the question of the difference in the levels of civilization is implicit in the wish of some nations to resemble others or to resemble them in some respects, and also in the opinion that prevails among the advanced that they should share the basis or the fruits of their progress with the backward. Some nations must borrow the means and arts of war and subsistence, other nations are compelled to draw on foreigners for the theoretical goods. We will not try to say whether being a receiver in one of these senses is outweighed by being a giver in the other. But we can say with ease and certainty that to be a receiver in both senses is the mark of being in a backward state of civilization. Manifestly the human race is a unity as it is distinguished from everything non-human, just as each family is a unit in distinction to everything outside it. But within each family there is an unmistakable subordination and superordination of the members, and similarly in the articulated unity of the human kind as a whole. Surely all the members of a family are equal in belonging to the human race; but they are unequal in so many other respects that it would be absurd to speak only of the duties of parents and the rights of children, never of the duties of the subordinate members and the prerogatives of the more competent. The duties are different on the one side from those on the other: the duties of providing and educating on the side of superior competence, and the duties of obedience and helpfulness on the other side. Those who would persuade us that there is a duty to extend foreign aid can scarcely expect to succeed as long as they appear to argue that that duty carries with it no corresponding prerogative on our part nor a correlative duty on the part of the nations whose condition compels them to sue for assistance. It is false and harmful to argue from subordination and superordination as the grounds of duty in the superior, and then to deny all other consequences because they do not flatter our undiscriminating prejudices.

The distinction between those imagined to have a duty to extend help and those who, being backward, need it is the distinction between those who stand at a certain stage of life and those who hope to be set in motion toward it. It is elementary that every thing which is in a state of change should be discussed and treated in the light of where it is at the moment, as well as by reference to what it might some day be. The child who is treated as if he were already wise is at a disadvantage in comparison with the child who is treated as if he is now ignorant but may be impelled toward a better state. Only by a compounding of cant and illogic can it be asserted that the difference between greater and less must positively be eradicated and is at the same time of no significance. If it be thought that the practical consequence of such notions is a tutelage of the lesser to the greater, then that possibility must be faced; and though it be granted that such a state would be deplorable, yet it would be as nothing in comparison with the effects of a doctrinaire abdication by the greater of their wealth, their influence, and eventually their fate to the concourse of rude and barely emergent humanity.

Men wish it were possible to treat with potentiality as if it were actuality, with childhood as if it were maturity, with cannibals as if they were citizens, with what is not as if it were. To act so is to give way to self-deception and to deny that there is a necessity in things to which we must bend our wills, however freely we may exercise them after acknowledging the ascendancy of that necessity.

To appeal to necessity is not to make a ground for renouncing the discipline of moral obligation. By a too simple view, necessity can be made synonymous with the demand of self-preservation, and then a man who preserves himself by deserting his friends, betraying his country, and sheltering behind a parapet of his heaped-up victims can be exculpated by the rule of necessity. Worse yet, the man who murders in a blinding rage or from the prompting of a cruel and perverted nature could be said to act from necessity and thus to be exempt from blame and punishment. We must evidently discriminate the end to which necessity is properly directed if we are to avoid criminal mistakes, for it is not enough that vice is necessary for a bad man's pleasure, that he be exonerated or even encouraged.

I take it that "to be" or to continue to be is the impulse and tendency of everything that is; and that a thing most emphatically is when it is self-sufficient, or as little as possible exposed to being put out of existence because of the presence or absence of something alien to itself. Moreover, a thing "is" more emphatically or more completely when it is capable of all the acts that one of its type can in principle attain to: a dog is more a dog with four legs than with three, and with a courageous heart than without one. This double meaning of "to be" is reflected in the double meaning of "perfect": complete in itself, and excellently good. I take it to be necessary or of the nature of necessity that things and men strive to be in this double sense.

To obey necessity and thus to seek the means of their being is the law of the nature of men and nations. The precept of that law is delivered in tones that ring with the call to duty. To be bound to the necessary means to shun superfluity and insufficiency. Men deviate from the necessary when they fail to make prudent provision and when they wallow in a surfeit. To kill wantonly is to kill superfluously, unnecessarily, and therefore to commit an act of vice. Gossip differs from testimony in that it is gratuitous, there is no reason for it; and it generally earns contempt. When an act is unnecessary, there is no reason for it or behind it. The things men do for which they do not strictly speaking have a reason are strictly speaking not reasonable. This does not mean they originate without a cause. It means they originate from an unreasonable cause: envy, lust, malice, megalomania, avarice, or any one of a baker's dozen. The rational and the moral find a common ground in the necessary: the avoidance of the insufficient, the superfluous, and the inessential or untrue. From this maxim we learn our duty with respect to the backward or the simply needy.

We have indeed a duty as a nation not to deprave ourselves in a glut of baubles; and as citizens, not to decay into a brawling pack which spends its manliness in squabbling over the same baubles. It is not immoral to provide for oneself; it is immoral to provide in ways that are at the same time repulsive and incapacitating. Our duty to lighten the load of human misery is derivative from, indeed it is the reflex of our duty to bear ourselves as a great nation—firmly to wield a mighty power in a mighty cause. Liberally we must feed those mouths that will not confuse the hand with the aliment; grimly we must struggle against suffocation in our own abundance; and confidently we must draw the connection between liberality and authority. Grandeur has liberality as a sign, authority as a prerogative. That is the ground and the right of foreign aid.

Toward Reflection on Property and the Family

Paper presented at the Symposium on the Origins and Development of Property Rights, University of San Francisco, 19 January 1973.

If recent strictures on the private acquisition and possession of wealth and on the so-called nuclear family do not entirely persuade us, they certainly lead us to be reminded of the great age of the oldest reservations against property or family advanced by philosophy and theology. One of the most famous provisions of Plato's *Republic* is the abolition of privacy and property among the guardians, and the abolition at the same time of the family. The freedom of the guardians—who are the nearest approximation to a ruling class that one finds in the just city—to enrich themselves would be prejudicial to the unity of the city, for it would encourage the powerful to make victims of their wards; and it would deprive the guardians of the virile toughness necessary in the defenders of a country. Property is divisive and inconducive to spiritedness or martial virtue.

As for the family, it too is suppressed in the *Republic* among the guardians in favor of the practice of bringing together pairs of individuals who are matched with a view to eugenics. The matings would not be permanent, for women and children would be "in common." This great contribution to the unity of the city, whereby private "possession" even of wives and children is precluded, is of course a reinforcement of the thrust against divisiveness that had already been delivered against acquisition of property. But it is more than that. It is the direct obstruction of the expression of erotic desire through free selection by mutually attracted individuals. The disposition regarding property must be viewed in its connection with the disposition regarding family and sex: in the interest of the city and its unity, what tends to divide the members, to damp their spiritedness, or to give a precedence to their eroticism, is to be suppressed.

It is evident from the poverty as well as the celibacy of the Roman Catholic clergy that Christianity is understandable as leaning against acquisitiveness, which it might call avarice, and against eroticism, which it might call lust. This leaning, which is of course not intended as a support for patriotism or strength of the city, arises rather from the depreciation of the flesh, which is death, and magnification of the soul, which is life. The preservation of life is seen as requiring—though only within limits—not property and procreative intercourse but abstention from both. At the same time, the *amor habendi* is reprobated as inimical to charity, charity being the bond of love among men the rupture of which would be the dividedness that Plato and all others can see as a threat to sociality. This brief sketch must at least mention the heavy emphasis put upon the injunction, "Be fruitful and multiply," and the fact that matrimony is a sacrament while divorce is forbidden. The view of Christianity is that property and the procreative family are concessions to the fleshly estate, the existence of which cannot be dispelled but the primacy of which must be controverted in the practice of living human beings. In the merely fleshly estate, love in the form of charity (sociality) takes precedence of love as sexual passion, not because the latter is divisive but because it is of the flesh. Virile spiritedness does not enter in. To express this in a way that facilitates comparison between the pagan and Christian dispensations, Christianity has preached sociality without patriotism or spiritedness; and it has preached also sacramental domesticity as the check on erotic love, matrimony extenuated by procreation and always under the accusing shadow of the celibacy of clergy and religious.

The reminiscence of classical and Christian antiquity would be instructive if it did no more than call to mind the fact that property has been discussed without reference to rights during a much longer period than that in which it has seemed indispensable to make the investigation turn on rights. It is since the work of Hobbes that the visible focus has been rights, and the issue most often regarded as the crucial one concerning property is, whether the right to it is natural or merely civil. The question is thought to be crucial on the supposition that, if there is a natural right to property, then property stands legitimated, whereas if the right to property is only civil, then property stands impugned and the door is opened to communism.

How far this oversimplifies the issue is revealed by a glance at the doctrine of Hobbes. In the condition of mere nature, before the institution of civil society, every man had a right to everything, in the interest of his own preservation. This is the meaning of natural freedom or natural right, limited only in the exercise by such calculations as reason dictates on behalf of peace, that is, general preservation. There is a natural right to things and for that matter to human beings, if by a natural right is understood a right that derives its force from the conditions characteristic of man's natural or prepolitical state; but there is only a civil or legal right to property as such because the term itself implies precisely the *legal* differentiation between mine and thine, that is, the differentiation established through the supersession of the natural condition and the "renegotiation" of the natural rights. Certainly the natural right to preservation is inalienable and survives intact into civil society. It is Hobbes's understanding that that right is better exercised or more fully realized when men agree to such terms of common existence as make it unnecessary and indeed punishable to avail themselves of all of their natural rights, especially the right to "everything." What men do have a right to, by way of property, is at the discretion or assignment (not the caprice) of the civil sovereign.

Man's natural right to preservation—whatever that right may itself be conceived to rest on—implies an equally effectual right to the means necessary to preservation. This suggests that a political institution that deprives a man or men of their subsistence is in violation of their inalienable natural right. It must be recognized that Plato's city, which prohibits property among the "elite," in guaranteeing the means of life is wholly legitimate by the criterion of natural right while a system of private ownership that led to anyone's death by starvation on the streets would have to come under censure according to the same criterion. It would appear that the sounder defense of property is empirical and prudential rather than theoretical: property conduces better or more reliably to the natural end of preservation than does common ownership.

Perhaps however one should look beyond Hobbes to Locke, who gave more attention to the questions of property and might have provided a theoretical foundation for private ownership in the so-called labor theory of value: a man who mixes his labor with a thing imparts something of himself to that thing and without any intervention of convention or legislation acquires a claim to call that thing his own. It is a natural basis of property. It does not furnish the premise of a theoretical construction that sets property unassailably on the foundation of natural right, as is evident if one considers how tenuous is the hired shepherd's claim to the lamb whom he has seen into the world, born in a flock on which the rightful owner has never laid eyes. When one considers further how well adapted to Marxian communism the labor theory of value proved to be, it becomes clearer still that the origin of wealth in labor, directly or indirectly, in whole or in part, leads no more unequivocally to the natural right of property than to communism.

Before leaving the subject, it deserves to be remarked that the right to a thing that a man acquires by mixing his labor with it is, in Locke's thought, most absolutely undiluted in the state of nature; but it is precisely in the state of nature that a man's possession of what is "his" is most tenuous, and his natural right a precarious near-nullity. In the civil state, where property is rendered effectual by law or convention and not by appeal to nature, the institution of private ownership recommends itself on the ground of the function that it performs within the plan of the regime as a whole, not necessarily on the basis of rights. We shall return to this theme later. In the meantime, it may be stated that the writers who laid down the theoretical basis of liberal capitalism did so in terms of nature and the rights that are present to or in a man by virtue of the meaning of nature, for the impulsion to continue in being cannot be separated from the meaning of nature, according to the emphasis imparted to that meaning by modern philosophizing. It is easy to see the source of the thought that the right of property can be and perhaps must be perceived as a natural right. It is not equally clear that this thought will prove durable, or prove more useful than a more prudential or pragmatic alternative in giving an account of the system of private ownership.

Locke's formulations on property grow out of the more fundamental premise of man's natural freedom and his right to preserve himself. It is noteworthy that Locke's fairly extensive reflections on "the family" grow out of the same premise. In fact, Locke's reflections are not directly on the family but are rather on "paternal power," which he wishes to show is not based on the natural subjection of one human being (son) to another (father) but is based on the duty of both parents—mother and father—to see to their child's preservation, i.e., to help secure the preservation of the race. Something not insignificant does follow for the family itself: when the mother and father have discharged their obligations of procreation, the connubial bond is subject to some loosening, just as the paternal-filial bond is. Locke's "economization" of the family is broadly consistent with his thought on society at large. For this reason one is led to wonder why in fact so much of capitalist society did not, for so long a time, "rationalize" its domestic dispositions according to Locke's understanding but rather continued under the influence of old and received practices and conceptions—the monogamous, lifelong mating known to Greeks, Romans, and Christians, and to the Jews if not to all the Patriarchs. Capitalistic

society is not the "integrated" whole that Marxian communism especially
is pledged to find it—the total coherently made product of a certain mode
of production. Liberal capitalism is officially neutral with respect to
morality. The positive morality of the capitalistic societies has been,
necessarily, something exogenous to capitalism in the respects that are not
simply and directly in touch with money matters. Poor Richard's maxims
do not define a morality; they are a counsel of earthly advantage that
might guide a man fairly adequately from 9 to 5 between Monday and
Friday in times of peace if he has no dealings with women, the sick or
distressed, the public, the government, the clergy, the arts and sciences,
the schools, and other people, institutions, or things not definable directly
by reference to the acquisition of external goods. It is instructive to
consider how much of the morality that has regulated life in a capitalistic
society has been, until recent decades, not capitalistic but Christian or at
any rate scriptural. It is also evident that psychoanalytic psychology has
recently contributed a potent ingredient to the moral consciousness of
important capitalist societies, an ingredient that conflicts with the
traditional. It may be discovered, upon consideration, that the revised
morality indicated by psychoanalysis is the long overdue modern morality
that fits harmoniously with the system of private ownership. To determine
if it is so, one must begin by asking whether capitalism is essentially
inclined to austerity or to hedonism, to accumulation and saving or to
enjoyment and consumption. The answer is not as obvious as it was before
Keynes. If capitalism has passed from frugality to indulgence, then
perhaps the harmonizing morality would be that which opens new vistas of
guilt-free enjoyments of all kinds. Until this question is thoroughly
investigated and affirmatively resolved, the decay of the authority of
traditional morality cannot be viewed with indifference, for we do not yet
know whether in a system based on self-preservation, there exists the
moral energy adequate to generate a comprehensive moral conception of
suitable dignity. One might of course maintain that, as its morality has
been supplied to it from without heretofore, so will a new morality be
supplied again from without, not inadvertently as by psychoanalysis but
deliberately. There are signs that a new morality is indeed in the making,
but it presents itself as unsympathetic to private ownership or to that
morality which it takes to be the morality of capitalism, but which is as
much the morality that was received into capitalism as it is the counsels of
acquisition peculiar to capitalism.

The principal intention of this paper is to discuss and to begin to
investigate the possibility of a moral understanding consistent with liberal
capitalism, one not generated by predecessor or hostile moralists. Implicit
in the expression of such an intention is the thought that "capitalism" is
not a regime in the strict sense, for it lacks a moral understanding that is

continuous and integrated with itself and that brings it to completion as a framework of human life. Also implicit is the thought that liberal "capitalism" is not a Weltanschauung, for the ideal of "life, liberty, and the pursuit of happiness" leaves so many important elements of the way of life unspecified that crucial aspects of human existence remain at the discretion of governmental or merely private parties who successfully assert a claim to prescribe for them.

Since our premise is a certain defect or incompleteness of the liberal dispensation, we might conceive a need to turn to the hostile critics of that dispensation in order to obtain the least indulgent, hence perhaps most helpful, appraisal of the object of our concern. As it happens, it is not necessary to resort to a hostile assessment, because there is a most impartial clue to the moral difficulties presented by the system of natural liberty that emanates from so well-disposed a moralist as Adam Smith himself. Smith believed that "the understandings of the greater part of men are necessarily formed by their ordinary employments." In a civilized society, and thus especially in a commercial society, the decisive ingredient of men's ordinary employment is the division of labor. Smith expected the effects of this aid to productivity to be inevitably stultifying, contributing to the sacrifice of men's "intellectual, social, and martial virtues," (*Wealth of Nations,* V. i. 3. 1). By this he meant that most men will be made boorish, narrow, and cowardly by the routine of their everyday lives as they carry on their productive function. In their commercial or trading function, they will, if permitted, inflate into authoritative principles of statecraft "the sneaking arts of underling tradesmen," or give way to the pettiest conceptions of their own and the country's interest (*Wealth of Nations,* IV. iii. 2). There is other evidence of Smith's apprehensive belief that the productive and commercial institutions of a civilized nation, and even of one in which private ownership is well liberalized, work to demoralize most of the human beings whom they affect, particularly in exciting their selfishness or corrupting their public-mindedness, and in destroying their spiritedness. If these apprehensions can be summarized as the fear that unity and spiritedness will suffer if not provided for by public attention to education, Smith's understanding can be described as bearing a partial and at least superficial resemblance to Plato's. Smith did not disclose his expectations, if any, of the effects of the private ownership system on the relations between men and women.

It is not clear, on the record, that capitalism has produced nations of cowards, or of stupid people who have a more confined view of their own and their countries' interests than has been characteristic of the people of other systems. The institutionalization of acquisitiveness does seem to have fostered a self-assertiveness, aggressiveness, or simple egotism that comports particularly well with egalitarianism, and that might be called the variety of spiritedness peculiar to liberal society. The versatility that Adam Smith found in the agrarians and that he feared for among men organized for the division of labor seems to be replaced, in urban capitalism, by the quick-wittedness of the multitudes who are wise in the wisdom of the markets and the streets and by the varied abundance of detailed experience that is the inheritance of those immersed in the energized society. And, strange though it may seem, there has not developed in capitalistic countries that lack of a sense of belonging to a single nation that would show itself as a decay of patriotism and would result in an unwillingness and inability to wage war. Or to speak more correctly, these deficiencies have not emerged in capitalistic countries through the operation of capitalism but have emerged, and not insignificantly, through the hostile intrusion of socialism and other doctrines that either are in no direct way akin to capitalism or that avowedly seek the demise of capitalism. At the same time it must be recognized that, insofar as the unity of the society is manifested not in its solidarity in facing outward but in the mutual caring with which the parts regard one another domestically, the "unity" of capitalistic societies owes something to socialism. We conclude, if provisionally, that the "spiritedness" of self-caring may be in a state of tension or contradiction with the "unity" of mutual-caring if not with the "unity" of outward-facing patriotism.

No one will be surprised to hear that self-assertiveness may contradict altruism, although some who recognize the tension of the two within capitalism appear to take the harmony of the two for granted outside of capitalism. Our purpose at present is not to pursue a suspicion that the latter thought breaks down in contradiction but rather to consider what behind the thought might prove to have a serious value. What could be meant by the harmony of self-assertiveness and altruism? Presumably, the conjunction, within a man, of, on the one hand, a character that is strong and true, unfearful and therefore not truculent but confident, truthfully forthcoming and innocently or naturally pleasure loving; with, on the other hand, a compassion and sociality that bring the sufferings of others straight into the mind of the man in question. This portrait cannot fail to remind of Rousseau's Emile. Emile overcomes, or overcomes as far as possible, the rift between himself and nature and between himself and other men. He overcomes alienation, in other words, to that extent. He does so under the influence of an upbringing that leads to transcendence of the division of labor (for himself, independently of the world) and to strictly domesticated monogamy. Emile's example seems to show how property need not be replaced by communism of goods and kin, but can be replaced by vigorous, versatile self-dependence sustained by the moral rectitude that grows up in serious domesticity. Plato's division of labor and communism of women and children are reproached by Rousseau's versatility and romantic monogamous domesticity.

If we return now to the question, What is the nature of a project for the harmonization of spiritedness and either sociality or mutual-caring? we perceive several answers. That of Plato seems to suppose that they can be "harmonized" in the society only in a manner of speaking: spiritedness will be inculcated in a ruling class, and "mutual-caring" or sociality will be the consequence of the dissolution of the natural bonds of family affection and their replacement by the myth-nourished custom of marking kinship according to the calendar; and by the suppression of acquisitiveness in the same ruling class. Rousseau's answer supposes free, largely self-governing individuals in whom spiritedness and sociality will emerge simultaneously out of innocent strength: the self-dependent have no occasion to develop invidiousness and hostility. This scheme would come to ruin among passionate men. The scheme for the formation of men fit for Rousseau's projected world would have to include the suppression of that imagination that leads to the multiplication of wants and thus to rivalries and hostility, as well as to excess. Not only would art have to be free of the salacious and the provocative, but sexuality would surely have to find its outlet in a strict monogamy the effect of which would be the limitation of the affection of one human being to one and only one other human being. By the standards that have been erected in very recent times, Rousseau's formulation cannot be said to have dealt sufficiently with the problem of "alienation": as can be seen from his prescriptions concerning the family, he by no means contemplated such a dissolution of the boundaries between human beings as would lead each to give himself to and to unite with any or many other human beings without regard even to difference of gender. To state the issue: Rousseau's understanding reconciles spiritedness and fellow-feeling in the presence of property and family, the "emancipation" of the social man taking place through transcendence of division of labor and also through the politics of self-legislation; while the formulations of our own contemporaries seem to demand that the incarceration of human beings in constricted sexual relations, the symbol of which is the traditional family, be partly or radically ended. It would be only too easy to say that to the requirement inherited from Rousseau but mediated by Marx that the restrictions of division of labor be overcome has been added the requirement adapted from Freud that the restrictions of heterosexual monogamy be overcome. The covering formula is, "Overcome alienation."

For the purpose of exploring the possibility of reaching a moral understanding consistent with the nature of liberal capitalism and also salutary and praiseworthy by itself, we may begin by considering whether the overcoming of alienation, as defined, would be the sufficient criterion.

Transcending the division of labor, if it is not to imply demoralizing dilettantism and dishonest incompetence, must presuppose discipline, care, and earnestness in the approach to work beyond what is called for in the acquisition of a single routinized skill. Transcending the bounds of heterosexual monogamy implies a full surrender to the promptings for union with other human beings, which unavoidably is accompanied by pleasure. The two approaches to transcending alienation, one addressing work and the other addressing love, apparently are opposed to one another. From this we do not know directly whether they would complement or cancel one another. But we do know that we cannot without further reflection claim them as a remedy or supplement to capitalism, for in the first place there appears to be a divergence of thrust between the two meanings of "transcending alienation"; and then, between either or both of them and the moral tendencies of capitalism if any, there may prove to be a further tension as serious as that which is internal to the branches of the alienation ensemble itself. Under the circumstances, the very least that can be said is that the criterion of "alienation" should be set aside until the theoreticians who propose it as a touchstone for the perfecting of the private ownership institution are clearer about its meaning.

We cannot continue any longer to avoid the question of the moral tendency of liberal capitalism, for we find ourselves obstructed at every turn by our ignorance of the nature of the thing to which we must make an addition or to which we are being asked by its critics to bring a corrective. In view of the variety of moral influences that are patently at work on the minds of modern men—scriptural religion, mechanistic natural science, socialism, pacifism, moral and legal relativism, liberalism, psychoanalysis, historicism, existentialism, and doubtless others—the greatest restraint should be used in referring any part of our moral education to the influence of capitalism proper, by which I mean the institution of private ownership and acquisition as known in the West. I do not at all mean to suggest that there is not a strong connection between some or many of the influences enumerated above on the one hand and capitalism on the other. To take a restricted example, it would not be hard to show that principles of mechanistic natural science, the supreme value of peace, and liberalism can be found in articulated juxtaposition in the thought of Hobbes, connected not only with one another but with the premise that the primacy of self-preservation paves the way for property. But the property institution by itself is our immediate concern, and I see no alternative to mere observation of our own circumstances as the means for informing ourselves of its moral bearing, always keeping in mind its indecisiveness, or inability to constitute a comprehensive moral influence.

The prevalent view that acquisitive economy is morally defective primarily in that it fosters an unloving disposition is a view that is dominated by a powerful bias, one that becomes visible when we remind ourselves of the degree to which acquisitiveness is in conflict with magnanimity. Acquisitive egotism, on the ground of its alleged tendency to disunite men, to make them mutually competitive, and to suppress their social sentiments, is obnoxious to socialism and to other doctrines that turn on alienation in a loosely understood sense. But acquisitive egotism is subject to a diametrically opposed criticism of at least equal force and depth: the avid pursuit of wealth evinces a deficiency in the dignity, self-regard, or true self-sufficiency of the man who practices it as a way of life, the man who personifies the moral habit of treating small things as if they are important and is not ashamed to manifest his passion for things wanted. If the judgment of capitalism were undertaken from the standpoint of magnanimity rather than alienation, the verdict would be that acquisitive egotism is offensive to self-regard rather than to altruism. It seems to me that mere observation of our contemporary circumstances supports the judgment from the standpoint of magnanimity better than it supports the judgment from the standpoint of alienation. For the present purpose I shall take this to be one of the governing facts about the system of private ownership in our time.

The critique of capitalism from the point of view of its "alienating" influence ignores, however, another equally important consideration: Does the system of private ownership promote self-indulgence, hedonism, and an inclination to yield to appetite that eventually threatens men's ability to defend their own preservation? This question might have been dismissed as absurd in the age when capitalism was linked with austerity directed toward saving, and with the so-called work ethic. It is less absurd in an age in which economics itself has proclaimed a doubt about the superiority of saving to consumption, psychology is widely construed to regard the frustration of desires as unhealthy, moral theory provides little support for a consensus in favor of virtue however understood, and regulated technology provides relief from overburdening labor.

Let us summarize the moral circumstances of the present-day system of private ownership with severity but without hostility. The competitiveness that is complained of as alienating is in fact an expression, if not a noble expression, of spiritedness. The acquisitiveness that is also complained of as alienating because egotistical is, however, more objectionable as a sign of deficient than of excessive self-esteem. On the whole, it is probable that the setting of capitalism in a matrix of individual freedom and equality leads to the growth of an active if plebeian self-assertiveness, or democratic spiritedness that might explain the flaw in Adam Smith's expectation of a decay in "martial" virtues. On the other hand, the property system, encouraged and assisted by outside influences, lends itself to the gratification of appetite and desire as it has never done before. I take this

summary to support the following contention: on a moral question
pertaining to the way of life where private ownership is the rule, the weight
of presumption is against the less demanding solution of the question. By
the less demanding I mean that solution which favors either the principle
of individual preference or the supremacy of the antialienation criterion
rather than a prescription favoring the moral fortitude of the individual or
the community. While acknowledging fully that the theoretical foundation
of our present system of property is a doctrine of rights and natural rights;
and perceiving that the most widely received criticisms of the system turn
on "alienation," I have sought to maintain that there is an alternative to
the principles of rights and alienation that deserves consideration when
problems of capitalism are under review.

The concrete question is the status of the family in a society where
private ownership is the rule. If the status of the family were to be derived
solely from the right to property, a case might be made for paternal
despotism (the father is the normal center of ownership and need respect
no claim of any dependent except the right of mere survival); perfect
libertinism (provided only that contraception prevents the dilution of the
estate); homosexual matrimony (the parties are self-supporting and thus
can constitute a household by right); and other practices more or less in
conflict with one another but more or less in agreement, amazingly, with
the indications drawn from the side of "alienation." It is not at all difficult
to see how the moral latitudinarianism of the natural rights basis for
property, and the moral latitudinarianism of identification-ideology (I use
"identification" as the antonym of "alienation") might happen to achieve
occasional consensus. Following, therefore, the "contention" set down in
the preceding paragraph, questions touching the status of the family—
equality of the sexes, matrimony, divorce, and discipline, only to mention
examples—should be approached with a view that recognizes a need to act
on the dubious tendencies that have found their way into liberal capitalistic life. The reader is now reminded of the sketch of Rousseau's understanding that was given earlier, the reminder taking the place of a detailed
development here. To provide a concrete description of the domestic
arrangements most useful to present-day capitalism would be an enormous task, to which I have not pretended to do more than propose a
prolegomenon. The core of that prolegomenon is the suggestion that
neither the sovereignty of rights nor the absolute worth of "identification"
(the contrary to alienation) nor both together should be allowed without
careful consideration to dominate the field of discussions about life with
property.

```
PPPPPPPPPPPPPPPPPPPPPPPPPPPPPPPPPPPP
PPPPPPPPPPPPPPPPPPPPPPPPPPPPPPPPPPPP
PPPPPPPPPPPPPPPPPPPPPPPPPPPPPPPPPPPP
PPPPPPPPPPPPPPPPPPPPPPPPPPPPPPPPPPPP
PPPPPPPPPPPPPPPPPPPPPPPPPPPPPPPPPPPP
PPPPPPPPPPPPPPPPPPPPPPPPPPPPPPPPPPPP
PPPPPPPPPPPPPPPPPPPPPPPPPPPPPPPPPPPP
PPPPPPPPPPPPPPPPPPPPPPPPPPPPPPPPPPPP
PPPPPPPPPPPPPPPPPPPPPPPPPPPPPPPPPPPP
PPPPPPPPPPPPPPPPPPPPPPPPPPPPPPPPPPPP
PPPPPPPPPPPPPPPPPPPPPPPPPPPPPPPPPPPP
PPPPPPPPPPPPPPPPPPPPPPPPPPPPPPPPPPPP
PPPPPPPPPPPPPPPPPPPPPPPPPPPPPPPPPPPP
PPPPPPPPPPPPPPPPPPPPP  PPPPPPPPPPPPPPP
PPPPPPPPPPPPPPPPPPPPP  PPPPPPPPPPPPPPP
PPPPPPPPPPPPPPPPPPPPP PP PPPPPPPPPPPPP
PPPPPPP PP PPPPPPPPP PP PPPPPPP PPPPP
PPPPPPP PP PPPPPP PP PP PPP PPP PPPPP
PPP PPP PP PPPPPP PP PP PPP PPP PP PP
PPP PPP PP PP PPP PP PP PPP PPP PP PP
PPP P P PP PP PPP PP PP PPP P P PP P
PPP P P PP PP P P PP PP PPP P P PP P
P P P P P  PP P P PP PP P P P P P    P
  P P P P  P  P P P  PP P P P P      P
  P P    P  P  P   P  P P P    P      P
  P      P  P      P  P  P      P
  P         P         P P         P
            P         P
                      P
                      P
```

Part Four

Political Life and a
Natural Order

Reprinted from the *Journal of Politics* 23, no. 1 (February 1961). ©1961 by the Southern Political Science Association.

Our problem is, whether political life is in some way guided by nature, and if so, in what way; or more particularly, whether nature is characterized by an order that affects the shape of political life. The question is suggested by the practice of political philosophers, who have generally thought it necessary to make their doctrines reflect the order of nature, or consist with nature irrespective of order. At the same time, the difference between natural philosophy and political philosophy has long been honored in the great literature: whatever might be the inner continuity between the *Republic* and the *Timaeus,* or between Aristotle's *Politics* and his *Physics,* the massive differences between the books on political life and the books on nature stand out, as they do also in the books of later ages.

There is, indeed, some tendency for those differences to be made less in recent times, and for the books on political life increasingly to resemble the books on nature. That tendency has developed concomitantly with the belief in the simplicity of nature, as will be explained, or in the essentially unordered, homogeneous and unitary character of the natural whole; and in the simple, direct domestication of man in that whole. The relation of political life and nature proper thus appears in some respects to be remote, in other respects intimate, but is in every respect obscure. Our purpose is to clarify the relation as well as we can.

I

We wonder, to begin with, why it is necessary to implicate the problem of political life with the question of nature. Why can we not simply confine ourselves to the political phenomena as they present themselves, or as they spontaneously arise? The political phenomena are singularly human; to concentrate on them is to refuse the distractions of the extra-human and perhaps irrelevant world of nature; and moreover, the political, human things are those of which men are immediately a part and into which they therefore can enter directly and thus most knowingly.

The political phenomena present themselves as an astonishing congeries of laws and orders, varying within and among the countries. In their great variety the phenomena are incomprehensible, as phenomena or "appearances" cannot fail to be; and although it is true that the political phenomena are singularly human, it does not follow that the truths about them are directly or easily accessible, any more than are the truths about the human mentality, which is not only close to but identical with the investigative agent. The need, or desirability, then, of ascending from the merely empirical is well understood. There is a question whether that need can in any way be satisfied. The well-informed skeptics of antiquity, cognizant of philosophy, not only admitted but insisted that the appearances differ from the judgments, as we know even from Sextus Empiricus. They did not claim that the empirical is intelligible, but only that the judgments are not any more so. Like skeptics of a later period, they doubted that the phenomena were made intelligible by recourse to nature. Others than the skeptics have doubted that recourse to nature is sufficient, and have recurred in turn to divinity or the generation of nature; or to the growth of nature, i.e., history. It cannot be necessary to say that in this paper there will be no attempt to dispose of skepticism, or to arbitrate the claims of revelation and history against nature. Nothing more will be sought than to sketch the meaning of the appeal to nature as a means of avoiding the confusions of gross empiricism in political science, and to do this by reference to the possible order of nature. Our first task, then, will be to show why the recourse to nature gives any promise of rendering any object, say the political society, intelligible. By rendering an object intelligible we shall mean, at the outset, sufficiently defining the thing in question by showing what is characteristic of the individual examples of it. For instance, we should speak of the state as intelligible if we showed what about the British, French, and other states caused all of them to *be* states.

"Nature" is taken to mean many things, but primarily it means the things, or the principle of the things, that do not owe their being to human agency. The natural is opposed in the first place to the artificial. Now the artificial things are known to us to originate with beings in which intelligence is joined to corporeality. That is to say, in human making there is a clear connection between the purpose or intention of an individual being, and the action performed by that identical intender. There is no mystery about human making, for the human maker possesses, in his rationality, the means of conceiving his purposes; and in his corporeality, the visible means of acting as the efficient cause of his products, or giving effect to his conceptions. We are satisfied that human making is intelligible because, in virtue of man's corporeality and individual mentality, the visible acts of men are preceded and guided by the same acts conceived in thought in the body of the same agent: in man, the nexus of act and agent can be localized in demonstrable, not postulated existents. As to the artifacts, therefore, there would seem to be great clarity.

What is the case with respect to nature and the natural things? These perplex us because they live and move, and come into being without any prefiguration of their life, motion or generation in any intelligence that we can localize in body. The "ideas" that govern the changes of the natural things have no locus, for they are not in any body. The immediate source of each natural thing is some other thing that is destitute of intelligence: we speak of the living, motion and generation of the natural things as subject to necessity. This we do notwithstanding the fact that the animals and plants, as well as the celestial bodies, move or increase "by them-selves." In brief, the natural things exhibit motions and changes; and we connect motion and change with an intention on the part of some mover or agent. By nature, or the natures of the things, we mean that which gives the natural beings the appearance of having been the result of the action of an intelligence, or of moving as if with intelligence or by reason of intelligence, i.e., intention. Yet within the realm of nature there is no evidence for the existence of any intelligent, hence intending agent, one, moreover, with the corporeality indispensable to efficient causation. There is only necessity—which, as the alternative to intelligence, is not an explanation but a concession that we find the natural phenomena in principle unintelligible. As to the being of the natural things, therefore, there seems to be the greatest unclarity.

Now the laws and the political acts and orders are certainly artifacts, the products and doings of men. As artifacts they are, we have seen, quite intelligible. If they were natural things we should probably be at a loss to understand them, and would be limited merely to describing them more or less elaborately. It would appear unreasonable then to resort to nature, or to some notion of a natural order, for the sake of explaining the artificial things, when on the contrary the temptation is so strong in us, and the reasons apparently so compelling, to explain the natural things by analogy with the artificial.

We may begin to re-assess the claim of the natural to be the ground of the intelligible by considering more carefully the relation of the necessary and the rational. We shall speak of the necessary as meaning that which cannot be or move otherwise than as it does, and the things that live and move according to necessity may be said to exist according to inflexible rule, or to change changelessly, due allowance being made for the difference between the animate and inanimate things. So far as necessity means that which cannot be otherwise, necessity and truth or reason are indistinguishable. The numerical relations, for example, are necessary in the sense that there is no power that can alter them, just as no power can cause what is human to be at the same time non-human or what is non-human, human; the principle of the excluded middle is supremely necessary. The syllogism is perhaps the perfect example of pure necessity— and intelligibility. That nature is governed by, even exemplifies, necessity is not the source of conflict between the natural and the intelligible, but the reverse. The necessary, if by no means sufficient condition for intelligibility is that the object of study be foretellable: necessity is the guarantee of nature's regularity, whether necessity be conceived statistically, or probabilistically, or in any other way.

This seems to help vindicate the philosophers' habit of referring the political things to a natural standard: if a ground of being for the political can be made out in nature, then the intelligibility of the natural may be extended to the political. Unhappily, however, the same necessity which sustains the intelligibility of nature creates a difficulty with respect to the morality of nature or the natural. The necessary is taken to be contradictory of the moral, for the essence of the moral is believed to be choice, and choice implies that the immoral courses are as possible as the moral. Agents governed by necessity cannot be capable of morality; more exactly, morality does not exist for such beings; and still more exactly, for such beings morality collapses into and becomes indistinguishable from the rule dictated by strictest necessity. Readers of Hobbes and Spinoza will recognize this notion as playing a part in the political doctrines of those philosophers. We observe now that the attempt to reduce the variety of the political phenomena to intelligibility by recurring to nature for the standard of intelligibility has led to a difficulty: the natural, in virtue of its being essentially necessary, is at the same time essentially intelligible and essentially amoral. To deduce the political order from a natural order would thus appear monstrous. The most characteristic political phenomenon is law, and law is supposed to express the just. How can the diversity of laws, hence of notions of the just, be made intelligible by being referred to a natural order if the natural order is essentially alien to morality and hence to justice? The necessity that rules in nature seemed to furnish a foundation for understanding, even if it did not furnish a ground for morality: speaking metaphorically, nature punishes error, not crime. But when the object of investigation is itself inseparably connected with morality, as the body politic is, then the ground for understanding cannot be dissevered from the ground of morality; nature does not seem to provide us with a standard of political life. Our argument has led us back into confusion.

We began with the valid distinction between what is and what is not made by man, between the artificial and the natural. Our purpose was to understand the practice of the thinkers in referring the political things, which are artificial, to nature, in order to find the ground for them or the truth about them. The natural was represented as intelligible because necessary; and as amoral, also because necessary. The artificial was represented as intelligible because not necessary, rather the product of intention; for that which comes to be only if willed is surely not necessary; but on the contrary, when intended and generated, it is not mysterious. At the same time, what is willed or arbitrary is, as simply arbitrary, not intelligible, for will can in principle be guided by a multitude of purposes many or all of which are irrational. Finally, what is arbitrary is as such not moral, for the mere will is, as such, no more constrained to virtue than to reason; yet the necessary condition of morality is the freedom characteristic of a willing being. We are at a loss to discover an intelligible ground for morality, or say for political life, because neither the extra-human nature by itself, nor the purely artificial by itself, neither blind necessity, nor intelligent will, is sufficient to provide the ground for an intelligible moral order or political life.

We took as the premise of our argument the simple distinction between the natural and the artificial, a premise that has culminated in the perfect dichotomy of the natural and the political, or of the natural and the conventional. If it did nothing else, that premise, through its implication, would accuse a great part of political thought of a folly hardly to be imagined among competent men; for the political thinkers have almost from the beginning seen a need to find the connection between the political and the natural, and have indeed found it under various guises. The distinction between what is and what is not made by man is an unavoidable one which leads to anomalous conclusions when it is not applied with sufficient penetration. In applying the distinction, we must make provision for the fact that man himself is not in the first instance an artifact. Artifacts have, however remotely, a natural or quasi-natural ground in the natural constitution of their makers.

The natural whole is a comprehensive integer that culminates in man. The redintegration of man in the natural whole implies that it would be unreasonable to look for the ground of human life in the non-human part of nature, when nature is an entity of which man is a part and indeed the culminating part. Our problem is to state the connection of the all-including natural order with the political order, bearing in mind that man is part of the natural universe, yet not such a part that the difference between the natural and the artificial things may be neglected.

The natural ground of humanity furnishes the two characteristics of man which in effect are his nature: his corporeality, or the necessities and powers of the body; and a power of participating in the necessities or truths that are "in" the natural whole and its parts. Between corporeality and mentality are those intermediate signs of life, the passions, which draw the mind's attention to the body and assimilate the body to the mind; for the passions are, so to speak, the body's wisdom.

Man's mortality, or corporeal necessitousness, extorts from him the first degree of his rationality: he is compelled to view himself as object, to know himself as one of many, one whose claims are objectively no more serious than those of any other man, although to himself and for himself alone, no other claims might be worth considering. Man's first human reaction to natural necessity is to rise above it by that prudential calculation of self-denial which is social virtue. In the interest of self-dependence, out of a desire to emancipate themselves from brute nature, from want and from each other's brutality, they engage to practice a moderation with respect to the things hated and the things loved, or in other words to submit to be governed.

The spirited desire of man for self-dependence, or emancipation from nature, reaches beyond calculation in the interest of self-preservation. It carries him up to a morality higher than the social virtues, to morality which is the noble simulation of independence by the dependent, of considerate indifference to the things loved and the things hated, the things desired and feared. It is an expression of man's natural preference for being, i.e., being himself, and his natural aversion to non-being; and it takes the form of a uniquely human resistance against everything natural or non-human that man shares with the rest of the whole. Moral virtue thus presents itself as a fortifying of human nature, a prideful assertion against the external natural order.

The moral order is the outgrowth of man's prudent, proud self assertion in behalf of his human being, a defiance offered to the necessities that are laid upon him by the common nature, which he cannot escape, but towards which he can assume a posture of resistance. That posture is artificial, conventional, and could be called a sham and a mere formality. It is the formality, however, that stands off the brutalization of life or the surrender to mere nature. It is, indeed, the precarious conquest of nature. It cannot stave off appetite and mortality; it can only outface them and dignify the moral man.

We have said that the natural origin of humanity burdens man with a necessity and furnishes him with a power. That power is intelligence, which means the possibility of grasping the intelligible. The intelligible is primarily the truths which are in or about the natural beings, and which can come also to be in the mind of a rational being; the sense in which a truth is "in" either the object or the subject, and how it passes from the one to the other, without having location, is utterly mysterious. But the apprehension of it, or participation in it by an intelligent being, is precisely the exercise of the characteristic human power, the endowment of nature. Man's steady disposition toward his self-dependence, or the fullness of his being, expresses itself in his effort to be invested with those necessities that are the frame of the natural whole. Man's self-dependence as a rational being is consummated by his union with the external things over which conquest is unthinkable.

Man's corporeal necessities and his intellectual powers, bridged by the passions, are his natural constitution. So constituted, he repeats the constitution of the natural whole. We have seen how the moral order arises from his rebellion against the condition imposed on him by corporeal necessities; and how his intellectual life consists primarily in becoming united or reconciled with the natural necessities that are called the intelligibles. If political life were simply co-extensive with morality, then it would be true in a direct sense that political life is not guided by the natural order but is rather the expression of man's resistance to that order. But political life is not simply the legislation of morality; it is the full articulation of the moral and intellectual existence of man. It is the human construction by which a place is made for man's resistance to the gross nature and his surrender to the incorruptible nature. The dual organization of the natural whole emerges at last as the model of political life: that dual organization is microcosmically repeated in human community and in the human being. The duality of nature, repeated in humanity, dictates this constitution for human community: due allowance to both elements, for the grossly necessary can be resisted but it cannot be extinguished, while the incorruptible is therefore bound in its government by the nature of the governed. The redintegration of man in the natural whole, as the culmination of that whole, has led us to the conclusion that political life is the comprehensive work of man guided by the model of the all-including dual nature and the order of its duality.

II

In the course of this very rapid sketch, I have made use of a certain notion upon which the conclusion just reached may be said to depend. I have repeatedly described man as not simply part of the natural whole but rather as a part of it in the way in which the completing or culminating element is a part of some whole. This doctrine of the inegalitarian integration of man in nature not only might be questioned, but has been denounced as a crucial misunderstanding. It is what Spinoza described as the belief that man is a kingdom within a kingdom, or one dominion within another,[1] meaning of course that man and nature are thereby conceived as subject to two different laws.

The belief in the complex rather than simple integration of man in the whole presupposes an irreducible duality in the whole of nature. That duality has not proved to be demonstrable. On the contrary, it has had the appearance of being merely imaginary. Spinoza wrote, "... as things which are easily imagined are more pleasing to us, men prefer order to confusion—as though there were any order in nature, except in relation to our imagination."[2] Locke in turn speaks of the "general natures" as notions or ideas,[3] i.e., human cogitations. The view is, then, that the order of nature is a human supposition, and is not an objective truth as conceived. We will note in passing that there is no reason to believe that any animal besides man imagines an order of nature; and that this alone might be taken to establish the order of nature. But in any case, in ways well known to students of the sixteenth and seventeenth centuries, the essential homogeneity of the natural whole was linked to the essential unity of that whole. Spinoza's expression of it was very radical: "... only one substance can be granted in the universe."[4] From this he rightly inferred that "mind and body are one and the same thing," and thus that "the order of the whole of nature [is] ... the whole chain of causes,"[5] i.e., of efficient causes or mechanical causes. Blind nature is nature simply.

Into the whole chain of causes man is most absolutely and directly integrated: "... men believe themselves to be free, solely because they are conscious of their actions, and unconscious of the causes whereby they are determined; and further it is plain that the dictates of the mind are nothing but the appetites ... [A] mental decision as well as an appetite and a determined state of the body are simultaneous by nature or rather are one and the same thing, which we call decision, when it is regarded under and explained through the attribute of thought, and a determined state, when it is regarded under the attribute of extension, and deduced from the laws of motion and rest."[6]

In his own way, as Hobbes, Locke, and others did, Spinoza was fulfilling the oracle given in the *Novum Organum,* where Bacon despaired of progress in moral and political philosophy unless they were transformed into applications of natural philosophy: "... it is nothing strange if the sciences grow not, seeing they are parted from their roots."[7] We observe that it is nothing strange if a doctrine of society, assimilated to a natural philosophy that knows only the order of efficient causes, sees in the political order nothing but a power structure.

What, then, is the ground of the moral order, when the natural order is conceived to be an artifact or a product of the human imagination? We might take our answer from *The Wealth of Nations,* or from the *Federalist,* or we might ascend to their ancestor, Spinoza, or indeed to his progenitor, Hobbes. Spinoza wrote, in his *Ethics,* "... virtue is nothing else but action in accordance with the laws of one's own nature."[8] But there is no distinction between the individual nature and the universal nature, as he shows in the *Political Treatise* as well.[9] The plain ground of the moral order, in a radically integrated nature, is power.

If we consider together Bacon's plea in behalf of a natural philosophy that will give power over nature, and Spinoza's doctrine of the moral order, we notice this to be true: man is encouraged to cultivate a natural philosophy by which he triumphs over nature, even to creating its order out of his imagination, and a moral philosophy through which he capitulates to nature utterly. If we recall the implication of the old-fashioned dualism described earlier, it was very different from this. We saw there that moral and political philosophy was the field of man's strenuous rebellion against brute nature, and natural philosophy was his act of union with the intelligible nature. We are struck by the immense perambulations of the mind.

III

The natural laws that describe the homogeneous undifferentiated whole prescribe also, of course, homogeneous human society, when man is wholly absorbed into nature. In a remarkable way, the ages that are under the influence of the belief that nature exhibits an order live in political societies that exhibit an order; and the ages that believe in a homogeneous nature tend to live in homogeneous society. We have no reason to believe that varying nature induces the varying beliefs. It is human thought that generates the varying notions of changeless nature. The varying notions about nature do not alter nature, they alter political society. The deepest current of action is the production of the ground of human life by human thought. This could not be true if man were integrated in the unitary chain of causes as he is said to be by Spinoza.

We are led thus, as was to have been expected, from nature to the possibility of History. We may not now enter upon that subject, but we note that the modern doctrine of nature and political order brings us to the verge of it. As for the immediate problem, I will try very briefly to summarize my understanding of the state of the question. The traditional view of the order of nature saw man as within the natural whole, but within it as the perfection of it and as its microcosm. He was, so to speak, of it more than in it. According to the modern understanding, he is perfectly in it and of it, and its unitary un-orderedness is the inexorable guide of his political existence.

I do not know which of these doctrines is correct. The one nourishes a dream of humanity soaring into an empyrean of freedom, enlightenment and prosperity, a soul-swelling dream from which we awake to the imminent possibility of universal devastation. The other gazes piercingly through and beyond the multitude of mankind, holding aloft the symbols of a gallant, if hopeless, struggle to keep alive at least the vision of human excellence.

Notes

1. *Ethics*, III, beginning; *Political Treatise*, II, 6.
2. *Ethics*, I, Appendix.
3. *Essay Concerning Human Understanding*, III, 9.
4. *Ethics*, I, xiv, cor. 1.
5. Ibid., III, ii, note; II, vii, note.
6. Ibid., III, ii, note.
7. *Novum Organum*, LXXX.
8. *Ethics*, IV, xviii, note.
9. *Political Treatise*, II, 4.

Plato's *Phaedrus* and
Plato's Socrates

Paper presented at the 1976
annual meeting of the American Political Science Association, Chicago.

Plato's *Phaedrus* is about two things that seem to have little to do with each other: love and verbal utterance. (The awkward expression "verbal utterance" carries the necessary neutrality between speaking and writing.) The reader of the dialogue is called upon early in his reflections on it to reconcile these themes to one another, which he can do by referring both of them to the act and concept of soul-leading (*psychagogia*) in the following way: a lover tries to form the soul of the beloved, and the user of words aims at doing the same thing or something similar to his addressee (261A). One might expect then that the dialogue will be an examination of the question, which is the better way to shape a soul, the erotic or the dialectic way? In fact, the question with which the dialogue so to speak begins is, Is love good or bad, and the question with which it closes is, Is writing good or bad. By means that we will relate, the argument discloses that love is good and speaking is good. Love is good because it enables or induces a human being to draw close to another whose soul is of the same type as his own but is capable of becoming more perfectly so and thus of being led upward, as both souls ascend. Speech is good because, being face to face and, in fact, under the assumption that seems to rule the discussion, being one to one, the speaker assigns to the hearer precisely what his soul can accept and benefit by. Spoken *psychagogia* is apparently far wider in range than the erotic, for there is no intimation that a speaker as such is drawn to human beings who are of the same type of soul as his own; but there is a plain consistency between the argument for eros and the argument for speech: both arguments indicate than an education—erotic or verbal—is good because it is private, and as unpolitical as is the relation between one human being and another. It would be useful to consider the difference between this thought and that which the *Republic* makes famous, namely, that speech, love, and education altogether require to be politicized and eros itself subordinated to the requirements of the city. Perhaps when a discussion of the soul is preoccupied with political justice, the perspective in which the good will appear must be different from the perspective in which the good will appear when the discussion is dominated by a preoccupation with beauty, as it is in the *Phaedrus*. It certainly is true that the great myths of the *Republic* are subterranean while that of the *Phaedrus* is celestial. But we cannot stop to explore these things, and must rather press on to consider the peculiar importance for the lover and the speaker of being able to discriminate the soul-types of other human beings with great precision. If there were a man who was ignorant of what he himself is, who did not know himself well, or who was in confusion about his soul and the type of soul that it is, one could imagine that he would be also a confused lover, unable to match himself with another of like soul for want of the decisive information about himself. If he were a poor judge of other men, he would be a confused lover for want of the other, equally crucial knowledge, and his attempts to lead another soul toward the perfection of the type they both possess would be comical or pathetic but in any case ineffectual. Furthermore, a man who addressed speech to another man while under the impression that his hearer was of one type when he was in fact of another would be a blunderer in verbal *psychagogia*—as he would be a blunderer also in loving, if he attempted that.

As the reader makes his way through the *Phaedrus,* he encounters rather early (230A) this remark by Socrates: ". . . I do not examine these things [the meanings of stories about mythical beings] but rather myself, whether I am some wild beast more complicated and furious than Typhon or a gentler and simpler animal who participates by nature in some godly and unperturbed lot." At the end of the dialogue (278E–279B), Socrates, acknowledging Isocrates as his "favorite" (*paidikos*), prophesies for the young man a great future, marked not only by preeminence in rhetoric but by his being led by a godlier desire toward greater things, "for there is in the man's mind by nature something of philosophy." If one were to take

these passages on their face, without speculations about Socratic irony
and without presuppositions of Socrates' perfect infallibility, the two
passages would suggest that Socrates was unsure of his own soul and was
not an excellent judge of the souls of others. (A man who knew both Plato
and Isocrates, and was capable of acknowledging Isocrates as his favorite,
could not be a first-rate judge of human quality.) This and everything else
in the dialogue occurs in the course of a conversation initiated by Socrates
and conducted under the conditions of intellectualized intimacy that are
described in the dialogue as erotic. The action of the dialogue presents
Socrates as the lover of Phaedrus. One wonders why. One must suppose
that it was in order to elevate the soul of this kindred spirit, a supposition
that of course provokes troublesome questions. Was Phaedrus worth the
effort? Was he in fact improved? Was it desirable to deflect him from
public affairs toward philosophy? Above all, was Socrates serious in the
revelations that he made to Phaedrus about philosophy and goodness? At
least in one very important particular, it seems as if he was entirely
earnest. He shows how speaking is better than writing; and his deeds
testify to the sincerity of that argument. At least to some extent, the
problem of the *Phaedrus* takes on the shape of the problem of Socrates.
To that same extent, if we could interpret the dialogue, we would
simultaneously uncover the nature of Socrates.

One cannot speak of uncovering the nature of Socrates without
encountering the fact that we scarcely know what we know about him. By
this I mean that strictly as readers of Plato's writings, we might have the
greatest difficulty, or might perhaps find it impossible to tell whether a
particular thought or deed assigned to the persona "Socrates" belonged in
fact to the man of that same name. If we seek help outside Plato's writings
we encounter either the artistries of other authors whose works are equally
in need of interpretation, or an account like that of Diogenes Laertius, a
late miscellany that relies in part on Plato and Xenophon. Certainly I am
not proposing that we interest ourselves in the biography of Socrates as a
thing important in itself or as a test of the fidelity of Plato's account of
Socrates' mind. I am maintaining that Plato sets forth many arguments
and conceptions, put in the mouth of "Socrates," which might have been
the opinions of Socrates, or of Plato, or of both. If we could know that
"Socrates" means Socrates and nothing else, then we would know that we
should interpret a given Socratic dialogue by Plato as fitting into the great
conspectus of the world that the philosophic activity of Socrates comprised. But if "Socrates" is not simply Socrates, then it is to some extent a
mask for Plato. And if it is a mask for Plato, then in principle a given
Socratic dialogue by Plato *can* be part of a great conspectus of the world
that takes in not only everything looked at by Socrates but also Socrates
himself in his speaking, looking, and doing. Obviously, if a Socratic

dialogue by Plato includes Plato's scrutiny of Socrates, then the persona "Socrates" should resemble the man of that name sufficiently to avoid traducing the subject, and amply enough to be intelligible to readers who lack independent knowledge of the real man's life. In other words, in a Socratic dialogue by Plato, "Socrates" could or perhaps must portray Socrates and also speak for Plato. The modesty of this conclusion is largely deceptive. If it is correct, then the reader of Plato must, without independent information to guide him, interpret the Socratic dialogue before him mindfully of the question whether given words put in the mouth of "Socrates" convey the thought of Socrates and also of Plato, or of Plato though not of Socrates, or of Socrates but with so little concurrence of Plato that the "reporting" of them by the latter is or includes a tacit criticism of the real Socrates. If there were a flat statement of preference for Isocrates over Plato, it would illustrate the latter possibility. Because of Aristotle's openness, his readers need not exert themselves to perceive that he could detach himself from Plato's influence sufficiently to differ pointedly from his famous teacher. It should be obvious that Plato, if he was the genius that scholarship proclaims him to be, can hardly have been the echo that scholarly hermeneutics regularly assumes him to be.

Just a few more words on this perennially but inconclusively discussed question, to which Plato himself gave rise when, writing in his own name, he denied that there is or will be any *syngramma* (writing) by Plato, for the things that are now said to be so "belong to Socrates become beautiful and young" (Second Letter 314C). Plato reveals that "Socrates" is indeed a mask for Plato, but the revelation is enigmatic, and complicates the relation between Plato, Socrates the man, and "Socrates" the persona. Let us for the moment pay no attention to the alleged restoration of Socrates to beauty and youth, and ignore the fact that "Socrates" is seldom young and in any usual sense never beautiful in the dialogues. Let us ignore the fact that to be so restored to beauty and youth is to be reborn—not resurrected—and in what might be the only way in which a man can be reborn, through the writing of one who survives him rather than through that reincarnation of his immortal soul that the palinode of the *Phaedrus* will so beautifully paint. Plato's insistence that the writings called his are in fact Socrates' occurs in the context of a reproof to a somewhat aggressive monarchical pupil whose opinion of his own progress in independent thought goes beyond what his teacher had till then observed. Plato refuses to be plain with him in writing, sends him instead a puzzling precis about the Universe, and proposes a tedious arrangement by which further instruction in philosophy will be carried on through the intermediation of a trusted emissary who will pass back and forth, apparently one voyage per year, orally bearing questions to the east and riddles to the west. Here we see Plato conducting a philosophic education. I think it is fair to say that he has taken the measure of his man and has resolved to keep him at arm's length. (We cannot consider the vexed political relation between Plato and Dionysius. My premise, admittedly risky, is that it does not bear on what concerns us here.) At any rate, the contrast with "Socrates," who takes pains with everyone, is conspicuous. Plato now cautions Dionysius against revealing to the vulgar what he knows: write nothing down. It is at this point that Plato assigns all his writings to the persona "Socrates" (although there are dialogues in which Socrates does not appear, or is largely silent). Plato goes on by requesting Dionysius to memorize the letter and burn it, leaving one to wonder which of them published it. This performance is remarkable in several respects, of which we have time to notice only one. If there is a guilt that attaches to writing, how does an author purge himself of it by holding up before him the mask of another man's name, but in such a fashion as to leave his own intact on the title page? There is levity in the claim that one conceals his serious thought in so perfunctorily disguising his name. The imputation of levity would be removed, of course, if the use of the persona "Socrates" did contribute to the concealment of something serious in Plato's thought. Perhaps the clue to Plato's intention is contained in his choice of the name of Socrates, although any other could serve as a mere pseudonym. The use of that name would lend itself to the propagation of Socratism alone, which would expose Plato as a mere epigone. And if the substitution of one name for another had been the only subterfuge used, then Plato would automatically be guilty of profaning his master's mysteries. If more subtle instruments were employed, so that Socrates' own serious thoughts were decently protected, then one must ask why those same instruments were not simply applied directly for the concealment of Plato's serious thought, without the gratuitous—and in view of the fame of the original, somewhat unseemly—appropriation of a name to make a persona. Free from these difficulties would be a plan on Plato's part to use the peculiar device in order to convey Socratism at some times and Platonism at others, which would make no sense if the two did not differ significantly from each other.

In the Seventh Letter (341C ff.), Plato declares again that there is not and will not be any written exposition by him on the subjects about which he is serious. He then presents what looks like the very thing he says does not and will not exist. In a statement that makes no mention of Socrates, himself or as a persona, Plato radicalizes the argument against writing to the point that that argument becomes a proof of the futility of all language, written or spoken, to communicate the deepest truth. With regard to each natural or artificial thing, there is a name, a definition (*logos*), and an image (*eidolon*); and there is a knowing that is neither in words nor in bodily formations but in souls. Then there is a fifth to which he will make only allusions, but of which he says it is the thing itself (*auto*) which must be posited or postulated (*tithenai dei*) (342A), and it is the knowable and true. One is reminded, but we cannot afford to be more than reminded, of the hail of threes, fours, and fives in Book VIII of the *Republic* (546B-C) where Plato is somehow or other indicating the mathematical principle of all coming into being: the eternal that underlies the transient. To resume, we are told that the first four—name, definition, image, and knowledge itself—frustrate the mind because they confuse the attributes of a thing and its being or essential being (*to on*), and they do so because of the weakness of words or speech or language (*logos*). Hence no rational being would set down his highest understandings in words, for they are unchangeable or inflexible, and especially so when written. He supports this with the demonstration that everything said about the first four is beset with contradictions and can be overturned by arguments written, spoken, or interrogatory. Plato appears to be teaching that language is more rigid than true being and too supple for reasoning about it. We are surprised to learn that true being is less unchanging than anything at all. Of course he gives no reason for connecting this implicit reflection on essential being with the thought of Socrates. In fact, he makes it clear enough that the "Socratic method" of questioning, no less than any other use of speech, gains its victories because the verbal discussion of the four is necessarily beset with confusion of the inessential and the essential with regard to a thing under investigation. This would explain the sense in which the dialogues are merely playful; but in doing so, it would weaken an important distinction, made repeatedly in the dialogues, between philosophic discourse and the disreputable doings of sophists and vulgar rhetoricians. What remains of that distinction is not so much theoretical as moral: the proper questioning and answering is "well-meaning and free of envy" (344C). The same point bears on the possibility of teaching a human being anything of highest importance, and it does so without any reference to the doctrine of recollection, namely, that what we think of as learning is in fact recollection stirred up in the immortal soul by interrogation or, as in our dialogue, through eros. While Plato is willing to connect moral excellence with the immortality of the soul in the Second Letter, he presents theoretical success in the Seventh Letter as a purely terrestrial, transverbal insight achieved in an act of positing the very thing itself. Whether that thing is what is called the Idea is of course not intimated. In the last passage of the Seventh Letter that we may appropriately look into here (343E–344D), Plato makes both the theoretical and moral achievement of a man dependent on the good or bad nature of his soul, on what with a view to the contents of the *Phaedrus* could be called the soul-type. But there is no trace of a connection here between the natural constitution of souls and *psychagogia* or "soul-leading" or education or between the natural constitution of souls and recollection of eternal truths or beauties on the part of an immortal soul reincarnated. Nothing is present here, where Plato is writing in his own name, but a man's natural ability to learn "the false and at the same time the true about the whole of being" (344B). The perfection of a man is shown as the culmination of a private and terrestrial effort, open to the few equipped for it by nature. The truth that such a one would eventually possess needs no writing down for the sake of recollection: it is as short as it can be, and presumably is unforgettable in its simplicity. Perhaps it is some formula like "posit the fifth." Plato certainly does not say.

It became obvious in a general way that there need not be, and perhaps even presumably is not, a simple identity between the thought belonging to Plato, to Socrates the man, and to "Socrates" the persona. It is becoming obvious that there is not complete agreement between what Plato writes in his own name and what appears in the *Phaedrus* in the mouth of "Socrates." Whether Plato was more candid with his correspondents than he makes "Socrates" be in conversing with Phaedrus is a question that, fortunately, we need not try to resolve, for our task here is rather to formulate a certain problem. The problem might be stated in this way. How is the interpretation of a Socratic dialogue by Plato affected by the relation between Platonic irony—the inconspicuous self-effacement of Plato behind a mask—and the Socratic irony—a self-depreciation notorious to mediocrities among interlocutors and readers alike? Both ironies are subterfuges. We wonder whether they might conceal different insights. We become aware of the issue by pursuing the theme of writing that is raised in the *Phaedrus*. We turn now to the dialogue.

The *Phaedrus* consists of five quite clearly distinguished parts: a scene-setting prologue between Socrates and Phaedrus, a reading by Phaedrus of a speech written by the rhetor Lysias, an extempore speech by Socrates in which he outdoes the performance of Lysias, a second speech by Socrates in which he recants his first speech, and a lengthy exchange between Socrates and Phaedrus in which the relative worth of speaking and writing is a prominent theme. The three speeches that form the central material are about eros, the two sections that introduce and conclude the dialogue are generally about verbal utterance. The manifest unity of the whole follows from the fact that the three speeches, or at any rate the first two, are presented in connection with the immediate interest of Socrates and Phaedrus in speech making rather than in the substantive theme of love. Of Socrates' second speech, the famous palinode or recantation, the same could not so well be said, for he makes it out of a belief that he has erred by offending Eros with what he said about love in his first speech.

At the opening of the prologue, and hence of the dialogue, Socrates accosts Phaedrus and learns that the latter has been with Lysias the son of Kephalos. Phaedrus is impressed by a discourse in which Lysias makes an argument that one is wise to yield to a suitor who proclaims himself not to be in love rather than to one who says he is in love with the hearer. Socrates declares himself so taken with this notion that he will go anywhere with Phaedrus in order to hear him repeat Lysias' speech. Phaedrus denies that he could have memorized such a difficult production, to which both he and Socrates refer as something written. Phaedrus offers to give the gist of it, but Socrates has noticed that Phaedrus is concealing something in his left hand under his cloak, and demands that he come forth with the text and read it. From this point on, they are on their way to the place where they will recline while Phaedrus reads and, after he has read, while Socrates declaims and they converse. As they proceed, each has occasion to urge the other to lead on (*proage*), and it develops that they have at least one important characteristic in common: they are avid speech lovers. Mutually leading and also somewhat similar, they are rather like lovers as those will be described in the palinode. One presumes that Socrates has Phaedrus' spiritual education in view, and the dialogue roughly bears this out. Less evident is a reason for Socrates' love of Phaedrus, unless love encompasses every disinterested desire to alter another for that other's benefit.

Phaedrus, who is supposed to be the more familiar of the two with the country outside the wall, is leading them toward a towering plane tree, *platanos* in Greek, the name of which is mentioned five times (229A, 230B, 236E). The entire remaining dialogue will take place under the shelter of the tree *platanos,* and in one passage, Phaedrus will swear by it as by a divinity (236E). Just now, as they walk along the stream Ilissus, they are reminded of the events of a myth, the scene of which is somewhere nearby. Socrates knows exactly where. It is where Oreithyia, playing with Pharmakeia, was carried off by Boreas, the north wind. Socrates declines to speculate on a rational interpretation of the myth—perhaps simply that a girl was blown to her death from the rocks by the wind—because all his leisure is devoted to self-examination: he still does not know himself well enough, and finds it convenient to accept the conventional notions about such stories. Now Phaedrus will ask Socrates why he so seldom goes out of the city and into the countryside. The answer is that the countryside and trees do not teach him anything, but the city people do. However, Phaedrus seems to have discovered the *pharmakon* to procure Socrates' departing from the city. "Pharmakon" is appropriately rendered in the context as "charm," but it happens also to be the word used for the poison that slew Socrates, and it is obviously connected with the name of Pharmakeia just mentioned. (In this dialogue, Plato seems to avoid the use of *pharmakon* to mean a healing medicine. See 268A-B.) This *pharmakon* that Phaedrus has discovered is discourses in books, which Socrates says he will follow all over Greece or anywhere else. Now that he has been brought so far in pursuit of the charm-poison, and has in fact caught up with it, he will lie down on the earth; and so he does. This closes the prologue, in which Socrates has been led by a well-liked (228E1) young companion to the shelter of a tree called *platanos* from whom he cannot learn anything. As Oreithyia played with Pharmakeia and was rudely killed, Socrates played with discourses in books or in writing, among which he included laws and political writings (227D, for example), which were his *pharmakon* or poison—not that he broke the law but that he played with it, ostentatiously accepting the conventional notions while making it clear enough that he considered himself above them in wisdom: another of his penetrable ironies.

Now Phaedrus reads the speech of Lysias to the recumbent Socrates. I must refer to what happens at the end of the reading in order to complete a suggestion that arises out of the interpretation of the prologue. Socrates will say (235C-D) that he has "heard" from the men or women speakers and writers of olden times—Sappho, Anacreon, or others long dead—various things, and been filled through the ears like a pitcher, but he cannot remember how and by whom. He is in the state of forgetful reminiscence of a man between life and death, or one who is dead, or has been dead. Of course the great myth to come in the palinode could "explain" this, more or less; but we cannot yet turn to it. For the moment it suffices to notice that Socrates is stretched on the earth, absorbing what he calls his *pharmakon*. What follows in the dialogue should be read with that speculation in mind. If this conjecture has any value, then the *Phaedrus*, with *its pharmakon* and *its* discourse on the immortality of the soul, is like another *Phaedo*, one in which the proof of immortality differs markedly from that in the *Phaedo* and in which we can follow the soul of Socrates beyond death.

Phaedrus begins the reading of Lysias' speech, which is addressed to no one by name and commences abruptly with the supposition that the speaker's affairs and views are known to the hearer. The main point is that, under the influence of love, reason departs. The lover does things that he will regret when he returns to sobriety; but before he comes to his senses, he will injure his own interests and will corrupt the youth he loves in the course of making him weak, isolated, and dependent on the lover alone. Not only is the case made for sober and reasonable calculation of mutual benefit as against gratifying hot passion, but Lysias commends surrendering to the good rather than the urgent (233D). He closes this appeal for reason and in favor of common advantage with a formula, the equivalent of "any questions?" that rather stamps the performance as a display. The speech combines the paradoxical (yield to me because I do not strongly care for you), the sober ("no harm ought to come from love but benefit to both parties"), and the coolly calculating or unattractively rational. At the very least, it is not itself beautiful and manages to discuss love without making much of beauty at all.

When Phaedrus completes the reading of the speech by Lysias, he expects Socrates to join him in admiring it and is, of course, disappointed. Socrates affects to have ignored the thought and to have concentrated on the rhetorical character, which he finds undistinguished, particularly because the speech was repetitious. For some reason, Socrates points this out in a singularly repetitious way (235A), but Phaedrus takes no notice. Claiming now to have heard better things from the writers and speakers of old, who would refute him if he agreed with Phaedrus' praise, Socrates gives Phaedrus occasion to coax him to make a better speech than that of Lysias on the same theme. From this point on, Socrates pretends not to be merely coaxed but, falling in with the threat of Phaedrus to use force, positively compelled to make it. He adopts the theme of compulsion and necessity that permeates the speech he is about to give and that prepares in advance for his recantation of it on the ground that he gave it under compulsion. If his *daimonion,* which intervenes later on to prevent him from leaving without making a second speech (i.e., which causes him to do something rather than to forbear), had been alert, it would of course have forbidden him to make the first speech. The *daimonion* is an easily detectible subterfuge. Presumably, both of his speeches are seen by Socrates—or is it Plato?—from the outset to form a whole, the shape of which we must try to discover.

Before he begins, Socrates hides or covers his head or his face—out of shame, he says, and to avoid the embarrassment of meeting Phaedrus' eyes. As the end of the *Phaedo* attests, he was in the same state of concealment when the poison mounted toward his heart, and when he died. The "first speech" of Socrates in the *Phaedrus* is remarkable for being given while he is in the state of coveredness or hiddenness in which he went to death. Now he begins to speak by invoking the Muses, and passes on to the body of the speech as if it is a tale about a crafty lover who, wooing a certain boy, addresses to him most of what follows. The lover makes his argument by pretending not to love and urging everything he can against love and lovers. He opens by saying that deliberation should start with agreement or it will end in discord. He proposes an agreement on the definition of love: love is a certain desire for beauty. In order to distinguish it from the desire for beauty present also in the non-lover, he announces that in each of us there are two ruling and leading ideas (*idea*) which we follow where they lead, one an innate desire for pleasures and the other an acquired opinion that strives for the best (237D-E). The predominance of opinion leading through reason to the best is called temperance (*sophrosyne*); the irrational rule of desire drags us toward pleasure and is called, when it dominates, excess, insolence, or whatever best translates *hybris.* The compulsive, irrational desire for pleasure in beautiful bodies is called *eros,* after a word meaning force, *rhome.* Love is the victory of natural violence over conventional restraint and goodness. After this reflection on nature, Socrates takes up the effects of love on the beloved. In showing them to be deleterious, he mentions the need of the lover to induce defects in his beloved, unless nature has already planted them there. Now Socrates notes that there are other evils in the world, but "some *daimon*" has mixed pleasure with most of them, as nature has mixed pleasure with the doings of a flatterer (240A-B). Nature is some sort of *daimon* or godlike being, apparently, and therefore can be thought of as working with an intention for man or men; and to this point, there is nothing attractive about that intention, or thus about nature. So far as this speech of contest with Lysias is a speech about nature, it contains one additional element which must be observed. The words for necessity, the necessary, and being necessitated or compelled, all variations of *ananke,* occur with extraordinary frequency. Omitting the preliminaries in which the "compulsion" laid on Socrates by Phaedrus is being bandied between them, the word occurs once in the invocation to the Muses and thirteen times in the speech itself. The discourse ends with a verse that identifies eros with what might be the most appalling characteristic with which man's mind might endow nature—universal predatoriness: "As wolves love lambs, so lovers love lads." This is preceded by the only reference to the soul that occurs in the speech, a serious exaltation of the soul as the thing whose education is of as high importance as anything in heaven or on earth. There is no levity or flirtatious "irony" in the preparation for the somber verse about nature. Nature, as the principle of mutual harmfulness in beasts and men, is not on the side of the refinement of the human soul.

Socrates' speech is not the refutation but the elaboration of Lysias' speech. Lysias drew a picture of unappealing calculation devoid of any reminiscence of beauty or nobility. Socrates corrected this sketch with the introduction of beauty; but in so doing he exposed the ugliness of a nature indistinguishable from the power of necessity, compulsion, and violence even in the prosecution of love. As one might say, the natural impulse to possess and enjoy the beautiful cannot be cleansed of the violence that is even more fundamentally natural; and the merely human calculation of advantage that is so prominent in Lysias' speech is elevated in Socrates' speech by one degree to become knowledge of the forces of nature.

Socrates now (241D ff.) declines to continue his speech, and threatens to cross the river and depart lest he be compelled further by Phaedrus. Phaedrus replies by entreating him not to go away but to wait until the heat of the day has passed and then, when it is cool, they will go. (The word for cooling off, *apopsycho,* also means dying, and is close to the word used at the end of the *Phaedo* for the growing cold of Socrates' body.) Socrates responds by calling Phaedrus a great generator of speeches (cf. *Symposium* 177D) second of all those born in his lifetime only to Simmias the Theban—who calls forth in the *Phaedo* much of Socrates' discourse on immortality. In fact, it is to Simmias that Socrates says (*Phaedo* 66E) that we might have to wait for wisdom until we are dead, i.e., relieved altogether of the body; and that the philosopher, always striving for wisdom, is always striving for what only the soul alone can obtain and thus the philosopher's whole life is an approximation to death (*Phaedo* 67D-E; cf. 64A). Socrates now announces that his *daimonion* called him back just as he was about to cross the river, and restrained him from leaving before expiating some offense that he committed against a god, namely, Eros. So, like Stesichorus, who escaped the punishment of blindness by recanting his defamation of Helen, Socrates will recant his disparagement of Eros. One wonders whether the recantation by Socrates will be more truthful than the poet's denial that Helen went to Troy, which we still believe on the testimony of Homer. At any rate, Socrates declares that the speeches of Lysias and himself were shameful, and their authors shameless; he will now speak with face uncovered, unashamed. There is heavy, repetitive emphasis on shame and the shameful, explained, I believe, by Socrates' remark that the speeches against love would be scorned by any man of noble and gentle character. I think it is fair to say that Socrates' impiety consists less in an insult to Eros than in a denigration of nature or of the whole system of the world. In the picture of nature that has emerged, visible beauty is present, but as an irritant to violent passion, and nobility has been forgotten, and philosophy has been barely mentioned. It is up to Socrates to redraw and to beautify the picture of the whole. The palinode shows what must be asserted as true in order to achieve this reconstruction.

Socrates' progress toward his great recantation is through conduct that itself appears craven and shameless. He insists that the speech he made was not his, it was spoken by Phaedrus through his mouth that had been enchanted (*katapharmakeuthentos*) by Phaedrus. To escape some envisioned penalty, Socrates hastens to pronounce what he openly admits to be patterned after a saying that was made for the sake of avoiding a punishment. The palinode is presented to the reader as a song or poem that must be uttered for the sake of some end. As Socrates had claimed that his first speech was actually by Phaedrus, he will now declaim the second in the name of the great recanter Stesichorus.

The argument of the palinode begins with a retraction of the praise of sobriety implicit in the first two speeches and a strong praise of *mania* or madness. There is retrospective and prospective madness or prophecy, and there is madness that leads to poetry and to the education of future generations by embellishing the deeds of the ancients. To succeed in depreciating love, according to the argument, one must show that it is not bestowed by the gods for the advantage of lover and loved; while "we" must show that such (erotic) madness is given by the gods for our greatest happiness. To do this, we must first know the nature of the soul divine and human and its being acted upon and its acting.

Having set about to do something for piety to the gods, Socrates has, in deed and word, exhibited craven mendacity in terror of a punishing deity and has begun an encomium on madness, a fine gift from the beings aloft. One begins to wonder what direction will be taken by this effort to rescue mankind from a repellent nature.

"The beginning of the demonstration is this. Every (or all) soul is immortal." This is so because the ever-moving is immortal; for if something moves something else and is moved by something else, when it ceases moving it ceases to live. But the self-moving is the source and beginning of movement, and, as beginning, must be ungenerated. A beginning, if it were to come into being by generation, would have to be begun by a beginning; but it cannot be. In the *Phaedo,* one demonstration of immortality is the proof that everything is generated by its opposite, thus life must emanate from death as death proceeds from life. By that reasoning, a beginning should proceed from a non-beginning or an eternal or from eternity. But it is of the nature of beginning as such not to proceed from anything else, for it is that from which all else begins. Thus it cannot proceed from its opposite and it cannot proceed from its like. The proof of the immortality of the soul that rests on the premise that the soul is to be understood as the source of motion does not necessarily accord with reasonings about the soul that regard it primarily as the source or agency of good, or as mind. In any case, Socrates' demonstration proceeds through a showing that the self-moving, the always-moving, the ungenerated and the indestructible are all the same: soul. The reader is assured that, if someone were to say that self-motion is the essence and definition of the soul, he would not be shamed or disgraced, which might mean that he would not have to recant it for the reason that is acting on Socrates as he utters his present recantation.

What began as a proof of the immortality of the soul became immediately a description of the eternal principle of motion of an eternal universe or whole. The self-moving in man (or in a dog or mouse) is in no way distinguished from what causes motion in the heavens. The demonstration of the immortality of the soul obliterates the distinction between what is living and what is not; or rather it appears to give the universe as such soul and to make it an animal. In this discourse on the soul, which occupies less than one small page, Socrates has succeeded in integrating man in the whole so perfectly as to threaten to dehumanize him, for the sake of assuring him that his essence is imperishable. Concomitant with the autokinesis of the soul, however, is its absolute separability from whatever is corruptible or dissolvable, hence its absolute separability from body and unlikeness to body. By virtue of its incorporeality, soul should be closest to, most sympathetic with, or most combinable with the other absolute incorporeals, namely, the eternal ideas or truths. While the arguments for the autokinesis of the soul might not necessarily accord with those that trace moral and intellectual humanity to the soul, it appears at least that they might so accord or need not necessarily conflict. Such a harmony would be disturbed if the argument for the incorporeal soul as the seat of mind and good in man abandoned whatever is decisive for the demonstration of the soul as self-moving eternally. Let it be supposed that, for the soul to be eternal and eternally self-moving, it must be absolutely simple: not composed of parts that could and hence must separate from one another; and, of course, since by hypothesis not corporeal, then not conceivable as occupying space or suffering hetero-geneity of any kind. Then if the soul of man as noble and wise is shown to exist in parts and even in squabbling parts, one must wonder whether the autokinetic eternal soul is more like body than we had thought it is, or the argument for the immortality and self-moving essence of the soul is incompatible with its being the seat of human mind and goodness. I dare to intrude these remarks only because, after the brief metaphysical passage with which he begins the argument of his palinode, Socrates opens the great myth that takes up the rest of the speech; and, while the metaphysical passage is about immortality and self-movement, the myth is about love, beauty, the eternal truths, and man's openness to the good, true, and beautiful by virtue of the experiences of his soul in heaven.

Socrates passes from the immortality of the soul to its form or idea (*idea*), saying that, figuratively speaking, the soul is like the ensemble of a charioteer and a pair of winged horses, each of which in the pair can have either good or bad breeding or generation. One of the horses is fair and docible, the other is ugly, lecherous, and aggressive. The latter, while not itself and simply the same as eros, is surely the driving erotic force in the soul, amply infused with the madness whose praise we are, underneath everything, singing, but showing little else that one thinks of as divine except perhaps its great power of causing motion. The charioteer directs and, as the myth will develop, the fair horse collaborates in restraining the wicked one, but as for motion itself, the palm certainly goes to the brute. Naturally, the reader of the dialogue becomes uneasy upon realizing that the soul is not simple or homogeneous but is in parts which quarrel, and the motion for which the soul is responsible is in some large measure generated by something in us which we have little reason to admire.

The bare outline of the myth, which is all that we have time for, is this. "Soul altogether is in charge of (or, has the care of) everything soulless" (246B), moving across heaven now in one form, now in another. In its perfect state it rises and regulates the entire cosmos; when it loses its wings it descends and joins something somatic to which it lends the power of movement. Nothing whatsoever in Socrates' tale explains how all-soul that governs the cosmos can have parts that can be split off or in some other manner find their fragmentary way downward, i.e., earthward. If one had to give a literal turn to this vision, one would say that, by uniting in the act of generation, two human beings or two mice summon down from aloft a bit of soul and compel it to inhabit a body. The alternative would be that human souls and other animal souls do not become amalgamated with all-soul but retain their individual existence forever, entering now this and now that body to make it an animal—but not, as the myth will show, to make it over and over this or that kind of animal; for a soul can be incorporated in a beast as a kind of degradation. But what then becomes of "Soul" simply, upon the existence and characteristics of which was erected the immortality of the human soul?

Divine soul in heaven ascends freely and easily, human soul in heaven ascends with trouble and poor success, each kind of soul helped by wings which are wisdom, goodness and the like. The immortal gods drive their chariots upward to the roof of heaven and, poising themselves on top, contemplate the things outside heaven as the revolution of the heavens carries them around. It is worth repeating what might be the only reliable description of what lies beyond heaven, a description that could not possibly be furnished by any human being except one who has in a special sense returned from the dead: Socrates insists that he is speaking the truth in saying (247C) that "the colorless and shapeless and impalpable essential being of the kind that true knowledge is about keeps to this place, visible only to the mind, the pilot of the soul." Of the souls not divine, the best follow after god as well as they can, so that the charioteer's head is above the roof of heaven and he can see beyond as the revolution carries him past; but he sees little and poorly because the agitation of the horses is distracting him from the truths. A second sort of soul is so troubled by the horses that it only occasionally sees the truths; and the third sort never rise to see them at all because of the violence of the passions. Socrates at no point blames the charioteer for letting the horses get out of hand; he simply blames the horses for being unruly: *nous* itself and as such remains above reproach; but nothing can alter the fact that the horses have a terrible power to assert themselves. When the action returns to earth, Socrates will divulge that the ferocities of the erotic, ugly horse can be controlled only with the help of the fair and spirited horse in whom shame is made possible by pride. It should be said that, although one might speak of the action returning to earth, it becomes difficult at times to distinguish what is reported as occurring in heaven from what one can observe daily on earth.

It appears that everything depends, for a soul in heaven, on its success in following some divine leader as a model. (Zeus is called the great leader in heaven—246A—and is thus the cosmic pattern of all *psychagogia* or soul-leading, or teaching.) There are nine classes of souls, it now appears, and what kind of man each soul will inhabit depends on how much the soul observed in heaven before it became gravid for want of the nourishment on truth that levitates and keeps the soul from incarnation on earth. Socrates lists the nine ways of life to which the different souls are assigned, in an apparently descending order from philosopher to tyrant. Political and practical people rank high, and those concerned with the body, in fourth place, precede the mantics in spite of the latter's close relation to madness (cf. Aristotle, *Politics,* 1328b12). There are many more details in the same vein, but for the present limited purpose one main point emerges: human beings depend, for their ability to bring many perceptions under a single truth, upon a recollection of the pertinent unifying and real truth seen by the soul above heaven. Thus the famous doctrine that what seems to us like learning is in fact ultimately a remembering. The man who concentrates on and longs for the things aloft, the things somehow remembered, is thought mad by the many—and this is the madness, exacerbated by the sight of earthly beauty that stirs reminiscence of true beauty, that Socrates has been praising. The encomium on madness is an encomium on memory, on recollection of beauty in the presence of a beautiful body or face. Here (251A-D) follows a remarkable passage in which the perturbation of the amorous soul is described with great particularity in the most corporeal and atomistic terms, through the sprouting to the fuller evolution of feathers on the wings of the yearning soul, with assurances that moisture and warmth are conducive. The general impression produced by the dialogue that Socrates spiritualizes human existence mythically should be tempered by the tendency he shows also to corporealize the soul mythically. Perhaps love is especially interesting because, better than other passions, it indicates the mutual inextricability of the soul and the body. In any case, it is now revealed that men are drawn to others according to the way or kind (*tropos*) of the beloved, each lover attracted to the kind of man that resembles the god whom the lover followed in heaven, whom he himself imitates and in whose image he would like to form his beloved. A man must make an effort to identify the god who is his pattern (253A), and to do this he must look within himself rather than aloft. Thus eros brings about persuasion and education in the image of gods, who seem to be no more than types or patterns of human life. Remembering a god is certainly not the same as remembering one of the truths.

In the remainder of the palinode, Socrates describes the disciplined passion of the philosophic pair as they lie side by side, blessed with the blessing of having won restraint, than which there is no greater blessing. Presumably, the reason for this conclusion is that the consummation of such a union in an erotic gratification would be precisely that disturbance among the psychic horses that interferes with contemplation of the eternal truths aloft. Perhaps the corporealization of the soul then has this meaning: if one could persuade a man that in the soul of a lover there take place all those tinglings, sproutings, and moistenings that the untutored connect with the body, one might perhaps have put the capstone on his education, and thus completed the cosmeticization of nature by rendering a beautiful human being beautiful also within. Of course, satisfaction of the body would have to be fully replaced by satisfaction in the soul. It goes without saying that procreation becomes epiphenomenal, and indeed there has not been a reference to the duality of sexes in quite a few pages.

Socrates has, in the palinode, constructed on the foundation of the soul's immortality an immense edifice, with apparently edifying intent. He has indeed beautified the cosmos, altering the harsh picture of nature that Lysias' speech and his own first speech conjured. His strategy has been to praise love, that powerful signal of nature's force which had almost been swallowed and digested by the predatoriness to which it is akin. He had to rehabilitate love in a way that connected it with the good, the beautiful, and the true, and in so doing to save nature itself, or rather to save humanity from nature. In order to achieve this cosmic end, he must find or invent a link between the earthly or merely natural life of man and the eternals. He finds that link in or through death, through death by way of "immortality," in death in the sense in which the life of the philosopher is a kind of existence beyond merely natural or merely human life—the sense compatible with Socrates' being between death and life. At the end of the palinode, Socrates is praying that Phaedrus be made more philosophic, i.e., more like Socrates, his lover. Is there any sign that Phaedrus could believe all the things he would have to believe among the myriad poetic things said "on account of him" (257A)? The concluding section of the dialogue opens with unpromising indications.

After this tremendous performance by Socrates, Phaedrus says a perfunctory amen to the prayer with which Socrates had concluded and then gets quickly to what, he says, had been on his mind all along: how will Lysias do in competition with this second, very beautiful, speech? And will he consent to write a speech at all, since a politician has recently denounced him as a speech writer? Socrates reacts rather sharply: your point is ridiculous, young man. If one were to say that the grandeur and wisdom of the great story have gone past Phaedrus, one would not be far from the mark. In the ensuing pages, however, Plato will give speeches to Socrates blaming a man who badly adjusts his speech to his hearer—a thought to which we must make our way in due order.

Socrates now explains to Phaedrus that politicians are not in a strong position to attack speech writers: when they propose laws, they themselves are making speeches that they hope to see perpetuated in writing. Since a politician is in fact a speech writer, it follows that no politician will blame Lysias for writing speeches. Phaedrus is entirely reassured, having apparently forgotten that a politician has in fact already done what Socrates' argument proves he cannot, or at least should not, do. I am not suggesting that Socrates cannot reason well, but rather that, having failed with the mythical prestidigitation, he will next embark on the logical kind. Socrates infers that it is not writing speeches that is shameful, but speaking and writing badly are a disgrace. Socrates asks whether they should question Lysias and everyone else who ever did or will write anything of that kind. To this large proposal Phaedrus answers with unbounded enthusiasm, wondering what else there is to live for but to savor such joys, so unlike those servile pleasures of the body that are preceded by pains. Without explanation, Socrates calls his attention to the locusts overhead, dear to the Muses, who once were men before there were Muses. Those men became so infatuated with singing that they forgot to eat, and thus perished. Now they live as subhuman singing ascetics, needing no food, but reporting to the Muses on the devotion of humans to the Muses. The locusts have a gift from the gods that they can give to men; but Socrates does not say what this gift is until a few pages later (262D): the power of leading on one's hearer, if one knows the truth, with playful speech. Apparently, men who despise the facts of natural existence are punished for this by losing their human shape while becoming the embodiment of philosophy and Music that will be revealed as dialectic. Grasping at any straw in attempting to understand the interlude of the locusts, one is reminded of the place in Diogenes Laertius' life of Plato where the poet Timon's verse is quoted comparing Plato to the locust (III. 7). To us it seems more Socratic.

Now Socrates broaches the theme of the next section of the dialogue: the speaker must know the truth about the subjects he discusses. There is indeed spurious rhetoric by which ignorant speakers persuade ignorant hearers; but the true *art* of speaking must be philosophic, and it will not be necessarily or even primarily public. It is *psychagogia* (261A), soul-leading, but naturalized, altogether domesticated on earth. An artist in speaking is one who knows his subject so well that he can argue successfully on opposite sides of the point, proving to the same people first that something is just and then that it is unjust. This art depends on a thorough knowledge of the small similarities and differences among things, a knowledge that is used to lead the hearer step by step in either direction, toward or away from truth. Evidently, the end of the art of speaking is command over the soul of the hearer rather than arriving at truth. Rhetoric is an earthly *psychagogia* without *eros* or particular regard to the beauty of the hearer. In order to illustrate his meaning, Socrates brings on a contrast between Lysias' speech and his own first speech, acknowledging that the gift of the locusts, the prophets of the Muses, might have been important in helping him who knows the truth to lead on his hearer. Lysias' speech begins abruptly and without an agreed upon definition of a highly ambiguous thing, namely, love. Although, or perhaps because, he is a god, Eros belongs in the class of the debatable or ambiguous things. Socrates ostentatiously forgets whether he himself had not taken care to define love at the beginning of his speech but is much relieved when Phaedrus assures him that he had done so, and exceptionally well too. He probably has not forgotten, but he is not drawing attention to the fact, that the speech with which he is now exhibiting considerable satisfaction is the one he had so elaborately and piously repudiated in the palinode. Fortunate indeed that the *daimonion* had nodded and did not forbid him to blaspheme with the first speech.

Now Socrates bids Phaedrus read the opening of Lysias' speech, and Phaedrus complies, twice, both times reading the first sentence slightly differently from the way it was read early in the dialogue. (The order of two words is reversed.) This minute difference is not alluded to by either of the speakers. Since it is Phaedrus who is reading, the reversal has the appearance of a small trick played by Phaedrus on Socrates, perhaps in revenge for the unusual self-satisfaction of the famous ironist. The next thought developed by Socrates is, indeed, that order in a speech is highly important: everything should be where it must be. Phaedrus' reading, or misreading, seems related to the thought about minute differences and also to the rule of necessary order—whether as a trace of insubordination in this apparently impressionable youth would be hard to say. But in any case, Socrates passes on to his own speeches, using them to illustrate perhaps the supreme truth about the art of rhetoric: that art depends on being able to join the many details under the true one that unites them intelligibly, and on being able to separate what seems to be a one into the parts of which it naturally consists. Socrates was able to move from the blame of love to the praise of it because he knew that love was a part of madness but madness was divided into what comes from human diseases and what has its origin in divine release from customary convention (265A). This reticent sketch of the two speeches differs from the one given earlier in this paper in the following respect: Socrates does not now say that in his first speech, he explicitly put convention above nature in serving as a support for the human good. Joining our thought with that of Socrates, his two speeches appear to have this tendency: the first speech cures nature with convention, the second cures convention with "madness," but especially the madness of love, eventually philosophicized love. As the existence of the present section of the dialogue testifies, there is a need, for some reason, to go beyond love to discourse, to dialectic persuasion. Apparently, human mind or intelligence or wisdom needs to reassert itself over "madness" even if its independence of at least the poetic madness is not yet clear. Socrates declares himself enamored of division and conjunction, the art of one and many in thought, and will follow the master of that art, called a dialectician, as if that man were a god. The scene in heaven is apparently being assimilated to the life of man on earth. How far that assimilation can go will prove to be a or the supreme question for Socrates.

Socrates now leads Phaedrus through a lengthy examination of rhetoric, proving to him that technical knowledge is necessary but not sufficient to the end of persuasion. More important is knowledge of the nature of the soul and of the whole (270E), and of the kinds of souls and the classes of things and of speeches, or the speaker will not possess the true art of rhetoric, which rests on the highest speculations. However important are the unity and unities in the world, the drift of the discussion of rhetoric is toward multiplicity and variety, especially of souls, for rhetoric is an art and therefore acts on individuals. Now the difficulties multiply. Soul is one and cosmic, as we learned, the same in all moving, self-moving things from heaven down to the flea, and so it must be in the interest of immortality. But in relation to rhetoric or to art, the crucial fact is the existence of classes or kinds of souls, the variety of them so pronounced that what seems to one kind of man to be true will not seem so to another or perhaps to any other, and what persuades all but a handful is not truth at all but plausibility. The world before our eyes is in danger of dissolving into an ungraspable manifold permeated with deception and untruth, in spite of the fact that it has been perfectly explained in the language of eternity, intelligibility, and beauty. Socratism, as the investigation of rhetoric hints, has difficulty in keeping heaven and earth from flying apart. Is the soul's recollection of truths momentarily glimpsed in heaven a link strong enough to keep mankind in touch with the being that truly is? Is heaven itself, to say nothing of the mnemonic link with it, one of the mad or playful locutions of Socrates? I think the answer is not to be found in the *Phaedrus*. The dialogue continues for a few more pages, in which the subject is not speaking but writing (274B ff.). Socrates heard that Theuth, an Egyptian god of old, invented letters. The king of Egypt, also a god, was Thamus. The inventor brought his invention to the king and praised it as an aid to memory. The king corrected him: letters are for reminding, which makes memory superfluous. Socrates believes that writing serves to remind the writer and others like himself who know or once knew. As for teaching, that requires the inscription of the word in the present mind of the learner by the teacher before him, with questions and answers. Far nobler than writing is dialectical conversation, by which the generation of thought is begun that can go on immortally forever, leading to the peak of happiness possible for a human being (277A). Here is an immortality and a bliss descended, like a wing-wounded soul, from the great scene in heaven down to earth. It is the immortality of eternal fame passed from mouth to mouth—Socrates' own terrestrialization of his myth. He seems to have meant it in deadly earnest, for he acted on it. Yet this utterance, so solemnly pronounced by Socrates, might be among the most playful or frivolous things he ever said: if Plato had not written, who would know that Socrates gloried in despising the pen?

Now Plato gives Socrates an occasion for praising Isocrates to the skies. Having done so, Socrates invokes the comprehensive god Pan and prays to be made beautiful within and sensible about wisdom and wealth. Phaedrus, declaring himself a friend, joins him in the prayer, and they depart.

**Justice and Friendship
in the *Nicomachean
Ethics***

Presented as a Franklin J.
Matchette Foundation Lecture
at the Catholic University of
America, 3 November 1972.

The *Nicomachean Ethics* is probably the most famous moral treatise that
claims no debt to revelation. It is famous above all for depicting and
praising the moral virtues, which it describes as means between extremes,
and as indispensable to man's good and to his happiness. All the more
striking then is the fact that, although the work consists of ten books of
roughly equal length, the principal discussion of the moral virtues as
means occupies only two and a half books, or one-fourth of the whole
(from the middle of III through the end of V). Since justice has one entire
book (V) devoted to it alone, it appears that Aristotle dealt with all the
moral virtues but one in a mere one and a half books, less than he devoted
to a non-virtue or quasi-virtue, friendship, which is discussed in two
books.

One should not be surprised if a work contains more than that for which
it is most famous. On the other hand, if a notion is very widespread,
Aristotle himself would recommend caution in dismissing it. Aristotle
does then praise the moral virtues and describe them as praiseworthy; but
he is famous also for exalting the intellectual virtues and the contem-

plative life above all others. While intimations of his intention to do that may be discerned early in the *Ethics,* it is of course only in book VI that the foundation is thematically laid, and thereafter that the conclusion is drawn out. Having once noticed what a surprisingly small part of the *Ethics* is given over to the treatment of the moral virtues proper, the reader readily perceives that that treatment is ended by book VI, after which there is indeed a return to the subject of morality but on a different basis, namely, through the analysis of moral resoluteness (or continence: *enkrateia*), friendship (*philia*), and pleasure. None of these is simply or unequivocally a virtue, according to Aristotle, and they are not presented by being defined as means between extremes of deficiency and excess. We gain some confidence in the speculation that Aristotle intended us to perceive this, when we recall that book VI, on the intellectual virtues, opens by addressing the problem of the meaning or intelligibility of the mean. This problem rose to the surface, or became especially acute, in book V, on justice, a virtue that proved to be a mean only in a novel or mitigated sense, and to be describable only through the most mathematical discourses that occur in the *Ethics.* A somewhat remote look at the work as a whole gives it the appearance of a lever ten units long, the fulcrum being under the sixth unit, and the whole in equilibrium. The "mean," speaking metaphorically, is closer to the closing extremity than to the opening. I think that what one should say only metaphorically at this point will eventually rest on more literal support, and the portion of the *Ethics* following book VI will prove "weightier" than the portion preceding VI.

Our immediate subject is justice and friendship. Justice is the theme of book V, friendship of books VIII and IX. It is obvious that the two subjects are discussed on opposite sides of the decisive division, justice being a virtue and a mean, friendship only doubtfully a virtue and not truly a mean. On the supposition that the *Ethics* has an organization that is at least relevant to our immediate subject, we should make the effort to sketch that organization our first task.

The *Ethics* begins—almost literally—with an approving reference to the saying that the good is that at which everything aims (*hou pant' ephietai*). The formulation in Greek should be noticed, because it recurs twice, virtually or exactly, early in book X, where (through Eudoxus) it is applied to pleasure in the course of what may be called Aristotle's "rehabilitation" of pleasure as a human good. In book I, however, the good or the end for man is presented as happiness in its guise as concomitant of virtue: happiness, according to the famous formula, is the activity (*energeia*) of the soul concomitant with the practice of perfect virtue. The definition of virtue lies ahead, but, while Aristotle is far from foreclosing the inclusion in it of intellectual excellence, the heavy preponderance of the discussion is indicative of nobility and moral virtue. In book X there is a treatise on pleasure in which Aristotle declares that pleasure is not itself activity (*energeia*) but is the perfection of activity; and pleasure is attached to intellectual rather than moral virtue. Happiness in book I is made dependent on the affairs of a whole lifetime, and the question is raised whether it is not dependent on happenings after death: that is, the discussion of happiness in book I includes the suggestion of the immortality of the soul. Pleasure in book X is presented (in a theoretical passage whose closest parallel within the *Ethics* is the criticism of Plato on the Good in book I[1]) as not a motion, or a becoming of anything, but as instantly itself whole and complete, i.e., not in its own being affected by duration (1174ª18). There is no suggestion that pleasure is affected by questions involving the immortality of the soul. There is, to speak briefly, a change of emphasis between the first and last books of the *Ethics* from happiness dehedonized in the interest of noble moral virtue, to happiness constituted by pleasure and philosophy.

One cannot be satisfied with this formulation, however, because it both lacks precision and calls for interpretation. The last book of the *Ethics* is in several parts. The first part rehabilitates pleasure in preparation for the second part, which is Aristotle's final statement on happiness, a statement that rests on the redignification of pleasure but that itself goes on to do two more acts that are in need of reconciliation with each other. These two acts are the apotheosis of philosophy, and the transition to politics and the *Politics*.

Aristotle shows at length that perfect happiness is in contemplative activity, proving it among other ways by maintaining that the gods, who must be supremely happy, cannot be thought to practice the moral virtues, including justice. After proving the self-sufficiency and felicity of the philosophic, he asks whether all these speeches or words are borne out in the affairs of life—is it practically true that happiness crowns contemplation? This confrontation between words and doings (*logoi* and *erga*, 1179ª17 ff.) is resolved surprisingly: those same gods who have been described as being above justice compensate with felicity those men who most honor them and please them by participating in the most divine activity. The gods appear to return good for good, or at least, to practice distributive justice towards men. The question rises in the mind, is the happiness of philosophy assured in deed as opposed to speech by the evidence contained in such dubious speech?

Appropriately, what follows is a depreciation of the power of speech or reason to bring on a very important practical effect, namely, the moral virtue of the many. One wonders if the moral virtue of the many might be a condition for the perfect happiness of philosophy. However that may be, the rest of the *Ethics* leads up to the thought that the perfection of politics—i.e., the right moral education of the many—is a task not for politicians and not for sophists but for philosophy. The main reasons for this are that politicians are defective in theoretical understanding and sophists believe that speeches and writings are sufficient (without fear of bodily punishment) to the purpose. Neither politicians nor sophists can teach virtue. After this tacit evocation of the *Meno,* and thus of Plato, we are amazed when Aristotle remarks that his predecessors have left the subject of legislation uninvestigated, and he will now go on to furnish the *Politics.* It would appear that Aristotle believed himself to be the first man who saw correctly, not necessarily the end of life, and not necessarily the indispensability of the somatic-phobic means to that end, but rather how to teach the whole subject to mankind. This is not the place to try to judge the soundness of that belief, if, as it seems, he did entertain it.

One question remains before us. If the highest good is contemplation, why should the philosopher trouble himself with teaching virtue to the multitude? In the first place, it is not clear that Aristotle means to teach virtue to the multitude. It appears rather that he intends to show legislators how to do it. Perhaps we should make clearer, then, that he might believe himself to be the first man who solved the problem of enlightening lawgivers. But why should he wish to do that either? He gives his reason for investigating politics in one of the last sentences of the *Ethics*: "to perfect as far as possible the philosophy about human affairs." For the present we must content ourselves with a provisional statement about Aristotle's intention in investigating politics: he seeks and gains his own happiness through perfecting his contemplation of human things; one of the highest objects of that contemplation is the truth that the source of man's happiness is in contemplation. It is not possible to exhaust the question of the good of the contemplative life without achieving clarity about the articulation of the contemplative and the practical spheres of human affairs. Only the political philosopher can hope to attain the necessary clarity. An element in the understanding that he acquires is this thought: speech and thought do not rule the human world. Yet only he grasps thoroughly the ends and the means of rule. In his self-contemplation (or self-knowledge) and his grasp of the whole, he resembles divinity. He exceeds divinity because he can bring on human well-being through caring for human well-being. Why does he care for human well-being? Perhaps because he is closer to men than are the gods; and perhaps it is out of magnanimity, the moral virtue that most visibly evokes philosophy and is most visibly absent from the list of the "depreciated" moral virtues twice enumerated (1178a and 1178b) in book X. But in any event, the happiness in deed of the philosopher does seem to be assured by something like a divine act—the thinker's contemplation of himself as contemplative—and to be supported by his independence, so far as possible, of the external goods.

The initial and final points of the argument of the *Ethics* have now been indicated, and it remains to fill in briefly what intervenes. In book II, Aristotle shows what a moral virtue is; but he does not do so in the formal sense, that is, by saying what genus virtue belongs to, until well into the book (1105^{b}19 ff.). He first shows that moral dispositions proceed from our activities before they can go on to govern those activities. This of course raises a serious problem that is not made explicit here: Is there a circle of causation that vitiates either the efficiency or the voluntariness of the moral virtues as such? Leaving this issue aside, Aristotle connects the virtues with the mean by a loose comparison of moral with bodily well-being; shows that the virtues are by genus habits and not faculties or passions; and then returns, much more fully, to the theme of the mean, which he now introduces by referring to "all things that are continuous and divisible." These are the things that can be divided into larger, smaller and equal parts, thus a mean can be found, and that mean, as Aristotle says, can be the mean either according to the thing itself or in relation to us. The famous illustration is the calculation of six as the mean between two and ten pounds of food. Six is the mean simply, but not relative to us. If Aristotle had chosen one and two as the smaller and larger parts, and had been directing attention to justice as a proportion (book V), it would have appeared that the mean simply (equal of course to the square root of two) would be unavailable, for the reason that occurs to the reader when he sees the opening reference to "all things that are continuous and divisible." The reason is that there are irrational numbers which arise out of the attempt to express a mean proportional between unity and some numbers. (Perhaps to drive the point home, Aristotle mentions the Pythagoreans at the end of this chapter.) In brief, if the moral virtues are "about" (*peri*) pleasures and pains (1104b9); or if they are about actions and passions, which give rise to pleasures and pains (b15), then pleasures and pains, actions and passions, must fall in the class of continuous and divisible things. How they can be said to do so is unclear at least for now. If they should in fact fall in the class of things so constituted that the attempt to divide them rationally (i.e., to find the mean according to right reason) leads to something that can be spoken and written down but exists only so-to-speak and is called irrational, then the status of the virtues as strictly intelligible means is brought into some confusion. When it is remembered that the moral virtues are the virtues of the irrational part of the soul, their status as human attributes with an unequivocal foundation in right reason is rendered still more cloudy. At least for the moment, we must remain in doubt about the rationality of the moral virtues, whether because of the incommensurability of the ruled and the ruling parts of the soul, or because of a difficulty in assigning pleasures and pains and actions and passions to the class of continuous and divisible things, or for some other reason. We have already seen that Aristotle describes pleasure as being a "whole." At the same place in book X (1174b9–13), he puts pleasure among the things that are not divisible, along with an act of seeing, the arithmetic unity, and the geometric point. Although we know from Aristotle that the moral virtues are habits, and that they are means between extremes and that they follow the dictate of right reason, we have not attained to perfect knowledge of the virtues because there remains some unclarity about the sense in which the virtues are means. Aristotle is soon to shed some light on this. Going on to sketch the virtues one by one, he shows, to take only the first example, how courage is the "mediating" (observing the mean) concerning (*peri*) fear and boldness. The other virtues are defined equally loosely—well enough so that we know what they are about, but without precision of the sort that could dispel our unclarity as to the sense in which the moral virtues are both means and intelligible. We see now somewhat better why Aristotle has warned against demanding more exactness in a discourse than the subject matter will bear. As he is about to bring book II to a close, he mentions that the assignment of blame for departures from the mean is not easy to determine by reason, for they belong among the irreducible details, or the undefinables, of which perception (*aisthesis*), not reason, is the judge. In any case, let it be remembered that book VI, on the intellectual virtues, opens with Aristotle's saying that he must at that place consider what is meant by the thought that the mean is dictated by right reason; and book VI closes with his conclusion that virtue in the decisive (*kurios*) sense is not subsumed under right reason (*kata*) but comports with reason (*meta logou*), a subtle weakening to which he appears to attach significance.

We must conclude this sketch in broad strokes. After closing book VI on the note just described, Aristotle goes on to make another beginning, as he says, and this proves to have as its theme what is sometimes translated "continence," sometimes "moral strength," and which I will here render as moral dominion, since the term should convey the sense of mastery (*kratein*) (1150a35). (The word being translated is *enkrateia*.) Aristotle says that moral dominion is not the same as virtue, nor is it of a different genus (1145b1). That is, it is a *hexis* or disposition of the soul, i.e, of the same genus as virtue; but as it is not the same as virtue, it must differ from virtue specifically, i.e., either in not involving choice or decision, in not being observance of a mean, or in not concerning actions and passions. But the man of moral dominion (*enkrates*) is prudent, thus exercises choice (1152a7); and moral dominion is about the same things as temperance is (1148b13), namely, the pleasures and pains, but especially those of touch. And it surely affects actions. It is not said by Aristotle to be a mean, however, or rather, it is never said by him to be a mean by use of the word "mean."

Book VII on *enkrateia* is a redoing of themes that seemed to have been disposed of amply in book III, on temperance (*sophrosyne*). What is the difference between the *sophron* and the *enkrates*? Neither is led by bodily pleasure to act contrary to reason; but the temperate man does not have, while the man of moral dominion does have, low appetites (1152a1). In other words, the temperate man does not, while the man of moral dominion does, illustrate true, effective rule over a turbulent subject needing to be ruled. We may look ahead for a moment to notice that Aristotle says (book IX, 1166b8 ff.) that it is the *akrates* who does not (leaving us to infer that it is the *enkrates* who does) desire, wish, and choose one and the same thing, namely, what seems good to him. Then the *enkrates* is he who is at one with himself, in whose soul reigns that concord of parts described only metaphorically (i.e., incorrectly) by Plato's conception of justice. It should be remembered that book VII goes on to conclude with a section (4 chapters, 1152b1–54b35) that anticipates the rehabilitation of pleasure as an ingredient of humanity that occupies much of book X. This section begins by assigning the contemplation of pleasure and pain to the political philosopher—called so by name. It ends by referring to our twofold nature, a nature that demands change and that is, as not simple, not good.

Book VII is remarkable in a certain detail: it contains a blaming of overdone devotion to one's father[2] (1148b1) and a pair of repulsive little anecdotes palliating father-beating under the cloak of the naturalness of bad temper (1149b4–14). Suppose that one were to speak of a moral treatise in which the praiseworthy is shown as sometimes blamable and the most blatant recession from decency referred understandingly to the worth of our spiritedness as men; suppose further that the treatise in question replaced the teaching of the mean and of temperance with a teaching of moral dominion or moral hardihood or resoluteness; and suppose finally that the treatise revealed in this context the duality of human nature, and the consequent need for men to accommodate themselves to the change-ability of human things. If one knew only so much, by supposition one might imagine that the treatise in question emanated not from Aristotle but from Machiavelli. However tremendous the cataclasm' between classical and modern political philosophy, one is not justified in denying to the ancients, on historical grounds, access to the wisdom of the moderns.

We are now on the verges of our own theme of justice and friendship. As moral dominion or resoluteness (book VII) is presented through the reconsideration of what seemed disposed of under the heading of temperance (book III), so friendship (books VIII, IX) comes into view as a reconsideration of material apparently disposed of in the discussion of justice (book V). "Friendship and justice are about and in the same things" (1159b25). It is true that the books on friendship include important illuminations of liberality and magnanimity as well as justice, but those are outside our present scope. Let us now turn to the book on justice.

Some details of the formulations with which Aristotle opens up the discussion of justice in book V pose problems, or rather give intimations of the course of the discussion, and are therefore material to the interpretation. First of all, he states the subject to be, not justice, but justice and injustice. And he says that we must examine the kinds of actions that are involved, although in light of his previous definition of a virtue (as concerning actions and passions), we should expect him also to consider the passion or passions which operate through or are moderated by justice. If he does this at all, he does it tacitly. The *actions* that are just or unjust are what he discusses in full view. And then he characterizes justice as a disposition or habit (*hexis*) inclining a man in a certain way. Yet he proceeds immediately to contrast the dispositions with the sciences (or knowledges) and powers or faculties, in this way: a disposition can produce only that whereof it is itself the principle, while a science and a faculty can produce or deal with opposites. This leads him to observe that one of two opposite dispositions can thus be deduced from the other; but it might also be deduced from the thing in which it is residing. That is, justice might be found by examining injustice or by examining the man or thing in which justice is. Plato, as we know, finds it advantageous to investigate justice and the justice of a man not by looking at justice in a man but by looking at it where it is more conspicuous, "writ large," in a just city. Aristotle too chooses to investigate justice by looking at something other than itself. He tacitly rejects the example of Plato in one way while adopting it in another: for reasons that he (unlike Plato) does not divulge, he (unlike Plato) will not look at the just city, but will look at the unjust man (1129a31). It is a fact that there are more references to the unjust man and to injustice in book V than it would be useful to count; but the use of the word for the just man (*ho dikaios*) is exceedingly rare, perhaps only three or four occurrences altogether (1129a34, 1136a4, 1137a18 twice).

While it can be said that Aristotle does not say why he proceeds in this way, it should be added that he enables the reader to form an opinion of the reason. By the end of book V, the reader is left with the thought that the actions of the just man would not comprise a clear portrayal of justice in itself. Thus, if a just man possessed in addition to the *hexis* of justice (which inclines him toward the just) also some knowledge and some power or faculty, his actions would exhibit some "flexibility" with regard to justice.

This might explain why Aristotle would not rely solely upon the depiction of the actions of the just man as the source of the picture of justice; but does it explain why he relies so little, and at first not at all, upon the depiction of the just man's actions for this purpose? I think not. For more light, we must consider how Aristotle proceeds. The next large point is the connection of injustice and lawbreaking. The thought intrudes upon the reader that unjust actions are very conspicuous, and should not be made more so by ascription of them to just men, but, if at all, by denunciation. Unexpectedly, the exposure of the unjust man is more edifying than the exposure of the just man. Incidentally, it appears that Aristotle, like Plato, proceeds by examining what is most visible or conspicuous; but we sense something important about what is to follow when we realize that the conspicuous is not virtue writ large and nowhere but vice or non-virtue writ on many walls.

Aristotle now enters at length upon the difficult matter of the relation of justice and law or lawfulness. The unjust is both unlawful and unfair, the just lawful and fair. (Fair and unfair pertain to the things of gain and loss.) Of course a distinction has been introduced that leads to the question, is everything that is lawful also fair, and can there be anything fair that is unlawful. Aristotle will say after a while that not everything unlawful is unfair, though everything unfair is unlawful. We must now consider how he arrives at that thought and what it might mean.

The law-abiding man is just; thus everything lawful is "*somehow*" (*pos*) just. Now it is made to appear that legislators make two kinds of law—the kind aiming at the common advantage of all and the kind aiming at the good of the ruling class. Without saying that he is doing this, Aristotle addresses himself first to the former, and describes the law as prescribing virtuous conduct in general. He is thus enabled to refer to a sense in which justice means perfect (*teleia*) or entire virtue, though in the qualified sense of "toward others." Legality is virtue in the qualified sense of the advantage of others. (Apparently full virtue without qualification would be less characteristically altruistic.) He says next, however, that we are investigating the justice that is *part* of virtue, not coextensive with virtue. This partial justice pertains to the things of loss and gain rather broadly defined: honor, wealth, safety. It is in this vicinity that Aristotle declares that not everything unlawful is unfair, although everything unfair is unlawful. Evidently the law does more than make provision against greediness: it provides or tries to provide also for other goodnesses of men, and has care for their *social* education—which Aristotle explicitly distinguishes from education to human excellence without qualification. Now follows the discussion of partial or particular justice.

Aristotle had equated legality with justice qua perfect virtue. He is now about to take up partial virtue, and justice in the sense that corresponds thereto. Therefore we expect him to take up justice not as lawfulness, lawabidingness, or legality, but as fairness. He does so, but only in a manner of speaking. For it is in this place that he introduces the famous forms of Distributive and Corrective justice, which indeed look to the needs of fairness but are visibly founded in law. Aristotle makes clear that distribution is achieved along lines that are indistinguishable from the defining characteristics of the various regimes, as those lines are laid down in the basic laws or, as we would say, constitutions. Those constitutions, indeed, on reflection appear to be the very definitions of fairness from city to city. Corrective justice is also legal, for the judges are made by the basic law and administer it, and the statute law, in order to preserve the basic distributions as well as to insure ordinary fairness (punish thieves, make them restore what they have stolen, etc.).

The argument thus far seems to have this meaning: justice as perfect virtue in the sense of the good of *all* one's fellows in the community is expressed in the subconstitutional ("statute") laws of any or almost any regime. Partial or particular virtue, on the other hand, is particularly related to the justice peculiar to particular regimes as such, and is only fairness. It pertains to, or rather actively promotes, the advantage of some class in the community rather than that of all members of the community exactly to the degree that every regime expresses a judgment of the relative worth of the many, the rich, and the good. The question arises in the reader's mind whether there is something arbitrary or merely conventional in constitutions as such, or in all of them except those that express the true, natural proportion among the human beings. This question occurs also to Aristotle, but he does not raise it until he has discussed another possible meaning of justice qua fairness, namely, Reciprocity.

Reciprocity means returning good for good and evil for evil. Very little is said about returning evil for evil, only at the outset a remark indicating that reciprocity is believed closer to rectifying than to distributive justice, and that reciprocity does not hold between a policeman and a citizen. Reciprocity is farthest from justice as laid down by and enforced by the regime as such or as expressive of a judgment about desert. This is borne out by the fact that the entire remainder of the discussion of reciprocity deals with exchange or trade. Before leaving the return of evil for evil, however, Aristotle does say that men consider themselves slaves if they cannot return harm for harm—i.e., if they must submit to injury—and cannot give back good for good received—i.e., exchange. This is the basis of common life. The strong impulse to reciprocate is the only powerful motive to which Aristotle refers as a bond of common existence. Reciprocal justice is freely forthcoming between consenting parties, whose relations are mediated by money, of which he says rather amazingly that it measures all things, correcting this soon with the remark that want (or demands) is what in truth measures all things: the conventional money stands for the natural wants, and both are the measure of all things. One cannot speak with assurance, but certainly Aristotle's speech lends itself to the construction that money and want have a way of replacing man, or man's judgment, as the measure of all things. More concretely, the powerful desire to reciprocate evil for evil and the parallel desire to have good for good and to give good for good do not require the prompting of law. (The *initiation* of good is what requires public or religious encouragement.) And money or want or demand replace the constitutional distribution and the living judges as the mean or measure. Reciprocity, or shall we say commerce, appears as a mode of justice intimately related to the city yet neutral with respect to virtue or to that judgment of desert that finds expression in a good city's constitution. When Aristotle now makes a general statement about justice, he informs the reader that justice is an observance of the mean not as other virtues are but rather in being related to the mean—an obscure observation—and that justice is that by virtue of which the just man is disposed to do justly. Reciprocal justice seems to fit the description at least as well as do the famous Distributive and Rectifying forms of justice, though in saying this one ought to understand that neither distributive nor rectifying justice is, as such, in the citizen but is rather in the constitutional and judicial arrangements that govern the city's life. (In this sense Aristotle perhaps can be said to share Plato's understanding that justice is to be seen writ large in the city.) Reciprocal justice is the only form of particular justice that appears or is presented as being within the man as an active impulse. Its discovery and effectuation of the mean are infallible. But it does not arise from a disposition to justice so much as from an appetite for retaliation (harm) or preservation (good). The acts of justice proceed not from the *hexis* of justice.

It is after treating reciprocity that Aristotle introduces the discussion of Political Justice, which he describes as prevailing among men who are free and also equal either simply or proportionally, living a common life with a view to self-dependence (*autarkeia*). It is to be observed that their community is in the service of their autarky, a thought that should bring to mind the modern economy. Aristotle next makes the point, relevant enough to the foregoing, that there can be no relation of justice and injustice except where the parties are separated by a sufficient distance: it cannot occur fully within a household, and a fortiori, it cannot pertain to the relation of a human being with himself. Among fellow citizens, one supposes, the necessary distance can generally be found. If political justice truly presupposes the distance just mentioned, then a regime that destroyed that distance would, in making too close a community, destroy justice or political justice by assimilating the city to a household. Of course more hardihood would be needed to say than is needed only to suggest that Plato's proposals are inimical to justice. In any event, this is the context in which Aristotle makes or refers to the division of political justice into natural and conventional. Natural is everywhere and always the same; conventional is variable. He maintains that there is a natural political justice, yet among us, that is, among men, all the prescriptions of justice are variable. Perhaps among the gods this is not at all the case, he says. Among men it is surely true that the natural is changeable. The famous illustration of natural righthandedness being changeable into ambidexterity among all men indicates the difficulty perceived by Aristotle in the application of the notion of nature to law: nature means both the original power or disposition, or norm, and the capacity for altering that original power or modifying that norm, in fact producing a new norm by an act of art. In the immediate sequel, he asserts that only the one regime that is according to nature everywhere is the best. The best regime appears to be the only example of the natural-political just that is everywhere good. Aristotle of course knew that the best regime, everywhere good, is nowhere to be found. Next he maintains (1135a6 ff.) in effect that the human enactments as well as the natural order are the source of "universals" that contain the acts of justice and injustice as the forms or species contain the individuals that come to be under their several outlines. To say the very least, Aristotle causes the reader great difficulty in tracing the lines between the natural and the human dictates respecting justice, both in blurring the line between the natural and conventional political justice qua mutable or immutable, and in introducing the suggestion of artificial "species" of the Just and the Unjust.

The next section of book V treats the voluntary and involuntary performance of the just and unjust things. Of course it emerges that an act of injustice, or of justice, can be performed involuntarily; and an act of justice need not proceed from the justice of the agent but from fear of punishment, for example; while an act of injustice might come from a just man. Evidently, obedience to the law is not, in itself, the mark of a just man, however true it may be that perfect virtue is the dictate of law. Going on to consider whether men must suffer justice voluntarily or could possibly suffer injustice voluntarily, he shows that men by no means always suffer the legal punishments voluntarily, without saying that they ought to do so (cf. *Gorgias*). Moreover, a man may suffer an injury and yet not be the victim of injustice if the doer were not an unjust man. There is a noticeable drift in the argument away from law as the apparent sufficient guide to justice. In this vein Aristotle denies that a man can voluntarily commit injustice against himself: there must be some *other* man, who wishes to harm him, if there is to be injustice.

A remarkable thought, amply prepared, emerges: it is not easy, though men suppose that it is, to be just through doing the acts commanded by the law; and it is easy to do the injurious acts belonging to injustice if a man be just. We must remind ourselves how a disposition can produce only its affirmative product in action, while a knowledge or a faculty can produce contraries. The model of the just man capable of producing both just and unjust actions would be the just man possessing the sufficient knowledge and power. Having this in mind, it is not unduly difficult for us to understand why Aristotle moves, apparently erratically, to the remark that the claims of justice exist between those men for whom the things good in themselves are necessarily good to a certain extent, but only to a certain extent, i.e., necessarily not simply good.

Next he treats equity, which is the correction of the law's justice that is in need of correction because of its generality or universality. The equitable man is the one who, in a spirit of justice, demands less than legal justice allows him. He is perhaps silently counterposed to the man indicated in the preceding passage, who, in a spirit ascending above justice, demands more than legal justice would allow him. In fact such a man is outside the bounds of justice, in the same way that some men are said in the *Politics* to be above political life.

In the course of arguing that a man cannot commit injustice against himself, Aristotle fortifies the case for regarding reciprocity or retaliation of harm for harm as an element of justice or as being just. He does this partly by letting the reader reflect that the city retaliates when it punishes an injury (suicide) against itself, and partly in other ways (1138^{a}9 ff.). He also allows that doing injustice is worse than suffering it, because doing it betokens vice; but not every unjust act proceeds from injustice or vice, as he now repeats. Perhaps it would be better for a man for whom the simply good is good to take too much of it, in relation to some other men, than for him to suffer an unfair deprivation of it. As soon as one says this, though, one realizes that there is an element of unreason in the expression, "a man for whom the simply good is good taking too much of it." He can have too much of it, in a sense, if his having it deprives others of it to the point that they have less of it than is good for them. In another more obvious sense he cannot have too much of it. What he does to acquire it without measure cannot easily be blamed. We observe in the latter part of book V that Aristotle has shown, under the discussion of equity, that a man might do well to take less than lawful justice allows him. Aristotle has indicated also how a man might do well to take more, or to behave greedily with respect to some good that is absolutely good and good for him. Why may we not

combine these thoughts and wonder if Aristotle means to suggest that a
man may take less of something, say wealth and honors and power, while
taking or even in order to be able to take, something else, perhaps leisure
and what it brings to the best men, without measure? That this suggestion
does not point in the direction of the philosopher-king might serve to
make it either less or more plausible, as a conjecture about Aristotle's
meaning. For his last remark in book V is a denial that there is justice
toward oneself or even that there is justice among parts of the soul except
in a metaphorical and imperfect—merely despotic, thus not political—
sense. If Aristotle is correct in this regard, then of course one would
mislead himself in looking for the justice of the city in order to discover the
justice within a man, as if the justice of the city were merely the justice in a
soul writ large.

We must note briefly some of the elements of Aristotle's discussion of
justice. Early in the discussion (ch. i), it emerges that justice can have the
meaning of perfect or whole virtue, not merely one of a number of virtues,
and that in this meaning it is both the dictate of the law and the good of
others. As distributive, justice is giving to each what he deserves. As
corrective, it is restoring to everyone what was his own, whether he be a
good or a bad man, under auspices of law. (Under corrective justice, a bad
man could sue to recover his sword.) As reciprocal, justice means giving
back good for good and harm for harm. As political, justice, though in
part natural, is changeable and appears to participate not at all in the
eternal immutable things, but to be subject to art and deliberation. Justice
is such a thing that no man can suffer injustice voluntarily or at his own
hands. And it does not exist in the soul except figuratively. In the entire
discussion of justice in book V, the words for "noble" and "soul" are
astonishingly rare, the latter occurring only once, and then in a report of
Plato's thought, not Aristotle's (1138b9). I believe that it is because
Aristotle's treatment of justice is to such a large extent an "abstraction
from the soul" that the subsequent discussion of friendship is required.

Friendship is the theme of books VIII and IX of the *Ethics*. In the
course of developing the thought that friends and friendship are good,
Aristotle observes that friendship seems to hold cities together, that
legislators are even more in earnest about it than about justice, and that,
men being friends, there is no need for justice. This dignification of
friendship in relation to justice is to be understood in the light of the
remark occurring later in book VIII to the effect that friendship and
justice seem to be "about" (*peri*) the same things and to exist among the
same beings (1159b25). The point is made quite clear that any difference
of dignity between friendship and justice must be conceived in a way that
does not prejudge the question whether the one can simply replace the
other. I believe that this very question will prove crucial, and will be the

core of Aristotle's continued investigation of Plato's thought as presented in the *Republic*, where justice and friendship converge in communism, but converge on such terms that the difference between them is driven out of sight, and the sought-for definition of justice proves rather to define friendship, but also to frustrate the expression of friendship in love.

Conceding everything desired to the similarity between justice and friendship, how then do they differ? They differ in that friendship involves liking or even loving, and more concretely, liking other human beings for some good that they control or that resides in them and that can be had from, with, or through them. Aristotle maintains that there are three reasons that account for liking: usefulness, pleasure and goodness. These sometimes in the ensuing passage decay into two, pleasure and goodness, for useful means only productive of pleasure or good. Friendship involves also mutual wishing of good between the friends who must be known to each other as wishing, each, the other's well-being. It appears more or less directly to the reader that a relation of conscious mutual benevolence on grounds other than mutual usefulness is almost certainly not the political relationship.

Aristotle reveals that friendship expresses a man's liking for what is not necessarily good in itself or even truly good for him but for what seems to him to be good. Friendship therefore can and most often will exist between men for whom the simply good does not appear to be good; yet friendship at its best is the union of those for whom the good appears as good and is good. Justice, however, is characteristically and precisely the relation between those for whom the simply good is not good—those same men for whom some amount of a good thing can be too much. Friendship thus overtops justice, and should of course not be confounded with it, for reasons that will appear more specifically before we have finished.

Aristotle introduces early in book VIII the consideration of the durability of friendships, showing that those based on exchanges of utility and pleasure, and in general friendships between men who are unlike one another and who get mere pleasure or profit from the relation do not last. One could say that such "friendships" are the normal relation among fellow-citizens both as such and as parties to the division of labor. A city based in effect on friendship might be fragile if it were based also on the rule of "one man, one job," unless the parties to the relation loved one another for their characters, or virtues, or for what they truly are—provided that does not change. Aristotle eventually observes (1158ª10) and will repeat (end of book IX) that one does not feel true or warm friendship for many people. It is not of the greatest political importance.

The friendships discussed hitherto have been between unlikes but "equals." Since those friendships included those between rulers and subjects, one wonders what meaning Aristotle is attaching to "equality."

He explains that equality in matters of friendship means primarily "according to quantity" and secondarily "according to merit or worth," while equality in matters of justice means first according to worth and second according to quantity. He clarifies this by pointing out that too great a disparity in virtue, vice, wealth, or anything will destroy the basis for friendship. We now understand better why he introduced into this new section (on "unequals", 1158^{b}12ff.) the example of ruler and ruled along with others like father and son, and husband and wife: the earlier reference to rulers and subjects had in mind rulers who are not superior and may be inferior to their subjects. Here he takes into view those rulers who are truly superior to their subjects—and who are as little moved to friendship with them, or love for them, as the gods are for mankind generally. If the absolutely superior ruler were one such for whom the truly good things are good in unlimited degree, then according to the teaching of book V *justice* would not hold between him and his subjects; and according to the teaching of book IX, *friendship* would not hold between them. One wonders if Aristotle is not reflecting on the philosopher-king, and on the Platonic city. The passage ends with a remarkable thought: "we" (which must include "we philosophers") would not wish our friends to rise too high—even to become gods—for they would then have to lose us as friends, while also losing themselves through transformation. He says, moreover, that we wish our friend very well, but in truth, while we wish him the greatest goods, we perhaps do not wish him all of them, "for each one wishes the good things especially for himself" (1159^{a}13). I take this to mean that the philosopher-king would be estranged not only from the many but from those who were dearest to him and to whom he was dearest.

Aristotle goes on to observe that friendship brings a man affection, which is welcome, but that loving is more characteristic of friendship than is being loved. The leading illustration that he gives is that of the mother who clings to her love of her child even though the child is put out to nurse and does not know its mother, hence cannot reciprocate her love. The example seems poorly chosen, for Aristotle has already said that friendship implies reciprocal, conscious well-wishing. The example would however be pertinent to a reflection on the community of women and children. The remainder of the passage (1159^{b}2-24) develops the thought that true friendship is lasting. The passage as a whole may be taken to mean that the relation of mother and child, even if it is not strictly speaking friendship, bears some of the best, because most irrepressible, characteristics of friendship. It would be wrongheaded, perhaps, to attempt to stamp out this bond of union in the name of more perfect unity among human beings in a society. One might even condemn such an attempt as contrary to nature.

If the two preceding points are put together, Aristotle might appear to be saying that a proposal for rule by the philosopher-king and a proposal for dismantling the family aim, in unison, at joining what nature means to separate and separating what nature intends to unite.

The next passage (1159^{b}25ff.) deals, not altogether surprisingly, with the sharing of property. The point can be stated simply: sharing of good varies directly with the intimacy of the natural relation among the men. Brothers and "sworn-brothers" (*hetairoi,* comrades) share everything, parties to less intimate relations share less. Aristotle says in so many words, it is more terrible to defraud a comrade than a fellow citizen, and describes it as natural that the claims of both justice and friendship should increase with the intimacy of the relation. Therefore the community of property is naturally greatest at the level of association furthest from the city.

Aristotle concludes this section with a passage (1160^{a}8-30) in which he assigns to the subpolitical bodies that are the parts of the city, the function of catering to particular advantages (for example, sailors on a voyage) while the city as a whole provides for the benefit of everyone by securing the common advantage, or justice. I take him to mean that, where division of labor and nature itself both generate associations that need and administer property, associations smaller than the city and not political in their foundations, the basis for communizing property on the level of the city is unsound.

Now follows a fairly lengthy passage dealing explicitly with the various regimes (1160^{a}31ff.) The scheme is familiar: kingship, aristocracy, timocracy or políteia are the good regimes in descending order of goodness; tyranny, oligarchy, democracy are the respective corruptions in descending order of badness. (The corruption of the best is the worst; the corruption of the least good is the least bad. The reason is that tyranny is quite different from kingship while democracy closely resembles timocracy.) The point is made that in every regime there is the same scope for friendship as for justice between ruler and ruled. Aristotle makes it appear both that the king must be absolutely independent of his subjects with respect to "all goods," and as absolutely superior to them as a shepherd is to his sheep; and also that there will be friendship and justice between him and them. It is hard to reconcile this with the former statements making an excess of inequality between parties the destroyer of friendship and of justice between them. On the other hand he says in so many words that there is most friendship and justice between ruler and ruled—but perhaps only in the class of the corrupted regimes—in democracy, where equality prevails. Here the difficulty seems to be that equality is accompanied by the substantial identity of ruler and ruled, the demos. How can there be justice, or at any rate injustice, without a difference between the parties?

It appears that, abstracting for the moment from justice, friendship between ruler and ruled is not at a peak in the best regime but in the least bad one. Or rather, that this will be true if the best regime is the simply best one ruled by the philosopher whose superiority in excellence and power is absolute. In the city of Plato's *Republic,* it might seem, as between the ruler and the ruled, justice has no more basis than does friendship. Aristotle has not deceived us in saying that each regime exhibits these to the same degree, as between ruler and ruled.

In the next extensive passage (1161^{b}11–1162^{a}33), Aristotle enters particularly into the friendship and love that exist in the family, taking up first the relation between those united by blood and then those united by law of matrimony. Parents love their offspring as being their own selves or having the parents' being; children love their parents as the source of their being; brothers love one another as emanating from the same source: "the same being, somehow, though separate." Friendship between husband and wife appears to be natural, for man is by nature pair-forming rather than or more than (*mallon*) political. We infer that whoever would dissolve the family would attack the existence of that preeminently natural group in which is engendered that commingling of being, that overcoming of separateness in existence through a sharing of being, that will find its most perfect expression in the mutual love of two philosophic dialectic-partners. The family is made by Aristotle to appear as the subphilosophic prefiguration of philosophic *philia,* subphilosophic because based upon engendering of men by concourse of the bodies. To attack this preeminently natural community in the interest of the city would be perhaps to threaten the human association that is a shadow of philosophic and ontic-psychic unity in the interest of the human association that is capable of slaying the philosopher. I say this without an intention to romanticize the family in Aristotle's name or to suggest that one should banish from memory his references to and thus his awareness of father-beating.

Book VIII closes with observations on the grounds for complaint by a friend that he has been treated badly by his friend. It appears that when the bond of obligation between them is moral rather than legal, but the friendship is of the kind based on mere utility, the recipient's valuation rather than the donor's should govern. In friendships based on virtue, it is the intention of the donor rather than the estimation of the recipient that is decisive. Since the final passage reverts to the mutual claims or duties of fathers and sons, one is moved to wonder how Aristotle would determine the basis of valuation of those claims and obligations. The father has indeed bestowed being on his son; for this the son can never bring sufficient honor in recompense. This is apparently to adopt the son's standpoint, i.e., the recipient's standpoint, which is to suggest that the friendship is one of utility and not of virtue. This is confirmed in a way by our understanding that it is utterly impossible for a parent to generate a child out of an intention to give that particular child a being. It is more strongly confirmed by Aristotle's closing remark: a father might be disposed to sever all connection with an unsatisfactory son, but he would think twice about it, not only on grounds of natural friendship or affection but because "it is human not to repel assistance." Aristotle has been careful not to sentimentalize the friendship of fathers and sons.

In book IX, Aristotle takes up again the question of a difference between donor and recipient over the value of the good that has been bestowed. Here the case is put with the philosopher in the position of the donor, replacing the father: there is no doubt that the relation is based on virtue, and the intention of the benefactor is to benefit this existing human being. The beneficiary owes as unlimited a debt to his philosophic teacher as to his parents or the gods. Asking next whether there is an absolute obligation to respect one's father that would override the counterclaims of art and virtue (he puts the issue more decently than this), the answer proves to be that nobility and necessity are the rule, and no one man deserves consideration in every respect. It is notable that the present formula (*kalon, anankaion*) differs from the weighty characterization of the themes of the study of politics: the noble and the just (*ta kala kai ta dikaia:* 1094^{b}14). The rule for *philia* replaces the just with the necessary. Moreover, according to a point made in book VII (1148^{a-b}), the excess of filial piety is a distinct defect, the avoidance of which is *enkrateia* or moral hardihood. Putting these things together, one might say that in order to give everyone the honor of friendship due to him, including father, one must draw on the moral hardihood that permits the noble or beautiful indeed to rule, but alongside necessity or exigency. I believe that Aristotle might be defended against the charge that he has dropped justice from the highest human affairs by saying that moral hardihood in the service of the noble and the exigent, i.e., *philia* well understood, is justice. Everyone gets his due, and we gain an insight into Aristotle's reason for treating *enkrateia* and *philia* in contiguous books as an "alternative" to moral virtue in the mode of the mean.

Aristotle now raises the question whether a friendship should be preserved when the friends have changed. This is the inconspicuous introduction of the grand question of being, identity, or the sign or form of the seat of a man himself. At first (1165^b), a man is the same man if his "character" (*ethos*) remains unchanged; but soon the reader's attention is drawn to *mind* (*dianoia*) and the changes in it which would of course lead to the rupture of friendship when the inequality became excessive. Next, only apparently changing the subject, he shows five reasons for thinking that all friendship for others is patterned on a man's relation to himself.

After the enumeration of the five reasons, he discusses them: but he takes the fourth out of order and makes it first: the good man (*spoudaios*) is of a single mind in himself, and desires the same things with all his soul (he does not say "with all the parts of his soul"). He wishes his own good, in action, and with a view to the intellectual, which seems to be the man himself. The mind or intelligence (*nous*) seems to be the man, or more so than anything else, and the good of this is his good. Moreover he especially participates in his own pleasures and pains. Likewise is he toward a friend. Thus it appears that a friend is another self.

Bad men are not friends to their own selves: again taking the fourth point first, they differ from themselves, desiring one thing but wishing for something else. This is *akrasia*—moral weakness. Thus the condition of goodness, unity in the soul, and hegemony of the mind is moral hardihood (*enkrateia*) rather than justice as Plato might have it.

Through the rest of book IX, Aristotle pursues the issue of the union of a number of human beings, or their approach to a single being, and the manifold of a single human being and in what might consist his unity. He refers to likemindedness (concord, *homonoia*) and praises it as "political friendship." He then mentions that benefactors love their beneficiaries more than beneficiaries love their benefactors. The reason is that the benefactor's being *is* in his activity or actualization (*energeia*): Kant might say, the beneficiary is the mere object of his benefactor. Thus we can understand why Aristotle asks next whether one ought to love himself more than someone else. In this passage (1168^{b}28ff.) he portrays the man who seeks to outdo everyone else in virtue—in justice and temperance by name, but in virtue in general. Aristotle does not refer to the fact that Socrates shows Thrasymachus in the *Republic* that such behavior is unwise and unjust. He goes on to display the morally good man's justification for self-love in terms of his insatiable nobility. In a passage of about two octavo pages, he uses the word for noble or some derivative of it sixteen times. This athlete of nobility is characterized as being under the fullest control of the ruling element, the mind, which is the man himself; and his state is the state of moral hardihood—*enkrateia* (1168^b-1169^a). Everyone will praise him, and out of his self-regarding greed for the noble will emerge the common good—as if the scene were ruled by an invisible hand, we might say. But it appears next that this greed for the noble may well lead the man to death, poverty, and ruin, that is, to such great transformations that he must lose his being or open up such gaps of inequality between himself and his friends as to lose them. Or his competition to exceed in nobility will make him surrender wealth, honors, and offices to his friend for nobility's sake, and even to yield an opportunity to do a noble act. What Aristotle does not do is to describe the scene in which two such gluttons for nobility engage in the courtly rivalry to determine which one will exceed the other by ruining himself first or most. So far as friendship means likemindedness, beneficence, and union of beings through beneficence, it appears that nobility goes far but does not succeed in perfecting the paradigm of friendship. Nobility succeeds between a noble and a vulgar man, so far as it succeeds at all. It would fail between two likeminded men, or two men who resembled each other precisely in their desires, say two magnanimous men. But friendship should be most perfect between two such, if their desires be suitable. We are close to being shown that pair.

Raising the question whether friends are necessary to a happy man, Aristotle notes that happiness is something that arises or is generated by an activation, so that the man who is capable of it must be quickened to it by something. He now propounds the surprising notion that a friend might be a representation of oneself that a man can contemplate better than he can contemplate himself. It seems that happiness requires that one be able to contemplate oneself in action as good, and the way to do so is with the eyes. The other advantage brought by companionship to the happy man is the increased continuousness of the activated state with another to help keep it in being. Now Aristotle proposes to investigate the matter "more naturally." This results in the characterization of life as perception (*aisthanesthai*) or thought (*noein*); our perceiving that we perceive or think is our perception that we exist: "le sentiment de notre existence." This disturbingly fortifies the previous thought: one might need to "see" himself in act for happiness to be perfected, and to see himself with the two eyes in the head, not metaphorically. But Aristotle then reveals that "symperception" (*synaisthanesthai*) of the friend's being means being or living together and sharing discourse and thoughts. It also transpires that the friend's being is not equally but only almost as important to a man as his own. The more natural investigation leads beyond the seeing with the eyes of the body and restores the natural self-preference of even (or perhaps especially) the best man. It also confirms the need we have to be energized from without if we are to persist in the state of highest activity. It soon develops that friendship is at its best between a human being and one friend: two. Whereas it appeared in book VI that the compositeness or duality of a man interrupts his highest activity, it now appears that that interruption is overcome by the duality of minds lodged in two friends: *philia* repairs the imperfection in man arising out of the discord of body and soul—but on the level of philosophy, not of nobility; or between two men, not among a multitude; or dialectically, not politically.

Aristotle prepares to close the discussion of friendship. The last theme is pleasure and pain. A friend's presence helps take away grief; but if one cares for the friend, will one consent to get relief through grieving him?

We should have our friends in to share our pleasures, and discourage them from coming to us when we are in pain. We should go to them when they are in pain, not when it is time to share their good fortune. But Aristotle indicates a grave problem: one must not be a boor about declining their invitations. It might be very difficult to reconcile the noble benevolence of the friend in pain with the noble benevolence of the friend condoling; and similarly in pleasure. Unless the pleasure is gained through the activation of the contemplative mind, where the demands of gentlemanly rivalry do not enter and where rivalry of any sort is at a minimum, the consummation of friendship will be precarious. Thus the way is paved for the treatment of pleasure and happiness in the last book of the *Ethics,* and then the transition to politics and the *Politics.* Not friendship and not speech or reason can govern men but mind armed with a power to compel. Yet philosophy has no power to compel, and it must depend altogether on speech or reason and on a sort of *philia* that can grow up among good or earnest men, if only through some of them studying the books of others.

The city apparently needs the philosopher. Can the philosopher persuade the city that this is true? And why should he desire to confer this great good on those so far below him? He might succeed in persuading the city to accept his counsel if he refrains from exasperating it by insisting on friendship where mere justice will suffice. And he will desire to confer this benefit because, being beyond noble magnanimity, he does not despise but merely contemplates that multitude which is the greatest foil to his powers of activation.

Notes

1. Note that the pleasures, being inseparable from the activities in which they arise, must differ from one another as the activities differ: there is not a Good, but there are many goods; and there is not Pleasure, but there are many pleasures. A ranking or ordering tends to replace the Idea. Cf. *Philebus,* 53C.

2. The *Oresteia* may be considered as recording such an excessive devotion.

On Descartes' *Discourse on Method*

Reprinted from *Interpretation*
1, no. 2 (Winter 1970).

Descartes was born in 1596. The *Discourse on Method,* a work of his full maturity, was published in French in 1637 as the prefatory essay in a volume containing also his essays on geometry, optics, and meteors. The full title of the famous "preface" is "Discourse on the method of conducting one's reason well and seeking truth in the sciences."

The first of the six parts into which the *Discourse* is divided begins with the following famous reasoning. Good sense, or reason, which is the power of judging well and distinguishing the true from the false, is the best distributed thing in the world. One knows this because all men, even those who are the hardest to satisfy in every other respect, are content with the amount of it that they possess. It is not likely that all are mistaken in this. Rather, what follows is that reason is naturally equal in all men. Thus the diversity of our opinions does not signify that some men are more reasonable or rational than others but only that we conduct our thoughts along diverse paths and thus take different things into account. What is important is not the natural equipment but the right application of it, the right road or method for the mind.

It is obvious that from the fact that all men are content with their good sense it does not follow that all men are equally endowed with it. Whether they are equally endowed must be determined empirically. Descartes himself denies throughout the *Discourse* that men are equally endowed. His argument here in fact means that if men judge badly about their judgment, they will believe their judgment to be good, and in fact this is what they do believe—let us say, to overstate the case, "unanimously." Being deceived about their judgment, there is hardly anything else they may not be deceived about. It would appear that nothing but Descartes or his "method," not even the philanthropy of God, stands between mankind and wholesale deception. His vindication of the method, apparently based on a flattery of mankind, is in fact based on the unflattering notion that between himself and the rest there is a colossal inequality. If that inequality is sufficiently great, his method cannot be a method in the simple sense: the more it is a true description of the way in which *his* mind moved, the less can it prescribe the way in which other men's minds might move. I shall try to maintain that the *Discourse on Method* does not teach a method in the simple sense of "how to do it yourself," that Descartes' caution against mistaking his teaching for such a thing bears on the meaning of the scientific project, and that the irony of Descartes' introductory thought is characteristic of his expression throughout the *Discourse.*

Descartes' tacit reproval of the common opinion will animate his famous decision to doubt, i.e., reject at least provisionally, everything obvious and generally accepted as true. Aristotle's notion that the common opinion is not likely to be simply wrong is accepted by Descartes in the one context that shows it at its worst: the common opinion favoring common opinion. Descartes now confirms the thought that all men are equally endowed with reason by appealing to "the common opinion of the philosophers," i.e., the Scholastic Aristotelians, who teach that the essence of a species is in its entirety present in each member of the species. The success of Descartes' project will be measured, however, by the effectiveness with which that project discredits and supplants the Aristotelian-Scholastic conception of essences to which he here appeals. His ironic appeal to it is part of the foregoing rejection of the conclusion to which it seems to lead, and helps to prepare the elaboration of his intellectual autobiography, the core of which is his criticism and rejection of the sciences and arts as handed down to his time.

Descartes now opens the theme of his method as the means to something better than the vain and useless enterprises of almost all men, but he does so with what appears to be much modesty. He will show the story of his life as if it were a picture, gathering people's opinions about it through the common clamor (*"bruit commun"*), from which he will gain instruction. (This modest submission can be understood by juxtaposition with the state of his mind as expressed in Part Six, where he debates with himself the advantages of writing and publishing his thoughts. He admits there that he "almost never came across any critic of [his] opinions who did not seem either less rigorous or less balanced than [himself].") At any rate, Descartes now characterizes the ensuing autobiography as rather like a story or a fable in which, "among some examples that people can imitate there will perhaps be found some others which there will be reason not to follow." In the sequel, devoted to a showing of the value and the defect of each branch of received knowledge, Descartes will represent fables as harmful in leading men to believe impossible events to be possible; and history or "story" to contain distortions that lead men to conceive projects that exceed their powers. There is at least some reason, on the basis of Part One of the *Discourse,* to believe that Descartes was apprehensive not only of the dogmatists, his contemporary adversaries, but also of his epigoni.

Descartes has given the reasons for his dissatisfaction with the world of letters or books. In general, the learning of men is full of untruth and uselessness, contradiction and pretense. As soon as he could leave school—thus on the basis of a decision made while still a student—he abandoned books and resolved to cultivate no other science than what he could find "in [himself], or rather in the great book of the world." As he proceeds to describe the ensuing unlettered phase of his life, he shows that the preceding "or" was disjunctive, and that the order in which he enumerated the two unlettered studies was the reverse of the order in which he cultivated them. First, he studied in the great book of the world—as one might say, seeking to learn about the human things from and through conversing with men. His resolve to follow this course conflicts with the reason he gave, a few pages earlier, against too much study of the ancient writings: such study is like too much travel; it estranges one from his own country. Descartes tells us that he went abroad in order to learn what men by their actions prove themselves really to believe. He thus informs us how to resolve the tension between his criticism of travel, made in the name of good citizenship, and his actual travel, done in the name of learning. He was not averse to becoming a sort of stranger to his own land. More generally, he put science above the polity. Less generally, he was perhaps not devoted to the regime of his own country. What he might have preferred to it is, I believe, faintly indicated by the fact that, in the closing passage of Part One, where he speaks of his travels, he uses the expression "great peoples" which he uses once more, at the end of Part Three, to describe the Dutch. His description of the Dutch regime is laconic but weighty, and as close to enthusiastic as he allows himself to become.

However this might be, the earlier objection against travel, made on behalf of the country, is replaced by an apparently more serious objection, made on behalf of knowledge: no amount of travel helped Descartes to any certain truth. The practices of men are as confused as their theories. If he discovered an inclination among men to pursue good and avoid evil, he says nothing about it. What he does say is that he now gave up the quest for knowledge among men and began to seek it "in himself," which proves to mean literally in solitude. Apparently, in order to understand anything about man and the world, it is necessary to withdraw from the world of man, which is the world of common opinion, of the pretension to equal *bon sens* with which Part One began.

Part Two, which contains the famous rules of the method, opens with Descartes' remark that he was in Germany because the war known to us as the Thirty Years War had "called him" there. His expression in the Latin translation is more emphatic: he was there because of "[his] curiosity to see the war." He makes a point of his perfect detachment from the issues, doctrinal and political, over which the war was being fought. The meaning of this detachment will become clearer presently. At any rate, during the winter cessation of active fighting he found himself in complete isolation in the celebrated *poêle* or stove-heated chamber. There, for some reason, one of the first things to occur to him was that generally there is less perfection in productions consisting of several parts and made by several makers than in the things on which only one maker has worked. He gives examples: buildings; cities; constitutions including that of the true religion legislated by God and that of Sparta; sciences; and finally man himself.

These examples are noteworthy in several particulars. In the first place, there is something resembling facetiousness in praising the unity of design in the constitution of the true religion so soon after a reference to the terrific wars of the Reformation. Further, Descartes goes on to praise the laws of Sparta because, framed by one man, they all tended to the same end. Next, speaking of man, Descartes is forced to acknowledge that, because we are not born with the full use of reason and must therefore be children before we are men, we are inevitably pulled in opposite directions by our appetites and our preceptors, to the permanent impairment of our judgment. Implicit is a bold reflection on the creation of man by God in the image of God. First, according to Scripture, Adam was not made a child but was born perfect and entire. Any defects in his judgment had to arise otherwise than by Descartes' account, if childhood is inseparable from that account. But perhaps childhood is not necessary to the impairment of judgment. Descartes makes the conflict of appetites and preceptors responsible more directly. Did Adam have preceptors? He surely had one; or two, depending on the status of Eve. We do not have to ask if he had appetites. How can we doubt that Adam's appetites led him in one direction and the precept of his very creator urged him in another? He did not tend toward a single end.

The laws of Sparta had just been described as tending toward a single end. Is it imaginable that the fatal opposition of ends introduced into man's life by the war between appetites and preceptors could be overcome? Could mankind be directed toward a single end, as the Spartans apparently were for a time, by a grand constitution that reconciles precept with appetite once and for all? In Eden, man's appetite for knowledge was put in conflict with the precept that commanded obedience as the price of life. The rest of Part Two, indeed the rest of the *Discourse*, promises a way of making life the result of knowledge under a human constitution which resembles that of Holland rather than Sparta. If there is a political teaching in Descartes, and therewith in the scientific project of the modern age, this thought appears to be at its root.

Precisely for this reason, it surprises us not at all that the next paragraph of the *Discourse* contains Descartes' earnest disclaimer of any intention to reform any public affairs. He uses a striking argument to prove that he truly has no desire to meddle with public institutions. He says that he is merely recounting his own experiences and reporting the method that has worked for him, advising no one to imitate him. He goes further. He believes that most men will be unable to imitate him. Some, believing themselves more gifted than they are, would imitate him in rejecting the received opinions and would remain in confusion forever after, incapable of discovering the truth. Others, "having enough reason, or modesty, to judge that they are less able to distinguish the true from the false than are some other men by whom they can be taught, ought rather to be satisfied to follow the opinions of those others than to seek for better ones themselves." But according to Descartes the vain and the modest are almost all of mankind. His proof that he has no project for reconstituting the world seems to prove rather that if he had such a project, it would be based on a regime of which he might be the autocrat as well as sole maker, with perhaps no imitators but only a multitude of subjects. This bears heavily on the possible meaning of the method which is the chief burden of this Part of the *Discourse*.

Descartes now affirms that he would have been among the modest and docile part of mankind if he had had but a single teacher (*un seul maître*) or had not observed the differences that divide the learned. But things fell out otherwise; and moreover on his travels he learned that the differences among peoples and nations are so far-reaching, the effects of custom and example so profound, that they are hard to calculate. He is driven back on the conclusion that a man alone is more likely to come upon truths than is a whole multitude, that he himself must undertake the search, and that the figure by which he can be described is, a man who walks alone and in the dark. Conspicuous in Descartes' sketch are the following features: a docile man taught entirely by a single master and thus freed from confusion; the immense effect upon us of our environment; a solitary walker who frees himself and perhaps can lead the others. The anticipation of Rousseau is striking, and compels us to wonder, parenthetically, how deep Rousseau's criticism of the scientific project really went.

Next, in the paragraph that immediately precedes the statement of the four rules of the method, Descartes refers to the three arts or sciences that he had studied which seemed as if they might contribute something to his project: logic, geometry, and algebra. Each has merits and defects. Logic is merely didactic, at worst sophistic, never heuristic. It contains many good things—he does not mention any by name—but these are so confounded with bad things that the whole is unusable. Geometry and algebra, in their then state, are described as practically useless, geometry so limited to figure as to overstrain the imagination and algebra so bound to particular procedures and symbols as to be an obstacle rather than an instrument for the mind. Thus he must find his own method, one which, "comprising the advantages of these three, will be exempt from their defects." It is necessary to observe that, a few pages later, speaking of his method which has then been exposed to the reader, Descartes says that he has "borrowed the best of geometric analysis and of algebra." He has either not borrowed what is good in logic, namely, its power to explain to others what one knows, or he did not really find anything worth borrowing in logic—the only part of philosophy that he regarded as in any respect promising; or perhaps both. There is some reason to believe that Descartes believed that his combination of geometrical and algebraic reasoning was reasoning simply, replacing philosophy in general and logic in particular. What this would do to metaphysics, to which he devotes all of Part Four in order to prove the existence of God and of the immortal soul, is a question we shall not get to in this paper; but it deserves consideration. In any case, he declares that he has "taken a firm and constant resolve not to fail one single time to observe [the four rules.]" With this vow, so reminiscent of the traditional formula defining justice that one wonders whether obeying these rules is not the only obligation of justice he will acknowledge, he now enters on the enumeration of the famous rules themselves.

The first of these is to accept as true only what is evidently so, namely, what presents itself to his mind clearly and distinctly.

The second is to divide every difficulty into as many parts as is possible and necessary.

The third deals with the order of thinking: begin with the simplest objects and thus the ones easiest to know. Ascend to the most composite. Suppose an order among things if there is not a natural order.

The fourth is to make thorough enumerations and surveys in order to avoid leaving things out of account.

These rules, so economically presented, receive an important elaboration in the remaining few pages of Part Two. To begin with, Descartes asserts that the example of geometrical reason led him to *imagine* that all truths are linked together in a long, perhaps an indefinitely long chain, so that none is too remote or too concealed to be uncovered. Everything is knowable. I believe it is fair to say that this truth, manifested to Descartes' imagination, does not in any apparent way emerge from the four rules. Rather, it points in the direction of the remark that he makes in the succeeding paragraph, namely, that in his concrete studies, "every truth that I found was a rule that served me afterwards in finding others." What this means might be easier to say if we take note more particularly of what he thinks his method makes possible. In the first place, impressed by the achievement of mathematicians, he realizes that they do not deal with any specific material but with "relations and proportions" among things. He desires in effect a universal science bound to nothing particular and therefore true of everything. That science must be a science of proportions. As for any particular proportion, the simplest or irreducible element is the line: there was nothing else that he could represent more distinctly to his imagination and his senses. To work with a number of relations or proportions, however, he had to resort to symbols. Thus he borrowed the best from geometry and algebra, as was said earlier.

What does this mean? Can we not say that the element of the universal science is what is most clear to the imagination and to the senses, or that the primary and irreducible can be represented by what is visible and thus imaginable? This will be contradicted in Part Four, where the explicit intention is to prove that God and the soul are and are incorporeal, and that neither can be understood by reduction to the imaginable, namely, body. Yet Descartes here (at the end of Part Two) gives us to understand that this reduction to an imaginable is the very core of the universal science, which bears a similarity to what he will elaborate as physics (Part Five) but which seems to conflict with what he treats as metaphysics. Evidently this raises a doubt about the so-called dualism of Descartes, a doubt that students of Descartes do not entertain as often as they would if they respected their master's admonition to doubt all things at least once.

In summary, Part Two begins by praising the superiority of things made by a single maker, shows the defectiveness of man and his condition, and presents a plan for uncovering every truth in the world, thus acquiring the power to remedy those defects.

In Part Three, Descartes enunciates the "three or four" maxims of the provisional morality, described as provisional because, presumably, a final morality cannot be understood before the system of knowledge as a whole has been brought to perfection. In fact, however, it is not clear that the "provisional" morality is not in principle a final morality too. This point can best be considered after the maxims themselves have been considered, and we will return to it.

There is a tacit link or transition between Parts Two and Three: at the end of Part Two, precipitancy and prejudgment are held up as the great offenses against philosophizing. At the beginning of Part III, irresolution is held up as the offense against action that Descartes most desires to avoid. I believe that the text bears out the following thought: the prevailing way of life is defective in promoting premature conclusion, dogmatism, or immobility in theorizing; and wavering, inconstancy, or fluctuation in practice. The three or four moral maxims will be seen to be rules for flexibility and constancy in turn; to speak more or less figuratively, a presentation of morality in terms of the alternative of motion and rest: a reduction of morality to physics, very generally speaking.

The first maxim is to rest quiet in the laws, customs, religion, and opinions of the people and authorities with which he lives. More interestingly, he will avoid excesses or extremes. His reason is not that of Aristotle, which finds the virtues to be means, but is a version of the reason of Machiavelli: if he chooses an extreme which happens to be the wrong one, he will be further from the right road than if he had temporized. (At this point it becomes clear that the perfection of knowledge will enable him infallibly to choose the right extreme, and will transform the provisional rule into a final rule having the identical moral content.) More particularly, all promises by which one abdicates any of his liberty are extremes and to be avoided. Of course he excludes such things as legal contracts. His point is that, like all things, he is himself in a state of flux, and especially his judgment is subject to improvement. The promise that he makes *to himself,* i.e., the one unbreakable or unmovable, is to improve his understanding. This is, incidentally, the effectual retraction of the first part of this maxim in which he pledged allegiance to the prevailing opinions.

The second maxim is to be firm, resolute, and unchanging in his actions once he has made the best decision he can in the present state of his knowledge. He says, "this makes it possible to relieve me of all the repentings and remorse that agitate the consciences of weak and vacillating minds. . . ." The constancy that he avows here has a reflection on Christian morality, as his rejection of the mean in the first maxim had a reflection on pagan morality. One may notice that the final perfection of knowledge would if anything confirm this maxim and establish its intention beyond all provisionality.

The third maxim moves back to the theme of change or the goodness of his own flexibility. He must conquer himself rather than fortune and change his desires rather than the order of the world. More generally, he must learn to adjust his desires to what his understanding lets him know to be possible, which is the *natural* tendency of our will anyway. In this context he asserts that if we were to regard all goods outside ourselves (i.e., not our thoughts) as equally beyond our power, we would no more desire to be well, being sick, than to have incorruptible bodies or wings like the birds: But our thoughts, which he says are wholly within our power, have a great effect on the transformation of impossibles into possibles; and whatever he might have thought about resurrection of the body and immortality, he certainly believed that medicine was subject to vast improvement, making it quite reasonable for sick people to desire health. What then does he mean by resolving to change himself rather than the *order* of the world? Perhaps to change his thoughts, the only things wholly in our power; which done sufficiently, of course he need not desire to change the order of the world or of nature. In the present context, he refers to the limitations on us "due to our birth," or as one might say, due to our mortality, or perhaps our nature. He might limit himself to producing all possible changes, through changing his thoughts, within the order of nature. How far does that order itself limit us? Until we have exhausted the knowledge of nature, we do not know where it limits us, or how it limits our desires. Our understanding and our will are eventually one and the same, coextensive with the utter limits of nature. Man appears in the image of God. The third moral maxim is superficially provisional but in its intention it regards eternity.

The fourth maxim is a review of the grounds of the preceding three. This, I believe, is why Descartes says at the outset that there are "three or four" such rules, the last being on a higher level than the three maxims proper. The leading theme of the fourth "provisional" rule is ways of life; more specifically the excellence of Descartes' philosophic way of life: the sweetness and innocence of the happiness it brings beyond all others "in this life" as he says first and "ever" as he says soon thereafter. He plainly avows that the three maxims are entirely in the service of his philosophizing, and his happiness. As such they are neither provisional nor essentially moral. They are the declaration of his freedom to move by appearing to rest. They are an impressive sign that in its classic and its loftiest state, modernity and modern science were innocent of the notion that science is impotent to judge of the ways of life, beginning with its own.

It might appear that Descartes' morality is perfectly idiosyncratic, a declaration of his own unboundable freedom to do everything needful and possible for the increase of his knowledge—the ultimate subordination of moral to intellectual virtue in the interest of the man whom no one or almost no one can imitate. As the conclusion to Part Three shows, his claim of freedom for himself is not without an echo that speaks to the life of the multitude. He reverts to his sojourn in the *poêle,* and tells of his leaving that solitude for nine years of wandering in the world while he cleared his mind of error, always doubting yet avoiding irresolution. Now his words are these: "my whole plan aimed only at giving me certainty, and at rejecting the moving earth (*la terre mouvante*) and the sand in order to find bedrock and solid ground." The Latin translation omits the words, "reject the moving earth." Perhaps the Latin translation is bolder in eliminating the intimation that Descartes' project aims at overthrowing the doctrine for which Galileo was troubled, and troubled in ways that led to the publication of this very book rather than *Le Monde.* In any case, Part Three closes with Descartes' account of his withdrawal to a new solitude, one which takes the place of the *poêle.* His retirement was to "a country [namely Holland] where the long continuance of the war has led to such institutions that the armies one encounters seem only to enable one to enjoy the fruits of peace so much the more securely, and where, in the midst of the crowd of a great people, very active, and more careful of their own business than curious about other people's, lacking none of the conveniences of the most populous cities, I was able to live as solitary and withdrawn as in the most forsaken wastes."

Parts Two and Three form a unity as being the vehicle of the four rules of method and the four rules of morality. As a whole, these two Parts are enclosed within the brackets of an opening that speaks of war and solitude and a closing that also speaks of war and solitude. The war is the religious and civil war of western Christendom. The first solitude is the literal solitude of the Imperial desert, where the only convenience was the famous stove to which Descartes draws (I believe ironically) such extraordinary attention. The second solitude is civilized, convenient indeed, animated by the freedom and justice implicit in everyone's minding his own business, and consequently conducive to philosophizing. One is almost reminded of the transition from the City of Pigs to the City of Convenience. In the *Discourse,* the road between the *poêle* and the city of Amsterdam is the method of Descartes. The freedom that he claims for himself is most hospitably ensconced in a tolerant, commercial society. It is easy to understand his desire to assure the princes of Europe that the reform of their states is a thing far from his mind.

As Parts Two and Three form a certain unity, so also do Parts Four and Five form a whole, but on a different plan. Parts Four and Five have in common the subjects of God and the soul, presented as metaphysics in Part Four and as Physics in Part Five. Descartes says in so many words that he has presented the foundation of his metaphysics but only the order of the questions in his physics. I believe it would be unwise to overlook the possibility that he has protected his physics more thoroughly than his metaphysics—exposing answers in the one case but only questions in the other—because his physics is primary and more serious.

According to the early passages of Part Four, Descartes' metaphysical enterprise is and must be directed first of all to finding an indubitable truth and thus a perfectly certain one. The truth on which he alights is that he exists. The proof of this is that he cannot feign the opposite without absurdity. To sustain this point, he feigns a number of things, chiefly that he has no body, that there is no world and that he is not in any place; but he says nothing about what is the value of such feigning or the meaning of it. To indicate the problem, the reader must look ahead to the place at which Descartes will assert that clear and distinct ideas are as such true—a "general rule"—and to that other place just following where he holds that his false conceptions come to him out of nothing. Descartes does not explicitly consider the possibility that feigning myself to have no body is to feign an absurdity. He does later say, while proving the incorporeal soul, that man is a composite being, i.e., composed of body and soul; but to avoid the blasphemy of identifying man with God he affirms that the perfection of simplicity belongs only to God, while to man belongs the dependence to which all compositeness testifies. He does not say much about that dependence. He leaves one in doubt as to whether each component depends on the whole, the whole on each component, or—most portentous in the context—each component on the other. If this latter, then it is of the essence of man (adopting now the scholastic usage into which he falls in Part Four) that his soul and his body depend on each other, which is the tendency of Part Five, i.e., his physics. If body and soul depend on each other because we are not simple, i.e., not God, then to feign that we have no body is no more conducive to any truth than to feign that we do not exist; for in fact to feign that we have no body *is* to feign that we have no soul and no power to feign.

Descartes now reflects on his doubting, finds it the sign of an imperfection in himself, and sees that knowing is more perfect than doubting. How then did he, the imperfect being, obtain the power to conceive the perfect one? He explains that every conception of a thing less perfect than he is, is a dependency of his nature, while his conception of something more perfect than himself must depend on that more perfect being. Why this is so need not concern us for the present purpose, although it is quite important to bear in mind that, in Part Six, he will describe the truths of his science as consequences and *dependencies* not of more or less perfect beings but simply of more primary principles. What does concern us here is the formal argument employed by Descartes to sustain this proof of the existence of God: false ideas proceeding not from the truthful God but from nothing, if my idea of God's existence were false it would have to come from nothing. But ideas are real things, he says. Therefore it is as absurd that the idea of a perfect being proceed merely from a less perfect being as that more proceed from less or that something proceed from nothing. This remarkable proof of the existence of God depends on the self-evident absurdity of creation *ex nihilo*.

Let us consider one more attempt of Descartes to come to the aid of Scripture. He knows, from recognizing his imperfections, that he cannot be alone in the world. Something more perfect than himself must also exist and indeed must have been his creator. How does he move from his imperfections to the existence of God? By the simple reasoning that if he had made himself, he would have made himself not imperfect but on the contrary perfect, having all those desirable attributes that conduce to happiness and well-being—principally, of course, freedom from doubt. Having clumsily brought God's omnipotence into question in the one proof of his existence, Descartes seems to bring his philanthropy into question in order to strengthen that proof with another.

But Descartes wishes now to go on to other truths, in fact to further proofs of the existence of God. He begins by considering "the object of the geometers," which he conceives as a continuous body or a space extending indefinitely in all directions with parts divisible and movable. Now he observes that all the reasoning of geometers does not constitute proof that their object exists. This is his own example to illustrate his meaning: If one supposes a triangle, its angles must equal two right angles; but this gives no assurance at all that any triangle exists in the world. Whereas if one entertains the idea of a perfect being, the existence of that being is implicit in the idea of it as perfect. Thus the existence of God is at least as certain as any geometrical demonstration. In this reasoning there seem to be some difficulties, however. First, his thought apparently drifted from *the* object of the geometers to such particular objects as triangles and spheres. What he proves to be questioning is the existence of the latter, which merely have their being—if they exist—in the former. Second, he seems to adopt the view that triangles exist ("are outside") in extension or not at all. But is it not true that the definition of a triangle as the figure with angles equaling two right angles *is* the existence of the triangle? The existence of the triangle in the mind, clearly and distinctly, perhaps carries with it the clear and distinct conception of the great space that any figure as such presupposes in the way that a part presupposes the whole. If this is true, then reflection on the object of the geometers leads to this thought: there are some things whose existence is guaranteed by their definition. The guarantee rests on this: the existence of the thing being wholly in the mind, the clear and distinct definition of it is its real being. But if it cannot be clearly and distinctly known, i.e., if it cannot be perfectly known, its existence is to say the least jeopardized. Drawing the existence of God into this region of demonstration raises or at least seems to raise large questions.

The nominal subject of Part Five is the order of the questions of physics. Descartes says that he will not present the substance of his physics because he does not wish to become embroiled with the learned. What Descartes does offer to do is to give a brief summary of what he wrote and would have published under different circumstances. First, he explained light; then the sun and stars as the sources of most of it; then the heavens, which transmit it; the planets, the comets, and the earth which reflect it; and especially all the bodies on the earth because they are either colored, transparent, or luminous; and finally man as the spectator of it. He fulfills his promise to say nothing substantive here, but he has let us understand that the order of questions is important and we therefore give attention to that. We notice that there are six things or classes of things "explained," beginning with light and ending with man. To this extent, the sketch just presented is reminiscent of Scripture; but it has a defect that the account in Genesis does not have: it says nothing of any living or growing thing as such except man. It has another defect which, if one may say so, it shares with the Scriptural account of the beginning: it makes no mention of fire. Like the account in Genesis, it alludes in its own way to fire: Descartes described the sun and the stars as the sources of *most* light; the Bible simply has light created before the sun, moon, and stars. But the place of fire in the order of things will soon prove to be important, because fire introduces heat and heat is indispensable to the Cartesian explanation of life which will take up most of Part Five. If I am not mistaken, the first reference to flame in the Bible is in the verse describing the flaming sword threatening death to Adam if, punished for seeking knowledge, he should offend further by seeking life. Fire will have a different place in the world of Descartes. As we are about to see, he will present the matter again, immediately, in different parts and in a different order, this time including fire, heat, and life. Perhaps the time has come to remind ourselves of the four principal rules of his method: believe nothing not clear and distinct; divide the matter into the right parts; look to the order, beginning with the simple or irreducible, constructing an order if there is none by nature; and make careful enumerations to see that nothing has been left out. I believe that the correction of the "Biblical" account of the world and its replacement by the Cartesian one that I will describe next is the only illustration of the application of the method in its entirety in the *Discourse*.

Descartes abruptly commences again with these words. "All the same, in order to shade all these things a little, and to be able to say more freely what I think about them, without being obliged to follow or refute the opinions received among the learned, I decided to abandon this whole world to their disputes and to speak exclusively of what would take place in a new one if God now created somewhere in imaginary space enough matter to compose it and agitated [i.e., set in motion] variously and without order the various parts of that matter so as to compose a chaos, ... and thereafter to do no more than to lend his ordinary [i.e., non-miraculous] concurrence to nature and allow it to act according to the laws he has established." The Cartesian construction has this order: mere matter; motion; the laws of nature (which operate in such a way that, regardless of how many worlds God might create, those worlds must all be alike); the arrangement of most of that matter into forming the heavens; some parts of it composing an Earth, some going into planets and comets, and some into a sun and stars. Next he introduces light, and especially, its instantaneous traverse of the heavens and its reflection from planets and comets towards earth. Then, among other important things, he makes clear that he does not suppose any heaviness in matter, yet the parts of it nevertheless all tend toward the center of the Earth. Now such affairs as tides and air currents and geological features and, at last, fire. Fire leads to the remark that there is sometimes heat *without* light, as well as light without heat. Now he notices the transformations that fire, apparently through its heat rather than its light, is able to produce in things. It melts some and hardens others; converts things into ashes and smoke; and finally forms glass of those ashes. Now Descartes' words: "this transmutation of ashes into glass seeming to me to be as wonderful [*admirable*] as any other that occurs in nature, I took particular pleasure in describing it."

Now there is an interlude, which also serves as a connection, in which Descartes shows that it makes no difference to the honor of God whether the world was created in an instant or acquired its present appearance gradually; but supposing the latter makes understanding easier. For this reason he explains the nature of things through their development.

The next theme is animals and, especially, man. Having just drawn attention to his reason for explaining things in terms of their development, he claims to be unable to enter on the discussion of man except through assuming that God made him all at once, out of the same matter hitherto described, but without a reasonable soul to begin with, and without anything by way of a nutritive or sensitive soul except by the exciting in his heart of one of those "fires without light" already referred to. We may be permitted to pause for a moment to reflect on the articulation of the passages in the present context. First there was the "transmutation" of ashes into glass by the heat of fire, a change that impressed him immensely for a reason that he does not give. Then the thought that explanations of things in terms of their evolution (as we would say) ought not to be rejected as impious. Then the coming into being of man, whose mere life as such, as distinguished from his life qua rational for the moment, is explained through the animation of his mere matter by warmth. Scripture has it that "the Lord God formed man of the dust of the ground, and breathed into his nostrils the breath of life; and man became a living soul." Descartes shows us the wonderful but wholly natural transmutation of ashes by heat, and then the animation of man by that same power: heat is the great transmuter, the mediator between death and life. Descartes' conviction of this will inform that large section of Part Five in which he elaborates his notion of the circulation of the blood and the action of the animal spirits as thermal phenomena. The replacement of the "Biblical" enumeration has been in fact the replacement of light by heat.

There is one more point in this regard that is crucial. Descartes insists that he has not explained man's thinking, nor therefore his soul, that thing distinct from the body whose nature is only to think. Of course, the immortality of a man's soul requires that there be the disjunction between body and soul which Descartes is here maintaining. Descartes' position is therefore this: there is a principle of animation in body as such, and that principle is heat or anything more fundamental than heat to which heat itself can be reduced, say, the motion of particles. In addition there is a completely mysterious principle that accounts for reason or thought, and this second principle contributes nothing whatever to life as such, as is demonstrated by the living of the many irrational animals. The earthly death of a man is thus the cessation of whatever life as such means; and the survival of nothing but his reason. Immortality of the rational soul means the survival of a man's reasoning or thinking although his life itself does not continue. Men have found it easy to accept Descartes' famous dualism, but I find it difficult to reconcile its uninterpreted implications with reason. In order to progress on this theme, we turn directly to Part Six.

According to Descartes' prefatory synopsis of the *Discourse,* Part Six concerns "those things he believes necessary for moving further in the investigation of nature than has been done, and what reasons impelled him to write." He begins by alluding to the troubles which hover around him because of his beliefs, and again denies having any desire to reform the manners, politics, or religion of men. But the beneficent power of his physics is so great that ·he could not suppress that knowledge of his without sinning against the law that commands us all to respect the good of mankind. For he sees that there is a way to make use of everything in the world—stars, heavens, all things—"to make us as masters and possessors of nature." He holds out the vision of man's enjoyment, without any effort or pain (*sans aucune peine*), of the fruits of the earth; and more important, health, the well-being of the body on which not only life but the excellence of the mind itself depends. What he holds up to view is a new and better Eden, one in which man will enjoy all things without pain and trouble not under the condition of ignorance but in enjoyment also of the fruit of the tree of knowledge: a philanthropic Eden at last.

He goes so far as to give hope of resisting the enfeeblement of old age through the application of his physics—who can say for how long? And then he connects the conduct of his own studies with the term inevitably to be imposed upon them by the brevity of his own life. Thus he must share his accomplishments with the public: "joining together the lives and labors of many men, that we may all together go farther than any individual might do."

He undoubtedly expected his project to survive him by a great deal. He adopts for himself the metaphor of the general in command of armies, winning the battles of science and life by directing the strivings of subsequent generations. He says with perfect openness that no one is as likely to be able to perfect his project as he himself is; for it is his product—one is tempted to say his creation—and he says "one cannot so well conceive something and make it one's own if one learn it from someone else as if one discover or invent [*invente*] it himself." He discloses that he will be parsimonious with his truths in the interest of truth; in order not to deprive other men of the pleasure of discovery; and to· discipline his successors through hard work. Even the obstacles in the way to knowledge are planted philanthropically in the emerging Eden, without any animus to depreciate its denizens in comparison with its inventor— although their inferiority to him is real and probably incurable.

Descartes refers more than once to his need for the help of other men. He shares a bit of wisdom with respect to the gaining of men's assistance: do not depend on their good will but on their desire for gain. I believe that this maxim, the perfect paradigm for Adam Smith, might be understood as the thought that guides Descartes' presentation of his vast project as a whole to the world. So writing and so publishing as to charm mankind to a Mechanical Jerusalem, he achieves that conjunction of learning and politics which we saw anticipated at the end of Part Three in his praise of commercial Holland. Henceforth the city may love the scientist and may help him on his way for the most dependable because the lowest of reasons. In the new Eden it becomes difficult to distinguish the Lord from the serpent.

It is clear that Descartes expected his project, hence his thought and his reason, to live on in the minds and lives of untold generations. In this way, perhaps, his rational soul lives on and on, long surviving the extinction of that invisible heat which for a brief time quickened the ashes whose glory it was to harbor the audacious mind of Descartes.

Hobbes and the
Transition to Modernity

Reprinted from *Ancients and Moderns: Essays on the Tradition of Political Philosophy in Honor of Leo Strauss,* edited by Joseph Cropsey. © 1964 by Basic Books, Inc., Publishers, New York.

Thomas Hobbes cannot properly be called the inaugurator of the modern age, for his political philosophy is preceded by that of Machiavelli and his natural philosophy by that of Descartes, as well as of Copernicus, Galileo, Harvey, and others. Yet a claim can be made for the special importance of Hobbes as the philosopher who, at the inception of modernity, gave a comprehensive account of both man and the world, of political and natural philosophy, by articulating the two on novel principles and thereby produced a system which could stand as an alternative to the tradition. Hobbes's doctrine comprises the first modern system in which the political philosophy is ample and accessible (in a way that Bacon's, for example, is not) and is supported by a natural philosophy upon which the political teaching is meant to rest in a harmonious relation.

The significance of Hobbes's articulation of political and natural philosophy is not limited to the novelty (modernity) or the comprehensiveness of his system. Hobbes's thought is of special interest because when one attempts to grasp it and to perceive, moreover, the tradition against which it is directed, inevitably some of the most important characteristics of modernity, of antiquity, and of philosophy itself come to light.

Hobbes unquestionably believed his teaching to be novel or, as we would say, to be directed against the tradition or against what had been handed down to his time and received as true or sufficient. What was that tradition? It was the very long line of utterance beginning with pre-Socratic and Socratic philosophy and proceeding by various ways through the teachings of Christian theologians down to the writers of the seventeenth century. When the fundamental heterogeneity of this tradition and of the presuppositions on which its parts depend is recalled, the difficulty implicit in the notion of "rejecting the tradition" appears at once. It is possible to reject the tradition as a whole only to the extent that the tradition is not composed of elements which are mutually contradictory on any fundamental point. But the pagan and the Biblical elements of the tradition are in mutual contradiction on a number of fundamental points connected with the absence of revelation from the pagan doctrine and its presence in the Biblical doctrine. As to the contradiction between the teaching that the natural reason cannot be exceeded and the teaching that it can be exceeded, no synthesis or compromise is possible that would enable a thinker to reject both doctrines at once.

On the basis of this elementary reflection, it could occur a priori to a reader of Hobbes that Hobbes's doctrine cannot be simply novel. Yet Hobbes cannot be deprived of his place as an architect of the modern mode of thought and life. By reason of these facts, we are prepared for the conclusion that, to the extent that Hobbes is representative of modernity, modernity begins with, or in its beginning is constituted by, a rejection of some part of the premodern tradition and an acquiescence in some other part. The form taken by that acquiescence remains to be seen: it might conceivably be simple repetition, or a diluted or a fortified modification of the original. In any case, if the understanding of a phenomenon is assisted by an understanding of its genesis, then our understanding of modernity will be assisted by our understanding of Hobbes's relation to "the tradition," for implicit in that relation are the intention and the animus of classic modernity, which intention and animus are intrinsic to the genesis of modernity.

Hobbes's rejection of earlier thought and his presentation of his own thought rest, of course, on a common ground and may be approached in either order. If we begin with an affirmative as opposed to a critical statement, we find, early in *De Corpore,*[1] a comprehensive remark on the end or scope of philosophy, which end is "the commodity of human life," or "power"; whereas the "utility" of philosophy consists in the fruit of the arts which are perfected by natural philosophy and in that avoidance of

293 Hobbes and the
Transition to Modernity

evils which is made possible by moral and civil philosophy: "...all such calamities as may be avoided by human industry, arise from war, but chiefly from civil war...." This passage is amplified by a critical remark in *De Cive:* "...what civil war was there ever in the Christian world, which did not either grow from, or was nourished by this root [namely, the claims of clergy to be obeyed, and of laity to withhold obedience, 'under pretence of religion']?"[2] Hobbes's thought should therefore lay a foundation for technology and for civil peace, the former through natural philosophy and the latter through political philosophy. Insofar as he is, or believed himself to be, an innovator, he should by his philosophizing improve on the performance of the tradition in enhancing commodity and peace. As to commodity in the sense of a gain from technology, it will not be discussed in this statement. Hobbes did believe geometry to be fundamental to the precise study of motion or to be inseparable from the understanding in detail of matter in motion.[3] He also believed that, by treating lines as the paths of points in motion, he had become the first to solve the fundamental geometrical problem and in effect, therefore, the first "complete geometrician": "...no man hitherto hath compared any crooked with any strait line, yet many geometricians of every age have endeavoured it."[4] Whether Hobbes's geometrical mechanics, or mechanical geometry, did in fact produce or could have produced a revolutionary effect on technology must be left for others to say.

As to commodity in the sense of civil peace, Hobbes believed himself to have been the first to state the grounds of civil duty, namely, "a true and certain rule of our actions, by which we might know whether that we undertake be just or unjust."[5] Otherwise stated, Hobbes believed that his political philosophy provided a correction for the following errors, which are explicit or implicit in the tradition, which bear on political philosophy, and which militate against peace.

In the first place, Aristotle made a distinction between the good and bad form of each regime, emphatically between kingship and tyranny, thereby opening up to every man the possibility of privately passing sentence of death on the ruler.[6] Aristotle indeed had a republican, libertarian, perhaps even democratic inclination, and at the same time taught that men are by nature unequal in their qualification to bear rule so that only the wise or the best deserve to govern.[7] Moreover, Aristotle taught that the virtues and vices, and of course justice and injustice, are distinguished from each other by nature and not by positive law. Therefore, each man is not only free but compelled to judge of the goodness and badness of deeds and, incidentally, to govern his own conduct similarly by use of a standard that is not necessarily identical with the civil law.[8] This, too, means that Aristotle's teaching is productive of discord in that it transforms a characteristically social act—discrimination of the just and the unjust—into a private act, incidentally engendering the problem of the distinction between good men and good citizens.

Furthermore, Aristotle's physics and metaphysics laid down a doctrine of incorporeal substances or essences, existent things which are not accidents, but are the substrata of all accidents. The doctrine that incorporeal things can and do exist becomes the doctrine that men have souls capable of receiving punishment supernaturally. The administrators of that punishment are rivals of the civil authority for the obedience of subjects. In this way, the erroneous ontology of Aristotle contributes to discord in Christian countries.

Apart from the influence of Aristotle, revealed religion has engendered the belief that there is a sphere of "conscience" in which individuals are compelled to make wholly private judgments determining their actions.[9] Thus, on another basis, the conflict between the good citizen and the good man is forced on subjects to the detriment of the chief desideratum, which is peace.

Very broadly, the tradition is found by Hobbes to be defective in that it encourages or compels private judgment of the difference between good and evil. Hobbes's positive teaching on this fundamental point is a repetition of the first command addressed to mankind, according to scripture.[10] It is notable that Hobbes's objection to the tradition coincides largely with his objection to the state of nature: philosophy and revelation, the one by reflection upon nature and the other by a belief in the immanifest, imperil civil society by making men recur to essentially private judgments of the difference between virtue and vice or good and evil. Also, in the state of nature, every man must judge of right and wrong for himself. Perhaps it will seem strange that Hobbes should tax Christianity itself with leading to the violation of the earliest scriptural command; but much of Hobbes's doctrine suggests the departure of Christian practice and belief from the ways implicit in scripture regarded as the national law of a particular civil society. In any case, Hobbes teaches the conflict of revelation, reason, and nature itself with the civil life, to the extent that revelation, reason, and nature do not converge on or disappear in positive law, that is, convention. In order to give support to his doctrine, Hobbes must therefore provide for the assimilation of civil to divine authority, the latter understood in the scriptural rather than the Hobbean sense; the civil authority must be the supreme discriminator of good and evil and thus be the power that is fully obeyed. At the same time, Hobbes must show that the conclusion of reason is the abnegation of reason's authority to make the crucial moral and political distinctions: moral and political philosophy lead to the conclusion that law preponderates over philosophy in discriminating good and evil; but he must do this philosophically. He must show further that the preponderance of civil law or convention over nature follows from the meaning of nature itself; the conflict of the passions with the law of nature[11] signifies that nature is brought to effectual perfection in civil society, in which, and not in any prior condition, the law of nature is made law in the proper rather than the metaphorical sense.[12] To do all these things, Hobbes must go outside revelation and outside moral and political philosophy. He must have recourse to natural philosophy in order to perfect his political doctrine.

We may draw these provisional conclusions concerning the genesis of modernity: However prominent the definition of a "private sphere" as against the civil authority might have become in the modern time, modernity began with the assertion of the overwhelming power and range of the civil authority as against the judgment of individuals. Thus the development of modernity cannot be traced without comprehending the modification of modernity's own beginning. Moreover, the genesis of modernity has as one of its elements the reconstitution of the body politic by the redintegration of "church" and "state," or their submergence and re-emergence as civil society simply. The subsequent development of modernity will be unintelligible in an important respect without a clear view of how this redintegration gave way to "the separation of church and state." Hobbes, one may say, looked back to the *polis* in this connection while his successors looked elsewhere. So far as Hobbes looked back to the *polis*, the genesis of modernity was a restoration rather than a sheer innovation. The incentive for the restoration of a pagan principle may be found in the remaining characteristic of the genesis of modernity: the ground of human life was to be displaced from revelation to natural reason peculiarly understood, and for this purpose the intervention of natural philosophy into moral and political thought became, or was thought to become, inescapable. We see an intimation that, at the opening of modernity, the restoration of the supremacy of civil or human authority is in the interest of, or is at least inseparable from, an intention to restore the supremacy of natural reason somehow understood. The hegemony of the civil sovereign is a practical conclusion from the hegemony of natural reason; the hegemony of natural reason is the theoretical condition for the hegemony of the civil sovereign. To this extent it is legitimate to be reminded of antiquity by the opening of modernity.

Our task now is to sketch those governing doctrines of Hobbes by which he rectifies the tradition as far as he must, in order to procure a state of obedience within the limits of natural reason alone.

Hobbes's most perfected writings on political philosophy are *De Cive* and *Leviathan. De Cive* consists of three main divisions: "Of Liberty," "Of Dominion," and "Of Religion." *Leviathan* consists of four main divisions:

"Of Man," "Of Commonwealth," "Of a Christian Commonwealth," "Of the Kingdom of Darkness." One third of *De Cive* and one half of *Leviathan* are explicitly addressed to the problems of theology and religion. From his time to the present, men have suspected or known that Hobbes's obtrusive antihieraticism is not separable from a far-reaching latitudinarianism on fundamental points of Biblical religion. It is not necessary for the present purpose to consider whether Hobbes was a believer. It will be sufficient, with respect to this subject, to consider the extent to which what he taught about political life necessarily presupposed some reinterpretation of traditional Biblical theology. It will be possible to give an adequate indication of this by looking mainly at the nontheological parts of *Leviathan*, particularly Part I.

As Hobbes foretells much of his general enterprise in the first part of *Leviathan*, so he foretells it more pointedly in the first sentence of the Introduction: with respect to his own well-being, or the basis of it, which basis is political society, man has the same status as does the author of nature with respect to "the world." Hobbes proceeds to enlarge upon this thought by developing his famous mechanistic psychology through the reduction of man's psychic life to motion, which self-evidently means the motion of matter. As he proceeds, it is worth noticing that he affects the doctrine of the immortality of the soul in a way which almost makes it superfluous for him to argue later that all reward and punishment shall take place on earth (where the Kingdom of God must reside). At the same time, he adequately prepares—almost exhausts—his chief thesis with respect to prophecy when, in chapter II, he asserts that as "dreames are caused by the distemper of some of the inward parts of the Body; divers distempers must needs cause different Dreams. And hence it is, that lying cold breedeth Dreams of Feare...."[13]

It is of more than passing interest that the elaboration of his corporeal psychology gives Hobbes his first occasion to requite individual men for the right of discriminating virtue and vice, of which he deprives them in awarding it to the civil sovereign. He restores to them in return the right of discriminating truth and falsehood with respect to what is pretended about God. "...It is the part of a wise man, to believe [evil men] no further, than right reason makes that which they say, appear credible."[14] Hundreds of pages later, in the chapter "Of the *Word of God, and of Prophets*," Hobbes provides a more ample statement of this rather restricted thought. "Every man then [that is, in the time of the Old Testament] was, and now is bound to make use of his Naturall Reason, to apply to all Prophecy those Rules which God hath given us, to discern the true from the false."[15] It may be said that no part of his doctrine is quite free of the influence of his intention to reassert, simultaneously and inseparably, the claims of political life and of natural reason.

Hobbes's discussion of the "train of imaginations" or succession of
thoughts moves toward the definition of providence and toward a preliminary statement on the attributes of God and on the intrusion of absurdity
into the account thereof.[16] Providence, which is the foresight of things to
come, "belongs onely to him by whose will they are to come. From him
onely, and supernaturally, proceeds Prophecy." The difficulties inherent in
this remark do not become evident until, three chapters later, the will is
defined as "the last Appetite, or Aversion, immediately adhaering to the
action;"[17] and twenty-five chapters later still, it is asserted that "when we
ascribe to God a *Will*, it is not to be understood, as that of Man, for a
Rationall Appetite; but as the Power, by which he effecteth every thing.
Likewise when we attribute to him ... Knowledge and Understanding
... For there is no such thing in God...."[18] Considering that the passage
last quoted is preceded by the remark that "God has no Ends"[19]—that is,
his "power" cannot be understood in the light of the definition of power
given in chapter X, namely, "present means, to obtain some future
apparent Good"[20]—the difficulties generated in the third chapter may be
described as grave and far exceeding the scope of psychology.

In the fourth chapter of *Leviathan*, Hobbes treats of speech. Toward
the beginning of the chapter, he presents an outline of his material that is
interesting in itself, and more so by reason of the degree to which he
departs from it in developing the chapter. His outline[21] has this content:

I. General Use of Speech: to transfer mental into verbal discourse
    A. For mnemonic reasons (words are "marks")
    B. For reasons of communication (words are "signs")

II. Special Uses of Speech
    A. To record causes and effects (= right definition)
    B. To communicate knowledge; Counsel and Teach
    C. To communicate will and purpose [Command]
    D. To delight ourselves

III. Corresponding [Special] Abuses
    A. By misrecording thoughts, to deceive oneself (= wrong or no
       definition)
    B. By use of metaphor, to deceive others
    C. Incorrectly declaring the will
    D. To grieve others

The chapter as a whole appears not to cover the ground indicated by the
outline. All but the last three paragraphs are apparently devoted to II.A
and the corresponding abuse, III.A. However, for reasons that do not
urgently concern us, it is not entirely clear that this is so. Without any
doubt, the use and abuse of speech to express or dissemble the will is
overlooked, as is its abuse in the grieving of others. But in the last

sentence of chapter IV, Hobbes does allude to the abuse (III.B) that corresponds to the important use of speech which is to signify our thoughts to other men and thus to counsel and teach them. He speaks of "Metaphors, and Tropes of speech;" to the former of these he makes additional references that will demand further attention.

In mentioning metaphors (to leave aside the "Tropes of speech"), Hobbes says of them that they are not the most dangerous misleaders of reason, for "they profess their inconstancy, which the others do not." When the reader advances into the fifth chapter, he encounters the well-known distinction between error and absurdity, the latter peculiar to thinking and reasoning with the use of words. In setting forth the causes of absurdity in reasoning, Hobbes makes an enumeration that is immediately reminiscent of the parallel enumeration in section 12, chapter V of *De Corpore*. Comparison of the two shows a certain compression in the *Leviathan* account; yet the list of causes of absurdity, in *Leviathan*, includes (number 6)[22] "the use of Metaphors, Tropes, and other Rhetoricall figures, instead of words proper." The enumeration in *De Corpore* deprecates, as does the preliminary reference in *Leviathan*, the deceptiveness of metaphor. The increasing emphasis of Hobbes, in the political context of *Leviathan*, on the deceptiveness of metaphor begins to appear almost immediately. He writes, in a great metaphor:

> To conclude, The Light of humane minds is Perspicuous Words, but
> by exact definitions first snuffed, and purged from ambiguity; *Reason*
> is the *pace;* Encrease of *Science,* the *way;* and the Benefit of man-
> kind, the *end.* And on the contrary, Metaphors, and senslesse and
> ambiguous words, are like *ignes fatui;* and reasoning upon them, is
> wandering among innumerable absurdities; and their end, contention,
> and sedition, or contempt.[23]

Hobbes returns to the theme of metaphor in chapter VIII, "Of the *Vertues* commonly called *Intellectuall*; and their contrary *Defects.*" Here he makes the distinction between a man's facility in perceiving the similarity or dissimilarity between any of his thoughts, and his facility in perceiving how anything he is thinking of is related to another thing as a means is related to an end. The former is the basis of the virtues that he calls "wit" and "judgment," respectively: a good wit (or a good fancy) perceives similitudes, a good judgment recognizes differences. After linking, though not equating, similitudes and metaphors,[24] Hobbes asserts

> In a good History, the Judgement must be eminent; because the good-
> nesse consisteth, in the Method, in the Truth, and in the Choyse of
> the actions that are most profitable to be known. Fancy has no place,
> but onely in adorning the stile.

In Orations of Prayse, and in Invectives, the Fancy is praedominant;
because the designe is not truth, but to Honour or Dishonour; which
is done by noble, or by vile comparisons.

In Demonstration, in Councell, and all rigorous search of Truth,
Judgement does all; except sometimes the understanding have need
to be opened by some apt similitude; and then there is so much use of
Fancy. But for Metaphors, they are in this case utterly excluded. For
seeing they openly professe deceipt; to admit them into Councell,
or Reasoning, were manifest folly.

Some of the consequences of these remarks do not appear until much
later in *Leviathan.* In chapter XXXI, Hobbes represents worship as the
external sign of honor and of intention to praise. In chapter XXXVI, in
the course of his attempt to explain the meaning of the word of God and
of prophecy, Hobbes is compelled to distinguish between the utterance of
God himself and "the Words of him that wrote the holy History. The
Word of God, as it is taken for that which he hath spoken, is understood
sometimes *Properly,* sometimes *Metaphorically.*"[25] It is probably not an
overstatement to assert that the definitions laid down by Hobbes rather
early in *Leviathan* continually produce their effects on the understanding
of God's action and worship to the end of the book.

If we return to the end of chapter VII of *Leviathan,* we observe another
appearance of the theme of "history" in the context of the credibility of
statements about divine beings. Chapter VII is "Of the Ends, or
Resolutions of *Discourse.*" It differs from chapter V ("Of *Reason, and
Science*") in that chapter V deals with truth and absurdity, while chapter
VII sets out to deal with truth and error, that is, with knowledge of what
will be or will not be, or of what was and what was not. The beginning of
Hobbes's speculation on knowledge of matters of fact is that men cannot
have "absolute" knowledge of occurrences, past or future, through
reasoning. Certain knowledge of such things as are in the past is based on
sense and derivatively on memory; certain knowledge of what is to come is
tacitly allowed by Hobbes to be simply impossible. What is available to
men, however, is that kind of knowledge of things past and future which
Hobbes calls science or conditional knowledge: ". . . if This be, That is; if
This has been, That has been; if This shall be, That shall be. . . ."[26] By
this assertion and by the development of the consequences that he draws
from it Hobbes is able in this brief chapter to prepare a canon for judging
the credibility of all history: the test of fact is reason. He proceeds from
the definition of doubt through the definition of conscience, of belief, and
of faith; and he concludes having laid the foundation for his ruling thesis,
namely, that there may be things related to divinity that are "above"
reason, but there can be none that contradict it,[27] not in the entire sacred
record or history.

Between chapters V and VII is a chapter entitled "Of the Interiour Beginnings of Voluntary Motions; commonly called the *Passions. And the Speeches by which they are expressed.*" In this chapter Hobbes sketches his doctrine that all of a man's doings are reducible to motions either toward or away from objects that excite his appetite or aversion. This famous teaching may be said to commence with the premise that the real invisible which causes man's doings is the invisibly small motion called imagination, the relic of sensation, working through the submicroscopic motions that Hobbes calls "endeavor." The culmination of that teaching may be said to be the reduction of appetite and aversion to desire and fear: "Life it selfe is but Motion, and can never be without Desire, nor without Feare...."[28] The meaning of what intervenes between that commencement and that culmination is what we must consider next.

The body of chapter VI is divided, as the title indicates, between the passions and the speech in which the passions are expressed. The part on the passions proper consists of a dispassionate (that is, free from praise and blame) statement of the modes of the "simple passions," and its details are not pertinent to the present purpose. The part on the speech of passion, quite brief, is in the main a presentation of the grammatical moods and what they express, also not pertinent in detail to the present purpose. What is noteworthy is that in the enumeration of the modifications of the simple passions, Hobbes identifies one as being perfectly unique to man, and that is the "desire to know why, and how" or in other words "the care of knowing causes."[29] And in explaining the forms of speech in which passions are expressed, he draws a parallel by saying, "But of the Desire to know, there is a peculiar expression, called *Interrogative.*"[30] He indicates the direction in which he will develop this human peculiarity by following the definition of man's curiosity with the two paragraphs that he devotes to fear, of which the first begins as follows: "*Feare* of power invisible, feigned by the mind, or imagined from tales publiquely allowed, *Religion;* not allowed, Superstition." Thereafter he takes up "admiration" and "vainglory" in successive paragraphs in a way which continues the same subject, as may be seen by comparing the passage on vainglory with the passage on worship in chapter XXXI.[31] It comes as no surprise to learn that Hobbes believes, "the seed of *Religion,* is also onely in man."[32]

How Hobbes develops the joint theme of man's curiosity as to causes, and his fear, especially of things invisible, may be seen by looking ahead to the end of chapter XI, which has the misleading or at least unhelpful title, "Of the difference of *Manners.*" Hobbes explains that the subject he is treating in this chapter is "those qualities of man-kind, that concern their living together in Peace, and Unity." The reader is reminded in passing of the passage in *De Cive* cited in note 2. At the end of this chapter, in the paragraph in which Hobbes introduces the notion of the "natural seed of religion," and which precedes chapter XII itself, "Of Religion," he alludes to those "that make little, or no enquiry into the naturall causes of things." In this allusion he reminds the reader of the related passage in chapter VIII. Chapter VIII deals with the intellectual virtues and vices. The latter are dealt with in the second part of the chapter, in the course of an enumeration of the modes of "madnesse." Leading up to the remark by adjusting the content to the theme of the latter part of the chapter, Hobbes accounts for a certain opinion of the ancient Jews by appealing to no characteristic in them "but that which is common to all men; namely, the want of curiosity to search naturall causes...."[33] Man is the only being that is curious as to causes, but he is in almost every case not prone to seek for natural causes, for he is naturally too much under the influence of the fear that is bred by ignorance of causes to turn to the seeking of those causes. Following "some of the old Poets," Hobbes admits that perhaps the gentiles did indeed simply create their gods, passing from natural concern with their preservation, or "fortune," to irrational fear of powers invisible. Hobbes appears to argue that a better understanding of God is had by men who search for "the causes of naturall bodies, and their severall vertues, and operations,"[34] and hence necessarily for the first in the chain of all causes, as did the "Heathen Philosophers," than by men who are preoccupied with the causes of the good and ill fortune of human beings. This doctrine of Hobbes's is surely parallel to the very important distinction, made most explicitly in chapter XVI of *De Cive,* between God Almighty, or god simply, and the God of Abraham.

It might appear that Hobbes is attempting to teach men not to be afraid. He is of course very far from doing so. His doctrine concerning fear is sufficiently indicated in the abrupt transition from chapter XII, "Of Religion," to chapter XIII, "Of the *Naturall Condition* of Mankind, as concerning their Felicity, and Misery." Here he describes the natural war of all against all and shows how well founded is each man's fear of all others. The movement from chapter XII to XIII is a palpable break in the material of Part I, but the transition is itself quite orderly, and its nature is shown in the last passage of chapter XIII of which the crucial portion is this: "The Passions that encline men to Peace, are Feare of Death; Desire of such things as are necessary to commodious living; and a Hope by their Industry to obtain them."

Of the many important points made by Hobbes in the course of the two chapters on the state of nature and the law of nature, one is especially noteworthy for the present purpose. In elaborating his distinction between the naturally right and the just, he makes the latter dependent on contract. In engaging to be bound by a contract, a man expresses himself as voluntarily undertaking to give up something in exchange for something else. Breach of an undertaking is therefore a variety of self-contradiction, in which a man does the opposite of what he said he wished to do. Thus follows Hobbes's remark: "So that *Injury*, or *Injustice*, in the controversies of the world, is somewhat like to that, which in the disputations of Scholers is called *Absurdity*. For as it is there called an Absurdity, to contradict what one maintained in the Beginning: so in the world, it is called Injustice, and Injury, voluntarily to undo that, which from the beginning he had voluntarily done."[35] What makes injustice wrong is, of course, very different both from what causes men to abstain from it and from the reason it can be said to be harmful. Men are in practice deterred from it by fear of punishment. It is harmful in that it conflicts with preservation, bare or commodious. But what makes it wrong is that it offends against reason, for it is a form of self-contradiction.

Hobbes may indeed have given commentators strong reasons for describing him as a thinker who strove to put human life on the basis of the indefeasible passions. It should be recognized that his having done so did not prevent him from at the same time searching for the ground of justice in demonstrative reason or in the criterion afforded by the principle of contradiction. His thought is in this respect representative of, as it is in a way responsible for, a certain paradoxical quality of modern man's view of human and other things: reason is best, but the life of reason is not the best life. Thus Hobbes makes the principle of contradiction the touchstone of justice, which is effectual political right, and also of theology; for the omnipotent itself is bound to remain within the limit of that same principle, which is to say, it is bound up in the order of nature. This does not mean that to be is to be intelligible. How far it is from meaning that is a measure of Hobbes's distance from those classics to whom he recurred, in a manner of speaking, across the Christian centuries.

We have seen how, beginning with fear and desire, the argument came to a halt, and to a need for a new commencement. The first beginning culminated in religion, as distinguished from the grounds of peace. The recommencement, based upon a redirection of man's fears, desires, and incidentally his hopes, occurs where the political part of *Leviathan* begins—with the doctrine concerning the state of nature. One may say that Hobbes appears at that point on the threshold of presenting new objects of fear and desire, terrestrial objects obtainable by human means—natural objects obtainable naturally—and that he not only expounded politics by reducing life to desire and fear, which was novel, but that he sought to redirect desire and fear in ways and on objects which were less novel. Insofar as his ruling purpose was to restore the primacy of human authority as such, and of natural reason, he was an innovator through rediscovery. To this extent, he was of course a rejecter of the Biblical, and not of the classical, tradition.

Only a few things remain to be pointed out with respect to Part I. One is the contrast between "the Law of the Gospell; *Whatsoever you require that others should do to you, that do ye to them.* And that Law of all men, *Quod tibi fieri non vis, alteri ne feceris,*"[36] elsewhere called the law of nature. Another is the return to reflections on divinity in chapter XVI, the last chapter in Part I, entitled "Of *Persons, Authors,* and things Personated." Hobbes's general teaching concerning authors and persons is too well-known to be repeated. His doctrine as to the personation and authority of gods false and true ought not, however, to be neglected. It is contained in two consecutive paragraphs.[37] His statement has this outline: False gods can be personated but cannot, of course, be authors. As figments of men's brains, they can be personated only by the civil authority. The true God can, of course, be personated and was so thrice, a fact by which Hobbes can explain the Trinity. The continuation of Hobbes's discussion concerns a different subject. It is more than likely that his intention in giving his statement the form that it has may be perceived by comparing the statement in question with the passage in chapter XLVII of *Leviathan,* in which Hobbes considers the institution of priestly celibacy in a similar ellipsis.

We are able to return now to the first part of the question with respect to Hobbes's teaching, as that question was stated earlier in this paper. How does Hobbes confront the allegedly adverse effect of Aristotle's political philosophy? To begin with, he lays down, in Part I of *Leviathan* but in more detail in subsequent places, his well-known doctrine of the absolute authority of the civil sovereign. He does this in large measure by arguing that the civil authority is *the* authority, that monarchy is the best form of government, and that separation of powers is undesirable. Inevitably the question arises whether Hobbes was aware that Aristotle believed the civil authority to be *the* authority, that he showed signs of agreeing with Plato as to the excellence of rule by an outstanding man, and that he does not teach the separation of powers.

Hobbes asserts the natural equality of all men with respect to the right to participate in civil society, or so it seems. A famous passage in which he does so deserves at least one more glance. He writes, "The question who is the better man, has no place in the condition of meer Nature; where, (as has been shewn before,) all men are equall. The inequallity that now is, has bin introduced by the Lawes civill."[38] So far as this means that, without the restraints of political or other society, the relations of men are governed wholly or largely by brute force, one ought not to expect to find this contradicted by Aristotle or perhaps by anyone. Hobbes goes on to deny that the worse willingly submit to be ruled by the better qualified, a fact never gainsaid by Aristotle. "Nor when the wise in their own conceit, contend by force, with them who distrust their owne wisdome, do they alwaies, or often, or almost at any time, get the Victory." The opposite of this view cannot be found in Aristotle's teaching, not in Book I of the *Politics* or elsewhere. Hobbes adds, "If Nature therefore have made men equall, that equalitie is to be acknowledged: or if Nature have made men unequall; yet because men that think themselves equall, will not enter into conditions of Peace, but upon Equall termes, such equalitie must be admitted."

As to this, it is evident, on the one hand, that Hobbes argues for actual natural equality no more than he does for acting *as if* it existed, should no other course be open; and on the other hand, that Aristotle's elaborate discussion of imperfect regimes may be said to constitute tacit recognition of this by no means obscure insight. Nor is it by any means insignificant that Hobbes's allegation of equality describes the status of men engaged in contracting to leave the state of nature and to enter civil society, not of men engaged in asserting a right to participate in government. It is possible that no man was ever more conscious than Hobbes of the difference between men of mean capacity and men of intelligence, and of the obvious conclusion with respect to the question of who is fit to govern. Hobbes's doctrine of natural equality has extensive effects, but they obviously do not stretch in the direction of an argument that all men are fit to govern others. Rather, the practical consequence of his doctrine is that most men are fit to govern themselves in most things that concern only them. "A plain husband-man is more Prudent in affaires of his own house, than a Privy Counseller in the affaires of another man."[39] And more largely, "in all kinds of actions, by the laws praetermitted, men have the Liberty, of doing what their own reasons shall suggest, for the most profitable to themselves ... such as is the Liberty to buy, and sell, and otherwise contract with one another; to choose their own aboad, their own diet, their own trade of life, and institute their children as they themselves think fit...."[40] On the strength of these beliefs, Hobbes is much more susceptible to be accused of economic libertarianism by Aristotle than Aristotle is to be accused by Hobbes of anything comparable.

We cannot leave this part of the subject without noticing that, in his account of the intellectual virtues in chapter VIII of *Leviathan*, Hobbes distinguishes the natural and the acquired and, of course, includes among the natural virtues that same prudence possessed by plain husbandmen and privy counsellors. The inequality in prudence that manifestly exists among men must on that basis be called a natural inequality, regardless of what Hobbes might understand by the term "natural."

Hobbes's view that Aristotle's teaching is republican, libertarian, and democratic and that it is also based on the belief in natural inequality will stimulate some second thoughts. On the face of it, the two parts of the assertion seem capable of being made consistent with each other only if some explanations are supplied which are not furnished by Hobbes. Moreover, although to an antagonist of Aristotle and of democracy such as Hobbes himself, it may appear convenient to link the two, surely some weight must be given to the fact that sincere friends of democracy do not and have not regularly tried to make this connection, which is in truth implausible. The popular understanding of Aristotle, however, must not, indeed, be made too prominent, as can be indicated by reference to the quality of the popular understanding of Hobbes on this very issue. Hobbes's teaching is massively an advocacy of the absolute sovereignty of the civil representative, whether a man or an assembly of men, and is very widely understood in this sense. Still, it has some features of a qualifying character. For example, Hobbes must not only concede, he must on all occasions insist that the compact which brings civil society into being is an agreement among the future subjects and not between the subjects and their sovereign. This means, of course, that there is no compact at all between ruler and subject (except where rule is by conquest) and that they are *to this extent* in the state of nature with respect to each other, or in the state of "absolute liberty."[41] This is borne out by Hobbes's doctrine concerning the source of the sovereign's right to punish a subject: that right is nothing but an unimpaired vestige of the natural state in which

> every man had a right to every thing, and to do whatsoever he thought necessary to his own preservation.... And this is the foundation of that right of Punishing, which is exercised in every Common-wealth. For the Subjects did not give the Soveraign that right; but onely in laying down theirs, strengthned him to use his own, as he should think fit, for the preservation of them all: so that it was not given, but left to him ... as entire, as in the condition of meer Nature, and of warre of every one against his neighbour.[42]

In brief, an intimation of the subject's inalienable liberty does, of course, follow from a portion of Hobbes's doctrine.

There are other aspects of Hobbes's teaching which point in the same direction. In the chapter that deals primarily with property,[43] Hobbes grants that the sovereign may, in fact can be expected to, act many times in his own interest and contrary to the interest of his subjects (which, incidentally, is to grant Aristotle's definition of a tyrant). In the course of the remarkable paragraph in which he makes this assertion, he says both that when the sovereign disposes unfairly of property, his action "by the will of every one of [his subjects], is to be reputed voyd" and also that they may not so much as speak ill of him "because they have authorised all his actions, and in bestowing the Soveraign Power, made them their own."[44] Quite apart from any rudimentary intimations that economic life is privileged with a certain immunity from civil prescription,[45] readers could justifiably conclude that Hobbes had made an enclave of freedom for subjects, from which they might sally out on special occasions to much effect. Nor is there a profound difference between what a libertarian reader of Hobbes would conclude from the foregoing and what he would conclude from Hobbes's unconcealed doctrine that command (or law) expresses the will of him who commands and is uttered for that person's good, in contradistinction to counsel (or advice), which is intended for the benefit of him to whom it is addressed.[46] From this we may conclude that the general impression of any author's doctrine is indeed not to be unquestioningly trusted and that perhaps the failure of democrats to perceive Aristotle's libertarianism is merely an oversight. On the other hand, to vindicate Hobbes's view of Aristotle in this manner apparently raises a question as to whether Hobbes himself is not in a small way subject to be interpreted as a writer who cared more for men's liberty (or, out of respect to his prejudices, for their rights) than is often allowed.

Finally, it is to be noted that the passage (1317a 40 ff.) from the *Politics* that Hobbes quoted to indicate Aristotle's democratic tendency does nothing of the sort. It is a statement of the general opinion or what is commonly taken to be the case with respect to the relation of democracy and liberty, and, as the rest of the passage makes clear, it would not imply Aristotle's approbation or disapprobation of either democracy or liberty, even if it corresponded with his own view of that relation. This reference represents a rhetorical anomaly on Hobbes's part for the further reason that, a few pages later, while on the same subject (1318a 19-20), Aristotle makes the democrats say that "justice is whatever seems good to the larger number," an opinion remarkably similar to Hobbes's own view that the just cannot be separated from the legal or the agreed-upon.

Hobbes blamed Aristotle for having taught that the distinction between virtues and vices is a natural distinction and hence may be and must be discovered by reflection, a doctrine which is made tantamount by Hobbes to Aristotle's saying that discriminating between good and evil is a private act and thus an act done without respect to the will of the sovereign representative. Hobbes affects to discern in this view the same presumption of philosophers that leads them to believe that only they are capable of bearing rule. When Hobbes's own teaching is reconsidered, however, this particular criticism of Aristotle gives difficulty. Hobbes pre-eminently teaches that in the state of nature, in other words by nature, every man must be the judge of what he may and must do—guided by the principle of self-preservation, however it appears applicable under the circum-

stances. The law of nature is, however, eternal and immutable, strengthened rather than superseded by the passage from the state of nature to
civil society; and there is recognizable, therefore, an inalienable right of
men that descends to them from the nature of things and of themselves, in
and out of civil society. Howsoever little Hobbes might have intended to
prepare a doctrine of right of revolution and however much he might
blame Aristotle for putting the judgment of good and evil in private
hands, the fact is that men who assert a right of revolution often appeal to
a teaching concerning inalienable natural rights and rarely, if ever, invoke
the authority of Aristotle.

Hobbes's criticism of Aristotle on this issue deserves to be considered
briefly from the point of view of the question, Did Aristotle in fact put the
discrimination of good and evil into private hands to the derogation of the
law's authority? The claim that he did so must be based mainly on what he
says in the *Ethics,* rather than in the *Politics.* Surely it is true that the
Ethics is far more concerned with human excellence than with good
citizenship as a theme. It may be said to presuppose a decent respect for
the laws without dwelling on it and indeed without regarding it as
sufficient. The law does and can establish a minimum standard for men
to observe, the measure of bare impunity. Aristotle may be said to have
written with the thought in mind that political life can make the necessary
demand on men, but not a sufficient demand. He recognized a limit on
the scope of law and of political life generally and indicated that limit by
pointing to what lies above the city. Hobbes also recognized a limit on the
scope of law and of political life, but he did so with a view to what lies
below the city, namely, the indefeasible urge toward preservation. Each
writer recognized a claim of privacy: Aristotle above and Hobbes below
the law. In this respect, Hobbes's criticism of Aristotle can be defended,
although at the same time a very difficult question is raised as to which
reservation against the law would in the long run promote the more overt
or the more beneficial resistance to the law.[47]

From what has developed to this point we draw the following conclusions. Hobbes's reaction against the scriptural element of the tradition
pervades his work, and is fundamental. It might be said that a crucial
ingredient of that element survived in Hobbes's teaching, namely, that
men must not take it on themselves to judge of the difference between
good and evil. Such a remark would be without substantial merit,
however, for Hobbes's purpose was to show that there is no effectual
distinction between good and evil except what is concretely authorized,
recognized, and enforced by men. At the same time, Hobbes's reaction
against the political doctrine of his most prominently identified adversary,
Aristotle, if not less earnestly intended, yet loses some of its point upon
examination.

It seems that Aristotle's doctrines do not mean simply what Hobbes asserts them to mean, and that, moreover, Hobbes is occasionally more liable to the charges that he directs against Aristotle than is Aristotle himself. We find ourselves prepared for this fact by our realization that Hobbes's overriding purpose, which is to restore the hegemony of civil authority and natural reason, has something in common with the notion underlying the classic understanding of a *polis*. Hobbes's political philosophy, insofar as it concerns the relation of ecclesiastical and civil authority—which it most profoundly does—may be reduced to the following formulation, as appears with great clarity at the end of chapter XVII of *De Cive*. There are two realms of knowledge, and hence of controversy, one spiritual and governed by faith, the other belonging to natural reason. As to the latter, reason itself, following the meanings given to words by common consent, and observing the rules of logic, determines the issues satisfactorily as they arise. With respect to what is beyond reason, questions of faith concerning God, the issues must be determined by officers of the sovereign representative, that is to say by the clergy acting as ministers of the supreme arbitrating authority, whose function it is to execute the law of reason and to procure peace. A question, therefore, of utmost importance is, Who shall determine the boundary between temporal and spiritual questions? "But it is reason's inquisition, and pertains to *temporal right* to define what is spiritual, and what temporal."[48] It is in this sense emphatically that we say Hobbes unites the hegemony of civil authority and natural reason.

The point is made clearer still when it is recognized that, although Hobbes denies that there is a *summum bonum* for man, he argues everywhere that peace (or preservation) is above all to be desired. From the premise that peace is good follows the thought that what conduces to it is good, what jeopardizes it bad and contrary to reason. This practical canon of reason can with utmost ease be converted into the ruling principle of scriptural interpretation: no statement in scripture can have or can be allowed to have a meaning which is inconducive to civil peace. The dictate of peace, which is the dictate of nature and of natural reason, is both the ground of civil society and the guide to interpretation of scripture. Again, and it cannot be repeated too often, we find the conjunction of natural reason and civil sovereignty at the root of Hobbes's intention.[49] At the same time, what may be called Hobbes's recurrence to the pagans in opposition to the Christians is a recurrence on a lower level, as is indicated by his understanding of the sphere of privacy as being subpolitical and not superpolitical.

We turn now, if only briefly, to Hobbes's natural philosophy in its relation to his political doctrine. According to his statements in the Epistle

Dedicatory of *De Corpore*, there is a connection between the Aristotelian physics and metaphysics of the school divines, on the one hand, and the tendency of the Christian world to be embroiled in controversies and war over religion, on the other. More amply, Hobbes gives the order in which truths are to be demonstrated and in so doing starts with the definitions from which metaphysics follows, prescribes next geometry, then mechanics, then

> the motion or mutation of the invisible parts of things, and the doctrine of sense and imaginations, and of the internal passions, especially those of men, in which are comprehended the grounds of civil duties, or civil philosophy; which takes up the last place. And that this method ought to be kept in all sorts of philosophy, is evident from hence, that such things as I have said are to be taught last, cannot be demonstrated, till such as are propounded to be first treated of, be fully understood.[50]

His immediate purpose is to replace the Aristotelian element in school divinity with a natural philosophy based on the belief that "the gate of natural philosophy universal ... is the knowledge of the nature of *motion*,"[51] and hence necessarily of body in motion, as the name of the book implies. His further purpose is to destroy belief in incorporeal substances and thus to banish not only opinions as to the immortality of a passible soul, but also the influence of those who claim to control the afterlife of the soul, and also the controversy that must arise among men who discuss the attributes of that which is not.

As soon as the corporealist doctrine is stated, its impact upon the scriptural presentation of God is manifest. If nothing exists which is not body, then either God is corporeal or he does not exist. If he is corporeal, then he must possess the accidents of body. In addition, if he is to be capable of action, he must possess accidents. Moreover, if God is not to be either the same as the world or the soul of the world, but is to be the cause of the world absolutely, then he must be the cause *in toto*, which is to say the aggregate of all the passive and active conditions that are the necessary and sufficient conditions for the world. Plenary power, or as in the highest case it might be called, omnipotence, is the sum of the efficient and material causes which, when present, must inevitably produce and when absent in any detail cannot possibly produce the effect in question. The efficient cause or "active power" is motion, hence matter in motion. But there cannot be an unmoved, any more than an incorporeal movent. It is, then, impossible that God be without accidents or that he possess only negative attributes. If moreover he is One, then he is not indivisible and also he cannot be sole, for "one" has meaning only in relation to another. Similarly, if he is infinite, he must be so by virtue of a human imagining, for infinite means no more than that we do not imagine the thing limited or terminated. Also, if God is a whole being he must be composed of parts, for a whole means an aggregate of parts; but if he is infinite he cannot be composed of parts, for an aggregate of parts is a finite aggregate.[52] We can but barely allude to the fact that much of what amounts to the ground of Hobbes's natural theology is presented in the small number of sections that comprise the seventh chapter of *De Corpore*, "Of Place and Time," and at the same time refer to the remarkable discussion of many of the same themes in the General Scholium to Book III of Newton's *Principia*.[53]

It is hardly to be doubted that Hobbes considered his political philosophy to be as little separable from his natural philosophy as the latter is separable from his view of theology. Besides barely noting what a genuine departure from the practice of the classic ancients this constitutes, we are bound to examine Hobbes's belief that it was important to found his political teaching on deeply unpolitical truths or assertions in the realms of physiology, mechanics, and cosmogony. The question is inescapable since it is so far from clear that, of two men with an equal experience of, say, ambition or greed as it manifests itself to the eye, the one with a physiological or electrochemical explanation of its material concomitants will therewith have the advantage in dealing politically with the phenomenon. All the more doubtful does it appear that an expert in cosmogony will, as such, be qualified to generate important truths about right government.

To this Hobbes's legitimate rejoinder would be that he was addressing, not day-to-day politicians, but men concerned with the reforming and preserving of constitutions. For his addressees, two kinds of facts are of highest importance: what is desirable, and what is possible for man, the latter taking precedence, if either can. How important these facts are, and how far beyond politics their foundations extend can, if necessary, be shown by example. It is easy to imagine the case of a body of men who, overcome by their natural fear of death and under the influence of a gross superstition, would persuade themselves that immortality may be had through the sacrifice of human hecatombs to a vicious god made in the image of his vicious votaries. Would it not be best to prove to such men that what they desire is impossible; and would it not be necessary to do that by proving, physiologically, that death is inescapable, and, cosmologically, that their god is a nullity? And having proved it, would one not have shifted immeasurably the basis of their common life and, in all likelihood, their government? Is it not true, in brief, that human life, political life as well, is at last guided by the views that men entertain of the nature of things in the heavens and under the earth, as well as on the face of the earth? Does it not follow that truth is one because nature is one and the whole is one? And is it not so, finally, that political life which is guided by the truth about the whole, the truth, the whole truth and nothing but the truth, is the only rational and even viable political life?

Two difficulties appear immediately. How political life is to be "guided" by the truth is not evident. And moreover, modern men do not, and Hobbes most emphatically did not, claim to know the whole truth about the whole. As will presently appear, these two difficulties are capable of merging into one.

The first may be shown by example. Suppose the truth to be that justice means obeying the will of the stronger. Then men will eventually realize that in order to have whatever they want and to have it justly they need only to combine and make themselves the stronger. If true, this truth would be such that it would exercise its "guidance" by repulsion, not by attraction. That is to say, men who saw the truth of it and wished to avoid chaos would take cognizance of that truth by emphatically teaching its opposite as the truth. Thus they, and their government, would be guided by the truth.

To this it will be objected that the conclusion depends on a falsehood having been supposed true. In the case of all bona fide truth, the truth guides by attraction and not by repulsion, that is, it guides in its own name and not through the opposites that its own harmful character throws to the surface. This objection is not only a tautology ("the true is good, and if something is not good it could not be true"), it is conclusively self-destroying. If the true and the good must cohere, not to say coincide, then the highest form of truth consists in publicly replacing every lower form of truth on the ground that it is harmful, if it is harmful.

Of course this reasoning makes everything turn upon "what is harmful." In other words, it makes everything turn upon the study of man, or the philosophic study of moral and political things as autonomous with respect to physiology, mechanics, and cosmogony or, loosely, "science."

Whatever validity these remarks might have in general, they are not unqualifiedly valid as criticisms of Hobbes or, to the extent to which Hobbes represents the opening of modernity, to the larger movement of classic modern thought. They do not do justice to Hobbes because Hobbes did make the good, or what was in his view the desirable, namely peace, the criterion of the rational or the true in one important respect at least. It was his touchstone of exegesis proper; no scriptural passage can have a meaning inconsistent with the common good as the understanding of that good is derived from the law of nature. Of course Hobbes went much further than that, or proceeded in a different direction, when pronouncing on the natural things as opposed to the supernatural. To the extent that man's existence can be assimilated to the being of every other object in nature, and can be described by reference to the motion of matter, there is a single truth that overarches him and all, and that truth defines and is itself good, privately and politically. The difficulty arises at the point where it becomes necessary for Hobbes and for all others to recognize the uniqueness of the human being. At this point the truth about "nature" ceases to be simply identical with the truth about man, and man is confronted with the fact that it is good for him to know, but what he knows will include the difference between knowledge that fructifies the common life and other sorts of knowledge.

Hobbes's wish to establish political life directly upon the whole truth about the whole, a wish so nearly kin to the aspiration of the Enlightenment and of the modern time at large, may be said to have this notion as its premise: Peace is not possible on the basis of error, which is manifold and leads its errant adherents inevitably into contention; but it is possible on the basis of truth, which is one and must unify those who possess and serve it. Insofar as this is true, it animadverts generally on the ground of all human life lived in the realm of politics and history, or in other words, of the contingent. Hobbes was certainly content to admit that this difficulty is rooted in nature, and there is nothing in his teaching to suggest that a single rational order of the world will supervene over all diverse polities and extinguish war by extinguishing the differences which arise in the irascible or the concupiscible part of our nature; nor that the overbearing might of the sovereign is not one of those inconveniences of which man can never hope to rid his life. Hobbes, then, did not hope to solve the problem of sheer difference among men based on the inevitable departures from reason and truth. He did, however, hope to relieve the problem generated by the peculiar circumvention of reason which errs both simply and also in having such a character that what some venerate under its aegis others must inevitably contemn; yet by the very meaning of the veneration, death is, in the opinion of each, an insufficient punishment for the contemners of his opinion. One could not hope to understand Hobbes, or the advent or the development of modernity, without having done at least this much justice to Hobbes's intention.

Hobbes's work represents, as has been said, a kind of recurrence to the pagan wisdom that established political life on the basis of natural reason and secular supremacy. It is a recurrence on a plane different from that of the original. Hobbes regarded natural reason most highly, but he did not teach that the life of reason was the best life. He was prevented from doing so by the fact that his principles indicated to him a good for man which man had to share with the rest of the things in the world—the conservation of his motion. This feature of Hobbes's thought may be said to have been dictated to him by the absolutely urgent need to reassert the claim of intelligible nature in the most emphatic way. The ideological characteristic of modern thought entered, therefore, via the need to reassert the claim of nature as opposed to supernature, rather than as opposed to convention. In the light of this fact we may understand the respect in which Hobbes and incipient modernity are like an appeal to one part of the tradition against the other part; and why it may be said that the appeal takes place on a reduced level.

Notes

1. *The English Works of Thomas Hobbes,* ed. W. Molesworth (London: Bohn, 1839), Vol. I, Ch. I, secs. 6, 7, pp. 6–10.
2. Ibid., Vol. II, Ch. VI, sec. 11, note, p. 80.
3. Cf. *De Cive,* in ibid., Ep. Ded., II, iv, with *De Corpore,* Ch. XV, sec. 1.
4. *De Corpore,* Ch. VI, sec. 19; Ch. XVII, sec. 2. Cf. Ch. XII, sec. 4:". . . Let the conception of uniform motion upon [a] line, be time."
5. Ibid., Ch. I, sec. 6.
6. Cf. *Leviathan,* ed. W. G. Pogson Smith (Oxford: At the Clarendon Press, 1943), Ch. XXIX, pp. 251 ff.
7. Ibid., Ch. XXI, p. 166; Ch. XV, p. 118.
8. Especially ibid., Ch. XXVI, p. 212.
9. *De Cive,* Ch. VI, sec. 11, p. 79 n.
10. *Leviathan,* Ch. XX, p. 159.
11. Ibid., Ch. XVII, p. 128.
12. Ibid., Ch. XV, pp. 122–23; *De Cive,* Ch. III, sec. 33, pp. 49–50.
13. *Leviathan,* Ch. II, p. 16.
14. Ibid., p. 17.
15. Ibid., Ch. XXXVI, p. 336. Cf. Ch. XXVI, p. 208.
16. Ibid., Ch. III, pp. 21–23.
17. Ibid., Ch. VI, p. 46.
18. Ibid., Ch. XXXI, pp. 280–81.
19. Ibid., p. 279.
20. Ibid., p. 66.
21. Ibid., pp. 24–25.
22. Ibid., Ch. V, p. 36.
23. Ibid., Ch. VI, pp. 37–38.
24. Ibid., Ch. VIII, p. 53.
25. Ibid., p. 324. Italics in original.
26. Ibid., Ch. VII, p. 50.
27. Ibid., Ch. XXXII, p. 286.
28. Ibid., Ch. VI, p. 48.
29. Ibid., p. 44. In Ch. III, p. 20, however, he says that to seek the causes of some imagined effect is common to man and beast, but to seek the possible effects of some imagined cause is singularly human.
30. Ibid., p. 48.
31. Ibid., pp. 277–78.
32. Ibid., Ch. XII, p. 81.

33. Ibid., Ch. VIII, p. 61.

34. Ibid., Ch. XII, p. 83.

35. Ibid., Ch. XIV, p. 101.

36. Ibid., Ch. XIV, p. 100. Cf. Ch. XV, p. 121; Ch. XXVI, p. 209; Ch. XXVII, p. 225; especially, Ch. XLII, p. 388. But see Ch. XVII, p. 128.

37. Ibid., pp. 125–26.

38. Ibid., Ch. XV, pp. 117–18.

39. Ibid., Ch. VIII, p. 56.

40. Ibid., Ch. XXI, p. 163.

41. This point is admittedly made somewhat unclear by Hobbes's remark at the beginning of Ch. XXXI of *Leviathan.*

42. Ibid., Ch. XXVII, p. 239. The same is argued concerning God's right to punish: Ibid., Ch. XXXI, p. 276.

43. Ibid., Ch. XXIV.

44. Ibid., p. 191.

45. Ibid., Ch. XXII, p. 174; Ch. XXIV, p. 193.

46. Ibid., Ch. XXV, p. 196; cf. Ch. XXX, p. 268.

47. Consider Hobbes's remark in *De Cive,* Ch. III, sec. 21: "For every man is presumed to seek what is good for himself naturally, and what is just only for peace sake and accidentally...."

48. *De Cive,* Ch. XVII, sec. 14.

49. Cf. *Leviathan,* Ch. XXXVI, pp. 336–37, Ch. XXXIX, p. 363.

50. *De Corpore,* Ch. VI, sec. 17.

51. Ibid., Ep. Ded., p. viii; see also *Leviathan,* Ch. XLVI, pp. 524–25.

52. *Leviathan,* Ch. XLVI, pp. 524–25; *De Corpore,* Ch. IX, sec. 3; Ch. VI, sec. 10; Ch. X, secs. 1–7; Ch. XXVI, secs. 1, 7; Ch. VII, secs. 6, 12; sec. 11; secs. 9, 12.

53. Reprinted in *Newton's Philosophy of Nature,* ed. H. S. Thayer (New York: Hafner, 1953), pp. 41 ff. See also p. 183, n.

The Human Vision of Rousseau: Reflections on *Emile*

Paper presented at the 1973 annual meeting of the American Political Science Association, New Orleans.

Emile, or On Education is the story of the upbringing of a boy from the day of his birth to the day on which he announces to his tutor that his wife is expecting their first child. Besides Emile, there are two important protagonists of the book, both of whom happen to be crucial to the government of Emile's life and conduct: the tutor, who is, so to speak, Rousseau; and Sophie, Emile's eventual wife, whose existence and whereabouts were mysteriously known to the tutor even as he led Emile on a wide-ranging search for a mate. The tutor's foreknowledge of the real Sophie is the matchmaking mystery in the *Emile* that corresponds to the nuptial mathematics of Plato's *Republic*—Rousseau's mystery suggesting particular Providence and Plato's suggesting divine geometry. Sophie's name is given to her by the tutor while she is still only a vision in the eye of Emile's mind (*Emile* [ed. Classiques Garnier], p. 409), and the meaning of her name is broadly alluded to; but there is no explanation at all of the name of Emile, a word which disconcertingly resembles the Latin *aemulare*. Emile is for every practical purpose turned into an orphan at birth, coming absolutely under the charge of his tutor and out of the jurisdiction of his parents. To this extent Rousseau agrees with Plato that a radical new beginning requires the expulsion rather than the persuasion or co-optation of the grownups. But Rousseau's scheme will differ markedly from Plato's in ways that come to a point in Rousseau's celebration of the family in contrast to Plato's replacement of it with a communal-eugenic arrangement: apparently Plato had only limited confidence in his pedagogy in the strictest sense, providing therefore, however ineffectually, for the quality of the human stock; whereas for Rousseau the pedagogical discipline is presumed applicable to almost any healthy boy. Rousseau was, for all his descanting upon modern science, a true modern methodist.

The prominence of Sophie in the story and the emphasis that Rousseau places on the family are of course related to each other. Emile passes from the absolute tutelage of the tutor to the qualified hegemony of his wife, or from the influence of a man who knows and exploits the facts of nature to the influence of a woman who incarnates that most powerful of those influences, namely, the sexual. If a leading insight of modernity was that men do badly so long as they try to stifle rather than to compound with the passions, then surely the modern project must be said to have lain in a state of incipience until the sexual appetite, as well as those more visibly political ones disencumbered by Machiavelli and Hobbes, was itself at last reported on the surface.

Though Rousseau may be described, on the basis of the *Emile,* as a or the man of highest intellectual rank who first offered an account of mankind that brought woman into the active foreground, he did this by emphasizing the natural difference between the sexes. He was, in brief, interested in woman's influence rather than in her rights, which latter he might have supposed to find an adequate guarantee in the former. Though Rousseau may be described further as having brought to light for serious inspection human sexuality—which I distinguish from the more inclusive "eroticism" as being literally oriented upon a congener of the opposite sex—yet it is more than obvious that he in no way meant to throw down the constraints upon behavior that limit the expression of sexual desire to one and only one being, namely, one's spouse; the "wisdom" of Sophie is in large measure respect for convention, or opinion. Rousseau sought to exemplify, in Emile, a certain type of virility. This might appear to be simply another way of saying that Emile exemplifies the virtues, or is the portrait of the virtuous man. Rousseau's well-known preference for goodness over virtue, if nothing else, causes one to hesitate before accepting the alternative formulation. However the matter might stand in that regard, Emile emerges clearly as a very manly man—one whose manliness is not manifest as great promise in exploits of love, nor in those of war, not yet in politics, but rather in 'living." Our first task in interpreting the *Emile* could in fact be stated precisely as being to explain in what consists the manliness of Emile, that is, his excellence. In order to set about formulating such an explanation, I shall in the first part of this paper concentrate on matters dealt with in the first two books out of the five in the *Emile,* in which Rousseau lays down the foundations of his project for the making of a man, and thereby reveals to a considerable degree the character of the construction that he aims to produce.

The early pages of the *Emile* draw attention to the tornness of man, especially the divergent demands put upon him by his nature and his civil condition or his status as a citizen. Apparently man is not naturally political, and a point of agreement comes into view between Rousseau and Hobbes, the more noteworthy because of Rousseau's explicit criticisms of the earlier thinker. On the basis of those criticisms, the reader might speculate that, Hobbes having dealt with the tension between man and citizen by teaching man to be a citizen, Rousseau should proceed by teaching citizens to be men. This formulation, while not wholly misleading, is defective by virtue of its vagueness. What are the lessons that comprise the education of a real man?

At the head of book I, and thus of the *Emile* as a whole, there stands an illustration that serves as a frontispiece. Each of the five books has one such, in every case the depiction of a scene from Greek mythology or poetry. The frontispiece to book I shows Thetis dipping her infant into the River Styx, and by thus exposing him, hardening him against injury. It is total immersion with a view to such "immortality" as is possible strictly within the limits of nature. There are two imperfections in the immersion of Achilles. First is the familiar one resulting from the need to hold him by the heel while dipping him. The other is that the immersion, in rendering Achilles invulnerable or virtually so, deprived him of the merit that belongs to courage. Anyone with his advantages would be an Achilles (p. 30). We are entitled to reason as follows: if the hardening of Emile could be accompanied by his literal invulnerability or by his obliviousness to all danger, then Emile would exemplify manliness without courage, because without grounds for apprehension. But it is obvious that Emile cannot be made invulnerable, and under the circumstances, ought not to be made oblivious of danger. He must be made aware of the precariousness of his existence while gaining a capacity for enjoying keenly the sense of that existence and not decaying into the gross hedonism of seizing the moment in order to exhaust its voluptuous possibilities. The deeper reason for not rendering Emile simply fearless, even if that were possible, is shown in the early part of book IV (pp. 262–66) where Rousseau presents certain "maxims" that connect the humanization of man's feelings for his fellow men with a fear of someday experiencing the disasters that flesh is heir to. Manliness such as Emile's is next to godliness, resting upon strength, simplicity of soul, and an unhesitating inclination to deal with whatever may befall. This, as the rest of the *Emile* bears out, is not a misleading, though it is an imperfect, sketch of Emile's eventual virility.

Returning now to the tension between citizenship and humanity, we can state the issue somewhat more precisely. Within civil life, so far as a man is a good citizen, his heart is hardened against the foreigner, and the hardness of his soul is in general tainted with cruelty and animosity; in brief, he is hardened by being denatured, like the Spartan mother. Moreover, as a member of a civil order, he has a station in life from which he can at any moment be tumbled by events over which he can never have control. Civil life is presented by Rousseau as characterized by a hardness toward the outside and a vulnerability to the flux inherent in the class divisions that mark the inside. Rousseau's project for overcoming, or overcoming so far as possible, the tension between civility and humanity has the immediate goal of hardening to the vicissitudes or flux of class-divided society without producing that variety of hardness that is ill-will, callousness to the suffering of other sentient beings, and an appetite to rule others or to be a tyrant. It is worth remarking that, while Rousseau's characterization of civil life brings to mind the term "alienation," his effort to deal with that "alienation" is not through a sentimentalizing "humanism" but through a toughening of the spirit by straining men with moral burdens of increasing severity. I believe that the painful deceptions and deprivations that the tutor inflicts on the love-sick, fully grown Emile are in the spirit of Rousseau's remark about the invulnerable Achilles: in one way or another, even if not necessarily theoretically, a proper man must have impressed upon him the basic truth about the natural as well as the civil world—all is in flux, and therefore peril and tears are the human lot. The pedagogical problem is, how to let the man be formed to this truth without his becoming either enfeebled and emasculated, or brutalized, by the knowledge.

Through the reflection upon the tension of civility and nature, the reader is brought closer to the tendency of Rousseau's project. If the virilifying pedagogy is truly the dictate of nature, and if the hardening that ensues from that pedagogy is the condition for successful, i.e., full and happy, life in civil society, then of course one should cease to speak of the tension of civility and nature and should instead consider speaking of Rousseauan hardness or toughness as *the* mediating condition for reconciling the demands of nature and society. The fundamental demand of both nature and society is for resiliency; durability in the face of changes and shocks; adaptability to what Machiavelli called "the times," and what anyone might call fortune. It is because both nature and society make the same demand, namely, that a man be able to face at need in all directions, that Rousseau can claim very early in the *Emile* that he is presenting the education of a man and not of a being who is good for himself rather than for others or for others rather than himself.

Now it might appear from the foregoing that Rousseau has sketched the "virility" of man in a way that has led him roundabout to what Hobbes at least had sufficiently elaborated: man's natural, and therefore also his civil, goal is preservation. But Rousseau's conception of preservation goes beyond that of Hobbes in ways that, to speak historically, reflect the enrichment of that concept by Spinoza. Preservation was given a moral, not to say metaphysical, bearing by the latter that directed the concept far beyond the ends achievable by political means as such, i.e., by agreements not to injure, to accept a sovereign's hegemony, and so forth. In Rousseau's case, the surplus of durability (what I have called virility or manliness) over mere preservation consists in versatility and resignation.

By versatility I mean the characteristic that the tutor imparts to Emile by suppressing, so far as possible, the development in the boy of any habit except the habit of having no habits, to the point even of having no fixed meal times; and that he imparts to Emile by having him learn so many skills that he can earn a living anywhere and anytime. Versatility is as important an element of Rousseauan morality as its opposite, the rigid division of labor, was to the Platonic.[1] It is to be stressed again through the frontispiece to book II, showing Chiron the centaur, the exemplar of good judgment who partakes of two natures in the combination praised by Machiavelli. And it might be added that freedom from habituation is, at least to begin with, as important to Rousseauan morality as habituation is to the Aristotelian; for Rousseau's man of endurance is an athlete ever poised on the brink of declassification or worse, while Aristotle has in mind a gentleman who, if he ceases to be one, falls below the scope of Aristotle's eye. It should be understood, however, that habituation has a distinct place in Rousseau's pedagogy. It is the instrument for the mechanical conditioning against the fears proposed to a man by his reason. Rousseau gives as an illustration the discharge of larger and larger amounts of gunpowder in the presence of a child in order to inure him to frightening noise (*Emile,* p. 44). This is an example used by Descartes, with special reference to the training of dogs but with general reference to the education of men (*Passions of the Soul,* L.)

An element of the versatile durability that will be imparted to Emile that is of the highest importance is a capacity for skilled labor in many crafts. When he goes on the travels that will later be prescribed for him, he will be capable of supporting himself by the work of his hands anywhere and regardless of conditions. The conquest of flux is through labor that is untrammeled by the division of labor. The significance of this point will emerge at the end.

By resignation I mean recognition of the inevitable and the overwhelming to be what they are, and acceptance of them without hope, despair, resentment or any other irrational response. Ultimately, such a posture means perfect acceptance of and thus reconciliation with the order of nature, surely and at the very least so far as that order touches man. It is easy to see how the acceptance of what can only be accepted is an attribute of strength in the mode of stolidity, and that it could contribute to the imperturbable manliness of a man. It is equally easy to see that, by itself, the bare recognition or acceptance of the inevitable as such (apart from all possible confusion in detail of the evitable with the inevitable) might be a decisive ingredient of craven passivity or of unremitting anguish. Consider only the widely accepted inevitability of death, and how compatible the recognition of its inevitability is with the highest degree of untranquillity over the prospect. Precisely in connection with the issue as posed in relation to death, one is led to ask why, if resignation is a goal of Rousseau's teaching, he does not simply propagate Christian faith. To restate the question, is it possible to devise a teaching of resignation which is not only compatible with but contributory to a healthy, active, joyful life in the world, tranquil and happy? The problem of Rousseau's pedagogy, and thus necessarily of his morality, bears a striking resemblance to crucial concerns of Epicurean, and concretely Lucretian, thought: how to discern and appropriate tranquillity in an infinite and on the whole dumb environment of restlessness.

A clue to Rousseau's conception of the answer is given by his precept, stated explicitly and also frequently applied to the training of Emile, that any condition may be imposed upon a human being if it can be made to seem to him to be necessary in the sense that the hardship or restraint does not emanate from a will. Evidently, what emanates from a will may be in the given circumstances inevitable, compelling and irresistible, but it is not in itself or absolutely compelling and irresistible. Only what is of the nature of things might be so described. That which compels or coerces a human being out of some other, stronger will cannot be accepted with tranquillity but will or may provoke resentment or craven collapse of the spirit. Alternatively, resignation that is to include tranquillity, and that thus satisfies an elementary condition of compatibility with happiness, must not be the state of a mind that knows or thinks itself to be crushed by an alien consciousness to which the relation of the ruling and the subservient is present. To be subjected to a will is not only corrosive of contentment but plants the seed of a tyrannizing disposition in the one subjected. (Thus it is not at all clear that the impulse to dominate belongs to human nature rather than arising from a faulty education.)

From the foregoing one is led to wonder if Rousseau conceives nature itself as a mechanism not activated by any will. If nature were that, then of course a man's resignation to natural necessity would not be tainted with the deception that the tutor repeatedly practices on Emile by dissembling his will under the guise of "necessity." Thus an important condition of Enlightenment would be satisfied in that the lives of ordinary people would be lived both happily and rationally. On the other hand, if nature is indeed responsive to a divine will, and Rousseau believes that the good of man requires that he think himself free howsoever determined and foreordained his existence in truth is, then a valid question arises whether the overwhelming god would not be called upon, for the sake of man, to conceal himself to the utmost, wrapping himself in his creation and never revealing himself through any commandment, threat, or punishment, to say nothing of deeds of guile or entrapment. Remote as these themes are from the proper management of an infant, they are present, if sometimes tacitly, in the first two books of *Emile*.

In book I (pp. 46–48), Rousseau develops his thought as follows. One must exercise care in responding to an infant's crying, because if one deals with it angrily, the child's innate sense of injustice will be provoked to all the signs of resentment, rage and despair. Now, citing R. Boerhave on children's diseases, Rousseau gives a somatic explanation of the child's dispositions toward anger, and recommends that exasperating people be kept away from him lest he be provoked. The source of a state of mind is apparently some effect of an interaction between an outside stimulus and the constitution of the body. (I take this to be the only possible meaning of any notion of a sentiment of the just and the unjust in the heart of man that is active in an infant.) Rousseau writes, "So far as children encounter resistance only in things and never in wills, they will not become rebellious or irascible and will remain healthier." This is only one of many places in which Rousseau adopts some form of the doctrine of parallel of mind and body. At any rate, if the child's tears are met not with harshness but with indulgence, he will acquire an appetite for commanding. Now Rousseau, citing the Abbé de St.-Pierre without disagreement, assimilates children to adults and vice versa, and in this connection makes an important observation. "All badness proceeds from weakness; the child is bad only because he is weak; make him strong and he will be good: he who can do everything never does any evil. Of all the attributes of the omnipotent Deity, goodness is that without which one can least conceive him." Compressing the argument, we discover that it has this core: commanding is bad; the bad proceeds from weakness; strength is good and is the source of goodness; absolute strength, such as God Almighty's, is the source of absolute goodness; and one cannot conceive of God Almighty except as absolutely good. It is impossible to escape the conclusion that God cannot be the source of commands. The fact that the passage quoted above ends with the remark, "See below the Profession of Faith of the Savoyard Vicar," informs us that that profession either agrees with this present line of thought or, if it disagrees, must be read with a view to its not being owned by Rousseau as his own words.

In the immediate sequel (pp. 48–49), Rousseau rejects the doctrine, which he attributes to "philosophy," that there are natural vices—a thought no more characteristic of philosophy than of theology. Advancing beyond the simple assignment of weakness as the cause of badness, he shows that the old are as weak as the young, yet they are not destructive but are rather inert. The explanation is in the "physical state" (*l'état physique*) of each, or in the difference between an ascendant and a declining "active principle" (*principe actif*). Rousseau at the same time strengthens the connection between the purely natural-corporeal condition and the moral state of a man, and prepares to remark that a highly charged active principle is as such not destructive out of badness but out of precipitancy. "The action that forms is always slow." This is followed by a reference to the author of nature. Rousseau's argument indicates that an active principle is embedded in a physical state, and that the constructive acts of an active principle are slow. In sum, an omnipotent active principle would not, as omnipotent, issue commands nor, as active, work except very slowly.

In further pursuit of the issue as stated above, attention should be given to an episode in book II that Rousseau contrives for the moral instruction of Emile in the context of a discussion of rational persuasion as a means of inculcating moral maxims. In order to account for the significance of the context itself, one must survey the argument from the beginning of book II. The conscious life of a human being consists in enduring pain and enjoying the sense of one's existence as oneself. Death can destroy that sense at any moment. Man should therefore return to the here and now and give up the preoccupation with providing for a doubtful future that carries man beyond himself (*au delà*) and spoils life. "O homme! resserre ton existence au dedans de toi ... Reste à la place que la nature t'assigne dans la chaîne des êtres ... " (*Emile*, p. 68)—"Man, confine your existence to within yourself ... Remain in the place assigned you by nature in the chain of beings." This non-Christian resignation means that a man should conceive no desires that he cannot unaided fulfill. The definition of happiness follows: doing what one desires without help, which is the condition of man in the state of nature. Rousseau appears to believe that the ancient connection of happiness and autarky need not be thought applicable only to the lives of aristocrats. As we shall soon see, labor is of utmost importance.

To proceed: taking one's place in the great chain of natural beings means coming under the subjection of things, never of wills (p. 71). Rousseau indicates the political bearing of these thoughts by showing how they point toward republican legality. In further animadversions that bear equally on monarchy as on child-rearing, he reflects on the unnaturalness of the subjection of strength to weakness. There is no mention here of a mechanics of politics, or of the abominable effects that a politics of comparative masses might entail. Rousseau now considers how to implant in a young mind the lesson of man's full absorption into the order of nature. He first takes issue with Locke, by name, on the ground that Locke advanced the mistaken notion that one must reason with children and inculcate virtues by demonstrative arguments. The disagreement with Locke is of interest because the preceding advocacy of a politics of comparative masses can be found sketched in Section 96 of the *Second Treatise*, and the labor theory of property rights will soon be adopted by Rousseau. It appears that Rousseau means to convict Locke of the following inconsistency, which it will be Rousseau's intention to avoid: to hold at the same time a mechanistic view of nature and of politics, and a rationalistic view of the soul's formation. Locke apart, the general reason for rejecting the teaching of virtue as such, surely to the young, is that moral doctrines that are not understood or are misunderstood can have only harmful effects on the pupil. Rousseau will of course have much to say on the unwisdom of the use of fable for communicating moral precepts. We however are now on the verges of the episode contrived by Rousseau to show the proper manner of teaching a moral lesson.

First occurs this rather striking remark: "On this earth, of which nature made man's first paradise, dread making use of a tempter in desiring to endow innocence with the knowledge of good and evil" (p. 86). The danger is, apparently, that the innocent will be harmed by the bad example. Soon Rousseau is launched on the immediate task of moral instruction, which is to teach the lesson of the right of property, and thus of the origin of property. His method is as follows. He sets the scene in a garden that has been planted already by Robert the gardener, with whom he is in conspiracy. Rousseau, present by name as Jean-Jacques, has suborned the innocent Emile to plant and tend some beans in the already-cultivated garden. When the bean plants have begun to grow and the child's delight is keen, Robert pulls the plants up and expostulates with Emile and Jean-Jacques, accusing them of ignoring his rights and so on. The upshot is an agreement by which Emile will have certain privileges of use if he keeps his promise not to disturb the product of Robert's labor.

In Rousseau's garden, the will of the master never appears, and the lesson is taught altogether by the natural unfolding of events. The master of the garden issues no commands or prohibitions; there is no show of anger on his part, and far from there being any expulsion from the garden, Emile is invited to share in its occupancy—on terms of respect for labor. Never in this garden could labor be characterized as a punishment and a curse. And least of all can one imagine the master of the garden denouncing death upon, and making it seem fearful to, an innocent whose transgression was mere disobedience. Later on (p. 96), Rousseau criticizes the master who asks the suspected culprit, "Was it you?" The question suggests entrapment or encourages lying, and in either case is bad moral pedagogy. In all ways but one, Rousseau's garden is conducted on different principles from those that ruled in Eden: there is a tempter in Rousseau's garden too, but the tempter and his victim go on to a life of love and trust together rather than of mutual fear and injury, because the tempter-master had no need to exhibit himself as the source of command but was willing to let the mechanism he had contrived do its own, and thus his own, work silently.

Later on (p. 99), Rousseau returns to the theme that man's portion in the world is to remain "within himself," and his task to overcome the impulse to go *hors de soi*. He reformulates the thought in the form of the maxim, "Never harm anyone"—an obvious corrective to "Do good to others." "Never harm" is unobtrusive beneficence, unostentatious, unimpressive to the world, unadapted to gaining approbation, and thus the most demanding expression of philanthropy. It is perhaps the maxim of conduct that more successfully than any other reconciles true goodness and true self-care with each other, with the necessary hardness of a human spirit, and with that indifference to the judgments of opinion that is tantamount to the true suppression of pride.

To state the case broadly, Rousseau's project on behalf of the virilification of man is joined with his reflection on the universe in which man's moral existence must be conceived and maintained. I have attempted to suggest that Rousseau prepares to move away from the conception of that universe that was laid down in Scripture, old and new. God revealed himself, and that leads to infinite difficulties. Even the *imitatio Christi* is insufficiently self-effacing. Rousseau is in search of the natural morality that works, and leads its subjects to do their advantageous work, in benign invisibility.

Book II deals with the forces or powers of man, concretely the powers of the organs of his body by which he is put in relation to the environing world. The subject is important because happiness depends upon the exercise of one's powers without any of them lying dormant but also without any of them being directed upon objects proposed by the extravagant imagination. To aim at what requires outside helps is to invite dependency. Freedom and happiness are thus inseparable. But the subject is important also because it furnishes the context in which Rousseau's famous notion of the natural goodness of man may be seen in a certain light. He remarks, "Let us posit as an incontestable maxim that nature's first motions are always right: there is no original perverseness in the human heart ..." (p. 81). The so-called natural goodness of man is simply an aspect of the perfect articulation of pre-social man in the order or chain of natural motions. Fantasy, opinion and convention disrupt that articulation; proper education would help to restore it. The precise basis of that articulation is a profound problem, to which Rousseau gives perhaps a clue in a passage that is redolent of Cartesian thermal-vitalism (p. 101): "Treat him in accordance with his age, in spite of appearances, and fear exhausting his powers through a desire to overemploy them. If the young brain heats up, if you see that it is beginning to boil, allow it at first to ferment freely, but never stimulate it lest all be exhaled; and when the first spirits have evaporated, hold back, compress the others until, with the years, all will turn into vivifying heat and true strength. Otherwise you will lose your time and your trouble, you will destroy your own work; and after having imprudently become intoxicated with all the inflammable vapors, you will have nothing left but dregs without strength."

There follows a passage (pp. 105–15) in which Rousseau expels from the child's curriculum the study of languages, of history, and of fables, which should be compared with the parallel material in Descartes's *Discourse on Method,* part II. It is in the course of his declamation against fabulous instruction that Rousseau describes Alexander the Great's act of confidence in his physician (who had been accused of plotting to poison Alexander), by saying, "never did a mortal make so sublime [a profession] of faith]" (p. 108). The relation of the Profession of Faith of the Savoyard Vicar to the beliefs of Rousseau himself is a difficult question in its own right, into which we cannot go. Rousseau blamed people who assumed that the Vicar's words simply expressed Rousseau's thought. It is clear, because it is explicit, that the Profession of Faith is addressed in part to the philosophy of Descartes and Newton, and perhaps, through the question of the kind of motion that could be possessed by atoms necessarily (apart from divine action), to Epicurean corporealist atheism (p. 331). The Profession of Faith maintains that to the finite mind of man, everything important is mysterious, surely including ourselves and our "active principle" (p. 323). Furthermore, the Vicar proclaims, here with a note that appears as an intervention by Rousseau, his inability to conceive the motion of matter except on the analogy of the motion of his arm, that is, in response to the causal action of Will. This leads to his first article of faith: "A will moves the universe and animates nature" (p. 330). But it has already appeared that Rousseau refers more than once to our "active principle" as if it were not or need not be mysterious to us (e.g., pp. 49, 103); and he has made it reasonably clear that the human problems he seems dedicated to solving would be hopeless if the Vicar's first article of faith were simply true. My provisional conclusion is that the core of Rousseau's own understanding of man and his natural matrix is closer to that of Descartes than to that of the Vicar.

Returning now to the course of book II, we move to the latter portion, roughly pages 137–181, in which the theme is man's relation to the environing world, under two heads: the world as outside and remaining outside (object of sense); and the world as capable of being ingested (object of consumption as food.) Rousseau introduces the section on the senses with a short observation on inoculation against smallpox and a brief reflection on education (pp. 136–37). In the remark on inoculation, Rousseau makes the striking admission that to inoculate at an early age is rather consistent with "our" practice, apparently meaning that advocated in the *Emile*, which is to protect the more valuable advanced age at the risk of death (from the inoculation) at an earlier one, "if one can call a well-administered inoculation a risk." On the other hand, not inoculating is "more in the vein of our general principles of letting nature take its course in everything." Rousseau does not arbitrate between his practice and his principles except by leaving the matter to be settled according to the time, the place, and the circumstances. The rehabilitation of medical science of nature accompanies the withdrawal from the rigid position of surrender to mere or unmastered nature. The brief observation on education expresses Rousseau's desire, if it were possible, to make Emile at home in, or unthreatened by, all the elements—water, air, and fire as well as earth. It is useful to recall occasionally the extent of Rousseau's concessions to the scientific conquest of nature as well as the sense in which his teaching promotes a moral acquiescence to nature; for if the two postures toward nature can be reconciled to each other successfully, modernity is not without hope.

In the course of the discussion of the sense of touch (p. 147), a tension appears among various natural goods. For the sake of its sensitivity in judging of the nature of things, the organ of touch must be soft. In the interest of the durability of the whole man, the skin should be hardened to the impacts of air, the action of which is described in the terms and concepts of the simplest mechanical atomism (p. 133). And finally, in a passage that cannot be wholly irrelevant to man's sexual existence (p. 147), Rousseau prescribes that attention be given to the condition of the hands. Knowledge, hardness, and love make claims that are equally natural and equally tax the formation of man. In discussing sight, Rousseau makes the point that the illusions or deceptions intrinsic to our vision are indispensable to our perception of things as they are related in space (p. 149): it is by perceiving things as larger and smaller, though they are not in fact so, that we locate them in relation to each other and to ourselves. It is in this vicinity that the reference to Chiron occurs that

accounts for the frontispiece to book II. The point is that the duplicity of a
bi-natured being would not exceed what is needed to induce a young
gentleman (Emile)[2] to perform the exercises out of which will grow his
hardness and his judgment of the relations among things. Repeatedly,
the lessons are taught by deceiving and cheating him, as apparently nature
teaches us. In the treatment of taste, the sense that governs our relation to
the things outside us with a view to the possibility of their being
incorporated in ourselves, Rousseau reflects (p. 165) that the tastes that
belong to the state of nature, that are themselves natural, are at the same
time the most simple, the least durable, and completely supplanted by
habitual ones that are nourished on fantasy and are unchanging.
Rousseau quotes a lengthy passage from one of Plutarch's essays on
sarcophagy, in support of his own strong reprobation of meat-eating.
According to that passage, the earliest men were driven by hunger—by the
extreme scarcity of those first ages in which the parts of the earth were still
arranging themselves—to devour living beings. The reproach against
civilized meat-eaters, put in the mouths of those early men, is that we now
perform deeds of unnecessary cruelty against creatures like ourselves (*nos
semblables*) while surrounded by the abundance provided by law and
agriculture, or by the state of civil society.

To summarize: there is an equivocalness of nature as between sensitivity
and durability, or softness and hardness; and there is a duplicity in nature
that enforces the method of learning and teaching through deception.
Finally, the natural states of things are fragile while the post-natural are
the unalterable; and the post-natural provide the conditions in which the
simple yearnings of nature could be satisfied materially but will for moral
reasons probably suffer frustration. One cannot fail to doubt that there is
a general solution to the problem of man's wellbeing on the plane of
nature, except if the dictate of nature is understood to be the dictate of
supple reason in accordance with circumstances.

The last of the senses to be discussed in book II is the sense of smell.
This is "the sense of the imagination" (p. 173). The pleasure that it gives
is connectible with the pleasure imagined to be obtainable from the source
of the savored odor. Rousseau gives as illustration the stimulating effect of
the perfumed air of the boudoir, and speaks specifically of love. The sense
of smell is the adjunct of that power of the mind by which it looks forward
to the pleasures, and pre-eminently to the keenest pleasures, of earthly
life. Pursuing the theme of imagination through the grave subject of
reason, Rousseau first (p. 174) defines human or intellectual reason as the
formation of complex structures of sensations, and then (p. 175) maintains that the enchantment of our finite lives consists in the augmentation
of sense by the imagination of future good. He prepares to bring book II to
a close by assimilating old age to autumn, when there is no future, i.e., no

life, to imagine. In brief, the imagination of love is contrasted with the nul-imagination of death. If indeed there is nothing to be imagined hereafter, then it might be fair to say more simply that the image of love replaces the nul-image of bliss hereafter as an ingredient of human happiness.

Early in book III (p. 187), there is a description of a sunrise that precedes Emile's initiation into the laws of nature (p. 222), just as a sunrise precedes the Profession of Faith of the Savoyard Vicar, in book IV. The sunrise of book III is described by Rousseau in a passage of considerable beauty, followed by the remark that such beauties would be entirely lost on Emile as on anyone without the necessary preparation in experience. "How might the song of birds produce in him a voluptuous emotion if the tones of love and pleasure are still unknown to him? With what ecstasies will he watch the birth of so beautiful a day if his imagination cannot paint for him those with which it might be made replete? And how will he be melted with the beauty of the spectacle of nature if he knows not what hand took pains to beautify it?" From this it appears that there are two conditions for the appreciation of the beautiful: experience of love and knowledge of God. I believe that the context of the Profession of Faith of the Savoyard Vicar goes far to eliminate the latter of the two named conditions, except if it is blasphemously understood. The Profession of Faith is a statement by a priest who, though sworn to celibacy, admits that he is given to carnal love, though only with unmarried women. (The family is inviolate.) The addressee of the Profession is a youth whose fault is a resentful, envious ire (p. 318). The intention of the Profession of Faith seems to be the conquest of anger by love that has mollified Christianity and purged the Almighty of his own misanthropic ire. Long after the Profession of Faith, Rousseau will repeat that love is a channel to beauty (p. 495). But he says in the same place, "All is but illusion in love, I admit it." This is in fact a considerably weaker form of what he had said when preparing to give the phantom of Sophie her resplendent name: ". . . and what is genuine love itself if not chimera, lie, illusion?" (p. 409). Love is the myth that opens the heart to the beautiful. It also, and not incidentally, brings man under the influence of woman, bringing into his life that respect for propriety and conventional opinion (pp. 455, 473) that might be an important part of the wisdom he has to live by.

Surveying the scene of Emile's preparation for life, one gets a glimmer of Rousseau's conception of the human condition. An average man at his best, in the fluctuating, paradoxical setting in which humanity exists, will have the qualities of hardness that will fit him to struggle for life and also to accept what overwhelms his power to struggle. And he will enjoy love, for, in truth, it is a need. His bulwark against the flux and coldness of the world is, eventually, his own versatile labor. Love is the illusion that will make him accessible to beauty. The Rousseauan combination of work and love is domesticity (cf. p. 558). To speak by reference to Plato, in Rousseau's scheme the principle of one man, one job is replaced by versatility; gymnastic is replaced by labor; music is replaced by love; and communism is replaced by domesticity. Rule appears to remain in the hand of a philosopher.

Notes

1. Lest the point be overdrawn, the "adaptability" of Socrates himself—who wore the same light clothing in all seasons, and who demonstrated his imperviousness to poverty (while only praying for exemption from undue wealth)—should not be forgotten; but his virtue was the adjunct of unusual wisdom rather than of a system of conditioning, of freedom rather than necessity as we would say.

2. The youth is somewhat arrogant and lazy, and is described as destined for a military career. That he is Emile is made probable by the remark in book V, p. 556, in which Emile's former racing is referred to with laughter. It is equally clear that Chiron is Rousseau. Cf. also p. 168, where it is suggested that the boy was Emile.